RARE MASTERPIECES

OF PHILOSOPHY AND SCIENCE

EDITED BY DR. W. STARK

★

THE DISCOURSES

OF

NICCOLO MACHIAVELLI

VOLUME TWO

PUBLISHED ON THE LOUIS STERN MEMORIAL FUND

THE DISCOURSES OF NICCOLÒ MACHIAVELLI
TRANSLATED FROM THE ITALIAN
WITH AN INTRODUCTION
AND NOTES
BY
LESLIE J. WALKER
S.J., M.A. (OXON AND LONDON)
DEAN AND SENIOR TUTOR OF CAMPION HALL
OXFORD
FORMERLY PROFESSOR OF MEDIAEVAL PHILOSOPHY
AT HEYTHROP COLLEGE
praesidibus adprobantibus

THE
DISCOURSES
OF
NICCOLÒ
MACHIAVELLI

NEW HAVEN

YALE UNIVERSITY PRESS

1950

THIS EDITION FIRST PUBLISHED

IN THE UNITED STATES

BY YALE UNIVERSITY PRESS

NEW HAVEN CONNECTICUT

DESIGNED BY SEÁN JENNETT

AND PRINTED IN GREAT BRITAIN

BY BUTLER AND TANNER LTD

LONDON AND FROME

CONTENTS
OF VOLUME TWO

*For abbreviations used in the Tables and Notes see Vol. I,
pp. vii and viii*

NOTES

In the page-headings are given: (i) *on the outside* Book, Chapter or Chapters, and the numbers of the notes to them which occur on that page; (ii) *on the inside* Book, and the first and last Chapter and Section to which the notes on that page refer, so that in using the Indices, which give Book, Chapter, and Section, it may be possible to look up the note on any particular topic or person or event without first consulting the text in order to find the Index-number of the note

NOTES ON BOOK ONE

DEDICATION

ZANOBI BUONDELMONTI belonged to an old Florentine family, dating back to the twelfth century. They had been leaders of the Guelph party and were strong republicans. Zanobi was one of Machiavelli's most intimate friends and took part in the discussions on politics and war held in the *Oricellarii* gardens in 1516. He appears as one of the interlocutors in *The Art of War*. Ten years later he retired to Naples to organise a revolt against the misrule of the Medici, and died there of the plague in the same year as Machiavelli, namely on 11 September 1527.

COSIMO RUCELLAI was the grandson of Bernardo Rucellai (1448–1514), the brother-in-law of Lorenzo the Magnificent. Bernardo built a palace in the Via della Scala and laid out the beautiful gardens described by Machiavelli in *The Art of War*. His eldest son, Cosimo, died in 1495, the year in which the younger Cosimo (originally called Bernardo) was born. He lived with his uncles in the palace which was renowned for its hospitality, and, though an invalid, gathered round him a circle of friends, politicians, poets, and men who had an interest in literature and philosophy, just as his grandfather had done. An account of the meetings with Fabrizio Colonna, recently returned from the Milanese war, is given in *The Art of War*. Cosimo died in 1519, while still a young man, and in the opening paragraphs of *The Art of War*, Book I, Machiavelli records his death, and praises alike his virtues and his poetical skill.

1. Of Hiero II, king of Syracuse (272–216 B.C.), Polybius says that 'when quite a young man, he had a natural aptitude for kingcraft and the politic conduct of affairs. Having assumed command [of the Syracusan army in 275 B.C.], he gained entrance to the city by means of some of his agents and so got hold of his political opponents; but then ruled so mildly and in so lofty a spirit, that the Syracusans, though not usually acquiescing in officers chosen by the troops, unanimously approved Hiero; whose conduct from the outset made it plain to close observers that his aspirations soared above the position of a mere general' (I.8).

2. Perseus, son of Philip V, and last king of Macedonia (179–168 B.C.), was defeated by Paulus Aemilius at Pydna in 168 B.C., largely owing to his incompetence. Having fled from the battlefield he was pursued and captured, and taken to Rome to grace the triumph of Aemilius. (Cp. Plutarch's *Life of Paulus Aemilius*, nn. 23–4, 26–7, 32–4.)

3. The reference is clearly to Books II and III, which at this time were not yet

complete. The date cannot have been much later than 1513, when *The Prince* first appeared, for in Chapter 2 Machiavelli says that he will say no more of republics 'because elsewhere I have spoken of them at length'; which suggests that Book I of the *Discourses* may already have been written. (See Pref. n. 6, below.)

PREFACE

1. On the originality of Machiavelli's method of proving that there is a pattern in history, see Introduction, Section VIII. Machiavelli here claims that the path he proposes to explore is as new and also as dangerous as were the voyages Columbus made to the Bahamas, the West Indies and South America between 1492 and 1504. Cp. Valerius Maximus: *'Animadverto in quam periculosum iter processerim'* (III.6, opening words).

2. Polybius, who in Book VI analyses the Roman constitution with a view to discovering whence Rome derived her greatness, also points out the difficulty of the task (VI.3).

3. It is as vain to call to the administration of public affairs a man who knows nothing of the causes of political events, says Polybius, as it is to call in an ignorant physician to minister to our diseases (III.7).

4. In the Filadelfia edition the reading is *'la presente educazione'*, not *'la presente religione'*. (Cp. D. II.2.6.)

5. Machiavelli, like Polybius, holds that the laws of cause and effect govern politics in the same way that they govern inanimate nature, and are to be discovered in the same way—by the empirical method. Given that we can discover the causes of political events by the consideration of what is already past—as is possible, Polybius holds,—it should be possible to foretell the future by conjectures, based on the past, especially if in examining precedents we pay attention to the motives governing political conduct, which is precisely what Machiavelli does. See Polybius III.31 and cp. I.1, 35; II.35; VI.1. Quotations both from Polybius and from Diodorus Siculus are given in the Introduction, §§ 96, 97.

6. The words *'tutti quelli libri che dalla malignità de' tempi non ci sono stati intercetti'* make it clear that Machiavelli intends to comment only on Livy's first ten books, after which the first break occurs. There is no suggestion that he intended to supplement his work by commenting on the remaining books, XXI to XLV. Nor is this likely, for (i) it is in the causes of Rome's rise to power that he is primarily interested, and both this and her success in maintaining that power he ascribes primarily to her constitution (cp. D. I.1.1), which in its essentials was complete by the year 293, with which Livy's tenth book ends. Moreover, (ii) in the second book of the *Discourses*, which is concerned with the building up of her empire, and in the third, which draws lessons from the examples set by her great men, Machiavelli has no hesitation in narrating incidents taken from the later books (e.g. from Livy's account of the war with Hannibal), and even of citing these books (see Index *sub* 'Livy').

BOOK ONE

1. *Concerning the Origin of Cities in General and of Rome in Particular*

1. Cp. Polybius: 'The chief feature in my work and the most instructive for students is that it should enable them to know and realise to the full in what way and under what kind of constitution it came about that nearly the whole world fell under the power of Rome within a space of slightly under fifty-three years—an event certainly without precedent' (Book VI.1).

2. For the founding of Athens by the legendary Theseus in 1234 B.C., see Plutarch's *Theseus*, nn. 24–5. For the founding of Venice in consequence of the invasion of Attila (A.D. 451), see H.F. I.29 and cp. I.3 and 5.

3. On Roman colonies, cp. H.F. II.1 and see Index *sub* 'Colonies', and cp. also P. 3, E.18–19.

4. On the origin of Florence and of its name, see H.F. I.5 and II.2, where we are told that it came into existence first as a market-town, and that it was Sulla who first set up a Roman colony there.

5. At Ragusa, an easily defended spot on the Dalmatian coast, there was a colony from Corinth, and later a Roman colony of considerable wealth. It was then known as Epidaurus (cp. Livy X.47; XLV.28). After the Avar invasion of 656 it was occupied by refugees, who were joined later by some Slavs. It survived as a republic, under the overlordship first of Constantinople, then of Venice, of Hungary, and finally of the Ottoman Turks till Machiavelli's own time, and owing to its position enjoyed comparative tranquillity.

6. On the fertility of Egypt and the labours undertaken under the direction of her kings, see Diodorus Siculus—*Gesta Regum Aegypti*—I.30 *sq.*, and I.45 *sq.*

7. The Mamelukes ruled Egypt as sultans from 1252 to 1517 when Cairo was taken by the Ottoman Turks under Selim I. Their policy and their persons were at the mercy of the army, by which they were frequently deposed and murdered. They none the less more than held their own against neighbouring peoples and against European powers.

8. Deinocrates was the architect who designed Alexandria in 322 B.C. for Alexander the Great. His proposal to re-shape Mount Athos is mentioned both by Strabo (Bk. XIV.23) and by Lucian (*pro Imag.* 9), but, as Ellinger points out, neither of these passages agree with what Machiavelli says. The relevant passage will be found in Vitruvius (II, Pref., 2–3), where, on being introduced to Alexander, Deinocrates explains that he is 'a Macedonian architect, who brings you ideas and plans worthy of you as an illustrious prince'. For, he adds, 'I have shaped Mount Athos into the figure of a man's statue'. Alexander is delighted with the plan, but asks whether there are any fields about whence a supply of corn can be obtained. When told that this was not the case, and that supplies must be brought by sea, the king rejects the plan, but keeps Deinocrates with him. The story is also told by St. Thomas in *de Regimine Principum*, II. c. 3, and Vitruvius cited as his authority; but the name of the architect is given as Xenocrates. In the next chapter (II. c. 4) St. Thomas asks: *Quid sit locus amoenus?*

9. For the story of how Aeneas fled from Troy to Rome where he made friends

with king Latinus, whose daughter he married, see Livy I.1–3; and for the story of how Romulus and Remus, the sons of Mars and the vestal Rhea, were nourished by a she-wolf and then brought up by Faustulus (which Livy prefers as being more appropriate for a city whose 'power was to become next to that of the Gods'), see Livy I.4–5.

10. The topics to be discussed in the *Discourses* are here briefly indicated, namely:

Book I: what was done in the city by public enactment, i.e. constitutional changes and new institutions and laws.

Book II: what was done abroad by public enactment, i.e. the making of war, conquests, and alliances.

Book III: what was done on the initiative of private individuals, i.e. the example set by Rome's great men.

11. Cp. Polybius' Book VI.1: 'What is really educational and beneficial to students of history is a clear view of the causes of events and the consequent power of choosing the better alternative in a given case.'

Guicciardini *in loc.*, i.e. in his *Considerazioni intorno ai Discorsi del Machiavelli*, points out that the colonies sent out by the Gauls and the Cimbri were not dependent on the parent peoples, and that, after the decline of the Empire, Rome's colonies often became magnificent and powerful cities. Rome itself was situated in a fertile spot, but, being confined to a small space and hemmed in by powerful neighbours, it had to expand, unless it was prepared to live philosophically *(alla filosofica)*!—For Aristotle's views on the situation of cities and its effect on the inhabitants, see *Politics*, VII, cc. 5–7.

2. How many Kinds of Commonwealth there are and of what Kind was that of Rome

1. Cp. D. I.1.4–5. It is clear from what follows, if read in conjunction with D. I.1.6, that two conditions must be satisfied by a 'free city' or 'free state'. It must be (1) independent of any other state, and (2) must have chosen its own form of government, whether it be a republic or a principality.

2. See below, § 17; and cp. D. I.18.2.

3. Cp. D. I.9, where special stress is laid on the advantages of cut-and-dried constitutions formulated at the start by a single person. It is odd that Machiavelli should have thought this so important in view of the fact that admittedly Rome's constitution was developed and modified as occasion arose, and that Rome is his model state and the most successful of all. It was, doubtless, the instability of governments in Florence as contrasted with the stability of Sparta that caused him to adopt this view.

4. Thucydides (I.18) says that 'Sparta obtained good laws at an earlier period than any other state', and that she 'preserved the same form of government rather more than 400 years, reckoning to the end of the Peloponnesian war' (404 B.C.). Aristotle says that, according to tradition, Lycurgus was the guardian of Charilaus (*Politics* II.10). Charilaus began to reign in 884 B.C., if Apollodorus is right in saying he began to reign 108 years before the Olympiad of Coroebus. Hence, if the laws of Lycurgus lasted more than 800 years, they ceased to obtain some time during

the first century B.C. They were suspended temporarily in the time of Cleomenes, 226–221 B.C.; and in 146 Sparta became part of the Roman province of Macedonia. Both these dates are too early. Hence the date Machiavelli is assigning as the end of the Spartan constitution is presumably 27 B.C., when Sparta became subject to Augustus and to the governor of Achaea. (Cp. A.W. Bk. I, B.277b, F.18, where Sparta is again said to have lasted 800 years. Cp. also § 15 below.)

5. In 1502 Arezzo revolted against Florence and Caesar Borgia seized Urbino. The Florentines, whose security was thus threatened, appealed to Louis XII, and sent Francesco Soderini and Machiavelli as envoys to Urbino, where they met Caesar Borgia. He demanded a change in the government of Florence. This was on 24 June, and on 26 August a law was passed appointing a Gonfalonier for life, to which office Piero Soderini was elected in September.

6. On 29 August 1512 Prato was sacked by the Spaniards, and the Medici party, now all-powerful, demanded the deposition of Soderini. He was deposed on 1 September, and on the same day Giuliano de' Medici entered Florence. A *Balìa* consisting of 40 citizens was appointed to reform the constitution. They abolished the *Consiglio Grande*, the *Dieci di Balìa,* and the national militia which Machiavelli had organised. The republic thus in reality came to an end, though nominally it still survived.

7. Between what Machiavelli writes in the rest of this discourse and what Polybius says in Book VI of his *Histories* there is a close correspondence, especially in regard to §§ 3–14. Not that Machiavelli is translating Polybius either from the Latin or the Greek. What he gives us is a condensed version of Polybius, with numerous omissions and frequent remarks of his own thrown in. I give under each paragraph the corresponding passage in Polybius, so that the reader may see for himself the extent to which the correspondence holds good. I translate from the edition published by Firmin-Didot (Paris, 1880), in which the Latin and Greek texts are given side by side. Schuckburgh's translation agrees with it in substance, but is based on the text of Hultz. Latin editions of Books I to V existed in Machiavelli's time, but not of Book VI (see Table XIII, B. 1, Polybius).

With § 3 compare the following passage from Polybius VI.3:

'In regard to the Roman Republic it is difficult to describe either its present state ... or to discern its future. .... Hence we must enquire diligently into the outstanding forms of government and how that of Rome differs from others. Since those who have dealt with this topic and have discussed how commonwealths differ in method and policy (*via et arte*), enumerate three forms of commonwealth (*tres rerumpublicarum formas*), and call one kingship (*regnum*), another the principality of the best men (*optimatium principatus*), and a third the rule of the populace (*populi imperium*), I think I have the right to ask them whether they are proffering these forms as the only ones, or as the best forms' (VI.3.3–6).

Though some critics have suggested that Aristotle's classification differs from that of Polybius, I do not think it does. The difference is merely in terminology. Polybius prefers to use πολιτεία in its generic sense for a 'form of government' (*reipublicae forma*); and to call government by the *populus* (or πλῆθος) δημοκρατία, whereas Aristotle in his *Politics* III.7 restricts the term δημοκρατία to the corrupt form of 'populi imperium'. Machiavelli replaces βασιλεία by the more general term '*Principato*', and for the other two types uses '*Ottimati*' and '*Popolare*', terms derived from those which occur in the Latin version of Polybius, '*optimatium principatus*' and '*populi imperium*'.

8. With § 4 compare the following passage, which occurs in VI.3-4 after a passage which Machiavelli omits, but uses later:

'It cannot, however, be admitted that there are only these forms of state (*reipublicae formae*); for we find some monarchical and tyrannical regimes which ill accord with kingship, yet are like it in some respects. . . . So, too, there are many cities governed by the few that are not wholly unlike an aristocracy (*optimatium principatus*), yet—if I may so put it—are very far removed from this. . . . It must be reckoned, then, that there are six kinds of states, three commonly called by the names we have given above, and three analogous to them in nature, namely, domination by one man, by a few, and by the mob (*turba vulgaris*). The first of these is brought about without artificial aid in the natural course of events, namely, domination by one man. After which, and out of which, when men learn better and become more skilled, there arises kingship, which, when it degenerates into the evils congenital to it, becomes tyranny. When kings are got rid of, aristocracy (*optimatium principatus*) arises, and then gets turned into domination by the few, man's nature being what it is. When the masses (*multitudo*) become incensed and take vengeance for the injuries inflicted by these princes, the rule of the populace (*populi imperium*) comes into being; and in due course, owing to its insolence and its contempt for the laws, there emerges mob-rule (*turbae potentatus*). That what we have said about this is true, is easily understood by anyone who calls to mind the basic character, origin and mutability of each of these kinds of state' (VI.3.9-4.10).

Machiavelli abbreviates considerably here, because what Polybius says of transitions he says again later in a passage which Machiavelli uses. The main point in which he is interested here is the sixfold division of states. This sixfold division is common alike to Aristotle, Polybius, and Machiavelli, and, for that matter, is also to be found in Plato. Thus, having first distinguished between states in which the supreme authority lies with (i) a single person, (ii) the few, and (iii) the many, Aristotle subdivides each of these forms according as they are good or perverted, (*Politics* III.7). He thus obtains six forms for which his technical terms are: (1) βασιλεία—τυραννίς, (ii) ἀριστοκρατία—ὀλιγαρχία, (iii) πολιτεία—δημοκρατία. The corresponding terms in Polybius are (in Greek): (1) βασιλεία—τυραννίς, (ii) ἀριστοκρατία—ὀλιγαρχία, (iii), δημοκρατία—ὀχλοκρατία; and (in Latin): (i) *Regnum—Tyrannis*, (ii) *Optimatium principatus—Paucorum dominatio*, (iii) *Populi imperium—Turbae potentatus*. Machiavelli's terms are: (i) *Principato—Tirannide*, (ii) *Ottimati—Stato di pochi*, (iii) *Popolare* (or *Governo popolare*)—*Licenza* (or *Governo licenzioso*). All of which forms are in his opinion bad, either of their very nature, or because they are incapable of lasting (cp. § 17). There is a fragment ascribed to Plutarch entitled: '*De unius in republica dominatione, populari statu, et paucorum imperio*', cp. also Aristotle, *Ethics* VIII.10 on the tendency of governments to pass over into their opposites.

9. To the hypothetical state of the world which Polybius supposes to have been denuded alike of inhabitants and of knowledge, political, social and scientific, by floods and pestilences (cp. D. II.5), Machiavelli gives substance by supposing that at the beginning of the world men were actually in this state. Otherwise there is a close correspondence between § 5 and what Polybius says in VI.5:

'What are we to say of the origins of civil societies, and how shall we say they arose? . . . From the seed of the survivors in course of time a multitude of men would again be propagated. Men would then, doubtless, as is the case with other animals, herd together—for it is reasonable to suppose that they would herd with animals of the same kind on account of their natural weakness. It would then inevitably happen that he who excelled the rest in strength of body, presence of mind and audacity, would become their leader and ruler' (VI.5.4–7).

The question with which this passage opens has already been discussed from a different standpoint by Machiavelli in D. I.1.

10. In the next paragraph (§ 6) Machiavelli gives the gist of a long passage in VI.5–6 in a very few lines, but omits altogether what Polybius says about family life, and, by so doing, conveys the impression that moral notions have an origin which is purely political. Polybius, on the other hand, holds that they are aroused by a display of ingratitude toward a benefactor and the sympathy felt for him when ill-used. Whether ingratitude be toward parents or toward a ruler the reaction is the same in both cases. Thus, of ingratitude toward parents Polybius says that 'since men differ from other animals, it is improbable that they would let it pass unnoticed, as other animals do . . . seeing that, looking to the future, they would easily perceive that the same mischief might befall themselves. Or, if anyone after obtaining help and protection from another in time of danger, should not repay his benefactor with gratitude but should even injure him, who doubts but that such a man would stand condemned by everyone who knew of it, since all would be indignant at the other's lot (reading "*vicem*" for "*vocem*") and for themselves would fear the same thing? Whence arose in every man's mind a certain sense of duty and a recognition of its binding force, in which lies the beginning and end of justice. Similarly, when any man in time of danger fights valiantly in the common defence . . . the crowd will undoubtedly acclaim and extol him, become well-disposed towards him, and honour him as their patron. But one who does the opposite, will evoke the contempt and disapproval of all; so that again it is likely that there will arise in the minds of the populace some recognition of the shameful and the good, and of the difference between them' (VI.6.4–9).

11. The next paragraph (§ 7) is concerned with the distinction Polybius makes between 'Monarchy' (or the rule of the strong) and 'Kingship' (or the rule of the wise)—μοναρχία and βασιλεία. 'That government where one alone rules, ought not to be called kingly government,' he says, 'but only that which is given voluntarily, and where authority is not obtained by fear or force, but by reason and good counsel' (VI.4.2) '. . . Monarchy, which comes first, establishes itself without skill, and as it were by an instinct of nature. After it and out of it comes kingship proper, in which art is used to correct monarchy's faults' (VI.4.7). Kings distribute justice, and at the outset live as their subjects live; and, adds Polybius in the passage which Machiavelli seems to be using, 'for the time being those whom the people choose to carry on the king's rule, are presumed to have the same faculty for distributing justice, but, should they displease them, they choose as magistrates and kings, not those who excel in bodily strength, but those who are pre-eminent for wisdom and prudence' (VI.7.2–3).

12. A short account of the transitions which Machiavelli now proceeds to relate will be found in Aristotle, *Politics* III.15, 1286b, 10 *sq*. But it is the longer account given by Polybius in Book VI that Machiavelli follows almost *verbatim*.

Thus with § 8 compare the passage in VI.7 which deals with kingship when it ceases to be elective and becomes hereditary:

'But when later sons obtained kingdoms from their fathers by right of succession, and had gathered together not only what was required for their security and for the necessities of life, but many things that were not necessary, then, blinded by passions evoked by this excessive wealth, they thought that princes should have a different standard of life from their subjects, should indulge in the pleasures and display which goes with luxury, and that no one should say them nay, even when they gave way to the forbidden pleasures of the flesh; and when by some of their crimes they aroused envy and hostility and by others caused anger and hatred to blaze up against them, kingship became tyranny.' (VI.7, 6–8.)

13. With § 9, which deals with the next transition, corresponds the closing passage in VI.7 and the opening passage of VI.8:

'In doing this, they paved the way for their downfall, for against those who ruled conspiracies were formed, not by the worst amongst the citizens, but by those who excelled in liberality, large-mindedness and courage; for such men least of all could put up with the injuries inflicted by their princes. Moreover, when leaders arose, the people rebelled against the perverseness of kings for the same reasons, with the result that, when kingship and the domination of one man had been removed from the state (*respublica*), the principality of the best men came into being. For the people, as a kind of reward for their having got rid of monarchy, adopted them as their rulers and submitted themselves to them; while they on their part were content with the honour bestowed on them, set the common advantage of the state before aught else, and administered all affairs, both private and public, with special care, diligence and solicitude.' (VI.7.8–8, 3.)

14. The passage corresponding to § 10 follows on immediately:

'But when sons obtained this power from their fathers, they being men who had had no experience of the danger evil causes or of equality and civic liberty, but being accustomed from their youth to the honours and dignity of their fathers, some abandoned themselves to avarice and covetousness without restraint, while others gave themselves up to drunkenness and to the bestialities which accompany it, such as the violating of women and the raping of boys; and thus transformed the principality of the best into domination by the few. Hence they, too, aroused in the minds of the populace the passions of which we were speaking, and ended in the same way tyrants ended when calamity befell them. For when someone noticed how much envy and hatred they had aroused in the populace, he at once tried to egg it on by word and deed, and soon had the whole population ready to second his efforts.' (VI.8.4–9.1.)

15. The transition to democracy now follows both in Machiavelli and in Polybius:

'Finally, when some of the aristocrats had been killed and others banished they did not dare to commit their affairs to a king, since they were afraid of the injustice former kings had displayed. Nor yet did they feel disposed to commit the state to the many, since the errors they had been guilty of were still there before their eyes. Since, therefore, their only real hope lay in themselves, what happened was that the state was taken out of the hands of the few and committed to the sovereignty of the people (*ad populi imperium*), who themselves took over the charge of public affairs and the ruling power it involved.' (VI.9.2–3; cp. § 11.)

16. 'So long as there remained any who had had experience of the power and domination of the few, they acquiesced in this form of government and held nothing in higher esteem than the original equality and liberty of the citizen. But when offspring came along and the sovereignty of the people passed to their descendants, they made little of equality and liberty since they were accustomed to it, a vice which is especially common amongst those who excel others in wealth, and then turn to ambitioning honours which of their own efforts and virtue they could not attain; so that, to win the people over they distribute lavishly largesse, and thus at once corrupt the people and ruin their own estates. Moreover, when once such people in their stupid greed for honours have taught the mob to imbibe, and to live on, largesse, the rule of the populace at once begins to break down, and is replaced by force and physical violence. For, when the populace grows accustomed to living on others, and places its hope of a livelihood in the fortunes of others, and there comes along a magnanimous and bold leader whose poverty precludes him from obtaining public honours, the rule of the populace is transformed into a regime of physical violence. When the mob has joined up with him, it expresses its fury in massacre, banishment and in re-dividing up the land, to such an extent that it becomes like a wild beast, and then, once again, there arises a master who takes sole charge of things.' (VI.9.4–9; cp. § 12.)

I have given this passage in full because it contains so many ideas with which the readers of the *Discourses* will soon become familiar—the importance of equality if liberty is to endure, the dominating power of avarice and ambition, the means taken by a wealthy citizen, such as was Cosimo and Lorenzo de' Medici, to gain control of the state, the vengeance of the populace when such powers are abused. Though Machiavelli does not cite the passage in full, he none the less read it, and, in doing so, must have found it in complete accord with his own experience and his own reading of history.

17. The sentence which deals with cyclic change (in § 13) is based on Polybius VI.9, in a passage which follows on that quoted above:

'This is the cycle through which states in rotation pass, whereby they are changed and transformed until they get back to the start.' (VI.9.10.)

Polybius goes on to say that a person seeking to apply this theory to existent states, might mistake the time at which a change would take place but ought to make no mistake in regard to its being in process of decay or as to the form likely to supervene, provided he looks at the matter impartially. Machiavelli, on the other hand, shrewdly remarks that the cycle is rarely completed; nor does he ever mention cyclic change again. What he is interested in is the transitions, particularly those from some form of servitude to liberty (cp. D. I.16 to 18); and also the converse transition, which he discusses in P. 5 to 9 from the standpoint of the prince, and in D. I.46–55 from the standpoint of those who are anxious to preserve liberty.

18. The next paragraph (§ 14) is based on a remark Polybius here makes in regard to Lycurgus, and on an earlier passage in which he speaks of the best form of constitution. Of Lycurgus he says that:

'This distinguished man was aware that all these changes take place in accordance with a necessary law of nature, and held it to be dangerous to set up an unmixed form of state with a government of one particular type, since it would easily succumb to the vices in its nature.' (VI.10.1–2.)

Also in regard to the three 'good' forms of state, he says earlier:

11

'It is a mistake to regard these forms as the only forms, or either of them as the best form; for it is obvious that one should regard that state as best which is built up of all the aforesaid forms' (VI.3.7).

On this point Machiavelli is wholly at one with Polybius. The best form of state is one that has a strong central authority, and in the government of which both the aristocracy and the populace have a voice (cp. n. 21).

19. Polybius in VI.10 explains this somewhat more fully than does Machiavelli, who in § 15 summarises what he says. For Polybius writes:

'Lycurgus, therefore, foreseeing this, did not constitute a simple or uniform state, but conjoined in one all the best virtues and properties of each, so as to prevent one factor, should it gain ascendancy, from lapsing into its congenital vice.... For, fear of the people, who themselves were an integral part of the city, prevented the kings from behaving arrogantly and abusing their power; and by fear of the elders the people were prevented from treating the kings with contempt, for the elders, being chosen to their rank on account of virtue, would be on the side of justice in every question that arose. So that, the elders being the mainstay of the ancient discipline, if any factor became weaker than another, at the behest and with the backing of the Senate, it grew stronger and pulled its weight. Lycurgus, therefore, in thus constituting the state, preserved liberty amongst the Lacaedemonians for a longer time than it has lasted amongst any other people known to us.' (VI.10.6–11.)

For the data on which Machiavelli relies in assigning 800 years as the duration of Sparta's constitution, see n. 4 above.

20. Solon is not mentioned by Polybius. He became prominent in Athens about the year 595 B.C., and began to institute democratic reforms. Of them—so Plutarch tells us in his *Life of Solon*—he said: 'To the common people I gave so much power as is sufficient, neither robbing them of dignity, nor giving them too much; and those who had power and were marvellously rich, even to these I contrived that they suffered no harm. I stood with a mighty shield in front of both classes, and suffered neither of them to prevail unjustly,' (Solon 18). Plutarch also quotes Heracleides Ponticus as having said that Solon lived for a long time after Pisistratus had made himself tyrant, but Phanias as having said that he lived on for but two years (*ib.* 32). Pisistratus was tyrant of Athens three times. He set up his first tyranny in 561, and on his death was succeeded by his sons, of whom one, Hipparchus, was murdered in 514, and the other, Hippias, was expelled in 510. The period covered is, therefore, fifty years, but, of this, part was spent in exile. Aristotle says that Pisastratus' tyranny lasted in all 17 years and that of his sons another 18, making 35 in all (*Politics* V.12). But the dates of the earlier tyrannies are uncertain, so that it may be Machiavelli is right when he says the tyranny lasted 40 years. Cleisthenes, who was mainly responsible for expelling the Pisistratidae, restored Solon's laws, increased the number of tribes from four to ten, and introduced ostracism. These were all democratic measures. Other changes of less importance were made by Themistocles and his rival, Aristides; and again by Cimon, Ephialtes, and Pericles. From the expulsion of the Pisistratidae in 510 to the temporary abolition of democracy in 411, when a Council of Four Hundred was set up to administer the state, is just less than one hundred years.

21. In § 17 we return once again to Polybius who, after speaking of Lycurgus, says in VI.11:

'He indeed used a certain amount of reason, and in constituting the republic of

Sparta took note of what usually happens and why it happens; but, though the Romans so constructed the government of their country that they attained the same result, they did not obtain it by any rational process, but arrived at it after many conflicts and disputes, in which it was always what happened in particular cases that taught them to choose the more advantageous course.' (VI.11.1–3; cp. D. I.47.)

Having elaborated this point, Machiavelli then explains how the three factors which Polybius holds to be essential to a perfect state were brought into being in the case of Rome. Polybius, on the other hand, merely states the fact that they existed, and how they contributed to form a well-balanced whole:

'There were then three factors, the nature of which we have already explained, each of which obtained its full rights in the republic (of Rome), and in and through them everything had been so equably and advantageously constituted and was so administered that of the republic as a whole no one could say for certain whether it was an aristocracy, a democracy, or a monarchy. And they were right; for if we look at the power of the consuls it seems to be purely monarchical and royal; but if at the senate's authority, to be an aristocratic regime; and if at the power of the populace one would clearly take it to be a democratic state' (VI.11.4–5).

22. Note that, though Machiavelli says in this paragraph that the development of Rome's constitution followed roughly the lines laid down in §§ 7–12, it did not, after the fall of the monarchy, lead first to a purely aristocratic, and then to a purely democratic, government, but to one in which all three forms were combined; and again that there is no question of the sequence repeating itself, though it did end in the re-establishment of principality.

Guicciardini *in loc.* agrees that a constitution in which all three types of government are combined is the best form, but maintains that the Venetian constitution was better than that of either Rome or Sparta, because it had a head who was appointed for life, but who was an elected, not a hereditary, ruler, and whose powers were strictly limited. He also calls attention to the importance of having a large senate, chosen from all who are eligible for a magistracy, and perpetual, i.e. composed of life-members, but not hereditary.

3. *What Kind of Events gave rise in Rome to the Creation of Tribunes of the Plebs, whereby that Republic was made more Perfect*

1. For the institution of tribunes of the Plebs see Livy II.32–3, and for the class-conflicts which led to it see the preceding chapters in Livy. Machiavelli not only approves of classes in spite of the conflicts to which they inevitably give rise owing to the tendency of the upper class to dominate and of the lower to resent domination (cp. D. I.4.2; 5.3–7), but he also looks on the conflict between them as in the long run beneficial, since, given some one who can discern their cause and find a solution, out of the turmoil arise institutions beneficial to the state as a whole. That is the point of this and of many other chapters (cp. D. I.4–5 and see Index *sub* 'Class-conflict'). Polybius also calls attention to the inevitability of class-conflicts and to the dangers involved. He writes in VI.57:

'When a city has emerged triumphant after many and great dangers, and has already acquired an empire and undisputed power, it is evident that, when good fortune has been firmly established in that city over a considerable period, it will take to luxurious habits, and ambition will get obstinate hold of the minds of its citizens in regard alike to offices and other undertakings; and once such evil ways have crept in, men will begin to deteriorate when they seek to obtain or fail to obtain office moved thereunto by ambition, and will become corrupt, too, in their private conduct owing to their arrogance and luxury. But for completing the transformation the populace will be responsible, since they will ascribe the ill-treatment they suffer from some to avarice and exploitation, and, having been corrupted by the ambitious display of others, will acquire a false sense of their own importance. For, when this comes about, burning with rage and acting only as anger dictates, they will scorn to obey any longer, or to share on equal terms with their former magistrates, but each will demand everything in so far as he can. The appearance of the commonwealth having thus been transformed, it will be given some extremely high sounding name, such as a free people or a popular regime. But in fact it will experience the tyranny of an undisciplined mob, which of all forms of evil is by far the hardest to bear.' (VI.57.5–9.)

Writing somewhere about 150 B.C., and foreseeing all this as a possibility, Polybius says it is difficult to tell what the future of Rome will be. With every word in this passage Machiavelli must have found himself in wholehearted agreement, for he says much the same thing himself. Polybius in this book seeks to discover how Rome managed to control the turbulence of the populace during the centuries which preceded 150 B.C., and incidentally to point out how, when she failed any longer to do so, the tyranny of army commanders who, later on, were to become emperors, was the inevitable result.

2. Note that Machiavelli does not say that all men are wicked, but that the legislator must act on this assumption. Nor does he regard all men as wicked. (Cp. D. III.29, where he denies that the wickedness of the world is due to the wickedness of man, as some say, and ascribes it to princes. Cp. also Introduction, XIII, and see Guicciardini's comments below.)

3. The Roman senate, like most senates in ancient times, was an exclusively aristocratic body. It originally consisted exclusively of patricians representing the various tribes, but, after the expulsion of the Tarquins, plebeians of equestrian rank were 'conscripted'. Hence the term used in addressing the senate, *'patres conscripti'*, i.e. *patres et conscripti* (Livy, II.1.11). Both, therefore, may be classed as nobles, and it is by this term that Machiavelli usually designates them.

4. The traditional date for the expulsion of the Tarquins is 510 B.C. (cp. Livy I.58–60). Dissensions between the patricians and the plebs led to the secession of the latter in 494 B.C. (II.32), in consequence of which two *'tribuni plebis'* were appointed (II.33.2). Their number was subsequently increased.

Guicciardini *in loc.* writes: 'The statement that men never do good except when needs must and that he who is constituting a republic should suppose that all are bad, is too absolute, because there are many who, even when they have the chance to do wrong, do right, and all men are not bad.' . . . On the contrary, 'All men are naturally inclined to the good, and to all in like conditions good is more pleasing than evil'. He grants, however, that legislation envisages those who would be bad.

Aristotle in *Politics* III.15, 1286*b*. 26 *sq*. admits that a king must have force in order to coerce the refractory, even in a constitutional monarchy, but adds that this force, whereby he is to maintain the law, need not be equal to that of the whole people, but will suffice if it be a match for one or more individuals; i.e. he agrees with Guicciardini that most people will not want to violate the law. Law is for him the outcome of custom, and customary laws have more weight than written laws. A man may be a safer ruler than the written law, but not than customary law (III.16, 1287*b*, 5–7). For 'law is reason unaffected by desire', and 'he who bids the law rule, may be deemed to bid God and Reason alone rule, but he who bids man rule adds an element of the beast; for desire is a wild beast, and passion perverts the minds of rulers, even when they are the best of men' (*ib*. 1287a, 28–32).—Cp. Cicero, *De Legibus* II.4:

'Law is not the product of human ingenuity and thought, but is something eternal which should rule the whole world, its commands and its prohibitions being based on wisdom. Thus the wise used to say that the primary and ultimate law was reason (*mens*), all its prescriptions being rooted in the rational commands or prohibitions of God.'

The poor view Machiavelli takes of human nature is probably based mainly on his own experience and on his reading of history; but if one desires a parallel there is one in the speech which Thucydides puts into the mouth of Diodotus:

'All are by nature prone to err both in public and in private life, and no law will prevent them. Men have gone through the whole catalogue of penalties in the hope that, by increasing their severity, they may suffer less at the hands of evil-doers. In early ages the punishments, even of the worst offences, would naturally be milder; but as time went on and mankind continued to transgress, they seldom stopped short of death. And still there are transgressors. Some greater terror, then, has yet to be discovered; certainly death is no deterrent. For poverty inspires necessity with daring, and wealth engenders avarice, pride and insolence; and the various conditions of human life, as they severally fall under the sway of some mighty and fatal power, lure men through their passions to destruction' (III.45).

4. That Discord between the Plebs and the Senate of Rome made this Republic both Free and Powerful

For the discord, see Livy II.7–9, 18, 23–4, 27–32.

1. Cp. D. II.1.

2. Cp. D. I.5, 3–7 on the dispositions giving rise to such conflicts. Cp. also P. 9 (Burd 238, E.77), P. 19, (E. 155) and H.F. III.1 on conflicting humours. See also Aquinas, *Politics,* Book I, *Lect. III: aliquibus natura servire conveniat, aliquibus autem dominari.*

3. Krappe thinks that § 3 may have been suggested by a passage in the Roman Antiquities (*Archaeologia*—'Ρωμαικὴ' Ἀρχαιολογία) of Dionysius Halicarnassus in which he points out that 'the plebeians in their conflict with the patricians never forgot the latter's rank nor resorted to arms to kill them'; and adds:

'If I take somewhat more space in relating this than it seems to merit, it is because I want to forestall the astonishment of readers who shall find it difficult to convince themselves that the patricians of so extensive a power should have agreed to make the populace so absolute without being forced to it either by the murder or by the banishment of their great men, as often happened in other cities' (VII.66).

4. Cp. Cicero, *De Amicitia* XXV, 95: 'A public assembly (*contio*), though composed of ignorant men, can usually see the difference between a demagogue, i.e. a shallow, smooth-tongued citizen, and one who is stable, true, and grave (*constantem et verum et gravem*).' Cp. also a little further down: 'Now if on the platform, I mean in a public assembly (*in contione*), where there is the great opportunity for deceit and dissembling, truth yet prevails provided it be made plain and brought to the light of day', what of friendship, etc. (XXVI.97). Machiavelli is not *quoting* Cicero. He gives but the substance of his remarks, and the context would seem to indicate that it is this passage, XXV–XXVI, that he has in mind. (Cp. also D. I.54 on the influence exercised by a grave man on a tumultuous crowd.)

Guicciardini *in loc.* denies that conflict between the plebs and the senate caused Rome to become great. Such conflicts were harmful. The most one can say is that they did less harm in Rome than in many other cities. The consideration is long, but these are the main points Guicciardini makes.

5. Whether the Safeguarding of Liberty can be more safely entrusted to the Populace or to the Upper Class; and which has the Stronger Reason for creating Disturbances, the 'Have-nots' or the 'Haves'

1. The constitution of Sparta is mentioned in D. I.2.15 as an instance of a constitution in which kings, the aristocracy and the populace each play a part. In D. I.6.2 we are told that Sparta was ruled by a king and a small senate, and in D. I.6.4 that the plebs played no part in the administration, but that the kings safeguarded its rights. In saying this Machiavelli is following Polybius VI.10 (cp. D. I.2, n. 19). Aristotle also says that the Spartan constitution combined all existing forms, i.e. was made up of 'oligarchy, monarchy and democracy, the king forming the monarchy, the council of elders the oligarchy, the democratic element being represented by the ephors; for the ephors are selected from the people.' He adds, however, that 'others regard the ephoralty as a tyranny, and see a democratic element in the common meals and the routine of daily life' (*Politics* II.6). Other democratic factors are mentioned in *Politics* IV.9, amongst them that the people elect the senators and share in the ephoralty. Some, however, prefer to regard it as an oligarchy, since all offices are filled by election, and none by lot, and the power of inflicting death or banishment rests with a few persons (*ib.*). That the constitution lasted so long Aristotle ascribes to Theopompus's having restricted the power of the kings, in particular by establishing the ephoralty. For 'the more restricted the function of kings, the longer their power will last unimpaired, for then they are more moderate and not so despotic in their ways, and are less envied by their subjects' (*Politics* V.11).

2. See D. I.6.2–3 for a further account of the government of Venice. Venice was administered by a Doge, who was elected for life, and was assisted by nine citizens

who formed the *Signoria*. There were two councils, the '*Pregati*' (or senate), and the Great Council. On occasion the people were summoned to a kind of Parliament, called the *Arrengo*. But reforms instituted between 1297 and 1319, abolished the *Arrengo*, restricted the powers of the Doge, made the Grand Council hereditary, and placed the supreme power in its hands. To the Grand Council only the members of certain families, inscribed in a golden book, were eligible. Some of these families were extremely wealthy merchants, known collectively as the '*popolo grasso*', in contrast with the '*popolo minuto*', which comprised artisans, sailors, and the working-class generally. Many aristocratic families, on the other hand, were extremely poor, and in consequence were continually plotting against the state. In 1310 the conspiracy of Tiepoli Baimonte was suppressed with considerable difficulty and much bloodshed, and a Council of Ten was established, which by summary trials and executions sought to eliminate the least sign of revolt. (Cp. Burckhardt, *The Civilisation of the Renaissance in Italy*, I, c. 6, pp. 62–4, for an account of its activities).

3. That Venice should have remained secure for so many centuries Burckhardt ascribes to its isolation, to a common commercial prosperity and trade interests which united all classes, and to the barriers set up between the noble and the burgher class (*ib.*, pp. 65–6). On the duration of Sparta see D. I.2, n. 4.

4. Caius Marius, son of a labourer, rose from the ranks to become so successful a general and so popular with the masses that he was elected consul by a large majority in 107 B.C., and again, after further military successes, was consul from 104 to 100 B.C. During this year there were continual riots in Rome and even a pitched battle in the Forum between his supporters and those of the optimates, or aristocratic party. Marius suppressed the revolt by cutting off the city's water-supply. In 88 by the use of armed force he obtained his coveted appointment to the command of the army against Mithradates, but Sulla marched with another army on Rome and Marius was driven into exile. In 87 he returned at the head of an army, drawn largely from slaves, seized Rome, and put to death all who had opposed him. He became consul for the seventh time in 86, but 18 days later he died at the age of 71. His wife was the aunt of Julius Caesar, who also led the popular party, and it is to Caesar that Machiavelli ascribes Rome's 'ruin'.

5. Cp. Livy IX.26.5–22, for a full account of this incident, which took place in 314 B.C. In the Teubner text we have, however, Caius Maenius as dictator, and Marcus Folius as his Master of Horse, instead of Marcus Menenius and Marcus Fulvius. Maenius was sometimes read for Menenius in the older texts, e.g. in VI.19 and VII.16. Similarly Diodorus reads 'Falinius' for Folius, in XII.58 (cp. Livy IV.25). The Folius or Foslius who became Maenius's Master of Horse was surnamed Flaccinator, and had been consul in 318 (IX.20.1). L. Fulvius was Master of Horse to Lucius Aemilius in 317 (*ib.* 21.2).

Guicciardini *in loc.* points out that the function of the tribunes of the plebs was to protect the rights of the plebs, not to defend the liberties of Rome.

Aristotle also ascribes the origin of class conflicts to opposite and conflicting tendencies. 'The universal and chief cause of the sentiment which leads to revolution', he says, 'is the desire of equality on the part of men who think they are equal to others who have more than themselves; or again the desire of inequality or superiority on the part of those who, regarding themselves as superior, think that they have not more, but the same or less, than their inferiors. . . . Inferiors revolt in order that they may be equal, and equals that they may be superior. Such is the state of mind which creates revolution; and the motives are the desire of gain or honour or the fear of dishonour or loss' (*Politics* V.2, 1302a, 22–36). But, though care should be taken that loyal citizens should outnumber the disloyal, salvation cannot be found on party principles, for if anyone attempts to push either oligarchic or democratic principles to extremes, 'he will begin by spoiling the government and end by having none at all'. The same law of proportion must hold between classes as holds between the parts of the human body (*ib.* V.3, 1302b, 33 *sq.* and V.9, 1309b, 14–35. Cp. also the passage from Thucydides cited at the end of the notes on D. I.46).

Sallust in his *Jugurthine War*, c. 41, points out that: 'Down to the destruction of Carthage, the people and senate of Rome between them administered the state peacefully and soberly; there was no strife amongst the citizens for glory or supremacy, and fear of its enemies kept the state to the exercise of honourable qualities. When, however, men's minds were relieved of this fear, as a natural consequence, wantonness and arrogance, the favourite vices of prosperity, made their appearance. Thus the repose for which amid their calamities they had longed, proved, when they had obtained it, more troublesome and bitter than calamity itself. The nobility now made dignity, the people freedom, the objects of party passion, and everyone seized, plundered, and robbed for his own hand. Thus everything was drawn to one side or the other, and the state which had stood between them, was torn asunder. Of the two parties the nobility were the stronger, owing to their power of common action; the force of the commons, weakened and scattered in a multitude of hands, was less effective.'

Though there is no parallelism between this passage and what Machiavelli says in this and in the preceding discourse, they agree in certain points, for Sallust also ascribes class conflict to a clash between appetites, opposed one to the other, wantonness *versus* arrogance, dignity *versus* the demand for more freedom; points out the disastrous consequences, and also accounts in the same way for the strength of the senatorial party. Hence it may well be that Machiavelli had this passage in mind. But it is on Livy that he is relying for his facts.

6. Whether in Rome such a Form of Government could have been set up as would have removed the Hostility between the Populace and the Senate

1. The Gracchi become prominent in the third part of the second century B.C.; Tiberius during his tribunate in 133, and his brother, Caius, in 123. The much-needed land reforms initiated by Tiberius led to riots which were ruthlessly suppressed by supporters of the senate, in the course of which Tiberius was murdered. It was alleged that he had tried to make himself king. The proposals of Caius in regard to land-reform, colonisation and the extension of the franchise were no less unwelcome to the senate. Though supported by the wealthy equites, to whom he gave a new status, the movement was eventually crushed, and Caius was brutally murdered in 121. Marius, who was mentioned in D. I.5.4 as the cause of Rome's

undoing, headed the reform movement some twenty years later, but, unlike the Gracchi, had an army to support him. His action, therefore, marks the second stage in Rome's failure either to control or to find a solution for class-conflicts. For further references to the Gracchi, see D. I.37.5 and 9; D. I.4.3.

2. At the outset Venice did not exclude newcomers, for in H.F.I.29 we are told that the original settlers were joined by fugitives from Lombardy.

3. The use of the term 'gentlefolk' (*gentiluomini*) in this chapter must be distinguished from its use elsewhere; cp. D. I.55.7, where gentlefolk are defined to be 'those who live in idleness on the revenue of their estates', and 55.10, where we are told that in Venice the term does not signify this, but is indicative merely of rank.

4. That the Spartans should cease to exclude foreigners was one of the demands made by Pericles in his speech to the Athenian Assembly in 432 B.C. (Thucydides I.144; and cp. 139 where the Spartans complain that Megarians were excluded from Athenian markets). Plutarch says that Lycurgus 'excluded foreigners who could not give a good reason for their coming'; not, as Thucydides states, out of fear lest they should imitate the constitution of that city and emulate its virtuous practices, but lest they 'teach his own people to do evil' (*Lycurgus* 27). Aristotle says that 'there is a tradition that in the days of their ancient kings, the Spartans were in the habit of giving the rights of citizenship to foreigners, and therefore, in spite of their long wars, no lack of population was experienced by them; indeed at one time Sparta is said to have numbered not less than 10,000 citizens'; but at the time of the Theban invasion it had fallen to 1,000 (*Politics* II.9, 1270a, 30 *sq.*).

5. With this passage compare what Polybius says in VI.48:
'In the matter of preserving concord amongst citizens and of providing for the security of Lacedaemonian territory, I think it was to the laws of Lycurgus that Sparta owed the maintenance of her liberty, and that in all such matters his prudence was so outstanding that I cannot but think of it as divine rather than human in origin. For the equality in landed possessions and the easy simplicity of the common meals, which caused moderation to be the ruling note in the lives of her citizens, were to be his doing, and were to prevent civic strife; just as habituation to hard work and to the facing of danger was to turn out courageous and public-spirited men. But when both these factors, I mean fortitude and temperance, are present together in the same man or in the same city, it is not easy for vice to spring up in their midst or for such a man or such a city to submit to a yoke imposed by force from without.'

With which contrast what Aristotle says about inequality of property in Sparta and about this being due to her faulty laws (*Politics* II.9, 1270a, 15 *sq.*)

6. As in D. I.2.15 no mention is here made of the Ephors, though it has been claimed that their function corresponded closely to that of the plebeian tribunes in Rome (cp. D. I.5, n. 1), and they were, so Aristotle says, 'chosen from the whole people, so that the office was apt to fall into the hands of very poor men, who, being badly off, were open to bribes,' (*Politics* II.9, 1270b, 7).

7. Neither Venice nor Sparta relied wholly on their own people in their wars. On land the Venetians relied almost exclusively upon *condottieri*, and Sparta relied in part on her serf population, called Helots, and on troops supplied by the Perioci who dwelt in neighbouring cities which acknowledged her supremacy.

8. Machiavelli assigns the same causes for Sparta's decline as does Polybius in VI.48 where he writes: 'For obtaining dominion over her neighbours and for

enforcing her supremacy and rule, Lycurgus seems to have made no preparation whatsoever', and yet, adds Polybius, 'he left the Spartans extremely ambitious in regard to the rest of the Greeks, and eager to dominate them and to grow rich at their expense, for, as everyone knows, the Spartans were the first of all the Greeks to become inflamed with greed for their neighbours' lands'. The rise of Thebes and the decline of Sparta began with the overthrow by Pelopidas and Epaminondas in 379 B.C. of the tyranny which Sparta had established over that city. This was followed by her alliance with Athens, and culminated in her unexpected victory over Sparta at Leuctra in 371.

9. For an account of the conquests made by Venice in Italy see H.F. I.29; and for her collapse at Agnadello or Vaila in 1509, see D. I.53.3; II.10.6; III.31.3; and P. 12 (Burd 262 *sq.* and note 6; E. 101 *sq.*).

10. Note that the outbreak of wars is here ascribed to precisely the same appetites that have been set down in D. I.5.3 as the cause of class-warfare, namely, the desire to dominate and the resentment it arouses. Cp. D. II.14.1, where envy and hatred are said to be the causes of war. Wars, however, may also be made in order to preserve peace (D. II.11.3).

11. Several typical Machiavellian maxims and principles occur in the course of this chapter. Thus in § 6 we are told that 'it is impossible to remove one inconvenience without incurring another' (see Index *sub* 'Inconveniences') and in § 8 that we must choose the course that leads to the fewest inconveniences. Again, in § 8, the general principle that some seek to dominate and others to resist domination (cp. D. I.4.2) is applied to nations. In this paragraph (9) we are reminded that all things are ever in a state of flux (cp. Preface to Bk. II, § 4; D. I.2.3 *sq.* and H.F. Pref. to Bk. V). While in § 10 Machiavelli points out that virtue does not always lie in choosing the middle course (cp. D. I.26.3; II.23; III.2.3; III.21.3).

For the general theme of this chapter, cp. Polybius 48–52, where the argument is much the same.

Guicciardini *in loc.* suggests that conflicts between the plebs and the patricians might have been avoided, had the patricians, instead of opposing the plebs on all counts, allowed their more distinguished members to become patricians.

7. How necessary Public Indictments are for the Maintenance of Liberty in a Republic

1. Polybius refers to the need for public indictments in VI.14. 'For what can go right', he asks, 'if the good and the bad are placed on the same footing.' The people [of Rome], therefore, exercise judgment, usually imposing fines wherever a grave offence has been committed, especially if committed by those holding the highest offices; and the people alone have the power of life and death. There exists also an excellent custom: those accused of any capital crime, while the cause is being tried, have the right to appeal to the public and to go into voluntary exile.'

2. Cp. Livy II.34–5, where Coriolanus' speech is given and all the data Machiavelli uses. Cn. Marcius Coriolanus, a descendant of king Ancus Marcius, won his cognomen in the siege of Corioli, when he drove back the Volscians, who had made a sally. On his return to Rome at the head of the army, says Machiavelli (in

A.W. Bk. VI, 8, 349b; F. 133), he saved the possessions of the nobility but burnt those of the plebs. Livy does not say this, however. But he does relate how after his impeachment Coriolanus joined the Volsci and led their army against Rome. This was in 491 B.C., so the legend goes.

3. In the disturbances which occurred later, use was made of private forces by the Gracchi (cp. D. I.6, n. 1) and for his attack on Rome Marius collected an army (cp. D. I.5, n. 4).

4. When Francesco Valori returned to Florence in November 1494 from an embassy to Charles VIII who was encamped near Florence, he found the Piazza filled with a turbulent crowd demanding vengeance on Piero de' Medici. Without dismounting, Valori, who had once been a friend of the Medici, told them of Piero's acceptance of the degrading terms proposed by the French king; then put himself at the head of the mob and led them against the Medici palace with cries of 'Down with the balls!', of which there were six in the Medici arms. Piero, unable to find support anywhere, was compelled to flee the city, and the regime of Savonarola presently began. Valori now became the head of the popular party which supported Savonarola, played an important part in the framing of the new constitution, and was elected Gonfalonier for the first two months of 1497. Opposed to him were the Arrabbiati, who were in favour of an aristocratic government, and the Compagnacci or 'Bad Fellows', a group of young men who went about armed and were out to kill Savonarola. In May there was a riot in the Duomo. By the end of the month Savonarola was excommunicated and the Arrabbiati were triumphant. In April 1498 the fiasco of the ordeal by fire turned the mob against Savonarola since they had waited for hours to watch it, but in vain. On the following day, 8 April, Savonarola's supporters, the Piagnoni, were attacked by the Arrabbiati on their way to the Cathedral, and the convent of St. Mark's was stormed by the mob. Valori was amongst its defenders, but, finding that the friars were not prepared to fight, he left to seek fresh forces. He was summoned to the Signory, but on the way was murdered by friends of Piero de' Medici. His wife was shot at her window; his house and those of several of his friends were pillaged and set on fire, for which no punishment was exacted by the Signory. On 23 May Savonarola and Fra Domenico were put to death, and in the following month Machiavelli began his public life.

5. On 20 September 1502, Piero Soderini was appointed Gonfalonier, or President, of the Florentine Republic. The appointment, by a statute passed on 26 August, was for life. Soderini was the intimate friend of Machiavelli, who served under him until his fall, ten years later, in 1512. He was a scrupulously honest man, and in 1510, when a conspiracy was formed against him, insisted on giving an exact account of his stewardship. His refusal to show any special favour to those who had supported him, caused many of them to join the party which was anxious to restore the Medici. His fidelity to the French alliance, his refusal to join the Holy League, and the support he gave to the Concionabulum of Pisa, alienated Pope Julius II, who placed Florence under an interdict and appointed Cardinal de' Medici as his legate in 1511. After the French victory at Ravenna and their subsequent retirement before the combined forces of the Pope and of the Spaniards, both sides solicited the friendship of the Florentines, and between them Soderini hesitated, thereby offending both. The Spanish Viceroy, Raimondo da Cardona, on arriving at the Florentine frontier, announced that he had come to depose

Soderini and demanded that the Medici be allowed to return to Florence as private citizens. Many Florentines were in favour of this, but Soderini, knowing full well that it meant the end of Florentine independence, imprisoned twenty-five of the chief suspects, and appealed to the city to support him in its defence. On 29 August, 1512 the Spaniards entered Prato and pillaged the town, killing several thousand of the inhabitants. The Spanish Viceroy now declared openly that he proposed to restore the Medici. A party of young men broke into the palace and threatened to take Soderini's life unless he at once released the citizens he had imprisoned and resigned his office. Soderini promised to resign, and, having sent for Machiavelli, despatched him to Francesco Vettori, their mutual friend, to ask for shelter in his house. Vettori called a meeting of the magistrates, who refused to consent to Soderini's deposition until Vettori explained that his life depended on it. They then consented, and Soderini was sent with an escort to Siena, whence he made his way to Castelnuovo, then under the rule of the Turks. The judicial body to which appeal might have been made, though too small to be impartial, was the Magistracy of the Eight, whose function it was to keep order and to try all common offences and offences against the state. Machiavelli suggests that, had this happened, Soderini might well have been acquitted, which is probable; but that the Medicean party would have been satisfied with this is extremely improbable.

6. It is basic to Machiavelli's republicanism that an outlet should be provided whereby the populace may air its grievances and let off steam (cp. D. I.4.4 and 8.2 *sq.*). To neglect to make such provision, or, again, to tolerate private vengeance or a citizen with an armed backing (§§ 3 and 4), is to endanger the state.

Note, too, the causal sequence—private vengeance, fear, defensive action, the arming of partisans, the growth of factions—in § 4. Such sequences are of frequent occurrence (cp. Index *sub* 'causal sequences'). Machiavelli's mistrust of oligarchy in any shape or form is illustrated by his remarks on the judicial system in Florence (§ 6). It will be noted that throughout his work he discusses but two types of government, principality and republicanism, save for an occasional remark (cp. *sub* 'republics and principalities' and *sub* 'oligarchy' in the Index).

7. Livy V.33. Aruns had been the guardian of Lucumon, the scion of an important family, and, according to the legend which Livy cites, had guided the Gauls over the Alps. The truth of this story Livy doubts, for the Gauls had already found their way over the Alps two hundred years before this. He admits, however, that Aruns or some other citizen of Clusium may well have betrayed the city to the Gauls. The incident occurred in 391, and is part of the prelude to the sack of Rome in 390. For the attraction Tuscany had to offer the Gauls, see D. II.4.2 and II.8.2.

Guicciardini *in loc.* agrees in principle, but does not think the populace would be competent to administer justice, since it is too easily moved by rumour and false charges.

8. Calumnies are as Injurious to Republics as Public Indictments are Useful

1. In 391 B.C. M. Furius Camillus was accused of having distributed unfairly the booty he had captured at Veii and went in voluntary exile to Ardea. In 390 the

Gauls laid siege both to Rome and to Ardea, but at Ardea Camillus made a sortie and destroyed the besieging army (V.44-5). Rome then recalled Camillus, made him dictator, and on his arrival at Rome he drove off the Gauls, and at his triumph was acknowledged as Rome's second founder (*ib.* 46-9). Other victories followed. This caused Manlius Capitolinus, who had saved the Capitol in 390, to become jealous, and in 386 he stirred up the plebs against Camillus (VI.11). The dispute was settled by the dictator, Cornelius Cossus, who called the disputants before him on his return to Rome in 385 (*ib.* 15-16).

2. Machiavelli, when in office, was not wholly free from calumny, for there is extant a letter from Biagio Buonaccorsi, informing him that 'a certain person, masked, presented himself to the notary of the Conservators with two witnesses, alleging that on account of his father, he was not qualified for the post of secretary'. What the trouble was we are not told, but it is clear from the letter that it was causing Buonaccorsi considerable anxiety. He also mentions that Machiavelli had few friends ready to help him. This was in 1509 when the opposition to Soderini was already strong (cp. Villari I.504).

3. For the 'Captain' see D. I.39.4 and *notes 5, 6 in loc.*

4. Cp. *Hist. Florence* IV.24 *sq.* In 1430 Giovanni, son of Luigi, Guicciardini was appointed commissary of the Florentine forces then besieging Lucca. The Lucchesi, then under the domination of Paolo Guinigi, appealed to Filippo Maria Visconti, Duke of Milan, who sent Francesco Sforza to help them. The Florentines bribed Francesco with 50,000 ducats to withdraw (IV.24). A conspiracy overthrew Luigi, who was taken by Francesco as a prisoner to Milan. The Lucchesi, now rid of their tyrant, appealed again to Milan and Niccolò Piccinino was sent to their assistance. The Florentine army under Guicciardini and the Duke of Urbino tried to intercept him, but was defeated, and the Commissary fled with the remnant of his men to Pisa. Those responsible, unable to blame the popular party, who had promoted the undertaking, says Machiavelli, 'renewed their calumnies against those who had conducted it . . . The person most fiercely attacked was Messer Giovanni Guicciardini, against whom it was alleged that having it in his power when Count Francesco left Lucca to bring the war to an end, he had been bribed with a sum of money which he remitted home, the amount, the names of those who had carried it, and of those who received it, all being given. These rumours and accusations went so far that the Captain of the People, moved by public clamour and urged on by the party hostile to Messer Giovanni, cited him before him. Giovanni appeared, fuming with indignation; whereupon his kinsmen for the honour of their house prevailed on the Captain to abandon the enquiry.' (IV.25). Nor was this an isolated incident, for the popular party 'set themselves with all skill and industry to calumniate the men employed in the war (amongst whom were many of the most distinguished citizens in the commonwealth), so that if, as frequently happened, a reverse was suffered, it was ascribed not to the good fortune or superior strength of the enemy, but to the scant prudence of the commissary' (IV.26). The result was that the so-called party of the nobles, led by Messer Rinaldo degli Albizzi, in 1433, entered the Piazza with armed forces, created a Balìa to reform the government, and caused Cosimo de' Medici to be arrested, and subsequently to be sent into exile (IV.28-9).

Guicciardini *in loc.* admits that calumnies are detestable, but does not think it possible in a free city to prevent them. To assert that calumnies made it possible for Cosimo de' Medici to acquire power is nonsense (*un sogno*); he owed it to his prudence and to his exceedingly great wealth. Nor did the calumniation of Giovanni Guicciardini give rise to divisions in Florence or intensify them. They already existed.

Cp. also on calumnies Plutarch's '*Praecepta gerendae reipublicae*'. Having remarked in n. 14 that the statesman in just causes should give testimony even on behalf of his opponents, and should assist them in court against the blackmailer, and should discredit calumnies about them if the charges brought are alien to the principles they profess (810A), in n. 16 he says: 'In every democracy there is a spirit of malice and fault-finding directed against public men, and if there be no party opposition and no expression of dissent, it is surmised that desirable measures are the result of conspiracy, and this subjects a man's associates and friends to calumny' (813A).

9. That it is necessary to be the Sole Authority if one would constitute a Commonwealth afresh or would reform it thoroughly regardless of its Ancient Institutions

1. Polybius cites with approval the saying of Euripides that 'one wise head is worth more than many strong hands'. For, he says, 'it is manifest in the case now before us'—the defeat of M. Atilius Regulus by the Carthaginians under the Spartan general, Xanthippus—'that the counsels and abilities of one single person subdued the Roman legions who, owing to their experience and bravery, were esteemed invincible, rescued a sinking and despairing commonwealth, and restored courage to a beaten and spiritless army, grown stupid by their misfortunes' (I.35). He also has an immense admiration for Lycurgus, to whom he attributes all that is good in the Spartan constitution (VI.48). But he does not, like Machiavelli, hold that in general constitutions and the reforming of a constitution are better carried out by one man, for what in his opinion—and also in Machiavelli's—is the best constitution, namely, that of Rome, did not arise in this way, but was constructed gradually and under the constraint of circumstances, as Machiavelli is careful to point out. (Cp. D. I.2.17.)

2. In spite of Livy's warning (*Praefatio* 6) that the early story of Rome's foundation is based on poetical fables rather than historical documents, Machiavelli makes no mention of this, but uses them as the basis of his political theorems in the same way he uses genuine historical incidents. Livy gives a brief account of the killing of Remus in I.7.1–2. After their womenfolk had induced the Romans and the Sabines to make peace, they lived as one people, the Romans on the Palatine hill under Romulus, and the Sabines on the Capitoline and Quirinal hills under Titus Tatius, who was killed by some Laurentines whom he had offended. Romulus was not directly responsible for his death, but 'took the matter less to heart than he ought to have done', says Livy (I.14.3), and took no action against the tribe responsible for the murder.

3. It is in the light of such passages as this that what Machiavelli says about autocrats in *The Prince* should be read. Though fully alive to their failings, Machiavelli always supposes that the true prince rules 'not in his own interests, but for the

common good; not in the interest of his successors, but for the sake of the fatherland common to all' (§ 2). It is because the removal of rivals is, in Machiavelli's opinion, for the common good, and only when it is for the common good, that he claims that it is justifiable.

4. This passage, which is perhaps the first clear statement of the famous dictum that 'the end justifies the means', provided the end be good, runs in Italian as follows: '*Conviene bene che, accusandolo il fatto, lo effetto lo scusi; e quando sia buono, come quello di Romolo, sempre lo scuserà.*' (Cp. the French dictum: *le fait accuse, l'effet excuse.*) This is the only passage in which Machiavelli explicitly formulates the principle that the end justifies the means, nor does he ever attempt to prove it either by appeal to experience or to reason. It is an assumption, but an assumption that is basic alike in the *Discourses* and in *The Prince*. The end he has in mind is explained in § 2: it is that of a prudent organiser 'whose intention it is to govern not in his own interests but for the common good, and not in the interests of his successors but for the sake of that fatherland which is common to all'. Given this end, the prudent organiser is justified, Machiavelli claims, in doing anything to promote its realisation, even though it be flagrantly and admittedly immoral. If a new prince, he can and should wipe out not only the ruler he has despoiled, but the whole of his family, even though they be his own kinsmen (D. III.4). If a republican regime has just been set up in the name of liberty, 'exemplary action must be taken against those who are hostile to the new state of affairs', where 'exemplary action' means 'killing the sons of Brutus', even though the prudent legislator is Brutus himself (D. III.3). Almost all the recommendations to which exception has been taken in Machiavelli's writings are based on the same principle; and towards the close of the *Discourses*, in D. III.41, we are told explicitly that 'it is good to defend one's country in *any* way whatsoever' and that whether the action taken 'entail ignominy or glory', i.e. be morally good or bad, is irrelevant. In my Introduction (XII, §§ 130 *sq.*) I have applied to this principle Machiavelli's own criterion, that of consequences. Here it suffices to point out that, fundamental as the principle is in Machiavellian theory, no evidence is adduced in support of it, and that it is this principle, more than any other, that has aroused, and rightly aroused, adverse comment.

5. Note that the term 'virtue' connotes here not merely 'efficiency', but efficiency used in the interests of the state and for the 'common good'.

6. This statement, though not explicitly made either by Livy or Plutarch, accords with what they say. Plutarch, however, in his *Life of Romulus* (26) says that after his last war he, 'like all men who had been lifted up by great and unexpected strokes of fortune to power and dignity, was emboldened by his achievements to take on a haughtier bearing, to renounce his popular ways, and to change to the ways of a monarch.' Cp. also the *Life of Numa*, 2.

7. This agrees with what Livy says in the opening chapter of Book II. (Cp. Arnold, *History of Rome*, c. 8.)

8. In the time of Agis IV, king of Sparta (244-240 B.C.), the laws of Lycurgus had been to a large extent abandoned, property was centred in the hands of about a hundred citizens, and there was much poverty and debt. Agis, supported by Lysander, sought to revive the Lycurgan laws, but was opposed by Leonidas, the Agid king, and by the ephors. He fled, but was caught and put to death. Leonidas died shortly afterwards and was succeeded by Cleomenes III (237-221 B.C.). He took up Agis's project of reform, but, instead of attempting to carry it out at once,

But his son, Dionysius II, was also tyrant of Syracuse from 367 to 343 (Cp. *note* 5 above, and *Politics,* V.10).

8. Round Lucius Sergius Catiline centred all the malcontents in Italy and Rome. In 66 B.C. he supported two consuls-designate who had been debarred for bribery, in a conspiracy to murder the consuls. When Cicero became consul in 64 B.C., he thwarted an attempt of Catiline to seize the consulship by force. A plot was formed to murder Cicero in 63 and Catiline sought to raise troops and to persuade the Allobroges to join him. The discovery of this plot turned the populace against him. The conspirators in Rome were arrested and strangled, and Catiline, who had collected some 6,000 followers near Pistoia, was defeated and slain. Of him Plutarch in his *Life of Cicero* says: 'Besides various other crimes he was accused of having debauched his own daughter and killed his own brother, and to save himself from prosecution induced Sulla to put his dead brother's name, instead of his own, amongst the proscribed as if he were alive. Under his leadership, a profligate set, sworn to secrecy, sacrificed a man and ate his flesh. He corrupted the youth of Rome by indulging their desires with every form of pleasure, providing them with wine and women and setting no limit to the expenses they incurred.' Vast inequalities in wealth, a nobility impoverished by lavish entertainments, and offices obtained by bribery, signified the tottering state in which the republic then was, and 'it needed but a bold adventurer to upset it' (*Cicero, n.* 10).

9. Of Marcus Junius Brutus, who murdered Julius Caesar, Plutarch in his *Comparison of Dion and Brutus,* writes: 'The greatest glory of both consists in their abhorrence of tyrants, and tyrannical measures. This in Brutus was mingled with no other motive. He had no quarrel with Caesar, but risked his life for the liberty of his country. . . . Even his enemies admitted that he alone of the conspirators, had no end save the restoration of the ancient form of government' (n. 3). On the prejudice displayed by historians, cp. Polybius II.56, 61, and Tacitus, *Histories,* I.1.

10. In this paragraph Machiavelli speaks only of the earlier emperors down to Marcus Aurelius. In *The Prince,* c. 19, he deals with the set which begins with Marcus Aurelius and ends with Maximinus, and discusses the more important emperors in considerable detail. In the next paragraph he discusses the two sets (26 of them in all) as a whole. Of those mentioned here three, be it noted, are bad, and six are good.

11. Before discussing what Machiavelli says of the Roman emperors in this paragraph, it will be convenient to draw up a list of them, and to tabulate what Machiavelli says about them in P. 19 and D. I.10.

LIST OF ROMAN EMPERORS FROM CAESAR TO MAXIMINUS

Column 1: A = assassinated (or suicide). d = died natural death.
Column 2: D = mentioned in D. I.10. P = mentioned in P. 19. P* = discussed in P. 19.
Column 3: G = classed as good. B = classed as bad. T = classed as a tyrant.
Column 4: Relationship to previous emperors.

	(1)		(2)	(3)	(4)
1. Caesar	A	44 B.C.	D	T	
2. Augustus	d	14 A.D.			grandnephew and adopted heir of J. C.

common good; not in the interest of his successors, but for the sake of the fatherland common to all' (§ 2). It is because the removal of rivals is, in Machiavelli's opinion, for the common good, and only when it is for the common good, that he claims that it is justifiable.

4. This passage, which is perhaps the first clear statement of the famous dictum that 'the end justifies the means', provided the end be good, runs in Italian as follows: '*Conviene bene che, accusandolo il fatto, lo effetto lo scusi; e quando sia buono, come quello di Romolo, sempre lo scuserà.*' (Cp. the French dictum: *le fait accuse, l'effet excuse.*) This is the only passage in which Machiavelli explicitly formulates the principle that the end justifies the means, nor does he ever attempt to prove it either by appeal to experience or to reason. It is an assumption, but an assumption that is basic alike in the *Discourses* and in *The Prince*. The end he has in mind is explained in § 2: it is that of a prudent organiser 'whose intention it is to govern not in his own interests but for the common good, and not in the interests of his successors but for the sake of that fatherland which is common to all'. Given this end, the prudent organiser is justified, Machiavelli claims, in doing anything to promote its realisation, even though it be flagrantly and admittedly immoral. If a new prince, he can and should wipe out not only the ruler he has despoiled, but the whole of his family, even though they be his own kinsmen (D. III.4). If a republican regime has just been set up in the name of liberty, 'exemplary action must be taken against those who are hostile to the new state of affairs', where 'exemplary action' means 'killing the sons of Brutus', even though the prudent legislator is Brutus himself (D. III.3). Almost all the recommendations to which exception has been taken in Machiavelli's writings are based on the same principle; and towards the close of the *Discourses*, in D. III.41, we are told explicitly that 'it is good to defend one's country in *any* way whatsoever' and that whether the action taken 'entail ignominy or glory', i.e. be morally good or bad, is irrelevant. In my Introduction (XII, §§ 130 *sq.*) I have applied to this principle Machiavelli's own criterion, that of consequences. Here it suffices to point out that, fundamental as the principle is in Machiavellian theory, no evidence is adduced in support of it, and that it is this principle, more than any other, that has aroused, and rightly aroused, adverse comment.

5. Note that the term 'virtue' connotes here not merely 'efficiency', but efficiency used in the interests of the state and for the 'common good'.

6. This statement, though not explicitly made either by Livy or Plutarch, accords with what they say. Plutarch, however, in his *Life of Romulus* (26) says that after his last war he, 'like all men who had been lifted up by great and unexpected strokes of fortune to power and dignity, was emboldened by his achievements to take on a haughtier bearing, to renounce his popular ways, and to change to the ways of a monarch.' Cp. also the *Life of Numa*, 2.

7. This agrees with what Livy says in the opening chapter of Book II. (Cp. Arnold, *History of Rome*, c. 8.)

8. In the time of Agis IV, king of Sparta (244–240 B.C.), the laws of Lycurgus had been to a large extent abandoned, property was centred in the hands of about a hundred citizens, and there was much poverty and debt. Agis, supported by Lysander, sought to revive the Lycurgan laws, but was opposed by Leonidas, the Agid king, and by the ephors. He fled, but was caught and put to death. Leonidas died shortly afterwards and was succeeded by Cleomenes III (237–221 B.C.). He took up Agis's project of reform, but, instead of attempting to carry it out at once,

waited until he had established his reputation in the war with Achaea. He then returned home, put the ephors to death at a dinner-party, and restored the constitution of Lycurgus with some modifications, such as admitting the Perioci to citizenship.

Krappe in his article 'Quelques Sources greques de N.M.' (see Intro. § 10), suggests that in this paragraph Machiavelli is relying on Plutarch's *Life of Agis and Cleomenes.* But (i) Plutarch does not say that the ephors took Agis to be a man aiming at a tyranny; (ii) he mentions as the source whence Cleomenes learned of Agis's designs, not some records which he had discovered, but Xenares, who gave him an account of Agis's doings and plans; nor (iii) does Plutarch say that Cleomenes realised that he could not carry the plans into effect unless he became the sole authority, though this is implied by his actions. Krappe, therefore, would scarce seem to have established his contention.

Incidentally, Polybius has no use for Cleomenes, and mistrusts Phylarchus, upon whom Plutarch relies (cp. II.56–63). Cleomenes' reforms, he claims, resulted in the entire destruction of Sparta's ancient constitution, presumably because of the admission of the Perioci to citizenship and of the imperial designs which Cleomenes entertained.

9. The Macedonian invasion of Greece took place in 338 B.C., when Philip II was invited there by the Amphictionic League. The Greeks were defeated at Chaeronia in August of this year, and in consequence Greece became subject to Macedon.

On the difficulty of introducing 'nuovi ordini', see *The Prince,* c. 6; E.46 sq.

Guicciardini *in loc.* admits that a ruler 'who cannot constitute a state otherwise deserves praise if he resorts to violence and fraud and extraordinary measures', but prays God that 'there may be no need to amend republics by such methods'. (For the full passage, see Introduction, § 122.) He adds that it is doubtful whether Romulus was looking to the common good, for, if he remembers aright, Romulus was killed by the Senate for having arrogated to himself too much authority (cp. Plutarch's *Romulus,* nn. 26–7).

Aristotle holds that normally legislation is the function of those who are equal in birth and power, but that if there be a man 'with whom the virtues of all the rest bear no comparison, so that he can no longer be regarded as a part of the state'—a 'God among men', then he will be a law unto himself, and it will be unjust that it should be otherwise (*Politics* III.13, 1284a, 3–14).

10. Those who set up a Tyranny are no less Blameworthy than are the Founders of a Republic or a Kingdom Praiseworthy

1. Cp. with the heading of this chapter St. Thomas, *De Regimine Principum* I, c. 3, 'Sicut autem regimen regis est optimum, ita regimen tyranni est pessimum.' The strong indictment of tyranny contained in this discourse makes it clear how intensely Machiavelli hated tyranny, and hence that the last thing he had in mind in composing *The Prince* was to help would-be princes to set up a tyranny. He believes that autocracy is called for in certain circumstances, and that those circumstances were

26

realised in the Italy of his day, but never tyranny. The indictment is the more remarkable in that at the head of the list of tyrants appears Caesar, of whose rule Plutarch says that it 'was a tyranny only in name and appearance, and no cruel or tyrannical act was authorised by it: nay, it was plain that the ills of the state required a monarchy, and that Caesar, like a most gentle physician, had been assigned to them by heaven itself.' (*Comparison of Dion and Brutus*, 2). Machiavelli's condemnation of Caesar is based simply and solely on the fact that he put an end to Rome's liberties and that in consequence there ensued later on a sequence of tyrants who brought ruin to Rome's name and imperial power. 'Tis the property of a tyrant', says Polybius (V.11), 'to lead a wicked life, dominating unwilling subjects by force and fear, and to be hated by the subjects who live under his yoke'—vices that all virtuous princes will studiously avoid. Caesar was not a tyrant in this sense.

2. Note that praise is here assigned to various classes of men precisely in proportion to the services they render to the state, and blame in proportion to their disservices. This constitutes for Machiavelli political virtue and political vice.

3. P. Cornelius Scipio Africanus Major (234–183 B.C.), who destroyed the power of the Carthaginians first in Spain and then in Africa, though he might have perhaps seized supreme power, preferred to ignore the charges of bribery that had been brought against him, and to live in retirement. In Machiavelli's opinion, Caesar's ambition was to become a king and to found a dynasty.

4. Agesilaus II (398–360 B.C.) was the nineteenth king of Sparta in the Europontid line. His victories were such that, down to the defeat at Leuctra, 'he was looked up as leader and king of almost all Hellas', says Plutarch in his *Life of Agesilaus* (40). 'I attribute to political virtue in Agesilaus that inimitable act of his in abandoning his career in Asia on receipt of a dispatch. For he did not, like Pompey, help the commonwealth only as he made himself great, but with an eye to the welfare of his country renounced such great fame and power as no man won before or since his day, except Alexander' (*Comparison of Agesilaus and Pompey*, 2).

5. Dion of Syracuse (assassinated in 354 B.C.) freed Syracuse from the tyranny of Dionysius II in 356, but in 354 he was murdered and Dionysius returned, to be again expelled by Timoleon, the friend of Plato, in 343. Timoleon died in 337. Plutarch's Lives comprise both those of Timoleon and Dion, whom he compares respectively with Aemilius Paulus and Brutus. In view of Machiavelli's contention that it is legitimate and even necessary to remove rivals in order to secure one's position, it is worth while pointing out that, according to Plutarch, Agesilaus 'got his kingdom by sinning against both gods and men, since he brought Leotychides under condemnation for bastardy' (*Comparison of Agesilaus and Pompey*, 1), and that Timoleon was responsible for the murder of his brother, Timophanes, who was seeking to set up a tyranny (*Timoleon*, 5, 6, and cp. *Praecepta gerendae reipublicae*, n. 12; 806A).

6. Nabis, tyrant of Sparta (207–192 B.C.). Polybius gives an account of his tyranny in XIII.6–8. He had constructed the figure of Apéga, his wife, which embraced his enemies and crushed them to death against spikes. (Cp. P. 9, 19; E.80, 150.)

7. Phalaris, tyrant of Agrigentum (570–554 B.C.), had a brazen bull in which his victims were burned. Aristotle refers to him in *Politics* V.10 and *Rhetoric* II.20. For Dionysius the Elder, tyrant of Syracuse (405–367), see Diodorus, Books 13 and 14; and c. xxi in Arnold's *History of Rome*. (Cp. also D. III.6.6 and n. 11).

But his son, Dionysius II, was also tyrant of Syracuse from 367 to 343 (Cp. *note* 5 above, and *Politics*, V.10).

8. Round Lucius Sergius Catiline centred all the malcontents in Italy and Rome. In 66 B.C. he supported two consuls-designate who had been debarred for bribery, in a conspiracy to murder the consuls. When Cicero became consul in 64 B.C., he thwarted an attempt of Catiline to seize the consulship by force. A plot was formed to murder Cicero in 63 and Catiline sought to raise troops and to persuade the Allobroges to join him. The discovery of this plot turned the populace against him. The conspirators in Rome were arrested and strangled, and Catiline, who had collected some 6,000 followers near Pistoia, was defeated and slain. Of him Plutarch in his *Life of Cicero* says: 'Besides various other crimes he was accused of having debauched his own daughter and killed his own brother, and to save himself from prosecution induced Sulla to put his dead brother's name, instead of his own, amongst the proscribed as if he were alive. Under his leadership, a profligate set, sworn to secrecy, sacrificed a man and ate his flesh. He corrupted the youth of Rome by indulging their desires with every form of pleasure, providing them with wine and women and setting no limit to the expenses they incurred.' Vast inequalities in wealth, a nobility impoverished by lavish entertainments, and offices obtained by bribery, signified the tottering state in which the republic then was, and 'it needed but a bold adventurer to upset it' (*Cicero*, n. 10).

9. Of Marcus Junius Brutus, who murdered Julius Caesar, Plutarch in his *Comparison of Dion and Brutus*, writes: 'The greatest glory of both consists in their abhorrence of tyrants, and tyrannical measures. This in Brutus was mingled with no other motive. He had no quarrel with Caesar, but risked his life for the liberty of his country. . . . Even his enemies admitted that he alone of the conspirators, had no end save the restoration of the ancient form of government' (n. 3). On the prejudice displayed by historians, cp. Polybius II.56, 61, and Tacitus, *Histories*, I.1.

10. In this paragraph Machiavelli speaks only of the earlier emperors down to Marcus Aurelius. In *The Prince*, c. 19, he deals with the set which begins with Marcus Aurelius and ends with Maximinus, and discusses the more important emperors in considerable detail. In the next paragraph he discusses the two sets (26 of them in all) as a whole. Of those mentioned here three, be it noted, are bad, and six are good.

11. Before discussing what Machiavelli says of the Roman emperors in this paragraph, it will be convenient to draw up a list of them, and to tabulate what Machiavelli says about them in P. 19 and D. I.10.

LIST OF ROMAN EMPERORS FROM CAESAR TO MAXIMINUS

Column 1: A = assassinated (or suicide). d = died natural death.
Column 2: D = mentioned in D. I.10. P = mentioned in P. 19. P* = discussed in P. 19.
Column 3: G = classed as good. B = classed as bad. T = classed as a tyrant.
Column 4: Relationship to previous emperors.

	(1)		(2) (3)	(4)
1. Caesar	A	44 B.C.	D T	
2. Augustus	d	14 A.D.		grandnephew and adopted heir of J. C.

	(1)	(2)	(3)	(4)
3. Tiberius	d 37 A.D.			stepson, son-in-law and adopted heir of A.
4. Gaius Caligula	A 41	D	B	great-grandson of A. and adopted heir of G.
5. Claudius	A 54			uncle of Gaius.
6. Nero	A 68	D	B	stepson and adopted heir of Claudius.
7. Galba	A 69	D	G	Elected.
8. Otho (suicide)	A 69			Elected.
9. Vitellius	A 69	D	B	Elected.
10. Vespasian	d 79			Elected.
11. Titus	d 81	D	G	son of Vespasian.
12. Domitian	A 96			son of Vespasian.
13. Nerva	d 98	D	G	Elected.
14. Trajan	d 117	D	G	Spaniard, adopted as son by Nerva.
15. Hadrian	d 138	D	G	adopted son of Trajan.
16. Antoninus Pius	d 161	D	G	adopted son of Hadrian.
17. Marcus Aurelius	d 180	P D	G	grandson of Hadrian by adoption.
18. Commodus	A 192	P*	T	son of Marcus.
19. Pertinax	A 193	P*D	G	Elected.
20. Julianus	A 193	P	B	Elected.
21. Severus (Septimius)	d 211	P*D	T	Elected.
22. Antoninus Caracalla	A 217	P*	T	son of Severus.
23. Macrinus	A 218	P	B	Elected.
24. Heliogabalus	A 222	P	B	reputed son of Antoninus.
25. Alexander (Severus)	A 235	P	G	cousin and adopted son of Heliogabalus.
26. Maximinus	A 238	P*D	T	Elected.

To complete the list of 26 emperors we must either include Julius Caesar or Geta, who for a brief space was co-emperor with Caracalla till the latter murdered him. As Geta is not mentioned in P. 19, presumably Machiavelli intends us to reckon Caesar as the first emperor, though he never assumed the title of *'princeps'*, or any other imperial title (cp. C.A.H. IX, p. 727 *sq.*). This is borne out by I.52.4, where he is said to have acquired a principality. In either case, 16 out of the 26 emperors met with a violent death if we include Claudius, who was suspected of dying of foul play, Otho, who committed suicide, and with Herodian reject the plausible legend that Commodus died of apoplexy brought on by over-eating. (*Hist. de Imperio Rom. Imperatorum post Marcum*, II.2).

12. A comparison of columns 1 and 3 shows a close correspondence between emperors who came to a violent end and those classed by Machiavelli as tyrants or as bad emperors in D. I.10 or P. 19. With three of the exceptions he deals, but of Claudius he says nothing. Hence presumably Claudius must be classed as a bad emperor, and so as no exception. Galba and Pertinax are easily explained, but

Severus presents some difficulty, for he is described as a wicked man (*scelerato*) who escaped a violent end in part owing to his virtue (!) and in part owing to his good luck.

Severus belongs to the later period with which Machiavelli deals in P. 19. During this period it was the army rather than the senate or the people that had to be placated. Hence, says Machiavelli, emperors who wished to maintain their power were 'forced to do evil for, when the body is corrupt, you have to submit to its humours'. The outstanding case is Severus, who 'committed every kind of iniquity against the people', yet was 'of such virtue', i.e. was 'so valiant a lion and so cunning a fox', that he surmounted all difficulties and kept the troops friendly, at any rate for the time being (P. 19). Hence, though in P. 19 Severus is classed as a wicked emperor, in A.W. Book I (B.282b, F.17) we find him classed with Hadrian and Marcus Aurelius as a good emperor. Similarly, in P. 8 Agathocles is described as virtuous in that he owed his position 'neither to fortune nor to friends, but to his own efforts carried out amid a thousand dangers and difficulties'. In both cases the term 'virtue' signifies efficiency; but of both it is important to add what Machiavelli actually does add in the case of Agathocles, that, though a great man, he is not to be classed with '*excellentissimi uomini*', nor—strictly speaking—is his success 'to be ascribed either to fortune or virtue'.

13. In the last section of § 6 Machiavelli distinguishes between 'emperors who acquired imperial power by inheritance' (*per eredità*) and those who 'acquired it through adoption' (*per adozione*), and tells us that of the former all, save Titus, were bad, and that the latter were all good. If, taking the emperors from Galba onwards, we exclude those who were elected (usually by the troops), a comparison of columns 3 and 4 will bear out the claim Machiavelli makes; for Trajan, Hadrian, Antoninus, Marcus, and Alexander Severus, who were adopted, are all classed as good. While of those who were hereditary, Titus is admittedly an exception; Domitian behaved tyrannically not only toward Jews and Christians, but also toward republicans and all whom he suspected of disloyalty; and in P. 19 Commodus, Caracalla, Heliogabalus, and Maximinus are all classed as bad emperors. But in regard to the earlier emperors a difficulty arises, for in that they all belonged to the *gens* Julia they all had a hereditary title, and yet, with the exception of Claudius, were all adopted by their predecessors. Moreover, except in the case of Julius Caesar, Caligula, and Nero, we do not know whether Machiavelli regarded them as good or bad. Hence in regard to the emperors from Augustus to Nero it is impossible to verify Machiavelli's statement. Incidentally, Gibbon in discussing the emperors from Augustus to Maximinus contrasts hereditary succession with election (not with adoption), and concludes in favour of 'the prerogative of birth'. In spite of the fact that men smile at the thought of the nation's property, on the father's decease, passing, like a drove of oxen, to his infant son, a mere glance at the list of emperors, says Gibbon, will suffice to convince us that almost anything is preferable to election by a turbulent soldiery (I. c. 7). This, however, is not Machiavelli's point. There is another alternative which Gibbon ignores: it is that kings and emperors should designate those who are to succeed them.

14. The preceding paragraph (§ 7) indicates plainly what Machiavelli means by a good or virtuous prince, and § 8 indicates no less plainly the consequences likely to ensue when an empire falls into the hands of a bad prince. In § 8 Machiavelli follows closely Tacitus, *Histories*, I.2.

Cp. with this chapter *The Prince*, c. 19.

Guicciardini *in loc.* agrees with the theorem that heads the chapter, but not with the way Machiavelli has used his examples. He distinguishes three cases: (i) Tyrannies acquired by usurpation. For these there is no general rule, but when brought about by civil disorders, the usurper who prefers his country to his own safety is to be praised. (ii) Hereditary tyrants. These deserve less blame than do those who found a tyranny, but rarely renounce their position of their own accord. (iii) Princes appointed legitimately, as were the Spartan kings. On the question whether adoption is preferable to hereditary succession, Guicciardini says merely that tyrants who are prepared to deprive their posterity of the right to succeed, exist rather in books than in point of fact. Aristotle agrees. 'That a king should not hand on his power to his children,' he says, 'is hardly to be expected, and is too much to ask of human nature.' He points out, however, that if the children who succeed are no better than anyone else, it will be mischievous (*Politics* III.15, 1286b, 23–6).

11. Concerning the Religion of the Romans

1. The arguments Machiavelli uses in this and the next four chapters, in defence of a religion of the type found in pagan Rome in its republican days, are similar to those used by Polybius. Both see in oaths, auspices and miracles an instrument which the civil authorities can use to serve political ends, and in religious rites a stimulus to the practice of military virtues. The relevant passages will be cited as occasion arises. But, though there can be no doubt that the general line of Machiavelli's argument is similar to, and was in all probability suggested by, Polybius, the way in which he develops and illustrates it is his own, and his examples, as usual, are taken from Livy.

The points with which Machiavelli deals in this chapter are (i) the importance of religion in general, (ii) the value of oaths, and (iii) the advantage of claiming divine authority especially in founding a new regime, given that the people are prepared to recognise such claims.

2. For the constitution ascribed by tradition to Romulus, see Livy I.8. For the religious institutions introduced by Numa, see Livy I.19–21. On the important part played by religion in the development of Rome, see Polybius VI.56: 'In my opinion the Romans excel all other peoples especially in their attitude to the gods, so much so that what with the rest of mortals becomes a vice seems to me to be the very thing which they used in order to control the republic, I mean superstition. For many quite rightly marvel at the exaggerated importance assigned to superstition, which alike in private and public life played a part that could not have been greater than it was.'

Note that it is of '*superstitio*', not of '*religio*', that Polybius says this, and that it is mainly with superstitious practices that Machiavelli is about to concern himself.

3. For an account of what Scipio Africanus Major did to prevent the Romans from fleeing to Sicily after the defeat at Cannae in 216 B.C., see Livy XXII.53. Scipio was one of the few Roman officers who survived the battle.

In regard to oaths Polybius remarks that, whereas it is almost impossible to get Greeks to keep their word even in regard to a small sum and no matter how many witnesses there be, 'with the Romans, on the other hand, though their magistrates and their ambassadors handle large sums of money, they keep their word simply and solely on account of their oath sanctioned by religion' (VI.56). Cp. also on the *'jurati'*, A.W. Bk. II, B.291b; F.41.

4. Cp. Livy VII.4–5. Titus Manlius Torquatus's father was Lucius Manlius Capitolinus Imperiosus, who had been dictator in the previous year, 363 B.C. He was accused of having been unduly severe, and of having been cruel even to his own son, who hurried to Rome to defend him against the charge.

5. On the use the Romans made of religion in controlling troops, see D. I.13–14. On the influence it had with the populace, cp. Polybius VI.56: 'The masses, I think, are the chief reason for maintaining it; for, if it were possible to have a commonwealth composed entirely of wise men, there would perhaps be no need for that sort of thing at all. But as the masses (*multitudo*) are always fickle, full of ill-controlled passions, and their anger is easily aroused, and by it they are moved to violence, it is essential to restrain the vulgar crowd by specious dreads and fictitious terrors of this kind. Hence the ancients do not seem to me to have been rash or to have acted without grave cause in inculcating belief in the gods and in punishment in Hell amongst the vulgar crowd.' (Cp. also on the value of oaths and of religion, A.W. Bk. IV, last paragraph, F.96–7.)

6. For the institution of the Senate, see Livy I.8.7.

7. For Numa's nocturnal meeting with the nymph, Egeria, see Livy I.19; and cp. A.W. Bk. IV (end; B.327a, F.97), where the victory of Charles VII over the English is ascribed to his converse with the Maid of France, sent by God.

8. Thus, Plutarch relates how Lycurgus went to Delphi to consult the god in regard to his proposed constitution, and was told that 'Apollo had heard his prayer and promised that the constitution he was about to establish should be the best in the world' (*Lycurgus*, n. 5). He also says that, according to some writers, when the citizens were still hesitating, Solon received from Apollo the oracle: 'Seize, seize the helm, the reeling vessel guide, with the help of patriots stem the raging tide' (*Solon*, n. 14).

9. For the use of the scholastic theory of matter and form, and its application to politics, see Index *sub* 'Matter and Form'; and cp. D. III.8, *note 7*.

10. Polybius also uses the analogy of a statue in VI.47 but for a different purpose. To compare Plato's republic with the actual constitutions of Sparta, Rome or Carthage, is like 'selecting a statue in order to compare it with living and breathing men' (cp. the opening paragraph in P. 15).

11. Cp. the passage quoted from Polybius in note 2 above.

12. Dante, *Il Purgatorio*, Canto VII, 121–3. Machiavelli reads *'discende per li rami'* in lieu of *'risurge per li rami'*, and cites the verse as follows:

> Rade volte discende per li rami
> L'umana probitate; e questo vuole
> Quei che la dà perchè da lui si chiami.

In a genealogical table the branches descend, whereas in a tree they rise. For shortness of life and its consequences, see Index *sub* 'Life, shortness of', and cp. P. 11, Burd 249, E.93.

13. For references to Savonarola, who was burnt at the stake on 23 May 1498, less than a month before Machiavelli entered public life, see Index *sub* 'Savonarola'.

14. The sermons to which Machiavelli here refers are those preached on 'the Ark

of Noah' in the Lent of 1494. In them Savonarola foretold how 'the sword of God (in the person of Charles VIII) was soon to smite the earth', and how the only remedy was to seek refuge in the Ark of God, which is his Church. (Cp. Villari's *Life and Times of Savonarola*, c. 10, pp. 185–9.) Villari cites from the '*Cedrus Libani*' of Fra Benedetto the following verse as a type of the kind of prophecy which electrified his audience:

> *Soon shalt thou see each tyrant overthrown,*
> *And all Italy shalt thou see vanquished,*
> *To her shame, disgrace and harm.*
> *Thou, Rome, shalt soon be captured;*
> *I see the blade of wrath come upon thee,*
> *The time is short, each day flies past.*

Charles VIII crossed the Alps on 2 September 1494; the Medici were expelled from Florence on 9 November. The French entered Florence on 17 November, and Rome on 2 December.

15. Cp. Preface, § 3.

Guicciardini *in loc.* remarks that though the early laws and religious institutions of Rome were mainly due to Numa, if her first king had not been warlike she would probably not have survived.

12. How Important it is to take Account of Religion, and how Italy has been ruined for lack of it, thanks to the Roman Church

1. This chapter comprises three parts:

(i) A eulogy of the religion of the Romans on the ground that, being based primarily on oracles, auguries, and miracles, it could easily be used by the government in order to persuade the people that the gods had given their sanction to what the government had decided to do (§§ 1–4).

(ii) An indictment of the Papacy as the main cause of the decline of religion in Machiavelli's day. (§§ 5–6.)

(iii) An indictment of the popes as temporal sovereigns on the ground that they were, and always had been, the chief obstacle in the way of Italy's unification. (§§ 7–8.)

2. On the importance of auspices and divination cp. Stuart Jones' account of Rome's 'Religious Institutions' in C.A.H. VII, 13.5 (pp. 429–31). Of auguries the second great priestly college, that of the Augurs, had charge. 'The object of Roman augury, and of divination in general, was not so much to ascertain the future as to secure that the favour of the gods was with them in the business in hand.' 'The augural college could pronounce an authoritative decision on the question whether the action of a magistrate was in accordance with or in defiance of the signs vouchsafed.' It is evident that 'this right might be used for political ends' (*ib.*). Machiavelli, be it noted, says nothing of the Roman pontifices in their capacity as judges of what was '*fas*' or '*nefas*'—what was lawful or unlawful in the eyes of the gods, nor of the moral influence which they thus exercised. Nor yet in

connection with oracles does he call attention to the moral and civilising influence of the Pythian Apollo (cp. *A History of the Delphic Oracle* by H. W. Parke, c. VIII). His main point is that governments could work the oracle, and, so long as they did not get found out, this served an extremely useful political purpose.

3. The oracle on the island of Delos was dedicated to Apollo, whose birthplace Delos was supposed to be. Ammon, later identified with Jupiter as Jupiter Ammon, was a Libyan deity, with numerous temples in Egypt and elsewhere, of which those at Thebes and Sparta were among the more famous.

4. On the encouraging of superstitious beliefs, even though based on a fallacy, cp. Polybius, who not only ascribes the growth of such superstitious beliefs to the encouragement given by prudent legislators, in the passage already quoted in D. I.11, n. 5, but at the end of it adds that 'those who nowadays reject such beliefs, do so rashly and without good reason' (VI.56).

5. Livy V.22.5. *Vis venire Romam?*—cited in Latin. The date is 396 B.C.

6. This statue of Juno was taken to Rome and set up on the Aventine in 391 B.C. in a temple specially built for the purpose. Polybius in VI.53 speaks of the Roman custom of clothing statues with ornamental robes, and says that this custom was 'a great incentive to young men to seek fame' (*ib.* 54).

7. Machiavelli has just been describing the religious spirit, devotion, reverence and credulity which characterised pagan religions, especially that of Rome; and has urged '*i principi d'una republica o d'uno regno*' to keep up the basic principles of the religion which sustains them in being (*i fondamenti della religione che loro tengono, mantenergli*), since this will enable them to keep the commonwealth they rule 'good and united'. He now says: '*La quale religione se ne' principi della republica cristiana si fusse mantenuta, secondo che dal datore d'essa ne fu ordinato*', Christian states and republics would be more united and much more happy than they are. '*La quale religione*' clearly refers to the pagan religion about which he has just been speaking. It has been suggested that *ne' principi della republica cristiana* might mean 'in the beginnings of the Christian era', but Machiavelli never uses '*principi*' for 'beginnings'; it is always '*principii*' (cp. D. III.1 *passim*, and D. II.13.2, where we have '*principi ne' principii*', 'princes in the beginning'). Hence '*principi*' refers here either to the popes as 'rulers of the Christian commonwealth', which fits in with what Machiavelli says later about 'the head of our religion' who is blamed for not keeping up this ancient religious spirit; or else to the emperors. The phrase '*secondo che dal datore d'essa ne fu ordinato*' clearly refers to Christ, who gave us the Christian religion, founded the Christian commonwealth, and intended that its religious spirit should be kept up. Hence the meaning of the passage would seem to be: If the religious spirit of Christianity had been kept up by the rulers of the Christian commonwealth as the spirit of Paganism was kept up by the rulers of the Roman commonwealth, and as Christ had ordained that it should be kept up, Christian states and republics would have been much more united than they are; for the effect of this spirit was to keep a commonwealth united, as has been pointed out above in § 3. Machiavelli is not regretting that Christianity replaced paganism, but that Christian rulers have been so slack.

8. For *il fragello* read *il flagello* (the scourge) with the *Filadelfia* edition. The forecast is correct, for Luther's revolt began a few years later in October, 1517. It should be noted, however, that it is not the Church, but the Court of Rome that is held responsible for the deplorable state of religion in Italy, (cp. Guicciardini *in loc.*

where a like distinction is made, and also § 8). That the conduct of many of the clergy in Rome and in Italy was deplorable Pastor frankly admits in his *History of the Popes*, Vol. V, p. 169 *sq.* where he writes: 'Although we must reject Machiavelli's picture of the condition of the Church as a caricature, it is nevertheless indisputable that a considerable portion of the Italian clergy, from the mendicant friars to the highest dignitaries, were participators to a large extent in most of the evils we have been describing. The more intimately the Church was bound up with the public and social life of the community, the more must the corruption of the world affect her, and its perils menace her members. Cupidity, manifesting itself in the prevalence of simony and the accumulation of benefices, selfishness, pride and ostentatious luxury were but too common amongst ecclesiastics. The extent of the corruption is seen in the complaints of contemporary writers, and proved by well authenticated facts.'

Machiavelli is also right in thinking that one cause of the trouble lay in the Court of Rome, for, as Pastor remarks: 'The lives of many cardinals, bishops and prelates are a sad spectacle at a time when one man could hold any number of benefices, and squander unabashed the revenues derived from them in a career of luxury and vice' (p. 170). The corruption, too, had spread throughout Italy, for Pastor admits frankly 'the immorality of the priests in almost every town of the Italian peninsula', and 'the deplorable condition of many of the monasteries' (pp. 171–2). But on two counts Machiavelli's description is open to criticism:

  (i) He gives us, as Pastor points out, but one side of the picture. Religion in Italy was by no means either dead or dying. Between 1400 and 1520 there were in Italy no fewer than 88 saints and *beati*, of whom 43 were Machiavelli's contemporaries. There were also numerous religious teachers, writers, and schoolmasters, such as St. Antoninus of Florence, Vittorino da Feltre, Agostino Dati of Siena, and Maffeo Vegio, whose works were published in 1491. Confraternities devoted to religious practices and pious works existed in every town and village and new ones were being founded, conspicuous amongst which was the Confraternity founded by some pious Florentines in 1488 and popularly known as the '*Misericordia*'; the *Confraternità di S. Rocco*, founded in 1499 by Alexander VI; and the Confraternity of Divine Love, approved in 1514. Preachers of penance, such as was Savonarola, still journeyed from town to town and from village to village, denouncing frivolities, urging enemies to be reconciled, and recommending that debts be remitted. In the trade guilds there was much solid piety. Each had its own physician and hospital, and made provision for visiting the sick and for assisting widows and orphans and girls without a marriage portion. In almost every village there was at least one confraternity devoted to pious and charitable objects, and in the cities they were numerous. In Florence at the beginning of the sixteenth century there were seventy-three such organisations. Alexander VI, Julius II, and Leo X all encouraged them and in each of these pontificates new ones were founded. Luther, who visited Rome in 1511, wrote: 'In Italy the hospitals are handsomely built, and admirably provided with excellent food and drink, careful attendants and learned physicians. The beds and bedding are clean, and the walls are covered with paintings.' None of the German hospitals, said John Eck, 'can in any way be compared with the splendid establishments in Rome, Florence, Siena, Venice and other places' (V, pp. 65–7).

  (ii) The lax morality prevailing amongst the Italian clergy and the bad example set by the Papal court was undoubtedly a contributory cause of the decadence, but the failure of the Popes to put a stop to it does not account for the decadence. The threatened ruin which Machiavelli deplores, supposes a positive, not merely a negative, cause. Nor can it be doubted but that this cause lay in the Renaissance itself. If the ancient culture provided examples of virtue, it also provided examples of vice which Italian princes and merchants were even more keen on imitating than they were on emulating the Romans in valour and austerity. This is exemplified in such customs as that of having Moorish slaves, male and female, about great houses, valued in proportion to their blackness; in the revival of the Hetaerae, now called not sinners, but courtesans; and in the spread of that vice which characterised Greece and is lauded in her myths and in the writings of Roman poets; and yet again—not least of all—by that very vice which Machiavelli regards as a virtue, the cult of fame, a fame which, as he points out in his Preface to the *History of Florence,* those who lacked the opportunity of gaining it by 'praiseworthy deeds' sought to obtain 'by deeds that were shameful'. It would, in fact, seem, as de Maulde-la-Clavière remarks in his *'Origines de la Révolution Française au commencement du XVIᵉ siècle'* (p. 125), that it was not the Roman Court that corrupted Italy, but the corruption of Italy that infected the Roman Court.

9. In this paragraph Machiavelli makes two main points. The old Roman provinces comprised for the most part people of the same race who had the same culture and spoke the same language. When the empire broke up and these provinces became independent countries, each of them ought to have been governed, he maintains, by some central authority, either republican or monarchic. In the case of France and Spain this was actually the case, but Italy was divided because right across the centre of it lay the Papal states, and the Papacy, as a temporal power, was neither strong enough to establish its jurisdiction over the whole of Italy, nor yet so weak but that it could maintain its independence by invoking the aid of foreign powers when threatened by other Italian princes. Thus the Papacy was, and always had been, he claims, the chief obstacle in the way of any national movement in Italy.

10. In support of this contention Machiavelli first cites the 'expulsion' of the Lombards by Charles the Great. The Lombards who had come to Italy in the sixth century, had by the eighth century assimilated the culture, religion, and customs of Italy to such an extent that they may be looked upon as genuine Italians. They had also, under Luitprand, Aistulf, and Desiderius, established their juris-diction over almost the whole of northern Italy, and in the south held the Duchy of Benevento. Each of these Lombard kings attacked the dominions of the Pope, and on each occasion the Popes appealed to the Franks, who, under Pepin and Charles the Great, invaded Italy and laid siege to Pavia, the Lombard capital. Had it not been for this, Machiavelli claims, Italy might in the eighth century have become united under the government of the Lombards. But, when in 772 Desiderius invaded the Papal states, Charles the Great crossed the Alps and the Lombard dukes acknowledged his jurisdiction, Pavia fell in 774, and the Lombard king was carried off to France. Hence it was owing to the Papacy that in the eighth century Italy failed to become a united kingdom. That it was the constant aim of the Popes to live at peace with their Lombard neighbours, that the Lombard kings frequently made treaties of peace with the Papacy, and as frequently broke them, that their failure to establish their jurisdiction over the whole of Italy was in large part due to their failure to establish it even over their own subjects, the Lombard dukes,

counts as nothing in Machiavelli's judgment in comparison with the salient fact that it was the coming of the Franks that saved the temporal power of the Popes and thus kept Italy divided. Moreover, the Lombards were not *driven out of Italy*: they remained there. (Cp. H.F. I.9–11, and for the Lombard invasions see also Aquinas, *de Regimine*, III, cc. 18, 19.)

11. Machiavelli now cites from his own times two incidents in which the Papacy played an important part: (i) the defeat of Venice at Agnadello in 1509, and (ii) the expulsion of the French from Italy in 1512. In the fourteenth century Venice had expanded to such an extent that it looked at one time as if she might establish herself as the 'monarch' of Italy (cp. D. III.31.3); but towards the close of 1508 the chief powers in Europe joined with Julius II to form the League of Cambray, and after her defeat by the French at Agnadello on 14 May 1509 her power collapsed (cp. D. I.53.3; II.10.6; III.11.5 and III.31.3). Julius, ever averse to the occupation of Italy by 'barbarian' powers, then changed sides and joined with Venice in a war with France (cp. D. II.17.7). The Holy League was formed in October 1511 with a view to driving the French from Italy, and, though its forces were defeated at Ravenna in April 1512, the arrival of 20,000 Swiss enabled the confederates to drive the French back into Milan, and before the end of the year they had withdrawn from Italy.

12. The futile endeavours of the Lombards and of the Venetians to extend their dominions over the whole of Italy were not the only attempt made by Italian powers to set up there a quasi-monarchy. There was also the attempt made by Caesar Borgia in the time of Alexander VI, an attempt which at one time Machiavelli thought might prove successful. Hence his eulogy of Caesar Borgia in P. 11; he thought then that 'a pope with money and arms might prevail'. He entertained similar hopes in regard to Julius II, 'who intended to gain Bologna, to ruin the Venetians, and to drive the French out of Italy' (*ib.*); and again of Lorenzo de' Medici to whom he dedicates *The Prince* and to whom he appeals in its last chapter, where he says of Lorenzo's uncle, Leo X, that 'if others made the Papacy great in arms, it is to be hoped that he will make it still greater and more venerated by his goodness and numerous other virtues' (P. 26). If, then, as it would seem, there was in Machiavelli's mind a genuine hope that Italy might be 'redeemed', it was because he thought the Papacy, so far from being a bar to its unification, the one power capable, and at that time possibly eager, to bring this unification about. But in Leo, who became Pope in 1513, his hopes were disappointed. Hence the resentment and bitterness displayed in this discourse, and especially in its concluding paragraph, as also elsewhere in the *Discourses*, a bitterness and a resentment which in *The Prince* is conspicuous by its absence.

Guicciardini *in loc.* agrees that during the period of which Machiavelli is speaking the Roman Court was infamous and a cause of great scandal. He also agrees with Machiavelli in thinking that 'the greatness of the Church, i.e. the authority which religion had given to it, has been the cause of Italy's never having fallen under a monarchy'. But, though holding that its divisions have been responsible for much misery, he does not think that it would have been more happy under a monarch, but, on the contrary, less happy, owing to the natural desire of Italians for liberty. Hence, he says, in opposing a monarchy, the Church 'has preserved in

Italy that manner of life which is more in accord with ancient custom and with its inclination'.

For the influence of Marsilius of Padua on Machiavelli's attitude toward the Papacy, see Table XIII, C.9, Marsilius of Padua.

13. What Use the Romans made of Religion in reorganising the City, in prosecuting their Enterprises, and in composing Tumults

1. Livy V.13–14. In 400 B.C. the plebeians, somewhat to their surprise, found that they had succeeded in obtaining the election of one plebeian tribune with consular power, the other five being patricians (V.12.9–11). The plebeian, Publius Licinius Calvus, administered his office so well that, to the annoyance of the patricians, in 399 five plebeians and only one patrician were elected (V.13.2–3). A severe winter was followed by an oppressive summer in which many animals perished. Three wars were being carried on at one and the same time, but the patricians were more anxious about the forthcoming elections than about the war, so they chose only the most distinguished men as their candidates, alleged that the severe winter was a prodigy sent by the gods, and that the pestilence which had affected both the city and the countryside indicated that the gods were angry. If a plague was to be averted, the gods must be appeased, as the books of Fate decreed, for it was an affront to the gods that honours should be prostituted and distinctions of rank be ignored. So on this occasion the plebs, thus overawed, elected only patricians as military tribunes with consular power (V.13.4–14.5 and cp. D. I.48).

2. Livy V.15–16. The unusual height to which the water had risen in the lake in the Alban grove in 398 B.C. caused the Romans to send a delegation to Delphi to enquire the meaning of the prodigy. By the time they returned, its significance had already been explained by an aged Veientian soothsayer, who said it meant that the Romans would not conquer Veii until the water should get away, and, on his being captured, he explained how they might drain it (V.15). The reply from Delphi confirmed what he had said, and the troops in consequence recovered their spirits (V.16.7–11). The story of the tunnel which the Romans are said to have made through solid rock to let the water escape is usually regarded as mythical, for, though there is such a tunnel, seven feet high, five feet broad, and over a mile in length, it is supposed to be of Etruscan origin.

3. See D. I.39.3.

4. Livy III.10.5–7. Caius Terentillus Arsa had carried a resolution appointing a commission of five to propose laws defining the powers of the consuls (III.9.5). In 462 the matter was dropped, but in the following year it was raised again by the tribunes as a body. Prodigies followed. The Sybilline books were consulted. They declared that danger would come from an assembly of foreigners, and warned the people against sedition. This was done, said the tribunes, to obstruct the law, and a great conflict ensued.

5. Livy III.15–18. The seizure of the Capitol by Appius Herdonius, the Sabine, in 460 B.C. is related in III.15.5–9; and the action of the tribunes in 16.5–6. The next incident is related in c. 17, but the text Machiavelli is using would seem to be

corrupt. The name of the person who intervened is given in the discourse as 'Publio Ruberio' in the edition I am using, and in the Philadelphia edition as 'Publio Rubezio'. In the Teubner text of Livy we have simply '*P. Valerius collega senatum retinente se ex curia proripit*'—Publius Valerius rushed from the assembly while his colleague held the senate back (III.17.1). P. Valerius Publicola was the consul and his colleague was C. Claudius, the son of Appius (15.1). There is no mention of a Ruberius, *alias* Rubesius; nor of his being one of those grave men who can appease the populace (cp. D. I.54). Nor yet was his intervention successful, for we are told that it looked as if the mob would resort to violence (17.9). There was, however, a second intervention when the troops sent to the consul's aid from Tusculum had been admitted to the city, and on this occasion the mob was wise enough to obey the 'authority of this distinguished man', and to help him to recover the Capitol, despite the protests of the tribunes (18.4–7). Publius Valerius had announced that he would not prevent the populace from meeting to discuss the proposed legislation, provided they undertook to be mindful of Roman traditions. During the attack on the Capitol both he and Appius Herodonius were killed. In December, 460, Lucius Quintius Cincinnatus (not Titus) was appointed in his stead (19.2). He declined to fulfil the promise Valerius had made, announced his intention of marching against the Volsci and Aequi, and reminded the people of the oath they had taken to obey Valerius. The tribunes objected that the oath had not been taken to obey Quintius, who was then a private person. But, adds Livy:

6. '*Nondum haec, quae nunc tenet saeculum, negligentia Deum venerat, nec interpretando sibi quisque jusjurandum et leges aptas faciebat*' (III.20.5 cited in Latin).

7. The compromise which eventually was reached is related in 21.2.

14. The Romans interpreted their Auspices in accordance with their Needs, were wise enough ostensibly to observe Religion when forced to ignore it, and punished those who were so rash as to disparage it

1. See D. I.12.2 and n. 2.

2. Cp. Livy X.40–1 for the story of L. Papirius Cursor the Younger and the Pullarii. The battle of Aquilonia took place in 293 B.C. during the third Samnite war.

3. The full name was Appius Claudius Pulcher, cp. D. III.39.2, where he is called 'Claudius Pulcher'.

4. Of the naval battle off Drepana in 249 B.C. Livy's account is not extant, but in the epitome of Book XIX we are told that 'Claudius Pulcher, the consul, who had set out in defiance of the auspices, ordered the poultry that would not eat, to be drowned'. In the engagement with the Carthaginian fleet Claudius was unsuccessful, and was recalled by the senate. Polybius gives a long account of this battle in I.49–51, and in VI.52 points out that the Carthaginians were always better than the Romans at sea, but in neither case does he mention the recalcitrant chickens. They are, however, mentioned by Valerius Maximus, who says that P. Claudius '*abici eos in mare jussit, dicens quia esse nolunt, bibent*' (I.5.3), and also by Cicero who says: '*mergi eos in aquam jussit ut biberent*' (*De Natura Deorum*, II.3.7). Both say that for this

Claudius was condemned. Valerius Maximus also tells the story of Papirius Cursor (VII.2.5), and is probably the source which Machiavelli is using.

Guicciardini *in loc.* lays more stress on the religious practices of the Romans than on the 'astute' use its generals made of auguries and auspices, of which he does not feel sure. He sees nothing wrong in Papirius having declined to accept the story told by a third person.

15. The Samnites had recourse to Religion as a last Resort when their Affairs were going badly

1. '*Nec suis nec externis viribus jam stare poterant; tamen bello non abstinebant, adeo ne infeliciter quidem defensae libertatis taedebat; et vinci, quam non tentare victoriam, malebant*' (Livy X.31.14—cited in Latin).

2. Cp. Livy X.38. The narrative in the text follows closely that given by Livy.

3. '*Non enim cristas vulnera facere, et picta atque aurata scuta transire romanum pilum*' (Livy X.39.12—cited in Latin). The Roman general is Lucius Papirius Cursor, son of the dictator of the same name who got annoyed with his master of horse for engaging the Samnites without permission in the second Samnite war (cp. D. I.31.3 and n. 6). This incident occurred during the third Samnite war after the Samnite general, Gellius Egnatius, had been defeated and slain in the battle of Sentinum in 295 B.C., and the Umbrians had submitted to Rome. In 293 both consuls set out for Samnium. Spurius Carvilius stormed Amiternum, killing 2,800 men and taking 4,270 prisoners. Papirius stormed Duronia where the slaughter was greater but fewer prisoners were taken. Carvilius then attacked Cominium, and Papirius, acting in conjunction with him, attacked the main body of the Samnites near Aquilonia, after taking the auspices as described in D. I.14.

4. An account of the victory is given in X.39. In view of Machiavelli's own views on the sanctity of treaties (cp. P. 19) and on the value of bloody sacrifices (cp. D. II.2.6), it is interesting to note that Papirius ascribes the Roman victory to the immortal gods who were angry with the Samnites '*propter totiens petita foedera, totiens rupta,*' and, 'if one can form any idea of the divine mind, were never more hostile to any army than to one which, smeared with the blood of men mingled with that of beasts slain in an unholy rite, on both counts had incurred the divine wrath' (39.15-16).

Polybius stresses the importance of the religious rites used by the Romans, such as funeral orations and the custom of dressing up men to resemble the deceased when a distinguished man died, but of sacrifices involving bloodshed he says nothing (cp. VI.53-6).

16. A People accustomed to live under a Prince, should they by some Eventuality become free, will with Difficulty maintain their Freedom

1. Cp. Polybius, VI.9.9 (cited in I.2, n. 16) for the analogy of a wild beast which eventually succumbs to a new master.

2. Cp. the next chapter, I.17. The distinction here made between a people which has become corrupt under despotic rule and one that has not yet become corrupt, is important, for the treatment demanded is radically different; cp. I.17 and I.18.7.

3. For the conspiracy of the sons of Brutus and of the dissatisfied Roman youth, and the motives moving them, see Livy II.1-5. Their father had taken a prominent part in the expulsion of the Tarquins. He was now consul, and not only consented to their death, but was present at their execution (Livy II.5). Machiavelli uses the phrase 'to kill the sons of Brutus' for the liquidation of anybody hostile and dangerous to a new government, a policy which he recommends both to princes and to republics (cp. P. 3, 4, and 7, E.17, 33, 40; and D. III.3.3 and 4).

4. The policy of making friends of the people is strongly recommended in the *Prince*. It is important when invading a foreign province (P. 3); or annexing a province (P. 5), and in forming a new principality, as Caesar Borgia did (P. 7). Even tyrants, like Agathocles, should confer benefits on the populace (P. 8). It is of special importance when a man becomes a prince through the favour of his fellow citizens, for he can place much more reliance on the populace than he can on the nobles (P. 9, cp. D. I.40.11). Nor will princes who have the affection of their people be likely to be attacked (P. 10 and P. 19). Cp. also Aristotle, *Politics*, V.9. He says that all rulers should profess to be maintaining the cause of the people, and should take an oath saying, 'I will do no wrong to the people' (1310a, 11-12).

5. The demand of an enraged populace for vengeance is one of the points on which Polybius lays great stress in the passage quoted in D. I.3, n. 1. (Cp. Index *sub* 'Vengeance' and see P. 5, concluding paragraph.)

6. Justin in his *Histories* XVI.4, says that the quarrel between the plebs and the senate of Heraclea concerned the distribution of the land of the wealthy. Clearchus, then in exile, having been called in by the senate to 'save his country', first betrayed it to Mithradates, then returned and was made prefect, for he saw 'in the quarrel a chance of making himself tyrant'. Having got rid of Mithradates, he then 'changed suddenly from being a defender of the senate's cause and became the patron of the plebs'. By threatening to leave them in the lurch, he induced them to give him supreme power, then put sixty of the senators in chains and the rest fled; at which the plebs rejoiced. Subsequently there was a fight between the senatorial party and Clearchus, in which he was victorious. Of its remnants he threw some into prison, tortured others and killed the rest (XVI.5). Diodorus Siculus also gives an account of Clearchus' tyranny in XV.81. Clearchus was murdered in 353 B.C., after ruling for twelve years.

7. In P. 19 France is described as one of the best ordered kingdoms of our time. This, we are told, was due to its 'founder', who devised a method of controlling both the ambitions of the powerful and the hatred and fear which the populace displayed towards them; parliament was to arbitrate between them. The founder is presumably Charlemagne, whose legislation was submitted to the approval of a general assembly, called by the annalists *'generalis conventus', 'placitum', 'synodus',* or *'synodalis conventus'*. All from the age of twelve upwards were required to take an oath of loyalty to him as 'Caesar'. The meaning of this oath was publicly explained. It meant that they were to live in the holy service of God to the best of their ability; were not to molest either by force or fraud the servants of the crown; nor to do violence to Holy Church, or to widows or orphans or strangers, seeing that the Lord Emperor has been appointed, after the Lord and his saints, the protector and

defender of all such (Bryce, *Holy Roman Empire*, c. V, pp. 65–6). It is plain from these words and from the fact that Charlemagne allowed himself to be crowned by the Pope, that he recognised a higher law by which he himself also was bound, namely, the law of God. Finance and the declaration of war he kept in his own hands, as Machiavelli says, but legislation was on a different footing: it expressed the will of God as understood by king and people alike, and to this will all were subservient. To the respect which French kings as a rule displayed toward the laws of their realm Machiavelli frequently calls our attention (cp. P. 19, E.153; and Burd's note on p. 314; D. I.19.4, and see Index *sub* France), and to this practice ascribes France's prosperity and long endurance. The *de Regimine* of Aquinas also calls attention to it in Bk. IV, c. 1.

Cp. also A.W. Bk. I (B.272a; F.10), where Machiavelli says:

'A kingdom that is well-ordered never gives the sovereign power to its prince in anything except the command of its armies, where it is essential that he shall have it, because sudden decisions may be necessary, and only if one man has command can they be carried out as speedily as they ought to be.'

He does not, however, mention finance here. Nor does he mention France, but, on the contrary says no such well-ordered kingdom now exists.

Guicciardini *in loc.* lays stress on the distinction Machiavelli has drawn between a people accustomed to tyrannical rule, and a people, such as in Florence, accustomed to liberty. In the former case there will be marked inequality in the standing and influence of the citizens, and a republic, which presupposes a considerable degree of equality, will in consequence be impossible (cp. D. I.17.5; D. I.55; and see Index *sub* 'Equality'). The revolution in Rome was possible because the replacement of kings by consuls did not involve any radical change in the constitution, and the creation of consuls had been suggested by the Commentaries of Servius Tullius. Liberty was introduced gradually as necessity dictated or experience required. Nor is it surprising that the Romans should have demanded liberty, since it was enjoyed by neighbouring tribes.

In order to preserve liberty, once it has been acquired, it is essential, on the one hand, to take action against those who machinate against liberty, but, on the other hand, to act with moderation, not to attack the rich and powerful without good cause, and to be ready to accept citizens who have collaborated with tyrants, provided they behave well and there is hope that they will not be hostile to liberty; for, provided there be good government and security for everybody, former collaborators will be content with such a government, as has been seen often in the experience of Florence. Hence, while those who machinate against the state should be punished promptly and inexorably, even though their offence be small, there should be no persecution of those who are merely suspected of disloyalty.

Good government is impossible if factions are allowed, and in such a case those who were the friends of liberty are apt to become its enemies, as happened in 1512 when the Medici were brought back, not by their former friends, but by many who had previously been hostile to them. So, too, after the revolution of 1526 many desired the return of the Medici owing to the severity of the persecution which followed it. Hence by the 'sons of Brutus' should be understood 'those who are by nature restless, rapacious, and with whose character liberty is incompatible'; not those whose character is such that there is hope they may be contented.

These comments deal not merely with what Machiavelli says in D. I.16, but with what he says elsewhere about the need of ruthlessly eliminating those who are opposed to a new regime, e.g. in D. I.17.5 and D. I.18, 6–7; and again in D. III.3. It is only with a view to establishing a tyranny that Guicciardini thinks ruthlessness is likely to be of use, and it should then be directed against the people, for it is futile to try to win over the populace, as Clearchus is supposed to have done and as Machiavelli recommends. The only way in which to set up a tyranny is by means of partisans. The people must be oppressed, or else be annihilated and replaced by others.

Guicciardini makes no comment on D. I.17–22.

17. A Corrupted People, having acquired Liberty, can maintain it only with the Greatest Difficulty

1. Since Machiavelli uses the plural in speaking of the corruption of Rome's kings, he presumably includes Servius Tullius, the last king but one, as well as Tarquinius Superbus, in spite of the fact that Rome owed to Servius many improvements in her constitution. He is probably thinking of the passage in which Livy says that Servius was chosen by the patricians, *'injussu populi'* (I.41.6), and of the troubles which arose later when he supported the populace against the patricians, which led ultimately to the revolt of Tarquinius and to his own assassination. Servius reigned 44 years (48.8) and the tyranny of Tarquin lasted 25 years (60.3), so that between them they cover two generations, during the second of which decadence had definitely set in.

2. Note the distinction here made between goodness (*bontà*) and virtue (*virtù*).

3. For Dion and Timoleon, see I.10.3 and note 5 to I.10.

4. The family of Augustus became extinct with the death of Nero in A.D. 68. His successor, Galba, was not a relative. Though the emperors who succeeded were by no means all of them tyrants, as Machiavelli admits (I.10.6–7), and Rome still remained nominally a republic, it was not a republic nor did it enjoy freedom, as Machiavelli understands these terms.

5. Livy II.1.9 *'Brutus . . . jurejurando adegit neminem Romae passuros regnare.'*

6. Marcus Junius Brutus, the leader of Julius Caesar's assassins. It was he who addressed the people after the murder. The assassins claimed to be acting in the cause of liberty, for Caesar was anxious to become king and Anthony had offered him the diadem in public, to the disgust of the people of Rome. Actually most of the conspirators were Caesar's personal enemies, but Brutus was his friend.

7. Julius Caesar's aunt Julia was the wife of Marius, the leader of the popular party in Rome (d. 86 B.C.), and his wife, Cornelia, whom he refused to divorce at Sulla's behest, was the daughter of Cinna, Marius' colleague and friend. At his aunt's obsequies in 69–68 B.C., 'Caesar's adherence to the "*populares*" was put beyond all doubt . . . He took care to recall her lineage—and his own—claimed origins which on one side were royal, on the other divine. In later days this passage was remembered' (Suet., *Div. Jul.* 6.1). When Caesar 'piled one dictatorship on another, and finally became dictator for life, men might be pardoned for wondering whether even at this early stage the young Julius had conceived monarchy to be

Rome's only hope and had begun to consider himself as a candidate for the throne' (C.A.H. IX, p. 342, art. by Prof. Last).

8. Filippo Maria Visconti, Duke of Milan, 1412–47, to whose doings a large part of Book V and the earlier part of Book VI of the *History of Florence* is devoted. 'On the Duke's death some of the Milanese desired to live free, some under a Prince. ... Those who were for a free form of government being more united, prevailed over the others, and devised a republic in conformity with their own ideas. From this government, however, many cities of the Dukedom withheld obedience. ... Hearing of these disagreements the Count [Francesco Sforza of Benevento] repaired to Cremona, where it was arranged between his agents and the envoys from Milan that he should be captain for the Milanese on the same terms as he had recently settled with Duke Filippo' (VI.13). He betrayed them, and in 1450 made himself Lord of Milan (VI.20–24). Cp. also P. 12 (Burd 258 and notes, E.100 *sq.*).

9. Three basic Machiavellian principles are contained in this paragraph: (i) Classes and class-conflicts are of advantage to the state when properly controlled. (ii) Only when matter is appropriately disposed can a given form—in this case a form of government—be imposed. (iii) In time of emergency it is essential that but one man should be in control of the state.

10. Epaminondas, Theban patriot and general, was the friend and colleague of Pelopidas who killed Leontiades in 379 B.C., thus putting an end for the time being to the tyranny which Sparta had set up in Thebes (cp. D. I.21.3 and n. 3). After several successful campaigns Epaminondas was killed in the battle of Mantinea in 362. No change in the form of government in Sparta ensued, nor did she at once lose her hegemony. But the death of Epaminondas caused Sparta's hopes of regaining her former hegemony to revive, and she declined to join in the treaty of peace or to recognise the independence of Messenia. (Cp. Polybius IV.32–3.) 'That things turned out well for Thebes', says Polybius in VI.43, 'was not due to the form of her government, but to the virtue of those who were in charge of things, as her fortune has made it plain to all. For it is clear that the progress, culmination and end of Theban prosperity took place during the period in which Epaminondas and Pelopidas lived, so that the splendour and glory which the Thebans acquired is to be ascribed not to the city but to these distinguished men.'

11. A marked inequality, especially in wealth, is in Machiavelli's opinion incompatible with a republican form of government (cp. Index *sub* 'Equality' and Guicciardini's comments on D. I.16).

12. See D. I.18.6–7.

For Guicciardini's comments, see D. I.16.

18. How in Corrupt States a Free Government can be maintained where it exists, or be established where it does not exist

1. Cp. D. I.3.3, where customs are said to be prior to laws.
2. The distinction between a law and an institution, i.e. a department of the state

to which some function and procedure has been assigned, is made clear by what follows. The constitution of a state comprises all such institutions.

3. The punishment for adultery was left to family jurisdiction and private vengeance until the time of Augustus, when it was regulated by the 'Lex Julia de Adulteriis' (cp. C.A.H. IX, p. 881). Sumptuary laws aimed at reducing that 'inequality' to which Machiavelli refers in D. I.17.5 (cp. Livy XXXIV.4). The Laws of the Twelve Tables restricted funeral expenses. The *Lex Oppia* in 215 dealt with dress and other feminine indulgences. The *Lex Fannia* in 161 limited the amount to be expended on dinner-parties and was reenacted in 143 as the *Lex Didia*. The *Lex Licinia*, circa 100, was to the same effect. There were also the *Leges Corneliae* passed by Sulla, the *Lex Aemilia* of 78, the *Lex Antia*, and the *Leges Juliae*, instituted by Julius Caesar. The *Lex Cornelia Baebia de Ambitu* controlled electioneering. The *Lex Plantia* forbade public violence; and the *Lex Tullia*, passed at the instance of Cicero, imposed severe penalties on corrupt practices.

4. Rome's main conquests took place between the year 200 B.C., when the second Macedonian war broke out, and 146 B.C., when Carthage fell. Asia Minor passed under Rome's dominion after the defeat of Antiochus at Magnesia in 190. The defeat of Perseus at Pydna in 168 brought not only Macedonia but also Greece under Rome's control. Africa became a province in 146, and Asia was organised as a province by M. Aquillius in 129.

5. Cp. the passage from Polybius, cited in D. I.3, n. 1, where he speaks of the luxury that is likely to creep in, once a state has surmounted many dangers and arrived at the zenith of its power; of the way in which the powerful and wealthy will either oppress the populace or cajole it into supporting their designs; of the effect of this flattery on the populace which tends to exaggerate its own importance and to demand for itself all appointments, or, alternatively, will become enraged when it is exploited or oppressed; with the result that there will be a revolution, and a new regime will be established, which, by whatever name it choose to call itself, will in fact be nothing but mob-rule. Polybius is writing of Rome as it was just at the period of which Machiavelli is speaking. He sees but one possible outcome—mob-rule, and for a time it looked as if this might come about, but eventually the mob succumbed to the dictatorship of distinguished generals.

6. Force and Fraud—the two weapons which all princes must be prepared to use if they would deal successfully either with foreign powers or with their own subjects. Caesar Borgia used them (P. 7), and in P. 18 and P. 19 they are recommended in the well-known passages dealing with the policy of the Lion and the policy of the Fox. The opposition here is between '*ingannato*' and '*sforzato*', and similarly in D. II.18.6. In P. 18 it is between '*astuzia*' and '*forza*'; but in P. 7 and in D. II.13 it is between '*forza*' and '*fraude*'. Cp. Cicero, *De Officiis*, I. xiii. 41, where he says that 'wrong may be done in two ways, by force or by fraud, fraud being, as it were, the way of the fox and force that of the lion'.

7. Machiavelli is here expressing himself in terms of the Scholastic doctrine of matter and form. Matter must be appropriately disposed before it can receive a form of a given type. Contrary forms, e.g. the hot and the cold, the dry and the moist, cannot subsist in the same matter. Nor can matter which has been disposed in some particular way, receive either of two contrary forms. So, too, with the governed, who constitute the matter upon which some governmental form is to be superimposed.

Either they must be appropriately disposed, or the attempt to introduce it will end in disaster.

8. The three discourses, 16, 17 and 18 illustrate how Machiavelli would apply to the transition from servitude to freedom the basic principle enunciated in D. III.9 and again in P. 25 that good or bad success in political undertakings depends upon their conforming or failing to conform with 'the times', i.e. with the circumstances, dispositions, and customs of the people with whom the politician is dealing. The case in which a people has recently recovered liberties which it has long desired is by no means the same as the case of a people which has become habituated to servitude. To maintain the liberties which have been recovered will be difficult in any case, as Machiavelli points out in D. I.17 and 18, and again in D. I.49, which should be read in conjunction with this set of three chapters; but in the case of a servile people it will be impossible unless they first be subjected to a quasi-monarchical regime in which good customs are imposed by force until such time as the people learn to appreciate them and to desire of their own accord to maintain them. There is only one other passage in which Machiavelli recommends a quasi-monarchical regime, namely, D. I.55.7, but it is, of course, strictly in accord with what he says elsewhere about the need of a dictatorship in time of emergency (cp. D. I.34; and on the need of introducing a *regale regimen* when nature has become corrupt see Aquinas, *de Regimine* II.9).

9. Cp. D. I.9.5 and *note* 8 for Cleomenes, and I.9, *note* 2, for Remus and Titus Tatius.

19. A Weak Prince who succeeds an Outstanding Prince can hold his own, but a Weak Prince who succeeds another Weak Prince cannot hold any Kingdom

1. Livy I.4–31. The salient features of the early history of Rome, given by Livy in his first book, though legendary, are almost certainly based on facts. Anyhow, according to tradition, Rome's first king was warlike and by the end of his 37 years reign had welded the three tribes he had conquered into a single state. The asylum he built for refugees flying from justice suggests that the population at this time comprised numerous gangsters (I.8.4–7). The second king, Numa Pompilius, devoted his attention mainly to religion and agriculture, and encouraged the practice of augury, which Machiavelli deems to have been so important a factor in the building up of confidence amongst the troops. Of these two kings Livy says: '*Ille bello, hic pace, civitatem auxerunt*' (I.21.6). The third king, Tullus Hostilius, was, like the first two, an elected king, who, according to Livy was 'fiercer even than Romulus' (I.22.2). He conquered Alba, and made war on Veii, Fidenae and the Sabines, but appears also to have devoted his attention to land-distribution and the housing-problem.

2. Cp. 3 Kings (= 2 Chron.) where we are told that 'Rehoboam, his son, reigned in Solomon's stead.' (11.43). His father's counsellors advised him, much as Machiavelli would have done: 'Speak soft words to the people, and they will be thy servants for ever.' He rejected this advice, boasting that 'as his father had beaten them with whips, he would beat them with scorpions'. Hence eleven of the twelve

tribes revolted to Jeroboam, leaving Rehoboam with only a twelfth—not a sixth—part of his father's kingdom, if we count by tribes (*ib.* c. 12).

3. The Mahomet here referred to is Mahomet II (1451-81). He was known as the Conqueror, for he not only took Constantinople in May 1453, but overran Asia Minor, Serbia, Bosnia, Albania, and the Crimea. He aimed at the capture of Italy, but failed to take Rhodes, and, though he landed at Otranto, he did not hold that city for long. His son, Bajazet II (1482-1512), was inclined rather to peace than to war. His brother, Prince Jem, revolted but was defeated, and took refuge in Naples. Bajazet then conquered Styria and Croatia, but in 1494 was driven out of Styria by Maximilian III. The Poles suffered severely from his incursions, and by the peace of 1500 he gained considerable territory. The Venetians were defeated at sea near Sapienza, and Lepanto fell into Turkish hands. When a landing was made in Venetian territory, the Pope, Alexander VI, in 1500 urged all princes to send representatives to Rome to deal with the Turkish menace. Selim I (1512-20) defeated the Persians and conquered Kurdistan; entered Cairo as a conqueror in 1517, and became Caliph. He then overran Egypt, Syria, and the Hejaz, and by the end of his short eight years reign had almost doubled the Turkish dominions. Machiavelli is clearly writing somewhere about the middle of this reign, after some of the main conquests. This suggests that Machiavelli was still engaged on the first book of the *Discourses* about the year 1517. Machiavelli's prophecy that, as things stand, Selim should excel his grandfather, was not fully verified in Selim's lifetime but he prepared the way for a further extension of the Turkish power in Europe under his successor, Suleiman I (1520-66), who overran the greater part of Hungary, captured Buda-Pesth, and at one time reached the outskirts of Vienna. Incidentally, though the Venetians were defeated in 1499 and many of the islands they owned were subsequently taken by the Turks, the peace of 24 December 1502 restored the *status quo ante*; which bears out Machiavelli's contention that this republic was given to gaining by diplomacy what it lost in war. (Cp. D. III.11.3; and for Guicciardini's account of the policy of Bajazet, which agrees with Machiavelli's, see *St. d'I.* VI.8, *sub anno* 1504.)

4. For France and the respect its kings had for institutions, cp. D. I.16.9, and see Index *sub* 'France'.

5. Cp. Livy I.32-4. Rome's fourth king, Ancus Marcius (640-616 B.C.), promulgated Numa's laws concerning religion. This led the Latins to think that he was devoting his attention to chapels and altars, so they invaded Roman territory, replied in arrogant terms to Ancus's protest, and were conquered by the Romans.

6. Cp. P. 2. Hereditary states are easier to hold than are new states, for 'given that a prince does not neglect the institutions of his ancestors and that he temporises when difficulties arise, he will need but ordinary industry in order to maintain his position, unless some extraordinary and overwhelming force deprive him of it'.

Aristotle says of hereditary monarchies that one cause of their destruction is that 'kings often fall into contempt (Machiavelli's weak monarch), and, although possessing not tyrannical, but only royal, power, are apt to outrage others. Their overthrow is then readily affected; for there is an end to the king when his subjects do not want to have him, but the tyrant lasts whether they like him or not' (*Politics* V.10, 1313a, 10-16—and cp. 1312b, 22-5, where he says that 'those who have inherited their power, have lost it almost at once, for, living in luxurious ease, they

have become contemptible, and offer many opportunities to their assailants.')
Aristotle also agrees with Machiavelli in holding that the strength of a monarch lies
in his respect for law and institutions. 'Monarchy is preserved by the limitation of its
powers. The more restricted the function of kings, the longer their power will last
unimpaired; for then they are more moderate and not so despotic in their ways; and
they are less envied by their subjects' (V.11, 1313a, 18 *sq.*). What Aristotle calls a
constitutional or limited or legitimate monarch is one who enforces the law, but
'does nothing arbitrarily or contrary to law' (III.15, 1286b, 31). This agrees closely
with what Machiavelli says of France in D. I.16.9; D. II.1.9; and cp. also D. I.55.2
and 58.3. Moreover, the chief fault for which Machiavelli blames the French kings
is their failure to realise the importance of arming their own people and of securing
their goodwill, and their folly in preferring 'the present advantage of despoiling
them', from which results the tribute they have to pay the Swiss for hired troops,
and that which they pay to the English king (D. II.30.4). And these are precisely
the defects to which Aristotle says monarchy is liable. For when a king seeks riches
in order to pay mercenaries, because he mistrusts his people and has deprived them
of their arms, monarchy becomes tyranny (V.10, 1311a, 5 *sq.*), and 'when kings
attempt to administer the state too much after the fashion of a tyranny, and to
extend their authority contrary to the law', they are preparing the way for their own
destruction, for, 'though the king is supreme in all important matters' (cp.
D. I.16.9), 'his rule is over voluntary subjects' (V.10, 1313a, 2–8).

20. *Two Virtuous Princes, of whom one immediately succeeds the
other, do Great Things: and, as in Well-ordered Republics
there is of necessity such a Virtuous Succession,
their Acquisitions and their Increase
also is great*

1. *potè venire a quella sua ultima grandezza in altrettanti anni che la era stata sotto i re.*—
Rome was subject to kings for 244 years. (Livy I.60.3). They were expelled
in 510 B.C. If it took Rome as many years again to arrive at its ultimate greatness
and we count from the year in which the city was founded, the year 266 B.C. is the
year in which it arrived at its ultimate greatness. In 266 Rome was on the eve of the
first Punic war. The period covered by Livy's First Decad, i.e. 753 to 293, was
over. Rome's constitution was complete. In 275 Pyrrhus was defeated at Beneventum. Tarentum surrendered in 272. Rhegium was taken in 271. The south of Italy
was now subject to Rome. In the north her dominion extended as far as Ariminium
whither a colony was sent in 268. In the same year the Sabines were admitted to full
citizenship. As yet Rome had made no foreign conquests, but her military organisation and the strength of the federation she had built up was now such that she was
ready to face the world. If, however, we measure greatness by empire, as Machiavelli
so often does, 266 cannot be the year he has in mind. We must interpret 'as many
years again' to mean twice 244, which brings us down to 22 B.C.; but, though by
this time Rome had acquired a world-wide empire, she had to all intents and
purposes ceased to be a republic.

2. Philip II of Macedon, father of Alexander the Great; cp. D. I.26, n. 3.
3. For Alexander the Great, see Index.

21. Princes and Republics which have not their own Armed Forces are highly reprehensible

1. For an account of the reign of Tullus Hostilius, Rome's third king (672–640 B.C.), see Livy I.22–31. Since Numa reigned in peace for 53 years, it is legitimate to infer that no Roman was familiar with war. To the Samnites, on the other hand, Tullus Hostilius could not have appealed, for as yet they were too remote; but since Romulus had made a pact with the Etruscans (30.8) he might have appealed also to them. Instead, he used his own men, whom he must have trained well since he not only conquered Alba but also defeated the Sabines and the Etruscans, and thus 'magna gloria belli regnavit annos duos et triginta' (31.8).

2. Since the *Discourses* were written after *The Prince* which was completed in 1513, and Machiavelli here speaks of the English king's invasion of France as *un esemplo freschissimo* and of the French troops having been continuously under arms in Italy, he must be referring to the invasion of France by Henry VIII in 1513. It was a magnificent affair and just the kind of thing to appeal to Machiavelli. According to a report current in Venice, the English king took with him 20,000 horse, 12,000 archers, 6,000 halberdiers, 12,000 mace-men; had a thousand men in his body-guard and fourteen horses at his disposal with 'housings of the richest cloth of gold'. At the battle of the Spurs, so-called because of the speed with which the French cavalry fled, the Duc de Longueville and the famous Chevalier Bayard were captured, and three thousand Frenchmen killed. Thérouanne, with its garrison of four thousand, capitulated, and Tournay, the wealthiest city in Flanders, was taken shortly afterwards. But, if this be the war, Machiavelli is wrong in saying that England had been *sanza fare guerra* for more than thirty years. He should have written more than twenty years, for the war waged by England to defend the independence of Brittany ended with the Treaty of Étaples in 1492. He also, when he says that the English were without experience in war, overlooks the wars of the Roses. (Cp. P. 14 on the need of keeping up military training in time of peace (E.116).)

3. Polybius in VI.43 takes a poor view of the constitution of Thebes and ascribes the transient glory and power it obtained rather to the stupidity of the Spartans and to the hatred they had aroused amongst their allies, than to the political skill of the Thebans. He then goes on to say—in a passage already cited in D. I.17, n. 10— that their victories over the Spartans, and the reputation and fame they thus won, were due wholly to Pelopidas and Epaminondas, and lasted only so long as they lived. These two great patriots and generals became the leading men in Thebes after Leontiades had been killed by Pelopidas in 379 B.C. This put an end to his tyranny; the exiles returned and a democratic regime was set up. Both men were ardent democrats, disinterested patriots, and distinguished generals. Plutarch in his *Life of Pelopidas* mentions that they armed all those who came over to their party. Both led numerous expeditions against the Spartans and to other states in which a democratic rising had taken place. Both were killed in battle, Pelopidas in an

49

engagement with Alexander of Pherae at Cynocephalae in 364 B.C., Epaminondas in an encounter with Agesilaus in 362 B.C.

4. The writer is probably Plutarch, who in his *Life of Pelopidas*, n. 17, says that the battle of Tegyra 'first taught the other Greeks that it was not the Eurotas nor the region between Babyce and Cnaeion which alone produced warriors, but wheresoever young men are wont to be ashamed of baseness and to be courageous in a noble cause'.

5. Aeneid VI.813–4, cited in Latin; but '*Desides*' should be '*Resides*'.

> *Desidesque movebit*
> *Tullus in arma viros.*

Cp. P. 10, E.85, on the need of having 'a sufficient army to join battle with any attacking force'; and P. 13 on the need of having one's own troops.

22. What is worthy of Note in the Case of the Three Roman Horatii and of the Three Alban Curiatii

1. The legend of the famous fight between the two triplets, one set Roman and the other set Alban, is told at great length in Livy I.24–6. Caius Cluilius, the dictator of Alba, had approached within five miles of Rome when he died and Mettius Fuffetius was appointed dictator in his place. Tullus Hostilius by-passed the Alban army and invaded Alba, and it was then that the fight was arranged which resulted in the death of the three representatives of Alba, and the victory of the surviving Horatius.

2. Cp. Livy I.27–30. The people of Alba were indignant, and the dictator repented of his folly. Hence when the people of Veii fell out with the Roman colony at Fidenae, and the Roman king, Tullus Hostilius, called upon Mettius to support him, the latter held aloof during the battle, with the result that after their victory the Romans surrounded the Alban troops, took Mettius prisoner, and killed him by tying him between two chariots driven in opposite directions.

23. That One should not stake the Whole of One's Fortune except on the Whole of One's Forces; and that, consequently, it is frequently Harmful to defend Passes

1. For details, see the preceding discourse, and cp. especially Livy I.24–5.

2. The arguments here used are peculiar to the *Discourses*. In the *Art of War*, Bk. IV, Machiavelli mentions that the Romans preferred to pitch their camp in the open, rather than in confined and rough places, but says nothing about the folly of defending passes.

3. Hannibal's difficulties in crossing the Alps are described by Livy in XXI.32–8 and by Polybius in III.50–6. His difficulties in crossing the Apennines or Italian Alps are described by Livy in XXI.58.

4. Since the Roman army under Publius Scipio was routed by the Carthaginians on the banks of the Ticinus and again on the Trebia in 218 B.C., and since after Hannibal had crossed the Apennines he defeated Flaminius, who had been awaiting him at *Arretium* (Arezzo) in the battle of Lake Trasemene, it is open to question whether the Romans gained anything by fighting in the open instead of defending passes. In the case of the Alpine passes, however, this would have been impossible since they could not have got an army there in time. Livy XXI.45–6, 54–6, 59; XXII.2–5.

5. The French retired from Italy after their defeat at Novara in June 1513. On the accession of Francis I he prepared an army of 35,000 men at Lyons, crossed the Alps by the Col d'Argentière, blasting his way through rocks and throwing bridges over chasms, surprised Prospero Colonna with his Milanese troops at Villa Franca on the Po, 12 August 1515, and took him prisoner. The Swiss, unprepared for this advance, fell back on Milan and began to lose heart, for the detachments from different cantons became separated and were quarrelling. Francis fortified his camp at Marignano, near Milan. The Swiss attacked on 13 September with 20,000 men, and, after a fierce battle lasting two days, were defeated, leaving thousands of dead on the field.

Note that this event is spoken of as a very recent incident, which indicates that this discourse was written not earlier than September 1515, nor yet much later.

Guicciardini *in loc.* urges against this theorem several objections. The fight between the three Romans and the three Albans is irrelevant, for the two peoples were kinsmen. And in regard to passes there are cases in which it has been of advantage to defend them when it could be done without serious loss. It may, for instance, delay the enemy's advance, as it did in the case of Flaminius Quintus in Macedonia. So too in the case of rivers. In our times Gonsalvo Fernando held the passage of the Garigliano and defeated the French. If the place is narrow and difficult to supply, the difficulty affects both sides. Nor did the Swiss suffer because they held the passes against Francis, who crossed the Alps by a new route. Nor yet is the case of Hannibal relevant, for the Romans could not defend the Alpine passes, which they did not hold; and, if they could have done, it might well have been to their advantage, for Hannibal suffered considerably from the peasants in the neighbourhood.

24. Well-ordered Republics, in assigning Rewards and Punishments, never balance one against the Other

1. Cp. D. I.22 above for a further account of the incident.

2. To the topic of rewards and punishments and gratitude Machiavelli devotes five chapters, D. I.28–32.

3. The defence of the bridge over the Tiber by Horatius Cocles, Lartius, and Herminius against the whole Etruscan army under Porsenna is one of the outstanding incidents in the story of the early days of the republic and is narrated by numerous historians and poets. Livy relates it in II.10–11. Polybius also relates

it in VI.55 as an example of Roman virtue. For its historical foundation, see C.A.H. VII, p. 397. Horatius the One-eyed was the sole survivor.

4. Mucius Scaevola (the Left-handed) killed Porsenna's secretary in mistake for the king. For this he was to have been burnt alive; but on his holding the hand that had offended in the fire without flinching, Porsenna let him off (Livy II.12–13). For his virtue he was given a piece of land on the other side of the Tiber, says Livy (13.5), which came afterwards to be known as the Mucia Prata.

5. What Livy actually says of the reward given to Horatius Cocles is that he was given 'as much land as could be ploughed in one day' (II.10.12). For this Machiavelli substitutes 'two *staiora*', the amount required for sowing two bushels of corn. A '*staioro*' is the equivalent of the Roman '*jugerum*' and it was reckoned that two '*jugera*' should be enough to support a man, and according to Varro (R.R. 1.10) this was the amount allotted by Romulus to each citizen as his hereditary property. (Cp. C.A.H. VII.416). The English acre was originally the amount that could be ploughed by a yoke of oxen in a day, and was slightly smaller than its Roman equivalent 'two *jugera*'. Livy adds that there was such a scarcity at the time that individuals deprived themselves of food for the public benefit.

6. For saving the Capitol during the invasion of the Gauls in 390 B.C., the populace were so grateful, says Livy, that they took to Manlius's house 'half-pounds of flour and quarterns of wine', and had to deprive themselves in order to do so (V.47). Manlius's attempted revolt and his death in 384 B.C. are described by Livy in VI.16–20. (Cp. also A.W. Bk. VI, B.345b, F.127.)

Guicciardini *in loc.* thinks that the Romans were justified in taking account of Horatius' merits under the circumstances. In general he agrees that it would be harmful to make it a rule that good should counterbalance evil, but circumstances may be such that in passing judgment the merits of a delinquent should be taken into account.

25. He who proposes to change an Old-established Form of Government in an Autonomous State should retain at least the Shadow of its Ancient Customs

1. For the doctrine that the masses are easily influenced by appearances, cp. D. I.53 and P. 15, 18. In P. 15 Machiavelli says that what 'appears to be virtue' may entail ruin, and what 'appears to be vice' bring prosperity. In P. 18 he argues that a prince cannot afford to observe the moral virtues or to abide by his promises, but that, since this is expected of him by his subjects, it is 'very necessary for him to appear to have these virtues'. (See Index *sub* 'Appearances').

2. Twelve lictors accompanied the king, bearing '*fasces*', bundles of rods from which protruded an axe, symbolising the power of life and death (Livy I.8; Cicero, *Rep.* II.17). When consuls replaced the kings the same number of lictors accompanied the officiating consul as had accompanied the kings. They and their insignia were retained, says Livy, that there might not seem to be any diminution of the '*regia potestas*' (II.1.7–8).

3. For the institution of the '*rex sacrificulus*', see Livy II.2. He was appointed

'*necubi regum desiderium esset*', and was made subject to the '*sacerdotium pontifex*', so that to those who had charge of divine service no 'new names' were added. For an account of these institutions, see the section headed 'Religious Institutions' in C.A.H. VII, p. 425 *sq.*

4. It was common amongst political writers in Greece and Rome prior to the Augustan era, to identify autocracy or one-man rule with tyranny. Thus Aristotle defines tyranny to be 'monarchy exercising the rule of a master over a political society' (*Politics* III.8, 1279b, 15), i.e. it is 'despotic power' or 'dictatorship' (IV.10, 1259a, 9 *sq.*). Previously, however, he has said that tyranny looks only to the interests of the monarch (1279b, 6), and it is in this sense that he normally uses the word. It is also in this sense that the word 'tyranny' is used by Machiavelli. His 'prince' is not a tyrant, for, if he is wise he will rule in the interests of his people; but he may be an autocrat, as was the ruler of Turkey, described in some detail in P. 4. Neither is a dictator a tyrant, though he may easily become a tyrant (cp. D. I.35). It is clear from what follows in D. I 26 that Machiavelli is here using the term '*potestà assoluta*' not in the sense of absolute rule which looks to the benefit of the state, but in the sense of absolute rule which looks primarily to the interests of the ruler. Hence I have translated it by the term 'despotism', not 'autocracy'. For Polybius's definition of a tyrant, see D. I.10, n. 1.

Guicciardini *in loc.* remarks that to retain appearances is more necessary in reforming a government than in introducing a radically new type. The retention of the Sacrificial king was a concession made to religious feeling, and obviously the Romans could not have increased the number of lictors, for this would have signified that the consuls had greater authority than the kings.—Livy's comments, none the less, seem to bear out Machiavelli's interpretation.

26. In a City or Province which he has seized, a New Prince should make Everything New

1. The quotation, which is given in Latin—*qui esurientes implevit bonis, et divites dimisit inanes*—is from the Magnificat, Luke 1.53, and is not said of David but of the Lord; nor does it begin with '*qui*'. The words used by our Lady refer to Psalm 33 (*Benedicam Dominum*), where David says '*Divites eguerunt et esurierunt, inquirentes autem Dominum, non minuentur omni bono*' (*v.* 11). The reference is to David's own hunger which Achimelech, the priest, satisfied by giving him holy bread (1 Kings 21.1-6). Machiavelli would often have heard the Magnificat sung, but appears to have but a hazy notion of what it is all about.

2. Though Machiavelli has Philip II of Macedon in mind, the description he gives of what a tyrant should do in a conquered province fits equally well the conduct of Philip V (220-179 B.C.), of whom Maurice Holleaux in C.A.H. VIII, p. 146, writes: 'His treatment of his subject-allies—Thessalians, Euboeans, Phocians, Locrians—while increasingly despotic, displayed demagogic tendencies; he gave orders as master to the cities, reduced their autonomy to nothing, imposed his nominees as magistrates, but tolerated and encouraged, especially in Thessaly, social disorders, hateful to the well-to-do and agreeable to the mob.'

3. The writer here referred to is Justin, who in VIII.5.7 says of Philip of Mace-

don: '*Reversus in regnum, ut pecora pastores nunc in hibernos, nunc in aestivos saltus trajiciunt, sic ille populos and urbes, ut illi vel replenda, vel derelinquenda quaeque loca videbantur, ad libidinem suam transfert.*' Philip II, king of Macedon from 360 to 336 B.C., began his career by getting rid of five rivals, of whom two were killed, two fled, and the fifth was won over by bribery. It was undoubtedly his policy to hand over populations from one ruler to another and to transport them from place to place. When he took Olynthus in 348 he sold its inhabitants as slaves and distributed Chalcidean lands amongst their Macedonian conquerors. When Phalaecus surrendered at Thermopylae in 346 Phocian towns were dismantled and their inhabitants distributed amongst villages not less than 200 yards apart and not containing more than 50 houses (C.A.H. VI. p. 240). After the Peace of Philocrates in the same year colonies were sent out to defend the new frontiers and the inhabitants of Chalcidice and Thrace were settled in the interior of Macedonia. To Thebes in 338 Philip promised slaves and flocks and herds from Attica if it would support him. When it was taken, after the battle of Chaeronia in that year, those hostile to Philip were executed or banished, their property confiscated, and the city placed under an oligarchy. Theban prisoners were sold as slaves. On the other hand, the Hellenic League which Philip organised for mutual defence and offence left the constitutions of the states composing it untouched; the independence of each member was guaranteed; no tribute was levied, and no garrisons placed in the cities. Polybius seeks to defend 'Philip, son of Amyntas' against some of the charges levelled against him by the historian, Theopompus, who 'set out to write a history of Greece, but, instead, wrote a history of Philip' which depicts him not only as 'shamelessly immoral', but as a tyrant who behaved with 'the grossest unfairness and perfidy towards his friends and allies, and treacherously seized and enslaved a vast number of towns by deceit and by seizing the right moment' (VIII.11). Machiavelli, on the other hand, adopts here the view of the prejudiced Theopompus.

4. Note the strong disapprobation of tyranny expressed in the last paragraph. There none the less are rules of which the tyrant should take due note.

Guicciardini *in loc.* says that the question of using violent measures only arises when the inclinations of a people are wholly averse to the new form of government. In that case mild measures will not suffice to eliminate the demand for liberty. Yet violence is indicative of weakness, especially in a prince whose regime has not been set up on the basis of his own armed forces. He should, therefore, use violent remedies when necessary, but at the same time should endeavour to stabilise his position by humane conduct and the conferring of benefits. 'What the writer says is not, therefore, to be taken as an absolute rule. He always takes immoderate delight in extraordinary and violent remedies.'

27. *Very rarely do Men know how to be either Wholly Good or Wholly Bad*

1. The facts here narrated are in the main correct, but in details open to question. Acting against the advice of France, of Venice, and of Caraffa and other cardinals, Julius II, at the urgent request of exiles from Bologna and Perugia who had taken refuge in Rome, determined in 1505 to expel the families under whose oppression

the inhabitants of these cities of the Romagna groaned. How he dealt with those powers which had declined to help is described in D. III.44. In August 1506 he announced his intention of taking the field in person. He set out on the 30th with nine cardinals and 500 fully armed knights, together with their retainers. After pausing at various towns *en route*, where he celebrated mass and was acclaimed by the populace, he entered Perugia on 13 September 1506, accompanied by twenty cardinals, the Duke of Urbino, and several Roman barons. Machiavelli in a letter dated 13 September says that the papal troops were near the gate and Baglioni's troops but a short distance away, so that the Pope and Cardinals were completely in his power; but Paris de Grassis, who was there, denies that the Pope was 'unarmed', and the Venetian envoy reports that he entered the city accompanied by 2,000 armed men. (Cp. Pastor, Vol. VI, p. 270 and note on this page.) The Pope remained in Perugia for eight days, celebrated solemn high mass, abolished the magistracy of Ten, and left Cardinal Antonio Ferreri as his legate in the city.

2. Other reasons besides his alleged cowardice determined Baglioni's decision to surrender. He feared the hostility of the Oddi party, and knew that he could not rely on the loyalty of the citizens. Nor did he surrender on the arrival of the Pope, as Machiavelli's narrative suggests. The Duke of Urbino and the legate, Cardinal Ferreri, who had gone there in April 1506, acted as intermediaries and came to meet the Pope at Orvieto. Thither, too, came Baglioni himself, and it was there that he promised to surrender Perugia, to recall the exiles, and to send his two sons as hostages, all of which took place a week before the Pope made his triumphal entry into the city.

3. Though the remark about gaining immortal fame is doubtless not meant to be taken seriously, the marked animosity displayed in this discourse calls for explanation. Julius II was but carrying out the policy of Alexander VI of reducing the turbulent barons of the Romagna to order. For this both he and Alexander are praised in P. 11, where we are told that the enterprises of Julius 'redounded to his credit, since he did everything to strengthen the Church, not any private person'. It is not, then, against the Pope that Machiavelli's sarcasm is here directed, but against the cardinals, for they in part were responsible for the disorders, notably the Orsini and the Colonnesi, whom for this reason Julius did not promote to be cardinals. (Cp. P. 11, last paragraph.) For the troubles these families caused to Pius III, see Pastor, VI, p. 204; and for the care with which Julius selected cardinals, see Pastor, *ib.*, pp. 218–22.

28. What made the Romans less ungrateful to their Citizens than were the Athenians

1. In view of the eight chapters which Machiavelli devotes to the Decemvirate and to the tyranny of Appius (D. I.34–5, 40–5), it is surprising that he should say that Rome had no great reason to be suspicious of her citizens until the time of Sulla and Marius (cp. Guicciardini's comments below). On the other hand, he is right in contrasting the leniency of Rome with the severity of Athens in her treatment of suspect citizens and in regard to its origin. Cp. Plutarch, *Praecepta gerendae reipublicae,* 3: the Athenian populace, he says, was easily moved to anger and prone

to suspect, e.g., it banished Hanno on the charge of having aspired to be a tyrant because on his campaigns he used a lion to carry his luggage (799E).

2. The rise of democracy in Greece in the fourth century B.C. resulted in the overthrow of the Pythagorean clubs in Sicily, the members of which belonged to the upper and cultivated classes, who, in and through them, were then exercising considerable political power. Of their abolition Polybius says that 'the burning of the Pythagorean clubs in Magna Graecia was followed by great constitutional disturbances, as was natural on the sudden disappearance of the leading men in each state'. Not only were the leading men exiled, but there was civil strife and confusion everywhere. Shortly afterwards 'there was a general movement to adopt the model of the Achaean constitution', but an attempt to make the Achaeans arbitrators on the points in dispute failed because the Achaeans had not been able to produce a leader worthy of the occasion. 'Whenever any man had given indications of such ability, he was systematically thrust into the background, and hampered, at one time by the Lacedaemonian government, and at another, still more effectually, by that of Macedonia' (II.39). (For Pisistratus, see D. I.2.16 and n. 20.)

3. By Solon's laws not only those who were guilty of subverting public liberties, but also those who failed to support the government during political disturbances, were banished, and their property confiscated. Ostracism, which was introduced later, differed from banishment or 'flight' as it was called, in that it was imposed for a specified time and did not involve the confiscation of property. Of ostracism Aristotle says that it was used by democracies against 'those who appeared to be pre-eminent amongst their fellow-citizens by reason of their wealth, the number of their friends, or any other means of influence' (*Politics* III.13, 1284a, 20-1; and cp. V.3, 1302b, 18, for its introduction on these grounds into Athens). The Romans, on the other hand, as Cicero points out (*Orat. pro A. Caecina*, 34), had no law to which the penalty of exile was attached. If citizens went into exile they did so voluntarily, '*confugiunt quasi ad aram in exsilium*'. Nor by so doing did they in general lose either their property or their status as citizens. Livy mentions several instances of voluntary exile (cp. I.41.7, II.35.6, III.13.8, 58.9, V.32.9). To the imposing of *exsilium* as a penalty, on the other hand, from the earliest times the Romans displayed a marked repugnance.

4. Cp. H.F. II.37: 'There can be no question but that a fiercer temper is displayed and worse cruelties inflicted on the recovery of freedom than in its defence.' Cp. also Cicero, *De Officiis* II.7.24: '*Acriores autem morsus sunt intermissae libertatis quam retentae.*'

5. It was the rape of Lucretia, the wife of L. Tarquinius Collatinus, by his cousin, Sextus, that led to expulsion of Tarquinius Superbus and the establishment of a republic in Rome in 509 B.C. (Livy I.57-60). Collatinus and L. Junius Brutus then became its first consuls, but owing to the hatred for the Tarquins, Collatinus was persuaded to resign and to go into voluntary exile. '*Hunc tu, tua voluntate, L. Tarquini, remove metum,*' said Brutus to his colleague (Livy II.2.7). He was succeeded by Publius Valerius, who suppressed the revolt which the Tarquins had stirred up. During the battle Brutus was killed and Valerius remained sole consul. Livy says he built an impregnable fortress *in summa Velia, alto atque munito loco* (II.7.6). Velia is usually identified not with the Caelian Hill, mentioned in the text, but with the ridge joining the Palatine to the Esquiline hill. Anyhow, the building of this 'citadel' aroused suspicion, so Valerius pulled it down and passed a law imposing death on anyone who sought to make himself king (II.7 and 8).

Guicciardini *in loc.* points out that, when the Romans were deprived of their freedom by the Decemviri, after the first outbreak of indignation they treated them humanely. Hence the reason why they were less ungrateful than the Athenians cannot be due to their having never been deprived of their freedom. It is to be sought rather in the difference between the two types of government. Athens was a democracy in which citizens could easily become eminent and so give rise to suspicion. Rome's government was 'mixed', and to become eminent one had to win favour alike with the senate and with the people. Hence there was less danger of tyranny and consequently less ground for becoming suspicious of, and attacking, men of power and position.

What Guicciardini says here of Athens, and what Machiavelli says in §§ 1 and 2, is borne out by the speech of Diodotus, given by Thucydides in III.42–8. In 42 Diodotus argues that counsellors whose advice is accepted ought not to be rewarded, nor those whose advice is rejected punished, since this will only cause them to give advice contrary to their better judgment. But, he adds in 43, 'we take an opposite course, and still worse. Even when we know a man to be giving the wisest counsel, a suspicion of corruption is set on foot, and from a jealousy which is perhaps groundless we allow the state to lose an undeniable advantage. It has come to this, that the best advice when offered in plain terms is as much distrusted as the worst; and not only he who wishes to lead the multitude into the most dangerous courses must deceive them, but he who speaks in the cause of truth must make himself believed by lying. . . . If he who gave and he who followed evil counsel suffered equally, you would be more responsible in your ideas; but now, whenever you meet with a reverse, led away by the passion of the moment you punish the individual who is your adviser for his error of judgment, and your own error you condone if the judgments of many concurred in it' (III.43).

29. Which is the more ungrateful, a People or a Prince?

1. There is no chapter in *The Prince* dealing expressly with the question of ingratitude; but P. 16 discusses the relative merits of liberality and meanness, and the ingratitude of Albinus, who sought to kill Severus, is mentioned in P. 19, E.158–9.

2. '*Proclivius est injuriae, quam beneficio vicem exsolvere, quia gratia oneri, ultio in questu habetur*' (Tacitus, *Histories* IV.3; cited in Latin).

3. For Antonius Primus's change of sides, see Tacitus, *Histories* II.86; III.2–3. For his victory over Caecina at Bedriacum see III.15–26; and his victory at Narnia, see III.58–63. For the quarrel with Mucianus see III.8, 46–9, 52–3, 78, and IV.39; and for the treatment of Antonius Primus by Vespasian, see IV.80. Antonius Primus was one of the first generals to declare for Vespasian when in A.D. 69 the fortunes of Vitellius were on the wane. He led the legions from Pannonia back to Italy, crossed the Alps, took Patavium and Verona, assumed sole command when the troops mutinied against his two colleagues, and defeated the army which had been sent by Vitellius to intercept him at Bedriacum, where in the night he was attacked by a second army which also he defeated. He then sacked Cremona, and marched on Rome, which he took, Vitellius and his army being put to the sword. He was then removed from his command by Mucianus, and was not well received by Vespasian on his going to Alexandria to complain of the treatment he had met

with in Italy—a treatment which was not wholly undeserved, since he had won favour with the troops by allowing them unlimited pillage and loot.

4. On 12 May 1495, Charles VIII was crowned King of Sicily and Jerusalem in the cathedral at Naples. On the 20th, having heard that the League of Venice had been formed against him, he left Naples, and appointed the Duke of Montpensier his Viceroy in the newly acquired kingdom. Ferdinand of Aragon sent Gonsalvo Ferrante, better known as Gonsalvo of Cordova, to assist Ferdinand of Naples to recover his kingdom. Gonsalvo landed at Messina on 24 May and crossed to Reggio. At Seminara, against his advice, the Spaniards engaged the French in battle and were defeated. Ferdinand fled to Sicily. Gonsalvo now began to drive back the French against whom many of the cities revolted. Ferdinand returned in July 1495, and by July 1496 the Duke of Montpensier had lost the whole of Calabria and was forced to surrender at Atella on 21 July. 'So ignominious a surrender had not been made before in our times,' says Philip de Commines (VIII.21), 'nor have I read of anything like it, unless it was that made by the two Roman consuls at the Caudine Forks.' In June 1507 Ferdinand of Aragon went to Naples to receive the submission of that kingdom. He deprived Gonsalvo of his command and in his stead appointed his nephew, the Count of Ribagorza, as Viceroy and Prospero Colonna as Constable. He took Gonsalvo with him to meet Louis XII at Savona, and at Louis's request Gonsalvo dined with the two monarchs and with the Queen of Aragon, and was treated by Louis as an equal. Gonsalvo returned to Spain with the king, who remained suspicious of him and never gave him any major appointment or adequate reward until his death in December 1515, when services were held in his honour at court and throughout the country. (Cp. Guicciardini, *St. d'I.* VII.8 and XII.19.)

5. On the need of making provision for expansion in the constitution, see D. I.6.5-10 and D. II.19.3; on three methods of expansion see D. II.4; on the advantage of using Rome's method and the defect of others, see D. II.3; II.19; II.23.2, and II.30.7.

6. In 52 B.C. Pompey induced the Senate to appoint him sole consul. Whereupon, says Plutarch, Caesar applied through his friends for another consulship (*Caesar* 28-29). Marcellus and Lentulus opposed this with great violence, disfranchised the inhabitants of Novum Comum, where Caesar had established a colony, and Marcellus, then consul, beat one of its councillors and told him to go and show Caesar his wounds. Caesar retaliated by distributing the treasures he had amassed in Gaul, but offered to lay down his arms if Pompey would do the same (*ib.* 29-30). Scipio, Pompey's father-in-law, proposed to the senate that Caesar should be declared a public enemy unless he laid down his arms by a stipulated date (*ib.* 30). Caesar again proposed moderate terms, but Lentulus treated his friends with great indignity, and many distinguished citizens and magistrates had to flee from Rome in hired carriages, disguised as slaves (*ib.* 31). Caesar then seized Ariminium and crossed the Rubicon which divides Cisalpine Gaul from the rest of Italy (*ib.* 32). The war with Pompey and the aristocratic party had begun.

7. Coriolanus, who had distinguished himself by gaining a victory over the Volsci, was subsequently impeached and banished in 491 B.C. for proposing to starve the plebs into submission (Livy II.34-5, cp. D. I.7.2-4 and n. 2). M. Furius Camillus, after having taken Veii in 396 B.C. (cp. D. I.13.2), aroused much resentment in Rome, first by riding in a chariot drawn by four white horses as if he

were a god (V.23.4–7); next by insisting that a tenth part of the booty from Veii be dedicated to Apollo (*ib.* 8–11); and then by opposing strenuously the proposal that plebeians should migrate to Veii (V.24.4–25). In 391 he gained further victories over the Falisci (V.26–7), but again aroused resentment by accusing the tribunes of violating their duty (29.8–10); with the result that he was indicted by Lucius Appuleius on account of his action in regard to the Veientian spoil, was heavily fined, and went into exile at Ardea (32.8–9). Coriolanus was never recalled, for he led the Volsci against his own countrymen; but Camillus was recalled when the Gauls took Rome in 390 B.C. (cp. D. II.29.4; and 30.1).

8. For the 'virtues' of P. Cornelius Scipio Africanus Major, see Livy XXVI.19.3–9. Already in 204 his success, conjoined with his style of living and fondness for Greek literature, had evoked the criticism of Fabius Maximus, but the commission sent to Sicily to enquire into the matter exonerated him. After his return from his final victory over Hannibal in 202, he received the title 'Africanus', and was made 'princeps senatus', but declined to become dictator for life. After the defeat of Antiochus in the consulship of his brother, Lucius, Africanus sought to obtain favourable terms for Antiochus, who had captured his son and then released him. On the return of the two brothers to Rome in 189, Lucius was accused of accepting bribes from Antiochus. Egged on by M. Porcius Cato, two tribunes insisted on an enquiry, but when Lucius was about to present his accounts to the Senate, Africanus snatched them from his hand and tore them up. His brother was found guilty and heavily fined. He was to remain in prison till the money was paid, but Africanus rescued him. In 185 Africanus himself was brought to trial by the tribune, M. Naevius. He declined to answer the charges, and on the anniversary of his victory at Zama persuaded the people to drop the case and follow him to the Capitol to give thanks (Livy XXXVIII.50–60; Valerius Maximus III.7.1). He then retired to his estate at Liternum, and the prosecution was dropped.

9. See D. I.30.3 and cp. also D. I.58.5–6, where princes and republics are compared.

Guicciardini's comments *in loc.* are unusually long. He says that ingratitude is due not merely to avarice and suspicion, but also to ignorance, malice caused by envy, or again to people being naturally ungrateful; and he rejects Machiavelli's thesis that princes are less grateful than republics. Princes can reward good service without touching their own pockets and do so generously, whereas peoples give rewards with a view to securing further services. They are, moreover, more ready to give credence to calumnies, and so are more suspicious. They are also less careful in judging of a given case, and are inclined to attack the rich and the noble out of envy. Nor are the examples Machiavelli cites relevant. The fall of Antonius Primus was due to his quarrel with Mucianus and to his arrogance, not to suspicion. Gonsalvo Ferrante was deprived of his command because he had acquired such power that to the king there remained but a name; yet he was not punished; but on his return to Spain ranked amongst the richer and more honoured of the king's subjects. If Rome was less ungrateful than other republics, there are yet numerous examples of her ingratitude, e.g. toward Camillus, Fabius Maximus, Cicero, Metellus, Publius Rutilius. Nor can Rome's treatment of Scipio be defended. It was due to envy and ignorance, not to suspicion; and Cato was moved to oppose him either owing to personal animosity or to his dislike of the nobles and to his austerity. 'Nor yet am I willing to overlook what the Discourse says about its being useful to the liberty of a republic, not yet corrupt, to maltreat those it ought to reward and to suspect those it ought to trust, for this is very far from the truth, since all ingratitude and all injustice is always pernicious, and a republic should so regulate its conduct that the good are always honoured and the innocent are free from fear.'

30. What Steps should be taken by a Prince or by a Republic to avoid this Vice of Ingratitude, and what should be done by a General or by a Citizen who does not want to suffer from it

1. It is characteristic of Machiavelli that he should here consider ingratitude alike from the standpoint of rulers, princely or republican, and from that of subjects to whom ingratitude is shown.

2. That a prince should lead his armies in person is implied by what is said in P. 14 about the need to study the rules and discipline of war, to organise and drill men, and to read the history of war. We are also told that princes who looked to their own ease rather than to arms have often lost their dominions. A prince is also recommended to 'go and reside' in a conquered province (P. 3), or in a newly acquired principality (P. 6). Cp. also P. 12 (Burd 257, E.99) where the maxim is applied to rulers in general.

3. Cp. D. I.27; and note that it is extreme courses, not a middle course, that is here recommended.

4. Resignations are mentioned by Livy in III.29; IV.47.6; VI.29.10, and XXIII.23.7, where we are told that Marcus Fabius Brutus resigned because he did not approve of there being two dictators at the same time, and that on his stepping down from the rostra a private citizen, crowds followed him to his house.

Guicciardini *in loc.* agrees that it is praiseworthy for a prince to go on expeditions in person, because in that case he will be better served. To tyrants and others whose position is insecure it is specially necessary, but it is not necessary for kings whose position is established, for there are numerous cases of kings today who have suffered no harm through entrusting expeditions to their generals.

31. Roman Generals were never punished with Extreme Severity for their Mistakes; nor yet were they ever punished for Ignorance or Bad Judgment even though it caused Harm to the Republic

1. Cp. D. I.28.
2. Philip V of Macedon against whom Rome waged war from 200 to 196 B.C.
3. The crucifixion of rebels was a common practice in Persia, Egypt, and the

East generally. (Cp. Herodotus III.125; VI.30; IX.120, and see the Appendix to Rawlinson's *Herodotus,* Vol. II.) It was also the common practice amongst the Carthaginians to crucify unsatisfactory generals. Polybius mentions several cases: I.11, a general for cowardice and folly; I.24, Hannibal, son of Gisco, for allowing himself to be blockaded by the Roman fleet in Sardinia; I.79, Hanno by mutineers for failing to hold Sardinia.

4. L. Virginius Tricostus Esquilinus and M. Sergius Fidenas were appointed consular tribunes in 402 B.C. An account of their quarrel and punishment is given in Livy V.8-11.

5. The battle of Cannae was fought by Varro against the advice of his fellow consul, L. Aemilius Paulus. Varro was one of the few who escaped. He reached Venusia with seventy horsemen, and then went on to Canusium, where he reorganised the remnants of the Roman army. It was this that accounted for the welcome he got on his return to Rome. For, says Livy, 'so magnanimous was the city that crowds composed of people from all ranks went to meet the consul on his return from the slaughter for which he himself had been chiefly responsible, and thanked him for not having despaired of the republic; whereas, had he been a Carthaginian general, no limit would have been set to his punishment' (XXII.61).

6. Quintus Fabius, afterwards called Maximus, was Master of Horse under the dictator, L. Papirius Cursor, during the second Samnite war in 325 B.C. He was left in charge with orders not to fight. He disobeyed and won the battle of Imbrivium. The troops, who disliked Papirius, threatened to mutiny if Fabius was punished. He fled to Rome, where his father interceded for him with the angry dictator, and he was pardoned (Livy VIII.30-5).

32. Neither a Republic nor a Prince should put off conferring Benefits on People until necessitated thereunto

1. Of the 'blandishments' which the senate at this juncture bestowed on the plebs, Livy, in II.9.6, mentions 'the obtaining of supplies of corn, the state-purchase of salt, which had hitherto been sold by private persons at a high price, and the remission of harbour dues and of tribute, which had now to be paid by the rich, since the poor had enough expense in bringing up their children'. Livy does not say that the tribute was connected with salt, but he does mention later in (XXIX.37) that a tax (*vectigal*) was imposed on salt in 204 B.C., presumably for the second time.

2. The date at which these benefits were conferred on the populace was 508 B.C., only two years after the Tarquins were expelled, and while they still remained a danger. The laws referred to are those made by Publicola, who acquired his name owing to the favours he conferred on the plebs, amongst them the right of *provocatio,* i.e. of appealing to the people against a sentence passed by the magistrates (Livy II.8.1-3).

Guicciardini *in loc.* remarks that it is wise to use benefits to make friends yet more friendly, but useless to try in this way to win over enemies; but in either case, if one has not done this in time, there can be no harm in attempting it later.

33. When either within a State or against a State an Inconvenience has made Headway, the Safer Course is to temporise, not to suppress it

1. In this chapter Machiavelli turns to the consideration of the constitutional changes which Rome made with a view to overcoming difficulties, external and internal. Chief amongst them was the appointment of dictators. According to Livy the first dictator was probably appointed in 501 B.C., when war with the Latins was threatening (Livy II.18 and cp. D. I.34, n. 1).

2. Of the events narrated in this paragraph Machiavelli gives a long account in his *History of Florence* IV.26-33. During the war with Lucca which ended in 1433, Florence had become very dissatisfied with its government, which was drawn from the nobility. The opposition centred round Cosimo de' Medici, the son of Giovanni, who by his wealth, his liberality, and his pleasing manners had gained great power. Uzzano, one of the leaders of the party in power, was urged to join with Rinaldo degli Albizzi in order to obtain either the banishment or the death of Cosimo. Uzzano in a long speech deprecates this course and admits that, if Florence ever came to be governed by one man, he would much prefer Cosimo to Rinaldo. On Uzzano's death Rinaldo induced the government to banish Cosimo. While in prison awaiting his trial, he was so afraid of being poisoned that for four days he ate nothing but a piece of bread. Had he not bribed the Gonfalonier he might well have been put to death. He was banished on 3 October 1433, but was recalled a year later by a Signoria to which several of his supporters had been elected. He returned in triumph, was 'saluted by everybody as the benefactor of the people and the father of his country'. From this time on alike the internal and external policy of Florence and all appointments to offices were controlled by Cosimo. Hence he was in fact, though not in name, the 'prince' by whom Florence was governed.

3. Cp. Plutarch's remark in his *Life of Julius Caesar*. By making Pompey and Crassus friends 'Caesar secured to himself the interest of both, and, while he seemed to be only doing an office of humanity, was actually undermining the constitution. For it was not, as most people imagine, the disagreement between Caesar and Pompey that produced the civil wars (49-47 B.C.), but rather their union. They first combined to ruin the authority of the senate, and, when that was effected, they separated to pursue each his own designs' (*Caesar* 13.3 and cp. *Pompey* 70.4; also for their friendship see *Caesar* 14, 21, and *Pompey* 47-8, 51, 53). On the actions of the senatorial party which provoked retaliation by Caesar, see D. I.29, n. 6. The main cause of the breach between them was Pompey's jealousy at the successes which Caesar had gained and at his ever increasing power.

4. Cicero. *Ad Fam.* XVI.11: '*qui Caesarem sero coepit timere*'. The quotation is not given in Latin in the text.

5. Cp. D. III.11.5, where procrastination is recommended to a power which is confronted with many enemies.

6. The mention of the dictatorship as a 'new device' resulting from this war, suggests that it is to the first Latin war of 501 that Machiavelli is here referring. But since this war occurred within ten years of the founding of the republic, when the

Tarquins were still trying to get back, it can scarce be said that Rome's power was already so strong that the Latins should have temporised. On the contrary, if they did want to crush Rome, now was the time to do it. No doubt the war was a mistake, as their defeat at Lake Regillus showed. The Latins would have done better to have disowned the Tarquins and to have continued their alliance with the Romans against the threat from the Volsci and the Samnites. This mistake, however, scarce falls under the head of a failure to recognise the need of temporising. Machiavelli, in fact, seems to be confusing two wars, the war which led to the appointment of a dictator in 501 B.C., and the Great Latin war of 340-338 B.C., which was against the Latin League mentioned in § 1. The first war is described by Livy in II.18-25; the second in VIII.1-11. In the list of Rome's wars given in D. II.1.3 this second Latin war is the only one Machiavelli mentions.

On the importance of giving medicine before it is too late, see. P. 3, E.21, Burd. 191, n. 17.

Cp. also Aristotle, *Politics* V.8, which deals with how to preserve states in general. 'In well constituted polities there is nothing which should be more jealously maintained than the spirit of obedience to law, more especially in small matters; for transgression creeps in unobserved and at length ruins the state, just as the constant recurrence of small expenses in time eats up a fortune ... Men, therefore, should guard against the beginning of change, and should not rely on sophisms' (1307b, 30-40). Yet 'no ordinary man can discern the beginning of evil, but only the true statesman' (1308a, 34-5).

34. Dictatorial Authority did Good, not Harm, to the Republic of Rome: it is the Authority which Citizens arrogate to Themselves, not that granted by Free Suffrage, that is harmful to Civic Life

1. Livy in II.18 says that it is doubtful when the first dictator was appointed. Some say it was Octavius Mamilius, son-in-law of Tarquinius Superbus, but this is incredible, says Livy. The oldest authorities mention T. Lartius as being the first, in which case the first appointment was in 501 B.C., and the occasion was the danger arising from the Latin war. M. Valerius is another name suggested, but Livy prefers T. Lartius on the ground that the law required that a dictator should be of consular rank, and Valerius was not then of consular rank. The outbreak of the Latin war did not occur till two years later (499 B.C.), when, during the consulship of T. Aebutius and C. Vetusius, A. Postumius was appointed dictator and Aebutius became his master of horse (II.19.1-3).

2. Caesar was appointed dictator by the praetor, M. Lepidus, not by the consuls, and without the approval of the senate—an unprecedented event. He held the dictatorship for eleven days (in 49 B.C.), but on being chosen as consul, resigned. After defeating Pompey at the battle of Pharsalia in 48, he was appointed dictator for a year. His third dictatorship began in 47, and the fourth in 46. In 45, after his victory over the sons of Pompey in Spain, he was appointed dictator and also imperator for life. (See Plutarch's *Caesar*, nn. 37, 51, 57, and cp. D. I.17, n. 7.)

3. The normal period for which a dictator was appointed was six months— Livy III.29, IX.34, XXII.23. Prior to the appointment of Sulla in 81 there had been no dictator for 120 years. His appointment was irregular, for (i) there were no consuls at the time, and his appointment was made by the people, before whom the *interrex* brought a *rogatio*; and (ii) the appointment was for as long as necessity should require. Actually he held the post for two years. Caesar, as we have seen, was appointed dictator for life. By the time of his death, the dictatorship had become so unpopular that it was abolished, and, though the title was offered to Augustus, he refused it.

4. Not only was the dictator '*rei gerundae causa*' appointed for six months in order to deal with some specific emergency in foreign affairs; but dictators were also appointed for other purposes, such as '*comitiorum habendorum causa*', and when they had accomplished their task their office came to an end. This indeed would seem to have been the general custom (cp. Livy III.29, IV.47, VI.29). Consuls required the approbation of the senate for what they did; dictators could act on their own responsibility (Polybius III.87). The dictatorship was also a '*magistratus sine provocatione*', i.e. there was no right of appeal from the dictator's judgments.

5. Note that Machiavelli's conception of dictatorship does not exclude a 'war cabinet', as is made clear by the example of Venice, where the reference is presumably to the Council of Ten (cp. D. I.5, n. 2).

6. According to Livy the proclamation of a dictator was always made by a consul '*qui oriens de nocte silentio diceret dictatorem*' (VIII.23.15 and cp. IX.38; XXIII.22), and it was by a decree of the senate that the consuls were authorised to make the appointment (II.30; IV.17, 21, 23, 26, and 57). According to Pauly-Wissowa, however, the first use of this '*senatus consultum ultimum*' did not occur until the time of Tiberius Gracchus (Supplem, Vol. VI, col. 756-7; cp. also C.A.H. VII. pp. 441-2 and VIII, c. 12).

7. The dictator was entitled to twelve lictors and to other insignia suggesting kingship, and the dictatorship was spoken of by Cicero (*de Repub.* II.17) and others as what Machiavelli here calls a '*regia potestà*'—the term he uses in D. I.18.7 to describe the kind of authority that must be introduced into a corrupt state before it can become accustomed to freedom.

8. 'The investing of consuls with dictatorial power' was first occasioned by the murder of one of the consul's criers in 121 B.C. The corpse was paraded before the Senate-house, and the fathers responded by a '*senatus-consultus ultimum*' urging the consul, Opimius, to take such measures as he thought fit for the safety of the state, but with the warning: '*viderent consules ne quid respublica detrimenti caperet*'. (Cp. Livy III.4.9, where the injunction is given to a consul who is being invested with quasi-dictatorial powers). Commenting on the action of Opimius, and on the practice of passing a '*senatus consultum de republica defendenda*' thus inaugurated, Professor Last says: 'The long-standing practice whereby in times of crisis a dictator had been appointed to act as a temporary autocrat found less and less favour with the Senate as the pretensions of that body increased, and at the end of the third century the dictatorship fell upon a period of disuse which was only ended when Sulla revived the office in a new and modified form. In the second century the Senate preferred to meet special dangers by giving special instruction to the ordinary magistrates.' On the other hand, 'defence of the public weal was no special or exceptional function for the magistrates to undertake; it was only the most important of their normal duties.

Consequently the substance of this decree was no more than an exhortation to the executive to attend to the business which it was appointed to perform. Moreover, the wording of the formula made no pretence of setting law aside, or even of encouraging the magistrates to disregard the legal limitations of their power' (C.A.H. IX, p. 84). In view, however, of the special '*senatus consultum*' required, of the warning attached which plainly envisages the possibility of abuse, and of the admitted fact that the consul could count on the senate's support should he have recourse to extra-legal action in order to 'save the state' (cp. *op. cit.,* pp. 84–5), Machiavelli is not far wrong when he says that the consul thus acquired dictatorial powers. The formula used in conferring these powers, on the other hand, was not new, for it is mentioned by Livy not only in III.4, but also in connection with the trial of M. Manlius Capitolinus for sedition in 384 B.C. Disregarding the exhortation of Servilius Ahala that strong measures should be taken, the senate 'had recourse to a decree which verbally was more lenient, though it had the same force, namely, that the magistrates should see to it that the state took no harm from the pernicious schemes of M. Manlius' (VI.19.3). The quotation '*Videat Consul ne Respublica quid detrimentum capiat*' is in Latin.

Aristotle says that a form of dictatorship called '*Aesymnetia*' existed in ancient Hellas, and was a kind of elective tyranny, which, like barbarian monarchy, was legal, but differed from it in not being hereditary. 'Sometimes the office is held for life, sometimes for a term of years, or until certain duties have been performed' (*Politics* III.14, 1285a, 29 *sq.*). See also IV.9, 1295a, 4 *sq.*; and cp. also V.8, where he speaks of the restriction of the tenure of offices to six months as a useful democratic institution since it enables all of equal rank to share in them, and 'prevents oligarchies and aristocracies from falling into the hands of families. It is not easy for a person to do any great harm when his tenure of office is short, whereas long possession begets tyranny' (1308a, 15 *sq.*). Cp. § 5 above, and I.35.1 and 2; and D. III.24.

35. How it came about that the Appointment of the Decemviri in Rome was harmful to that Republic in spite of their having been appointed by Free and Public Suffrage

1. Cp. D. I.34.3.
2. Livy III.32–54. 'That a beginning might be made in the writing out of the laws, it pleased them to appoint ten men, against whom there should be no appeal, and to abolish for that year all other magistracies' (32.6).
3. 'In the hope of getting a complete codex of all Roman law, there was a demand, when the next elections drew near, again to appoint ten men' (34.7). Appius then set to work to make his colleagues as proud as himself (36.1–2), with the result that the Decemviri became like ten kings, and everybody, even the highest in the land, went in terror of them (36.5). The date of the Decemvirate is 451–450 B.C.
4. For the constitution of Sparta and Venice cp. D. I.5 and 6. Sparta's two kings were 'watched over' by a small but powerful senate. In Venice the Doge, who was

elected for life, was 'watched over' by a Signoria, consisting of nine members, a senate, and a grand council the members of which were hereditary and together formed a closed circle by which the power of the Doge was much restricted.

5. The reference in the case of Sparta is presumably to the senate, to which the 'nobility' alone were eligible (cp. D. I.5.1), though the ephors also acted as 'supervisors'. In the case of Venice it is presumably to the Signoria, which 'watched over' the Doge, or possibly to the Grand Council (*ib.*).

6. For a further discussion of the Decemviri, see D. I.40-5.

36. Citizens who have held Higher Posts should not disdain to accept Lower

1. Livy II.43-7. Quintus Fabius Vibulanus was consul in 481 B.C. (43.1); and, the patricians being anxious that the consulate should remain in the Fabian family, Marcus Fabius, his brother, was chosen consul, with Gn. Manlius as his colleague in the following year (43.11). Quintus served under them in the war against Veii, and was killed. Wherein he set a remarkable example to the citizens, says Livy (46.4). (Cp. II.25.1 and III.12.5).

Cp. Plutarch, *Praecepta regendae reipublicae*: 'A statesman should not refuse offices if called to them by the people in accordance with law, but, even if they be too small for a man of his reputation, he should accept them and should exercise them with zeal, for it is right that a man who has been adorned with the highest offices, should in turn adorn the lower' (n. 17, 813 D).

37. On the Scandals to which the Agrarian Laws gave rise in Rome; and how great is the Scandal given in a Republic by passing a Law that is too Retrospective and contravenes an Ancient Custom of the State

1. This discourse, like several others, opens with some preliminary remarks on the appetites brought into play by the incidents about to be described (cp. Index *sub* 'Discourses'). In it there is a sequence of causes and effects to which also Machiavelli is partial (cp. Index *sub* 'Causal Sequences'; and for the views here expressed cp. D. I.5.4-7). For man's discontent, (see Preface to Book II, 7; and cp. Aristotle's views given below.)

2. Cp. D. I.3.

3. The first Agrarian law mentioned by Livy was that 'promulgated' by Spurius Cassius in 486 B.C. (II.41.3). It aroused the '*malignitas patrum*' to such an extent that, when Cassius' consulate terminated, he was indicted for having sought to make himself king, and was put to death. His proposal was that lands taken from the Hernici should be divided into two parts, one to go to the Latins and the other to the plebs, and that to it should be added public land which had become private property.

4. On keeping the public rich and citizens poor, cp. D. II.19.2; D. III.16.3,

and D. III.25. Cp. also Cato's speech in Sallust's 'Catiline' (52.22). It was industry at home and a just rule abroad that made our forefathers great, says Cato. 'But in place of these things we now have luxury and avarice, a needy public, but in private opulence' (*publice egestatem privatim opulentiam*).

5. Cp. Livy II.41.3: 'From then on up to the present day never was the question of this law raised without very great disturbances.'

6. Of these provisions the first was enacted by the laws proposed by C. Licinius and L. Sextius against which the patricians fought for ten years (377–367). The law '*de modo agrorum*' forbade anyone to hold more than 500 *jugera*—about 300 acres (Livy VI.35.5). The distribution of captured territory amongst colonists was already an established custom. In 418 B.C. a colony comprising 1,500 men from the city was sent to territory of the Labici, each of whom received the customary two *jugera* (Livy IV.47.6–7). Similarly in 385 a colony of 2,000 citizens was sent to Satricum, each of whom received 2½ *jugera* (VI.16.6). It has been suggested that this practice was confirmed by the Licinio-Sextian legislation, but Livy does not say so.

7. Cp. Livy III.1.7: '*Cetera multitudo poscere Romae agrum malle quam alibi accipere*' (but not cited in Latin). The date is 467 B.C. Antium was taken in 468 (II.65.7).

8. Tiberius Sempronius Gracchus caused himself to be elected tribune in 133 B.C. with a view to relieving the widespread distress he had observed amongst the peasant proprietors of Italy. For this purpose he proposed to revive the Licinian law of 367. Another tribune, M. Octavius Caecina, opposed the motion in the interests of the senate and the aristocracy, and, as he was obstinate, Gracchus took the unprecented step of getting the tribes to depose him. He then sought to enforce the law, which was modified only in one respect: it allowed a father with one son to hold an extra 250 *jugera*, and a father with two sons to hold another 250, making a thousand in all. All families holding more than this, and all individuals holding more than 500 *jugera* were to be deprived of the surplus, and in the case of those who had purchased their lands no compensation was offered. Hence the legislation, as Machiavelli says, was too retrospective, i.e. it revived an old law without adequate adaptation to present circumstances. When Gracchus put up for the tribunate of the following year there was a riot in which he and 300 citizens were killed. This left the popular party and the senatorial or aristocratic party at daggers drawn. (Cp. Plutarch, *Life of Tiberius and Caius Gracchus*, nn. 8–19.)

9. To obtain the seven consulships mentioned in the text, we must count as the seventh Marius' appointment to the command in the Mithradatic war in 88, for which Sulla had already been appointed consul. His first consulship was in 107, the second in 104 for the war with the Cimbri. This was followed by the three successive consulships of 103, 102 and 101 for which Machiavelli says that practically he appointed himself consul. Then in 100 he was elected for the sixth time. In this consulship he collected an armed force and seized the Capitol. When Sulla was appointed consul for the Mithradatic war in 88, Marius retaliated by proposing that the Italians who had just been enfranchised should be enrolled in the old tribes, and forced the measure through by entering the forum with an armed force. Sulla fled to Nola; Marius was appointed in his stead; but Sulla returned to Rome with the army from Nola, and Marius was defeated and fled. (For details, see the *Lives of Sulla and Marius* by Plutarch.)

10. On Caesar's connection with Marius, see D. I.17, n. 7. War broke out

between Caesar who was supported by the popular party, and Pompey who represented the aristocratic party in 49 B.C. (Cp. Plutarch's *Life of Caesar*, n. 6, for the reviving of the Marian faction by Caesar; and Aquinas, *de Regimine*, IV.1—cited in *Sources* B.8,x—for a statement concerning Caesar's tyranny similar to what Machiavelli says).

Aristotle in *Politics* V.8 remarks, apropos of the giving of honours, that 'men are easily corrupted, and not all men can stand prosperity' (1308b, 14). He adds that, if too great honours have been conferred, they should be taken away by degrees, and not all at once. He also remarks in II.8 that though 'laws ought not always to remain unaltered . . . since it is impossible that all things should be precisely set down in writing . . . yet the habit of lightly changing laws is an evil, and, when the advantage is small, some errors both of lawgivers and rulers had better be left; the citizen will not gain so much by the change as he will lose by the habit of disobedience' (1269a, 8-18).

Cp. also Aquinas, *Politics*, Book II, *Lect. XII: leges, etiam minus bonae, non sint facile immutandae.*

38. Weak Republics suffer from Irresolution and cannot reach Decisions; and, when they do arrive at one, it is due rather to Necessity than to Choice

1. The facts are supplied by Livy III.6. They occurred in 463 B.C. Rome was having a 'bad time' owing to a pestilence which was killing off both cattle and men. Hence the Hernici and Latins were told to look to their own defence. With these tribes Rome had formed an alliance in 493 B.C., so that they formed a bulwark between Roman territory proper and the Sabellian hill tribes, the Aequi and the Volsci, who were continually making raids. The comments are Machiavelli's, not Livy's.

2. Thus, when the Aequi invaded Latin territory in 494 B.C., envoys were sent to ask for Roman help or, alternatively, for permission to defend themselves, and in this case the Romans preferred to defend them rather than allow them to take up arms (Livy II.30.8-9). Again, when in 475 there was another invasion and the Latins got the Hernici to help and marched out without a Roman general or Roman troops, the consul, C. Nautius, protested that it was not the custom for Rome's allies to go to war without a Roman general or Roman help (II.53.4-5).

3. Of the three Florentine incidents cited in this discourse the first occurred in 1501 when Machiavelli was in his fourth year of office. During this year Caesar Borgia opened his second campaign in the Romagna, took Faenza on 25 April and became 'Duke of the Romagna' shortly afterwards. He next advanced on Bologna, but was stopped by the French and had to come to terms with that city. He then demanded provisions from the Florentines and a free passage through their territory. He had already seized Bersighella, the key to the Val di Lamone. Florence was alarmed, sent a present of 20,000 ducats to Louis XII, and under Machiavelli's direction began to prepare Florence for a siege. Meanwhile Ramazzotto had demanded in the name of the Duke the restoration of Piero de' Medici which would mean the end of republican government. They then gave the Duke permission to

march through Florentine territory but only with small bodies of troops; which so annoyed the Duke that he ravaged the country through which he passed. He then demanded a free passage to Piombino (which was granted), but dropped the question of Piero de' Medici's recall, which had been refused, and instead asked for an alliance and a '*condotta*', i.e. an agreement making him an officer in the pay of Florence. Both these requests were granted by a convention signed on 15 May. He then went on to Piombino, still ravaging the country; crossed to Elba, and finally returned in triumph to Rome.

4. The treaty which bound the French king to help Florence in the siege of Pisa was made on 19 October 1499. The Florentines were to pay 24,000 ducats a month toward the support of the French troops. The Cardinal de Rouen demanded that payment should begin at once, to which Florence had to agree, as well as to pay for 1,200 extra troops, not included in the contract. The French arrived at Cascina on 23 June 1500, accompanied by two Florentine commissioners with Machiavelli as their secretary. On the 29th, 8,000 men were encamped before the walls of Pisa, with their guns in position, but with a mutiny threatening on account of the shortage of provisions. It was Luca degli Albizzi who refused to accept the proposed terms of surrender in the name of the Signoria on the ground that hostilities had already begun and within a month the city might fall. On 7 July the Gascons deserted *en masse*, and the next day the Swiss mutinied and threatened Albizzi's life. He was held a prisoner till he agreed to pay 1,300 ducats to some Swiss who had just come from Rome; whereupon the French army withdrew, leaving the Florentines in the lurch. Hence, as Machiavelli pithily says, 'the net result was a fruitless journey to the camp from which they returned in disgrace.' (For details see Villari, I, pp. 270-3.)

5. That in rejecting Beaumont's offer the Florentines made a bad mistake there can in this case be no doubt; but in the next example which Machiavelli cites the issue is less clear. On 12 April 1502, Florence made an alliance with Louis XII who bound himself to supply 400 lances on demand in return for a promise to pay 120,000 ducats within three years. The Pisans had taken the offensive and planned to form an independent state stretching to the sea, with Borgia as its hereditary duke. In June, Vitellozzo seized Arezzo, which had revolted, and the Florentines applied for the four hundred lances which the French king had promised. Soderini, Bishop of Volterra, accompanied by Machiavelli, was sent to Urbino, which Borgia had obtained by treachery. The Duke, who had asked for envoys, promised peace on condition that Florence changed its government, and disclaimed responsibility for what Vitellozzo had done. The Florentines declined to change their government and, when Borgia became more threatening, temporised, relying on help from France. It came in July, whereupon Borgia left Vitellozzo and Piero de' Medici in the lurch, and Arezzo was occupied by Imbault. At the request of Florence, Imbault was replaced by de Lanques, and by the end of August she had recovered all her territory in this neighbourhood, and public festivals were held to commemorate the event. Hence the policy of Florence was in this case successful, though her success had cost Florence dear. In a short paper, entitled 'On the method of dealing with the rebellious peoples in the Val di Chiana', written at the time, Machiavelli blames Florence not for rejecting Imbault's offer, but for using half-hearted measures in dealing with the rebels. They ought rather to have followed here the example of Rome, as exemplified in the conduct of Furius Camillus, who

in his speech to the senate after the conquest of Latium recommended that rebellious cities should either be freely forgiven or destroyed. (Cp. Livy VIII.13, and for Machiavelli's treatise see Op. PM. III. 365 *sq.*; Villari I. pp. 296–7.) Imbault was replaced by de Lanques towards the close of the year, 1502, and de Lanques restored Arezzo to Florence. Cp. D. III.27.6.

39. To Different Peoples the same sort of Thing is often found to happen

1. From the logical standpoint the theorem which heads this discourse is basic to Machiavelli's inductive method, and is equivalent to the logician's Postulate of Uniformity applied to the realm of politics, which Machiavelli in his Preface and elsewhere holds to be but a part of 'nature' over the whole of which the laws of cause and effect hold sway. What he is here asserting is that, if due allowance be made for circumstances, the same causes will always give rise to the same effects, and that, in consequence, if we recognise the causes, we shall know what to expect, and also how to remedy the situation, provided in history we can find a similar situation to which a remedy has been successfully applied. The main point of this discourse was raised by Machiavelli in his treatise entitled: '*Del Modo di Trattare i Popoli della Valdichiana ribellati*' (Op. PM. III, 365 *sq.*; Detmold does not print this report). In it he discusses also the topic raised in the last chapter. (Cp. D. I.38, n. 5.) His report was probably written after Arezzo had been handed over to the Florentines by de Lanques on 26 August 1501, and is said to have been read before the Florentine magistrates. Having discussed at some length the way in which the Romans dealt with rebellious towns in the time of Furius Camillus, Machiavelli introduces the case of Arezzo and the Valdichiana with this remark, 'I have heard it said that history is the master of our actions and especially of those of princes, and that the world has always been inhabited by men who have always had the same passions, and that there were always those who were subjects and those who ruled, and that some were unwilling subjects and others willing, and that some rebelled and their rebellion was suppressed.' He then points out the similarity between the case of the Latins and that of the Valdichiana, and adds that, 'if it be true that history be the master of our actions it would not be a bad thing for those who have to pronounce judgment and to punish the towns in the Valdichiana, to emulate those who have been as fathers to the world'.

2. The writer whose sayings Machiavelli has in mind here and in the passage quoted above is almost certainly Polybius. For Polybius also claims that it is possible to draw parallels in history, and that, if history is to be a training for political life, it is essential that this should be done (I.1 and 2). Nor will a bare account of events suffice for this purpose; we must consider not only laws and customs, but also passions and inclinations (III.7). The diversities of states must also be taken into account, if we would 'foretell the future by what has gone before' (VI.1), and would use the misfortunes of others to benefit mankind (I.35). This has not been done by historians in the past, owing in part to their lack of impartiality (I.14) and in part to their failure to diagnose causes correctly (III.6).

3. The 'Ten of War', the committee to which Machiavelli was secretary, recom-

mended in 1499 that Venice be paid an indemnity to withdraw her troops from Pisa. Owing to this and to the increasing cost of the war and the demands of the generals for increased pay, new method of levying taxes had to be devised. Hence everyone began to grumble at the 'ten expenders', and, when the time came for their re-election in May, cried 'Down with the Ten and with Taxation' and declined to reappoint them. The result was incompetence in the management of the siege in 1500 (cp. D. I.38.5 and D. III.15.3), and the loss of Arezzo in 1502 (cp. D. II.23.3 and D. III.6.44), though by this time the ten had been reappointed. (Cp. Guicciardini's comments cited below.)

4. Livy gives an account of the proposal made in 462 B.C. by C. Terentillus Harsa and of the grievances which prompted it (III.9). The replacement of consuls by *'tribuni militum consulari potestate'* is first mentioned in IV.6. The date is 445 B.C., when the plebs was urging its claim to be admitted to the consulship. The new officers had the same power and function as the consuls, but were not entitled to a triumph and plebeians were eligible for the office. Tribunes with consular power were abolished by the Licinian law of 367 B.C., which threw the consulate open to plebeians (Livy VI.35, 38-42). For a discussion of the date of the institution of these tribunes see C.A.H. VII.14.5. Between the Roman and the Florentine episodes there are numerous points of similarity. In both we have (i) ill humour aroused amongst the populace by a prolonged war; (ii) resentment against the officials concerned in running it; (iii) who are blamed for what in fact was not their fault; and (iv) in consequence are replaced by others and their office is abolished; but (v) when the mistake is realised, there is a return to the original practice. The similarity is between sequences. Similar causes give rise, not merely to similar effects, but to similar sequences of effects; and in politics as in nature similar causes recur continually in the humours and desires which circumstances evoke. (Cp. Polybius III.6).

Guicciardini *in loc.* writes: 'I do not think that the complaint the Florentines brought against the magistracy of the Ten was altogether unreasonable; because ancient institutions of the city introduced under different forms of government had given this magistracy more authority than was befitting to the proper safeguarding of liberty. For it lay within its power without reference to others to make peace, war, treaties and alliances; to engage what generals, and as many as, and on what terms, it pleased; to spend all monies without any authorisation or restraint, and in general to have in matters pertaining to war as much authority as had the Florentine people. It was this too independent an authority which in large part accounted for the attitude of the populace and its reluctance to reappoint these magistrates. But, experience having shown that, if too much authority is pernicious, it is also very harmful to a city in difficult times to be without a magistracy of prudent men who shall watch over and direct affairs, a beating taught them what they were incapable of learning from reason, and they reappointed the magistracy of the Ten of War, limiting their authority in those matters which were deemed dangerous and prescribing that in such cases the Eighty should be consulted. It was owing to this decision that never afterwards, save in time of peace, was there any difficulty about appointing this magistracy, which was now called not the *"Dieci di Balìa"* as it was when it had absolute authority, but the *"Dieci di Libertà e Pace."* '

'The instance of Terentillus is different, for the authority of the consuls, when not on some expedition, was in no sense absolute, but was subject to an appeal to the people, restrained by the tribunes' right to intervene, and in all serious business the consuls were the executors of the senate's will rather than masters; and in consequence there was no need to modify this office. On the contrary, the motion to do so was altogether seditious, and aimed at introducing a purely popular and licentious government.'

40. The Appointment of the Decemvirate in Rome and what is Noteworthy about it; in which will be considered, amongst other Things, how such an Incident may lead either to a Republic's Salvation or to its Subjection

1. In what follows Machiavelli keeps closely to Livy's account of this episode in Roman history, and in the course of it quotes him no less than six times. I give below the references for the incidents and for the quotations, which are all in Latin.

2. Livy III.31.8. 3. 32.5–33.3. 4. 33.6–7. 5. 33.8–10. 6. 34.1–5.

7. 34.6–8, but Livy does not say Appius started the rumour. 8. 35.1–5.

9. '*Credebant enim haud gratuitam in tanta superbia comitatem fore*' (35.6).

10. 35.7–8.

11. '*Ille vero impedimentum pro occasione arripuit*' (35.9).

12. 35.9–10.

13. '*Appius finem fecit ferendae alienae personae*' (36.1—quotation not verbally exact).

14. 36.1–4. 15. 36.5–9.

16. '*et inde libertatis captare auram, unde servitutem timendo, in eum statum rempublicam adduxerunt*' (37.1).

17. '*ut ipsi, taedio praesentium, Consules desiderarent*' (37.3, but not verbally exact).

18. 37.4–8.

19. '*Quibus donis juventus corrumpebatur, et malebat licentiam suam, quam omnium libertatem*' (37.8—but not verbally exact).

20. 38.3–6, but Livy says the Sabines and the Aequi.

21. 39. 22. 41.5–6. 23. 41.7–8. 24. 44. 25. Cp. 48.5. 26. 52.1.

27. Cp. Livy: '*libertatem concordiamque civitati restitutam*' (54.7).

28. For the reliability of Livy's narrative see C.A.H. VII, p. 458–64. That ten men were appointed to codify Rome's laws in 452 B.C., and were given absolute authority; that they drew up ten tables and were reappointed to draw up another two; that they made this an occasion for setting up a tyranny which led to a secession of the plebs, modelled on that of 494 B.C.; and that, on the abdication of the Ten, tribunes, consuls, and an interrex were appointed and constitutional government restored, are facts for which there is considerable evidence. But for Appius's character and behaviour and end, as related by Livy, there is less evidence.

29. With §§ 9, 10 compare P. 9 in regard both to the methods used by the populace and by the nobles. In it we are told that 'a prince can never secure himself against a hostile people since they are too numerous, but against the nobility he can secure himself since they are but few.' Cp. also P. 7, in which Caesar Borgia, who

sought to eliminate the nobles in the Romagna, but to win over its people, is held up as an example.

30. To the dealings which Nabis, tyrant of Sparta (207–192 B.C.), had with Rome, there are numerous references in Livy, Books XXIX, XXXI–XXXII, XXXIV–XXXV. In 195 B.C. all Greece, except Aetolia, sent contingents to serve with Flamininus, and, though defeated in the end, Nabis for a time held his own. His method of 'making sure of a few nobles' on this occasion was to execute some eighty of them. For the brutalities practised in the early days of his tyranny cp. Polybius XIII.6–8. For the parallelism between Machiavelli and Livy on Nabis, see Burd, pp. 240–1, n. 19.

31. D. I.34.3–4.

32. Ferdinand V of Castile, II of Aragon, and III of Naples, 1452–1516.

Guicciardini *in loc.* writes: 'I am convinced that the principal error which Appius and his associates made was to have persuaded themselves that it was possible to set up a tyranny in the city of Rome in days when excellent laws prevailed and it had an abundance of sound customs, and was very ardent in desiring liberty, a liberty which, since the Romans were a military people, it was difficult to undermine. Hence the tyranny lasted as long as they had a pretext for continuing their magistracy in that they had to complete the laws; but, when this their deceit came to light, the first mishap, however small, destroyed their tyranny, which would not, I think, have been more stable even if they had set about maltreating the nobility with the support of the populace, for the populace was far too devoted to the name of liberty. The example of Manlius Capitolinus shows this, for, although he took action against the senate and employed purely popular devices, he was overthrown by this same populace as soon as it came to realise that he was trying to get rid of liberty.'

'In regard to the general question whether it is better for the would-be tyrant to cultivate popular favour or to make the nobility his ally, examples point both ways.' Sulla in Rome and the Duke of Athens in Florence availed themselves of the nobility. And there are reasons why it should be so; for 'he who has the populace on his side has a greater number of followers, and the populace will put up with a greatness which the nobles cannot stand; yet he who has the nobles with him, is relying on what is more sensitive, more efficient, and more reliable, and on what does not change its mind so easily and so frequently for little reason as does the populace'.

Aristotle agrees with Machiavelli that it is the people whom a tyrant should cultivate (*Politics* V.9, 1310a, 4 *sq.*—see note 3 to D. I.16).

41. A Sudden Transition from Humility to Pride or from Kindness to Cruelty without Appropriate Steps in between is both Imprudent and Futile

1. Cp. D. I.40.4. This discourse and the next four embody Machiavelli's reflections on the story of Appius Claudius and the Decemviri related in the previous chapter.

42. How easily Men may be Corrupted

1. Cp. Aristotle, *Politics* V.8, 1308b, 14: 'men are easily corrupted'.
2. The young nobles who in D. I.40.7 were corrupted with presents and pre-ferred licence to liberty (Livy III. 37.8).
3. Quintus Fabius Vibulanus, son of the Marcus Fabius mentioned in D. I.36.1. His father was one of the three Fabii killed at Cremera in a battle waged against the Veientes. He was three times consul, in 467, 465 and 459. It was he who suggested that a colony should be sent to Antium to prevent the passing of the Agrarian law (cp. I.37.4). He was victorious over the Aequi and the Volsci, and in 462 was *praefectus urbi*. After the fall of the Decemviri he was sent into exile and his goods confiscated. (Cp. Livy III.1, 9, 22–5; 35.11). In 41.8 he is spoken of with Appius as '*principes inter decemviros*', and as being 'inconstant in well doing, rather than assiduous in wrong doing'. For his exile see 58.9.

43. Those who fight for Glory's Sake make Good and Faithful Soldiers

1. The discourse on the Decemviri, D. I.40.
2. There had been no external wars since 457 B.C. owing to a pestilence which ravaged Italy, but in 449 the Sabines attacked and put to flight a Roman army under three of the decemviri at Eretum, and the Aequi defeated another army which had been sent to protect Tusculum (Livy III, 41–2).
3. In 448 M. Horatius Barbatus, who had delivered Rome from the tyranny of the Decemviri, gained a victory over the Sabines (III.62–3), about whom nothing more is heard for 250 years. The Aequi and the Volsci were also defeated in 448 and again in 446 (III.61, 66–70).

Ellinger thinks that this chapter is based on Herodotus V.78 (see Ellinger, p. 23). The passage in question runs as follows: 'The Athenians accordingly increased in power [after defeating the Boeotians and the Chalcidians]. And equality of rights shows, not in one case only but in every way, what an excellent thing this is. For the Athenians, when governed by tyrants, were superior in war to none of their neighbours; but, when free from tyrants, became by far the first. This, then, shows that so long as they were oppressed, they purposely acted as cowards, because labouring for a master; but when they were free every one was zealous to labour for himself ' (V. 78). The parallelism here is far from close.

Aristotle in *Politics* III.14 (1285a, 24) says that it is characteristic of a legitimate king, who seeks honour and not private interests, that he should be guarded by citizens, whereas the tyrant is guarded by mercenaries, for he mistrusts the people and deprives them of their arms (cp. the note to D. I.19).

44. A Crowd is useless without a Head; nor should it first use Threats and then appeal for the Requisite Authority

1. The story of Appius Claudius's lust for Virginia, daughter of an upright man then serving as a soldier, and the betrothed of L. Icilius, a former tribune, and of

74

the way in which he abused his position in order to retain possession of her, is told by Livy in III.44–8. To save her from Appius she was killed by her own father (48.6–7). The result was a secession of the plebs, who retired to the Aventine, where they were joined by troops from the camp at Tusculum (49, 50).

2. '*Non defuit quod responderetur*', says Livy; '*deerat qui daret responsum nullodum certo duce nec satis audentibus singulis invidiae se offerre*' (III.50.16). And in 51: '*admonet milites Verginius in re non maxima paulo ante trepidatum esse, quia sine capite multitudo fuerit, responsumque quamquam non inutiliter, fortuito tamen magis consensu quam communi consilio esse*'. The words quoted are not given in Latin.

3. Ten men, whom it was decided to call military tribunes, were appointed by the plebs and another ten by the troops, with M. Oppius and Sex. Manilius in command (51.10).

4. 50.16. 5. 51.12.

6. The mob now transfers itself from the Aventine to Mons Sacer (52.1), and there states the three points on which it demands satisfaction (53.4–5).

7. '*Crudelitatem damnatis, in crudelitatem ruitis*', whereas in the Teubner edition we have: '*quippe qui crudelitatis odio in crudelitatem ruitis*' (53.7), cited in Latin.

8. 53.9–10.

45. It is a Bad Precedent to break a New Law, especially if the Legislator himself does it; and daily to inflict Fresh Injuries on a City is most Harmful to him that governs it

1. Livy III.54.7; cp. I.40.8. 2. 56.1–4. 3. 56.5–57.5. 4. 57.6. 5. 58.6.

6. I.e. 1494, when Charles VIII invaded Italy and the Medici were expelled from Florence. The new constitution owed much to the influence of Savonarola's sermons preached in the Duomo in the Lent of 1495. He was strongly in favour of an appeal from the court called '*Gli Otto di Guardia e Balìa*', popularly known as the 'Court of the Six Beans' since six of the eight votes were required for a conviction. But whereas he advised that the appeal should be to a court of eighty or a hundred chosen from the Greater Council and comprising men with legal experience, the populace, egged on by supporters of Piero de' Medici, advocated an appeal to the Consiglio Maggiore of which all citizens over twenty-nine who had paid their taxes, were members, and it was in this form that the law of Appeal in the case of political offences was carried in March, 1495. Two years later a plot to restore the Medici was discovered and five of the conspirators were condemned to death and to confiscation of their property by the Eight of Guard and Custody, acting under the instructions of the Signoria. With this sentence the leading citizens who had taken part in the preliminary enquiries concurred. Hence, when the friends of the condemned men demanded an appeal to the Greater Council it was, after a long and turbulent discussion, refused, and in August, 1497, the sentence was duly carried out. It is true that Savonarola remained silent during the trial and made no protest against the refusal to grant an appeal. But he was living at the time in retirement and under the ban of excommunication, and it was not he who had proposed the law, but Vespucci. On the contrary, he and his followers had opposed it.

Hence, as Villari points out (*Life and Times of Savonarola*, p. 571 *sq.*), Machiavelli, Guicciardini, and other writers who blame Savonarola for his silence on the ground that he was responsible for the law, are by no means fair to the famous Dominican friar. (For a full account of the passing of the law, see Villari, *op. cit.*, pp. 278-88, and for the conspiracy and trial see pp. 557-75.)

7. Livy III.59.1-2. To allay the terror of the patricians at the sentences passed on the Decemviri and their supporters, M. Duillius in 449 announced that enough had been heard of our liberties and of the punishment of enemies, and that in consequence during his year of office he would tolerate no accusations and would put no one in chains.

8. Cp. P. 8, where Machiavelli warns those who have obtained a principality by brutal methods that 'the injuries which they have to inflict should be done all at once, so as not to have to repeat them daily.... He who acts otherwise, whether owing to timidity or evil counsel, has to keep the knife in his hand, and so cannot base his power on his subjects, since if he continues to inflict fresh injuries, he cannot win them over. For injuries should be done all together, so that they will be tasted less and so will give less offence' (E.72-3).

46. Men pass from one Ambition to Another, and, having first striven against Ill-treatment, inflict it next upon Others

1. The reference is to Rome's 'recovering the form of her ancient liberty' (D. I.40.8; cp. Livy III.54.7).

2. The laws of the twelve tables. After some preliminary remarks on the extent to which these laws as they have come down to us have been modified by glosses, Professor Last writes: 'Even the most callous critic of tradition must admit that the final successes of the plebs found expression, at least in part, in enactments of a kind which may be described as constitutional. The magistracy was opened to people who had been excluded so long as office remained a patrician preserve, and in general some greater say in the direction of public affairs was given to that section of the population which did not aspire to office at all' (C.A.H. VII, p. 463).

3. The remainder of this paragraph (§ 1) is a paraphrase of Livy III.65.7-11; but cp. also for the continuance of the conflict III.67-69 and IV.1-6.

4. '*quod omnia mala exempla bonis initiis orta sunt*' (*De Conjurg. Cat.* 51.27; but in Jordan's Berlin edition the reading is: '*Omnia mala exempla ex rebus bonis orta sunt.*')

5. See D. III.28 and 49, but in neither case is there an express mention of an institution; and cp. Aristotle, *Politics* V.8, 1308b, 20-4, where he says that there should be an institution to keep watch on individuals whose life is not in harmony with the government (with which compare the heading of D. III.28).

Cp. also Thucydides' description of the 'terrible calamities which revolution brought on the cities of Hellas, calamities such as have been and always will be while human nature remains the same, but which are more or less aggravated and differ in character with every new combination of circumstances.... When troubles had once begun in cities, those who followed carried the revolutionary spirit further and further, and determined to outdo the report of all who had preceded them by the ingenuity of their enterprises and the atrocity of their revenges. ... The cause of all these evils was the love of power, originating in avarice and ambition, and the party-spirit which is engendered by them when men are fairly embarked in a contest. For the leaders on either side used specious names, the one party professing to uphold the constitutional equality of the many, the other the wisdom of the aristocracy, while they made the public interests, to which in name they were devoted, in reality their prize. Striving in every way to overcome each other, they committed the most monstrous crimes; yet even these were surpassed by the magnitude of their revenges' (III.82—and see Machiavelli's account of what happens when the demands of parties for liberty or for domination become excessive, in D. I.40.9; cp. also the passage cited from Thucydides III.43, at end of notes to D. I.28 and from III.45 at end of notes to D. I.53).

47. Though Men make Mistakes about Things in General, they do not make Mistakes about Particulars

1. D. I.39.3 and 40.4; and cp. Livy III.9, and IV.2.1.

2. Livy IV.6.8. 3. 6.11.

4. '*Quorum comitiorum eventus docuit, alios animos in contentione libertatis et honoris, alios secundum deposita certamina in incorrupto judicio esse*' (IV.6.11, cited in Latin).

5. '*Hanc modestiam aequitatemque et altitudinem animi, ubi nunc in uno inveneris, quae tunc populi universi fuit?*' (6.12, cited in Latin). The incidents related and discussed in these two paragraphs took place in 445 B.C. four years after the tyranny of the Decemviri had come to an end. (For 'consular tribunes', see C.A.H. VII, pp. 519–20.)

6. For this incident and the state of affairs in Capua, see Livy XXIII.2–4. The date is 216 B.C. Livy speaks of Pacuvius Calavius Campanus as an '*improbus homo, sed non ad extremum perditus*' (2.4). For an account of the revolt in Capua, see C.A.H. VIII, p. 55–6. Machiavelli writes *Calano* for *Calavio*.

7. On 2 September 1494 Charles VIII crossed the Alps and took city after city in northern Italy. Piero de' Medici, the 'prince' who was then ruling in Florence, handed over most of the Florentine fortresses and promised to pay tribute. On 9 November the citizens rose in arms and expelled the Medici. The city was then in the state of anarchy which Machiavelli describes; but he does not tell us who saved the situation. It was Savonarola. 'The friar', says Villari (*Life and Times of Savonarola*, II, c. 2), 'was now the only man having any influence over the people, who seemed to hang on his words and look for safety to him alone. One hasty word from his mouth would have sufficed to cause all the houses of the principal citizens to be sacked, to revive past scenes of civil warfare, and lead to torrents of blood. For the people had been cruelly trampled on, and were now panting for a cruel revenge' (p. 214). Instead he preached repentance and 'so magical was the power of Savonarola's voice in those days that in all this great stir of public excitement, not a single excess was committed, and the revolution that seemed to be on the point of being effected by violence on the Piazza was quietly and peacefully accomplished within the walls of the palace' (p. 215). Though no name is mentioned it is presumably of Savonarola that Machiavelli is speaking in § 5, but, if so, he does him scant justice.

8. In this paragraph Machiavelli probably has in mind either Francesco Valori or Piero Capponi, both of whom displayed considerable impetuosity and violence after the revolution of 1494 (cp. Villari's *'Savonarola'*, pp. 221–2), but on being appointed arbiters or syndics behaved with moderation (*ib.* 234–5, and cp. 253). The proverb with which this paragraph ends was current in Florence in his time.

Guicciardini *in loc.* agrees that people are often mistaken at first but on acquiring further and more concrete experience revise their views, as the Florentine proverb suggests. 'In the case of the Romans one notes that it seemed to the populace unbecoming and scandalous that in general they should all be incapable of preferment, and that, when it seemed to them enough to have acquired the right to become magistrates with consular power, they remained partially satisfied with the honour and refrained from electing unsuitable men.' ... 'The other conclusion drawn in the discourse, that the populace is less mistaken in distributing preferment and magistracies than in anything else, I believe to be true, and the reason is apparent, for the facts here can easily be ascertained, and the popular judgment in this case is based not merely on what it knows of the worth of a candidate, but on that general opinion which in course of time and experience has been formed of this or that person.'

48. To prevent an Official Appointment being given to a Base and Wicked Fellow, either an Exceedingly Base and Wicked Man should be put forward as a Candidate or an Exceedingly Noble and Good Man

1. The point which Machiavelli seems here to be seeking to make is that, in order to prevent plebeians being elected to the newly constituted office of tribune with consular power, the senate which represented the patricians either put forward as candidates (*faceva domandare*) patricians of such standing that the plebs could not but elect them, or else put forward amongst respectable plebeian candidates some rascally fellow whom they would be ashamed to elect, so that the plebeian candidates all got turned down. Machiavelli cites no evidence, but his statement is correct. The law sanctioning the appointment of military tribunes with consular power came into force in 444 B.C. (cp. D. I.39, n. 4). Though the office was open to plebeians, none were elected because the plebs looked upon its own candidates as unworthy (IV.7. 9). Hence, rather than have their own candidates turned down as unworthy the plebeians preferred that consuls should be elected (*ib.* 7, 8–9), so that for some ten years there were no tribunes with consular power. Against this practice and the indignity it implied, the plebeian tribunes protested more than once; with the result that from 426 onwards sometimes tribunes with consular power, and sometimes consuls were elected; but still no plebeians (IV, 25.1; 30.1; 35). In 420, when some of their relatives had been turned down, the plebeian tribunes suggested that the failure of plebeians to obtain the military tribunate was due to trickery on the part of the patricians (IV.44.1–5). Ten years later we are told what the artifice was: the patricians, 'by mixing a crowd of unworthy candidates with the

worthy, turned the populace against the plebeian candidates, with whose palpable meanness they were disgusted' (IV.56.3). A similar artifice was adopted in the next year, 408, when not only were unworthy men put forward among the plebeian candidates, but as patrician candidates only the most distinguished men were put forward, so that again only patricians were elected (IV.57.11).

49. If those City-States which from the Outset have been Free, as Rome was, find it difficult to formulate Laws whereby to maintain Liberty, those which have just been servile are faced with a Quasi-impossibility

1. Livy IV.8. 'The censorship began in this year'—443 B.C., tribunes with consular power having been appointed in the preceding year. 'It began in a small way,' says Livy: the consuls were too busy with wars to undertake a census, so two censors were appointed to make the returns. 'But it grew to such an extent that Roman customs and discipline came under its control. The honour of belonging to the senate and to the centuries of the knights and the disgrace of being degraded, fell under its jurisdiction. It had complete control over public and private rights to property, and over the taxation of the Roman people' (8.2–3).

2. Tiberius Aemilius Mamercus was dictator in 433 B.C. (Livy IV.23.5), when he reduced the duration of the censors' office (24.3–6).

3. *ib.* 24.7–9.

4. In his *History of Florence*, II.2, Machiavelli says that from the time when Florence was rebuilt by Charles the Great (who ruled from 768 to 814) down to 1215, Florence 'followed the fortunes of those who from time to time had the upper hand in Italy', i.e. the descendants of Charles, the Berengers, and the German Emperors; but that, when 'the German emperors grew feebler, the Italian towns began to conduct themselves with less respect for the Imperial power'. Hence the 200 years during which Florence was abject count from *circa* 800 to *circa* 1000. After this there was the conflict between Guelfs and Ghibbelines, during which period 'down to the year 1215, the Florentines remained united, rendering obedience to whichever side prevailed'. In the ensuing period powerful Florentine families began to contend for supremacy in the city (II.3 *sq.*), and Florence became more and more divided into factions, factions in the nobility and factions in its populace whence 'there resulted deaths, banishments, and the extermination of families to an extent unheard of in any other city' (Preface to the *Hist. Florence*). None the less, Machiavelli adds, 'to my mind nothing affords clearer proof of the vitality of our city than that these divisions, capable in themselves of wrecking the very greatest and most powerful states, are seen constantly to have added to the strength of ours',—a view which ill accords with the contrast drawn in this discourse between the effect of conflicts in Rome and their effect in other city-states, where they led to perpetual disorder.

5. Cp. H.F. II.5. 'Moreover, to remove occasions for enmity in administering justice they provided for the appointment of two foreign judges, one of whom was styled "Captain of the People" and the other "Podestà", to try all causes, civil or

criminal, arising between citizens.' This was in 1250. For the behaviour of these Captains, see H.F. II.12, 25, 27, 32. It was usually bad.

6. On the change from Captains to the Eight of Guard, Machiavelli gives us very little information in his *History of Florence*. In IV.29 he says that to 'intimidate any who might be displeased with the expulsion of Cosimo a '*Balìa*' (or commission) was given to the Eight of the Guard (*Otto di Guardia*) and to the Captain of the People'. This was in 1433, so that in this year, it would seem, both tribunals were functioning. On the return of Cosimo in 1434 we are told that 'to the Eight of the Guard they gave authority to punish with death' (V.4). Villari in his *Life and Times of Savonarola*, p. 288, says that it was in 1477 that the office of Captain of the People was abolished, and cites in support the Florentine Archives, '*Provvisioni, Registro*' No. 190, sheet 5. He adds that the *Podestà* was also at this date near its end, and that 'as the greater part of their functions now devolved on the Signory and the Eight, the power of these bodies became greatly increased'.

7. Cp. D. I.7, 6-7.

8. The tribunal of Ten was a committee of public safety formed in 1310 after the revolt organised by Baiamonte Tiepolo, and made permanent in 1355 at which time the constitution of Venice was finally determined. The Quarantia was a Court instituted during the reform movement of 1171 and out of it grew the Great Council. It originally comprised forty members chosen from each of six districts, and its functions were primarily judicial. In 1296 an event of great importance took place: the Great Council was 'closed', i.e. membership was restricted to those who had already served on it, or whose ancestors had done so, and it was to the '*Quarantia*' that the function of determining who had a right to sit was assigned. The government of Venice thus became aristocratic or oligarchic. The Court of Rogation (*Consiglio dei Rogati o Pregati*), which had sixty members, came into being at about the same time and formed a kind of senate. Later on these two councils took over most of the functions of the Great Council. (Cp. Guicciardini, *St. d'I.* IV.6, where we are told that the *Consiglio de' Pregati* had taken the place of the senate in Venice; and *ib.* IV.12, last paragraph, for the trial of Antonio Grimanno at which this council declined to listen to calumnies).

Guicciardini *in loc.* writes: 'This Discourse and many others illustrate what I have said in another place (cp. the *Considerazione sul Cap.* iv) in criticism of the writer's view, namely, that the Roman government was in many respects defective; for, what more absurd than that it should lie within the power of a single man to hold up public affairs and not to allow the decision of the city to take effect, as these consuls did? Similarly, though the veto of the tribunes was good, none the less, if the tribune wished to cause disorders of this kind, there was no remedy. It was also a mistake that it should rest with two censors to drive from the senate on account of his good deeds Mamercus Aemilius, a highly honoured citizen who had deserved well of the republic; or rather in the power of one alone.' (Cp. D. I.50, where Machiavelli makes this very point.)

50. No One Department and no One Official in a State should be able to hold up proceedings

1. Livy IV.26. The depravity of the consuls, the discord between them, and the strife going on in all councils, says Livy, gave rise to terror. The date is 431 B.C. T. Quintius Cincinnatus was deputed to appoint the dictator, and selected his father-in-law, A. Postumius Tubertus, an extremely severe man.

2. The Great Council in Venice was exclusively a patrician assembly, but consisted at this time of about 15,000 members. Hence the term 'universalità' is used to signify a general meeting. The government and administration of justice was carried on by smaller councils to which members were elected by the Great Council (Cp. D. I.49.5, and n. 8.)

51. A Republic or a Prince should ostensibly do out of Generosity what Necessity constrains them to do

1. Livy IV.59.11 and 60. The Romans at this juncture, 405 B.C., were about to begin their campaigns of conquest by laying siege to the great Etruscan city of Veii. It was for this reason that the Senate deemed it necessary to pay the troops. It decided to do this without consulting the tribunes (59.11), and thus conveyed the impression that it was making the grant out of sheer generosity. The tribunes saw through this, and objected that the measure would mean an increase in taxation. To which the patricians responded by making generous contributions, sending wagon-loads of brass to the treasury when they were short of silver (60.6), thus confirming the impression that they were acting out of generosity. Their behaviour illustrates well the maxim laid down in P. 18, that rulers should always seek to appear virtuous in the eyes of the populace, even when they are not so in reality. The granting of pay to troops was first made in 405 B.C., after the capture of Auxur, from which immense spoils were taken. (Cp. D. II.6.3 and n. 5.)

Cp. A.W. Bk. I, B.281, F. 24–5, where we are told that troops should be paid only when on active service or when engaged in military exercises in the case of the militia. That he himself and other 'capi' should have been paid when not actually so engaged, Machiavelli regards as an abuse (ib. B.274a, F.13).

On the importance of being reputed generous, see the chapter on 'Liberality and Meanness' in *The Prince*, c. 16.

52. The Safer and Less Scandalous Way to repress the Arrogance of One who has risen to Power in a Republic is to forestall him in the Methods he uses to come by this Power

1. Machiavelli suggests that the payment of troops was subsequently dropped, and blames the nobility for this. It was certainly kept up during the siege of Veii, for in

403 Appius Claudius speaks of it in his address to the populace, and lays it down as a general principle that 'in no case should there be work without emolument, nor yet in general emolument without work' (V.4.4.). The *stipendium* paid to the cavalry was in fact trebled in 401 by Cn. Cornelius, owing to the difficulty of carrying on a campaign in winter (V.12.12). It may be that Machiavelli merely means that the patricians dropped their voluntary contributions and even evaded the tax. It was levied on the occupiers of public land, and, when this was inadequate, was supplemented by drawing on the tribute which all had to pay, and the land-tax might easily be evaded. Or, again, Machiavelli may have had in mind a passage in Polybius (VI.39), in which he states that it was customary in his time to deduct from a soldier's pay the cost of provisions, clothes and additional arms. Payment of troops was dropped for a time at least during the second Punic war, when the treasury was depleted, but this was done at the request of the troops themselves; for 'the generous spirit among the citizens spread from the city to the camp; not a mounted soldier, not a centurion would accept pay, and any man who took it they called a mercenary' (Livy XXIV.18.15).

2. Cosimo de' Medici was expelled from Florence in 1433 on the ground that, as Niccolò da Uzzano pointed out, 'he was trying to make himself prince of the city' by 'assisting everyone with money, not only private men but the community itself, and not only Florentines but foreign *condottieri*'—'all of which methods carry a man on wings to sovereignty, yet we cannot persuade people so to regard them, for our own conduct has deprived us of credit' (*Hist. Florence* IV.27). Hence Uzzano deprecated an appeal to violence, but Niccolò Barbadoro and his followers persisted and by the use of armed bands forced the Signoria to expel a citizen, who, says Machiavelli, was beloved of all the citizens, who were in tribulation at his loss (*ib.* IV.30). (Cp. D. I.33.4 and n. 2.)

3. In 1512, after the defeat of the French at Ravenna, troops under Raymond de Cardona marched on Florence, accompanied by the Cardinal de' Medici, demanding the deposition of Soderini, the Gonfalonier, and the re-admission of the Medici to Florentine citizenship. Soderini, for whom Machiavelli had the highest esteem and whom he had loyally served, offered to resign, but declined to allow the Medici back, thinking that Florence would be able to withstand so small an army —in which opinion Machiavelli concurred. But they were mistaken. Prato fell. There was an insurrection in the city in favour of the Medici. Soderini was deposed on 1 September and fled the city. The republic thus lost the freedom which it had maintained since the expulsion of the Medici in 1494. (Cp. D. I.7.6 and n. 5.)

4. After the murder of Julius Caesar in 44 B.C., his friend, Mark Antony, was declared a public enemy, and the two consuls, C. Vibius Pansa and A. Hirtius, were put in charge of the war against him. He was defeated at Mutina in April, 43 B.C., but the consuls were killed. Cicero in his Third and Fifth Phillipics had urged the Senate to entrust the command of the army to Octavian. Accordingly, he was appointed praetor, and on the death of the consuls assumed command of the army and was joined by Lepidus and the army in Gaul. Meanwhile Octavian had fallen out with the Senate, and through the mediation of Lepidus became reconciled to Antony, who together with Octavian and Lepidus formed the triumvirate which was to govern for the next five years. In the beginning of 43 Cicero was a man of great influence. By the end of it his head had been cut off and his hands nailed to the Rostra by the orders of Antony.

53. The Populace, misled by the False Appearance of Advantage, often seeks its own Ruin, and is easily moved by Splendid Hopes and Rash Promises

1. Livy V.24. The date is 395 B.C.

2. V.25.1–3; and cp. D. I.54.

3. *'E Dante dice a questo proposito, nel discorso suo che fa De Monarchia, che il popolo molte volte grida: Viva la sua morte! e Muoia la sua vita!'* The quotation *'Viva la sua morte! e Muoia la sua vita'* does not come from the *De Monarchia*, but from the *Convivio*, I.11, l. 54. The *Convivio* was first printed in 1490 at Florence. The *De Monarchia* was first printed by Oporinus in 1559 at Basle. It was published in MS between 1310 and 1313.

4. In 1481–2 Venice made war on Ferrara, and was supported by Sixtus IV, but on the Venetians seizing the territory of the Duke, the Pope demanded that they should withdraw. Of this request the Venetians took no notice. In 1505 Julius II insisted on their restoring all places which they occupied in the Romagna, but had to be content with a verbal promise which was not fulfilled. Hence in 1508 the League of Cambray was formed. It comprised the Pope, the Emperor, the King of France, the Duke of Savoy, the Duke of Ferrara, and the Marquis of Mantua. Venice was excommunicated, and at Agnadello was completely routed in a single battle (cp. D. III.31.3 and n. 5; P. 12, E.102 for Vaila, i.e., Agnadello).

5. Livy XXII.25 217 B.C.   6. *ib.* 27, and for authorisation 26.7.

7. *ib.* 28, 29.   8. *ib.* 34–5, and cp. 38–9.

9. *ib.* 46–9 216 B.C.   10. XXV.19.   11. Cp. Thucydides, VI, 8 *sq.*, and D. III.15.1, and n. 1.

12. Livy XXVIII.40 to 44. 147 B.C. This Scipio is Aemilianus Africanus minor.

13. In March 1505 the Florentine forces were defeated by the Pisans at Ponte Cappellese, and in July Bartolommeo d'Alviano invaded Florentine territory in the hope of seizing Pisa. On 17 August he was defeated at San Vincenti by Antonio Giacomini, the Florentine commissioner, and by Ercole Bentivoglio, who with a large force fell upon his flank. Elated at the victory, the Gonfalonier, Soderini, proposed at once to attack Pisa, urged on by Bentivoglio, who said it would be an easy task. He was opposed by a numerous *'Pratica'* (committee-meeting) called by the Ten of War, so appealed to the Council of Eighty and to the Great Council, who approved the project and voted supplies. Bentivoglio was appointed Captain-general, and Machiavelli was sent to him and to Giacomini with instructions for the siege. The besiegers were twice repulsed, and on 15 September withdrew and dispersed. Giacomini was blamed for the failure, and sent in his resignation. This ended his military career. (Cp. the last paragraph). On the method of besieging Pisa adopted later, cp. A.W. Bk. VII, B.361a, F.153.

Cp. Thucydides in the speech of Diodotus. After the passage in which he describes the proneness of Athens to suspect her best men, and if things go wrong to punish the individual who has advised them (III.42–3), Diodotus says: 'Desire and hope are never wanting, the one leading, the other following, the one devising the enterprise, the other suggesting that fortune will be kind; and they are the most ruinous, for, being unseen, they far outweigh the dangers which are seen. Fortune, too, assists the illusion, for she often presents herself unexpectedly, and induces states as well as individuals to run into peril, however inadequate their means; and states even more than individuals, because they are throwing for a higher stake, freedom or empire, and because, when a man has a whole people acting with him, he magnifies himself out of all reason' (III.45).

54. How Great an Influence a Grave Man may have in restraining an Excited Crowd

1. 'Tum pietate gravem ac meritis si forte virum quem
Conspexere, silent, arrectisque auribus adstant.'
Virgil, *Aeneid* I.155. (Dryden's translation has been used in the text.)
2. When in April 1498 the proposed ordeal by fire ended in a fiasco, resentment against Savonarola spread throughout the city. The Frateschi, better known as the Piagnoni, were his supporters. The Arrabbiati, a riotous gang of young men, were his chief opponents. On their way to the Duomo the former were pelted with stones and rushed home to get arms. There was a free fight in the Piazza, in which the Piagnoni were beaten. They then retired to the convent where Savonarola resided, and, despite his protests, tried to defend it. Francesco Valori was killed in trying to escape. The convent fell during the night, and Savonarola was taken to the Gonfalonier, and brutally ill-treated on the way. During the riot the houses of Andrea Cambini were sacked and burnt, while that of Paolo Antonio Soderini was saved in the manner described.
3. The proposed migration to Veii, mentioned in D. I.53.1; see the speech of Camillus in Livy V.51-5.

55. That it is very easy to manage Things in a State in which the Masses are not Corrupt; and that, where Equality exists, it is impossible to set up a Principality, and, where it does not exist, impossible to set up a Republic

1. Cp. D. I.16 to 18.
2. Livy V.23.8-11; 25.4-13. According to the legend in 395 B.C. the troops openly opposed the edict which their commander, Camillus, had caused to be promulgated, and the situation was saved by the ladies of Rome who sent to Apollo their jewels in lieu of the promised booty. Since the booty was never called in, Machiavelli's argument is based on pure supposition as to what would have happened, had it been called in; and so does little more than exemplify his firm belief in the probity of the masses.
3. On the deplorable state of Italy, cp. D. I.12.7-8.
4. Usually France alone is taken as an example of a kingdom ruled in accordance with constitutional laws and traditions; but here Spain is included, not without good reason. For though the policy of Ferdinand the Catholic, who by his marriage

with Isabella united the kingdoms of Castile and Aragon, and in 1492 expelled the Moors from Spain, was one of centralisation, and his chief aim was to reduce a turbulent nobility to order by depriving them of their castles, he treated the towns with consideration. His attitude toward the laws of the realm is well illustrated by the reply he gave to Barcelona when it reminded him of his oath to observe the ancient customs of that town, to which he answered that his oath obliged him no less to maintain the ancient rights of the throne. He was known as '*El Justo*' and '*El Honesto*'. He died in 1516.

5. The eulogy of German towns, with which Machiavelli had a passing, but not a long, acquaintance, has given rise to much controversy, (Cp. Villari I.470–80 for his mission to the Emperor in 1507; and 437–48 for the diverse criticisms to which this discourse, a passage in P. 19, and his Report on German affairs has given rise). Theodor Mundt in his work on Machiavelli says it is but a phantasy. Tout in C. Mod. H. I. pp. 298–9, says that his 'glowing eulogies of their liberty and capacity for resistance has misled most moderns as to the true position of the German cities', and is at pains to point out that the German cities did not, like Italian cities, rule over large districts, but were 'almost confined to their city walls'. In view of the fact that Machiavelli himself points this out, and of the German cities says that they had but little territory ('*hanno poco contado*'—P. 10) it seems to me that the moderns have misled themselves.

That Machiavelli has made some mistakes here cannot be denied. He is wrong, for instance, in looking upon the goodness and religious spirit of German towns as a survival of that spirit which pervaded ancient Rome; for their customs were of Teutonic, not Roman, origin; their religious spirit was the outcome of their Catholicism; and, fond as they were of liberty in the days of Tacitus they were ready to gamble it away (*Germania* 24). On the other hand, what he says of their good customs and their religious observances is amply borne out by the evidence which Janssen gives in his *History of the German People*, Book III.

He writes: 'With regard to all the relations of life and society each city formed an independent and exclusive association, looking on its collective inhabitants as one large family, for whose welfare it was no less bound to provide than is a father for his own household. This paternal care was looked upon as a sacred duty, and included not only moral supervision, but solicitude for material necessities also. With this object in view, "in the interest", that is, "of common needs and spiritual well-being", the ruling authorities regulated, according to the different conditions of each city, the general production, distribution, and utilisation of provisions and goods, as well as their prices and sale. In order that each inhabitant within the city radius should be supplied with food, clothing, lodging, hire, they aimed at having each trade represented' (Vol. II, c. 2, pp. 3–4). Of the guilds he says that their *raison d'être* 'was not the protection of trade rights, but rather mutual brotherhood or association in all the common aims of life' (p. 8); and both in their case and in that of workmen's clubs he shows that a high standard of professional honour was studiously maintained (p. 24).

6. Machiavelli is mistaken here. South Germany maintained contact with the outside world *via* Venice and Geneva; North Germany *via* Antwerp and the Hanseatic ports. Of Frankfort, Jerome Munzer wrote in 1495: 'Merchants from the Netherlands, Flanders, England, Poland, Bohemia, Italy and France, come to the [annual] Frankfort Fair and do large business' (Janssen, pp. 56–7).

7. Said the knight in the popular song: 'I am born of a noble race'. Said the peasant: 'I cultivate the corn: that is the better part. Did I not work, you could not exist on your heraldry.' (Janssen, Vol. I, p. 324.)

8. Cp. D. I.18.7; and for a list of the families with which Caesar Borgia came in conflict, see Burd, pp. 218-19, n. 15.

9. Florence, Siena, and Lucca all date back to Roman times and all passed through much the same vicissitudes. All were subject to the Emperor, who sometimes interfered and sometimes left them alone. In all there were violent and continual class conflicts, frequent revolutions, from time to time a tyranny, and between them wars were continually breaking out. The most prosperous period in Florentine history was when it was ruled by Cosimo and later by Lorenzo de' Medici; in Siena when in much the same way it was subject to Pandolfo Petrucci (1480-1512); in Lucca when it became subject to Castruccio Castracani, one of its own citizens (1316-28). Machiavelli sums up the situation neatly when he says 'they either maintain their freedom or would like to do so', and the trouble in each case was the same: unlike Rome, they failed to discover a means whereby to control class-conflicts. (Cp. D. II.21.6, and see Aquinas *de Regimine*, IV.8 on principalities in Italy.)

10. Cp. D. I.5 and nn. 2, 3; and for gentlefolk in Venice D. I.6.2 and n. 2.

11. For the importance of 'equality' in a republic, see D. I.2.10 and 6.4. On the way in which a monarch can maintain peace between his barons and his people see the paragraph on France in P. 19, E.143-4.

Aristotle in his *Politics* III.8 says that 'the real difference between democracy and oligarchy is poverty and wealth. Wherever men rule by reason of their wealth, whether they be few or many, that is an oligarchy, and where the poor rule, that is a democracy. But as a fact the rich are few and the poor many; for few are well-to-do, but freedom (which also is characteristic of democracy) is enjoyed by all, and wealth and freedom are the grounds on which the oligarchical and democratic parties claim power in the state' (1279b, 39-1280a, 6). This does not mean that in a democracy there will be no wealthy men, but that the poor will be in a majority, and, since all share alike in the government, the poor will be in control. (Cp. IV.4, 1291b, 34-8.) Neither oligarchy nor democracy can exist, so Aristotle claims, 'unless both rich and poor are included in it. [Hence] if equality of property is introduced, the state must of necessity take another form; for when by laws carried to excess one or other element in the state is ruined, the constitution is ruined—an error which is common alike to oligarchies and to democracies' (V.9, 1309b, 38-1310a, 3). Aristotle's conception of a democracy, as thus defined, approximates to Machiavelli's conception of a republic, and both agree that if the balance between the upper and the lower or poorer class be disturbed the state will be transformed. In a monarchy, on the other hand, the king 'is the resource of the better classes against the people, and he is elected by them out of their own number because either he or his family excel in virtue and virtuous actions, whereas a tyrant is chosen from the people to be their protector against the notables' (1310b, 8-13). Hence for Aristotle, as for Machiavelli, monarchy means the predominance of the upper class, and democracy means equality, if not absolute, at any rate proportional, as Aristotle would say (cp. V.1, 1301a, 28).

Furthermore, when discussing in III.17 the character of peoples suited respectively for monarchy, aristocracy, and 'polity' or constitutional government, he lays down as a condition for the latter that they should be 'a warlike multitude, able to rule and to obey in turn in accordance with a law which assigns office to the well-to-do according to their deserts' (1288a, 13–15), which is precisely the kind of multitude Machiavelli requires for a republic that is going to found an empire, save that for the 'well-to-do' he would substitute an aristocracy based on merit, not on wealth. This, moreover, is also Aristotle's notion of an aristocracy properly so called. For, though Aristotle envisages, and actually defines a 'polity' or constitutional government to be a combination of democracy with oligarchy (1293b, 34), i.e. a combination of rich and poor in which the majority (i.e. the poor) have in government the controlling power (1294a, 13–18), he looks on this as an inferior type of constitutional government. The best type is one in which offices are distributed according to merit, and this, it would seem, is the earlier form, since he speaks of his aristocracy of wealth as having replaced an aristocracy of merit (*ib.* 9–25).

56. Before Great Misfortunes befall a City or a Province they are preceded by Portents or foretold by Men

1. In his sermons on Noah's Ark, begun in the Lent of 1492 and continued in the Lent of 1494, Savonarola warned Florence of a scourge that was about to fall on the city and of a new Cyrus who would march through Italy in triumph without encountering any obstacle or breaking any lance. Charles crossed the Alps in the following August. Cp. D. I.11.6 and n. 14; and for the general character of Savonarola's preaching, Villari, *Life and Times of Savonarola*, I.131–44, and II.173–88.

2. Cp. *Hist. Florence* VIII.36. Lorenzo de' Medici died in 1492.

3. The evidence for this, and also for the previous incident, is of course first hand, since Machiavelli was in Florence at the time, i.e. in 1512.

4. Livy V.32.6–7. The Gauls took Rome and set fire to it in 390 B.C.

57. The Plebs United is Strong, but in Itself it is Weak

1. '*Ex ferocibus universis singuli metu suo obedientes fuere*' (VI.4.5, cited in Latin). Those who had preferred to occupy empty houses in Veii rather than build new ones in Rome, were recalled by a *senatus-consultum* in 389 B.C. Of them Livy says: *Primo fremitus fuit aspernantium imperium; dies deinde praestituta capitalisque poena, qui non remigrasset Romam, ex forcibus universis singulos, metu suo quemque, obedientes fecit (ib.).*

2. Livy III.50–51; cp. D. I.44.2.

58. The Masses are more Knowing and more Constant than is a Prince

1. The opening sentence sums up the views expressed by Livy in VI.17 in regard to the inconstancy of the multitude, though Livy does not use the actual words. The passages cited at the end of the paragraph are quotations. The first runs: '*Populum brevi, posteaquam ab eo periculum nullum erat, desiderium ejus tenuit*' (VI.20.15,

cited in Latin). Marcus Manlius Capitolinus, aroused by geese, had called enough men together to save the Capitol from the Gauls in 390 B.C. When Cossus was dictator he roused the populace against their creditors and was thrown in prison. On his release he urged the populace to violence and was charged with treason and condemned to death in 384 B.C. (Livy VI.14–20).

2. *'Haec natura multitudinis est; aut humiliter servit; aut superbe dominatur'* (XXIV.25.8, cited in Latin). An account of the accession of Hieronymus at the age of fifteen in 216 B.C., of his short-lived tyranny, and of his murder, is given by Livy in XXIV.4–7, to which subject Livy returns in XXIV.21 (cp. D. II.2.4 and n. 5).

3. Cp. Diodorus Siculus I.70–1 *'Gesta Regum Aegypti'*.

4. Cp. D. I.16.9; 19.4; 55.2.

5. Cleitus Melas saved Alexander's life at the battle of Granicus in 334 B.C. In 328 he was appointed satrap of Bactria. At a banquet celebrated on the eve of his departure he got drunk and used disparaging language of the king, whom people were praising up at the expense of Philip. Alexander sprang at him, and, seizing a spear, killed him as he was trying to leave the room. (Cp. Diodorus Siculus XVII.21.57; Plutarch, *Life of Alexander*, 16 and 50–2.)

6. Mariamne, or Marianne, as Machiavelli writes it, was the daughter of Alexander, son of Aristobulus II, king of Judaea and a Jewish patriot who in 57 B.C. defeated the Romans near Jerusalem but was afterwards defeated near Mount Tabor and executed by Pompey's orders. Her mother was Alexandra, daughter of Hyrcanus, high priest and king of the Jews (executed in 30 B.C.), by whom she was betrothed to Herod the Great, whom she married in 38 B.C. On two occasions when Herod went on expeditions he left word that, if he did not return alive, his wife was not to survive him. Since she took offence at this, her husband had her tried on a charge of adultery, and she was put to death in 29 B.C.—a deed which Herod subsequently repented. Machiavelli's authority is probably Josephus (Ant. xv, 2–7; *de Bell Jud.* i. 22).

7. Cp. P. 17, E.134 with Machiavelli's criticism of the proverb that 'He who builds on the people builds on mud' in P. 9. He admits that the populace is fickle and that it is difficult to fix them in any persuasion (P. 6, E.48–9).

8. Cp. D. I.29 and 30.   9. Cp. D. I.4.5 and 1.54.   10. Cp. D. I.53.   11. Cp. D. I.48.

12. For the progress made in Rome after the expulsion of the kings and in Athens after the expulsion of the Pisistratidae see D. II.2.2 and *note* 3.

13. Cp. D. I.9.   14. Cp. D. I.54.   15. Cp. D. I.29.4–5.

Guicciardini *in loc.* argues at great length against this theorem. To hold that the populace excels the prince in constancy and prudence is contrary to the general opinion, and 'no writer on politics ever doubts that, when a regime is regulated by laws, one-man government is better than government by a multitude even if regulated by laws, or that to this not only government by a prince but also by an aristocracy is preferable. For where the number is less, virtue is more unified and better able to produce its effects . . . but where there is a multitude there is confusion . . . and neither rational discussion, well-grounded decisions, nor resolute action' (and so forth, following the lines of arguments traditionally used). 'Examples of this confusion and of the tumults which result from it are too many and too well known to be worth citing. Nor are the examples adduced by the writer relevant. For a multitude which has to make decisions on its own is one thing, and a popular government so constituted that grave and important decisions have to be made by the more prudent is quite different' . . . and in Rome 'more important matters were decided by the senate, the consuls and the leading magistrates'. Furthermore, 'even if we call the decisions of the Romans decisions of the multitude, and compare a prince with the same degree of virtue relative to other princes as the Roman people had relative to other peoples, I am convinced that he will proceed in all his affairs with greater prudence and greater constancy than the Roman people displayed in their procedure. . . . And conversely that if we take a people loosed from law and a prince who is free and unrestrained as almost all are . . . I grant that in a prince one will probably find more vices and greater promptitude in acting viciously than in a people, though what the author claims on this head is beside the point; but I still maintain that in a prince one will ordinarily find more prudence and more constancy—the qualities mentioned in the author's heading—than one will find in a multitude. . . . And if one finds very imprudent princes, whose imprudence in the last resort is perhaps more harmful than that of the multitude, I maintain that if we take, for instance, a period of two hundred years, one will find in a kingdom prudent and imprudent kings, but that in a multitude during the same period one will find imprudence and changeability going on all the time. . . . Nor is it relevant to state that a city makes more increase under a popular government than under a prince; for this is due to different causes; nor if you give me fifty years under a good popular government and as many under a prince equally good, do I doubt but that greater increase will be made under a prince.'

Note that Guicciardini does little more in this consideration than to insist again and again that Machiavelli is wrong and the commonly accepted opinion right. Moreover, whereas Machiavelli almost invariably writes '*la moltitudine*' and is thinking of the part played by the masses or the populace in a republican government, not in a purely popular or democratic government, Guicciardini invariably writes '*una moltitudine*'—a multitude—and with government by a prince contrasts government by a multitude or government by the populace, to the exclusion of other factors, such as those represented by the senate and the consuls. This is the case of a populace 'loosed from the control of law' and must be compared with a prince who is in like manner contemptuous of law, and rules arbitrarily. But in the alternative case of a well-ordered regime what Machiavelli would have us compare with princely rule is a government in which the masses have a voice, but act constitutionally and are amenable to the influence of the upper class, which also has a voice in regard to all decisions, i.e. we are to compare in this case a principality with a republic, not with a democracy pure and simple.

59. What Confederations or Other Kinds of League can be trusted most; those made with a Republic or those made with a Prince

1. Demetrius I, surnamed *Poliorcetes* (the conqueror of cities—cp. Plutarch's *Demetrius*, n. 42), king of Macedonia, 294–283 B.C., was sent as a young man in 307 to liberate Greece from the power of Cassander and Ptolemy. Athens received him with open arms, decreed him divine honours, and later on admitted him even

to the Greater Mysteries. He spent two winters there and it became his favourite city. (Plutarch, *Life of Demetrius*, nn. 9, 14, 23–6). After his defeat at Ipsus in 301 B.C., he set sail for Athens, thinking, says Plutarch, 'that he could have no safer asylum than their affections'. They refused to receive him, and 'to find that their affection, so strong in appearance, was only counterfeit, cut him to the heart' (*ib.* 30). He again entered Athens in triumph in 303 B.C., and again met with the same servility, though shortly before a decree had been passed forbidding any man under pain of death to speak of reconciliation with him (*ib.* 34). Later, however, 'they abandoned his interests, and erased from their registers the name of the priest who served him as "god-protector"' (*ib.* 46).

2. On being expelled from his kingdom by the Alexandrians in 58 B.C., Ptolemy XI of Egypt (Auletes) went to Italy and endeavoured to persuade the senate to restore him. In this he failed. But in 55, Gabinius, proconsul of Syria, took up his cause, induced thereunto by Pompey and by a bribe of ten thousand talents, and after three successive victories Ptolemy was restored (Dion Cassius xxxix, 55–8.) After his defeat at Pharsalus in Thessaly in 48 B.C., Pompey, finding that there was no province of the Roman empire in which he could find a safe retreat, was advised by his friends to sail to Egypt, where Ptolemy XII (Dionysius) was now ruling, his father, Auletes, having died in 51 B.C. Two courses were open to Ptolemy, to give Pompey protection, which would offend Caesar, or to send him back, which would offend Pompey. So Theodotus a rhetorician, suggested that he should be killed, since 'dead men do not bite' (Plutarch, *Pompey*, n. 77). On his landing, Pompey was met by the king's officers, one of whom, Septimius, got behind him and ran him through with a sword. Machiavelli says that he was killed by the Ptolemy whom he had reinstated. This is a mistake. It was the son of Auletes, who ordered his death.

3. During the wars between France and Spain for the possession of the kingdom of Naples some of the Italian nobles and princes fought on one side and some on the other. Of those who fought for the French several were killed in battle and many captured and imprisoned during Gonsalvo's victorious campaigns in 1503 and 1504. Several, Guicciardini tells us, were drowned at sea together with Piero de Medici in 1503, and others, who were allowed to leave Gaeta in 1504, perished *en route* with their troops (*St. d'I.* VI, c. 7, pp. 123–4). Meanwhile the estates of those who had surrendered or were in exile were plundered by the soldiery. Nor, when in January 1504 a truce was signed, did the dispossessed French barons in any way benefit by it. Gonsalvo saw to that (*ib.* c. 10, pp. 137–8). They remained in prison, and the sad plight of those who had fought for him in Naples was one of the main reasons why Louis XII put off signing the terms of peace (*ib.* c. 12, p. 144). Most of them, therefore, had 'failed to find one of the king's enemies with whom he could come to terms'; but some were more successful, for Bartolomeo d' Alviano and the Orsini changed sides before the battle of Garigliano in December 1503. (Cp. Guicciardini, *St. d'I.* VI, c. 7, p. 121.)

4. Saguntum supported Rome in the war with Hannibal in 219 B.C., but in 218 was captured by Hannibal (Livy XXI.5–16).

5. The support given by Soderini to the French led to his expulsion by Raymond of Cordova in 1512, and to the restoration of the Medici. (Cp. D. I.7, n. 5.)

6. The story of this incident is told by Plutarch in his *Life of Themistocles* (n. 20) and also by Cicero in *De Officiis* III. xi. 49. Cicero cites it as a plan which was

apparently expedient, but which was morally wrong. The incident occurred after the battle of Salamis in 480 B.C.

7. Cp. for Philip II of Macedon and his methods, D. I.26.2 and n. 3.

8. On the grounds for breaking promises and treaties, see D. III.42.

60. That the Consulate and all Other Offices in Rome were conferred without Respect to Age

1. Caius Licinius Calvus Stolo in conjunction with his fellow tribune, Lucius Sextius, had proposed in 377 that no more military tribunes should be elected, but that, instead, consuls should be appointed, one of whom was to be a plebeian (Livy VI.35.5). The patricians resisted the motion for ten years, and it was not until 366 that the first plebeian consul was elected, namely, Lucius Sextius 'by whose law it had been obtained' (VII.1.2; VI.42.9).

2. *'praemium virtutis, non sanguinis'*—whereas Livy says: *'nec generis ut ante, sed virtutis est praemium'* (VII.32.14–15). Valerius Corvinus had already distinguished himself by his combat with the Gallic giant when serving as tribune under L. Furius Camillus, and in the next year, 348 B.C., was made consul, though only in his 23rd year (26.13). In his third consulate, 343 B.C., he defeated the Samnites near Cumae in a battle which Niebuhr says was one of the most memorable in the world, since with it began Rome's conquest of the world. We have now reached Livy's seventh book, and with it Machiavelli's first book appropriately ends. In his next book he turns to the conquests upon which Rome, now consolidated internally, was about to embark.

3. Cp. I.28.3; II.12.6; and see Index *sub* 'Necessity'.

4. Cp. I.6.6.

5. Cp. Livy XXV.2, where we are told that the tribunes objected to the appointment of Publius Cornelius Scipio as curule aedile since he was not yet of the legal age, to which he answered, 'If all the citizens of Rome wish to choose me as aedile, my years are sufficient.' The ages at which a citizen became eligible for office were determined by *'leges annales'*. By the Lex Villia, passed later in 180 B.C. (mentioned by Livy in XL.44) the age for the quaestorship was 31, for aedile 37, praetor 40, and consul 43. Scipio was elected aedile in 212, when he was but 22, and at the age of 24 he became consul and was appointed to the command in Spain. Pompey earned his first triumph in 89 B.C. He was then presumably 45 since he had been quaestor in 103. (Cp. Plutarch's *Pompey*, nn. 13, 14.)

Guicciardini *in loc.* points out that 'the Discourse omits to mention (1) that Scipio Africanus the Less could not have been made consul unless the barrier of age had first been removed by a special law; and (2) that Cicero says in ... [*De Legibus*. III.3] that a person of 33 needed ten more years before he could become consul; and if it was otherwise with Valerius Corvinus, there is need to add, what is true, that institutions in the beginning of the republic were different from what they came to be in course of time. For in the beginning there was no prohibition of a consul's remaining in office, or at any rate one who was consul could after a short interval become consul again. Later, however, a law was made requiring that between one consulate and the next there should be an interval of at least ten years.'

NOTES ON BOOK TWO

PREFACE

1. Cp. Polybius I.14, where of the historians, Philinus and Fabius, he says: 'Judging from their lives and principles, I do not suppose that these writers have intentionally stated what is false; but I think that they are in much the same state of mind as men in love. Partisanship and complete prepossession make Philinus think that all the actions of the Carthaginians were characterised by wisdom, honour, and courage; those of the Romans by the reverse. Fabius thought the exact opposite. Now in other relations of life one would hesitate to exclude such warmth of senti-ment . . . but directly a man assumes the moral attitude of the historian he ought to forget all considerations of this kind.'

2. Cp. Polybius III.31: 'In the case of contemporaries it is difficult to obtain an insight into their purposes . . . whereas the transactions of the past admit of being tested by naked fact.'

3. Cp. Polybius VI.57: 'To all things which exist there is ordained decay and change. . . . When a commonwealth, after warding off many great dangers, has arrived at a high pitch of prosperity and undisputed power, it is evident that by the lengthened continuance of great wealth within it, the manner of life of its citizens will become more extravagant; and that rivalry for office and rivalry in other spheres of activity will become fiercer than it ought to be. And, as this state of things goes on more and more, the desire of office and the shame of losing reputation, as well as the ostentation and extravagance of living, will prove the beginning of a deterioration'. (Cp. D. I.6.9.)

4. With § 5 compare the following passage which occurs in Plutarch's 'De Fortuna Romanorum', to which Krappe calls attention in his 'Quelques Sources Grecques de N.M.'; 'Thus fortune having abandoned the Persians and the Assyrians, flew lightly over Macedonia and quickly gave Alexander a shaking up; then took a short walk through Egypt and through Syria, dragging royalties after her and ruin-ing the Carthaginians whom she had often sustained; finally she drew near to Mount Palatine and, having crossed the Tiber, took off her wings, dropped her footgear, and let the ball run as it pleased; and so came to settle in Rome and make her habitation there. Thus did fortune comport herself, as if she were appearing in a court of justice to hear judgment pronounced' (Opera Moralia, XLIV—De Fortuna Romanorum, n. 4, as rendered by Krappe).

5. The term 'ultramontane' is used by Machiavelli for peoples on the Northern side of the Alps, whereas we use it for people on the Italian side.

6. Cp. the indictment of the Papacy in D. I.12.5–6.

7. Cp. D. I.37.1, where men are said to be never satisfied; and D. II.27.6, where there is said to be no limit to their desires.

8. It was also in order to benefit others that Polybius wrote, as he tells us in I.35 and II.35; cp. also I.4.

9. The contents of Books I and II are here neatly summarised.

Guicciardini 'sul Proemio del Libro II' agrees that too much praise has been given to the past; but does not agree that 'there has been the same amount of good in one age as in another'. The arts, military discipline, letters and religion have flourished in one age and in another have been almost entirely eclipsed. So, too, in one age peace has prevailed and in another the world has been full of wars.

Ellinger (p. 41) thinks the passage on praising the past may have been suggested by a remark of Velleius Paterculus: 'But we are naturally more inclined to praise what we have heard than what has occurred before our own eyes; we regard the present with envy, the past with veneration, and believe that we are eclipsed by the former, but derive instruction from the latter' (*Res Gestae Divi Augusti*, II.92, with which cp. § 2); or again by the remark of Tacitus: 'We extol the past and are indifferent to our own times' (*Annals* II.88, closing words).

BOOK TWO

1. *Whether Virtue or Fortune was the Principal Cause of the Empire which Rome acquired*

1. Cp. Plutarch's *Opera Moralia*, XLIV—*De Fortuna Romanorum*. In it Plutarch adduces several arguments in support of his contention that Rome owed more to fortune than to virtue. Amongst them in n. 5 he cites the fact that the earliest Roman temples were dedicated to Fortune, and only later were temples built to other gods. This shows, he says, that the Romans themselves recognised that they owed more to fortune than to virtue (cp. also n. 7). So, too, he argues in n. 8, 'the happy issue of their undertakings and their steady progress toward such great power and expansion clearly betokens to those who understand such things that it was not due so much to human hands and counsels and desires as to divine guidance and cooperation and to fortune's winds'.

2. There is another reference to this battle in D. II.8.2, where it is said to have taken place between Piombino and Pisa. Piombino lies to the south and Popolonia to the north of the promontory facing Elba. They are but a few miles apart. San Vincenzo is some ten miles further north on the route to Pisa, from which it is distant about 50 miles. The battle to which Machiavelli refers is commonly known as the battle of Telamon. It took place in 225 B.C., and of it Polybius gives a long account in II.25–35. The Gauls were encamped before Clusium, which lies on the same latitude as Popolonia. A Roman army was following on their heels, but, when they came in sight, the Gauls retreated along the road to Faesulae (II.25.4–6), i.e. they moved north. The Romans pursued them and were defeated after a fierce

battle (25.7–9). Meanwhile Lucius Aemilius came up with another army from Ariminum (26.1). Whereupon the Gauls held a council at night, decided to return home, and before daybreak were marching through Etruria by the road which follows the coast of the Ligurian Bay (26.6–7). Lucius Aemilius followed in their wake (26.8).

We are next told that the consul Gaius Atilius had landed at Pisa and was on his way to Rome (27.1), and that, when the Gauls were at Telamon their advanced guard fell in with that of Atilius and was captured (27.2). From them Atilius learned that Lucius was following the Gauls (27.3) who thus lay between the two armies. Thereupon Atilius with some cavalry seized some rising ground which commanded the road along which the Gauls must march, and told his legions to follow on (27.5). The Gauls at first thought that the cavalry of Aemilius had out-flanked them, but, on discovering that they belonged to the army of Atilius, decided to give battle, and drew up their army facing both ways (27.6–8). The battle, in which Atilius was killed but the Romans were completely victorious, is then described at considerable length.

The site of Telamon is given in maps as lying on the coast, near the mouth of the Osa, some 45 miles south of Popolonia (cp. Pauly-Wissowa *sub* Telamon, § 4). But this squares ill with what Polybius says about the route followed by the Gauls. To get to the coast from the road which leads from Clusium to Faesulae, they would have had to follow a route which would bring them out in the neighbour-hood of Popolonia, and to get to where Telamon is supposed to have been they would then have had to turn south, which would have placed them not between the two Roman armies, but to the south of both. Hence they must have turned north at Popolonia, and so may well have encountered Atilius at San Vincenzo, as Machiavelli says. Incidentally Orosius (following Fabius Historicus, *qui eidem bello interfuit*), says that Atilius was killed in the first battle, and that this took place at Arretium, which lies midway between Clusium and Faesulae (*Adversus Paganos* IV.13.6–8).

3. The dates of the wars mentioned in § 3 are:

493–431 War with the Aequi and Volsci.	238–225 The Gallic war (ending with the battle of Telamon, near Popolonia).
390 Rome taken by the Gauls.	
389–380 Renewed war with the Aequi and Volsci.	223–222 War with Ligurians and Gauls. The Insubrae and other tribes defeated at Clastidium.
343–341 The First Samnite war, ending in an alliance.	218–201 The second Punic war.
340–338 The Great Latin revolt	200–196 The (second) Macedonian war.
327–314 The second Samnite war.	
310–300 War with and invasion of Etruria.	193–188 War with Antiochus and in Asia, known as the third Macedonian war.
281–275 War with Pyrrhus and the Samnites.	(With this paragraph cp. D. II.8.2 and see Table II.)
264–241 The first Punic war.	

4. A treaty between Rome and Carthage was signed in 348 B.C.

5. Cp. *The Prince*, c. 3. The methods there mentioned are the sending out of colonies and the maintenance of friendly relations with lesser powers, care being

taken not to increase their strength whilst engaged in war with a greater power, e.g. keeping the Achaeans and Aetolians friendly until Macedonia has been humbled and Philip driven out of Greece. Thus the Gauls did not intervene in the first Punic war, nor did Philip V of Macedon during the second, nor Antiochus during the Macedonian war.

6. See P. 3 (E.20 *sq.*), and P. 5.

7. 'Fifth columnists', as we should say.

8. The dates and references to Livy are as follows:

(i) Capua and the invasion of Samnium. 340 B.C. Livy VII.29–32.

The Sidicines, attacked by the Samnites, appeal to the Campanian or Capuan League, which, on getting the worst of a battle in the plain between Capua and Tifata, appeals to Rome. (Cp. D. II.9.1 and 4). The historicity of this First Samnite war is, however, open to question. (Cp. C.A.H. VII, c. 18, p. 588.)

(ii) The Camertines and the invasion of Tuscany, 310 B.C. Livy IX.36.

A Roman whose name is uncertain explores the Ciminian forest and comes across the Camertini who become the allies of Rome, and whose youth enlists in Rome's service against the Etruscans. There was a pro-Roman party in several Etruscan towns at this time, e.g. in Cortona, Perusia, Arretium. (Cp. C.A.H. VII. c. 18, p. 605.)

(iii) The Mamertines and the invasion of Sicily, 264 B.C. (Polybius I.7–11, and cp. Scipio's speech in Livy XXVIII.28.6.)

The Mamertines, originally mercenaries employed by Agathocles in Sicily, seized Messana in 289 B.C. and when threatened by Carthaginian forces in 264 appealed to Rome, which sent them a garrison (Cp. D. II.9.2.) This led to the Punic wars. (Cp. C.A.H. VII.21.2, pp. 667–73.)

(iv) Saguntum and the invasion of Spain, 218 B.C. Livy XXI.6.

Saguntum, when attacked by Hannibal in 219, appealed to Rome, but was taken by Hannibal before assistance was sent. (Cp. D. II.9.2.) In 218, however, Publius Scipio sent his brother, Gnaeus, to Spain, and in 212 Saguntum was recovered (Livy XXIV.42.9–10). (Cp. C.A.H. VII.24.5 and 26.6; VIII.3.4.)

(v) Masinissa and the invasion of Africa, 205 B.C. Livy XXVIII.16 and XXIX, XXX *passim*.

Masinissa, the Numidian king of the Massyli when he heard that Scipio was about to invade Africa, deserted the cause of Carthage and became the ally of Rome and the rallying point of African opposition to Carthage, even when in exile. When the Romans landed in 204 B.C., he sent a detachment of cavalry to join them. He finally recovered his kingdom from Syphax in 203 B.C. (XXX.11.) (Cp. C.A.H. VIII.4.5.)

(vi) The Aetolians and the invasion of Greece. 211 B.C. Livy XXVI.24.

In 211 B.C. M. Valerius Laevinus appeared with a Roman fleet off the coast of Greece, and formed an alliance with the Aetolian League against Philip of Macedon. This led eventually to the Roman occupation of Greece (Cp. C.A.H. VIII.5.2.)

(vii) Eumenes and the invasion of Asia. 193 B.C. Livy XXXV.13.

Eumenes II, King of Pergamus (197–159), urged Rome to declare war on Antiochus, took part in person in the battle of Magnesia in 190 B.C. (XXXVII.37–45), and was granted extensive dominions in Asia Minor as a reward.

(viii) The Massilians and the Aedui and the invasion of Gaul 154 and 122 B.C. Livy *Epit.* 60, 61.

The Massilians helped Rome in the second Punic war, and appealed to Rome for help against the Ligurians in 154, and again in 125. On both occasions consuls were sent with Roman armies, and in 122 Rome founded her first colony north of the Alps at Aquae Sextiae. In the same year the Aedui appealed to Rome for help against the Allobroges. The Aedui were the first barbarians to be recognised by Rome as kinsmen, and the result of the war was that the Allobroges became Roman subjects.

2. Concerning the Kind of People the Romans had to fight, and how obstinately they defended their Freedom

1. The contents of this discourse fall under three heads:

(i) The advantages free cities (and states) enjoy, as compared with those that are subject to a foreign power. (§§ 1–5.)

(ii) An indictment of Christianity on the ground that it encourages humility and subservience rather than warlike virtues and 'ferocity' (§§ 6–8.)

(iii) A brief account of the resistance put up by the Samnites (§§ 9 and 12), in which are interpolated (*a*) some important remarks showing what Machiavelli understands by freedom (§§ 10–11), and (*b*) a comparison of the way in which subject cities are treated by a republic and by a prince (§ 11).

We hear of Lars Porsenna in Livy II.9–15. He was then king of Clusium (II.9.1); but when we next hear of Clusium in 391 B.C. and it appeals to Rome for help against the Gauls (V.35.4), the '*Clusini*' are no longer subject to a king. Porsenna may well have been not merely king of Clusium, but of Etruria. (Cp. C.A.H. VII, p. 397.)

2. Livy V.1.

3. The Pisistratidae were expelled in 510 B.C., and Athens remained free until it was taken by Sparta in 404 B.C.; see Herodotus V.78: 'The Athenians, when governed by tyrants, were superior in war to none of their neighbours; but when freed from tyrants became by far the first.' With the remark about Rome cp. Sallust's *Cataline* 7.3: *Sed civitas incredible memoratu est adepta libertate quantum brevi creverit* (cited by St. Thomas in *de Regimine* I.4). Similar remarks are made in D. I.58.7 (*q.v.*).

4. Usually cited now under its alternative title 'Hiero'.

5. Hieronymus, king of Syracuse (216–215 B.C.), reigned only thirteen months and was then murdered (Livy XXIV.7). The demands of the soldiers that the king's death should be expiated by the blood of the conspirators, and their change of mind when they heard that freedom had been restored is described by Livy in XXIV.21. Hieronymus was the grandson of Hiero II. For grandson Machiavelli uses *nipote* following Livy who uses *nepos* in XXIV.4.1. (Cp. D. I.58.1 and n. 2.)

6. The story of this massacre is told by Thucydides in IV.46–8. The Athenians had captured the Corcyrean oligarchs, promising to take them to Athens. The democratic party induced them to escape, alleging that in Athens they would be put to death. They then locked them up, and took them out twenty at a time—not eight or ten—and killed them. (427 B.C.)

7. Cp. the complaint Aristotle makes in his *Politics* V.9, 1310a, 12 *sq.*: 'What contributes most to the permanence of constitutions is the adaptation of education

to the form of government, and yet in our own day this principle is universally neglected. The best laws, though sanctioned by every citizen of the state, will be of no avail unless the young are trained by habit and education in the spirit of the constitution. . . . Two principles are characteristic of democracy, the government of the majority, and freedom. Men think that what is just is equal; and that equality is the supremacy of the popular will; and that freedom and equality mean the doing what a man likes. In such democracies everyone lives as he pleases, or in the words of Euripides, "according to his fancy". But this is all wrong; men should not think it slavery to live according to the rule of the constitution, for it is their salvation.'

8. This reference to 'sacrificial acts in which there was much shedding of blood' has been made famous by the speech which Donne puts into the mouth of Machiavel in '*Ignatius, his Conclave*'. Machiavel says: 'I my selfe went alwaies that way of bloud, and therefore I did ever preferre the sacrifices of the Gentiles, and of the Jewes, which were performed with effusion of bloud (whereby not only the people, but the Priests also were animated to bold enterprises) before the soft and wanton sacrifices of Christians' (The Nonsuch Ed., p. 371). Actually there was very little shedding of blood in the rites practised during the time of the Roman republic, as Warde Fowler points out in his *Religious Experience of the Roman People*, pp. 33–4 and 180–1. Moreover, everything was done with the utmost decorum; silence was enjoined and the priests veiled their heads (*ib.* p. 180). Machiavelli in this passage must be thinking either of Livy's description of a Samnite sacrifice in X.38, performed in secret by armed priests in which 'the promiscuous slaughtering of men and cattle, the altars besmeared with the blood of sacrifice and of murder, the horrible curse and the fierce chant invoking vengeance on family and relatives' were used to prevent the Samnite troops from running away; or else he is thinking of rites introduced during the Empire from the Orient—the *Taurobolium* and the *Criobolium*—in which bloodshedding played a conspicuous part. In Rome 'the general effect of the organisation of religion in the State-cult was deadening', not inspiring or terrifying, says Cyril Bailey in his article in C.A.H. VIII.14.6, p. 442. Moreover, its original aim, as Machiavelli himself points out in D. I.11.1, was to restrain the ferocity of the Roman people and to familiarise them with civic life and with peace. In his eagerness to make men bloodthirsty he would seem to have forgotten this, and to have been guilty either of a blunder or an anachronism. (Cp. Livy XXII.57.6, where he says that human sacrifices are not at all in accord with Roman rites).

9. This criticism of Christianity bears a curious resemblance to Marxist propaganda, which also ascribes the servility of the masses to the influence of Christianity, and in particular to its teaching in regard to humility. Machiavelli has no use for 'unarmed prophets'. 'Armed prophets have always conquered, whereas unarmed prophets have been ruined' (P. 6). The fact that Christ by his death on the cross established an empire which has proved far more lasting than that of the Romans, and that Savonarola, by his martyrdom, was to make an impression on history and on ages yet to come far greater than the impression created by Caesar Borgia's brutal methods and transient successes, are events of a kind in which he takes no interest, and of whose existence he scarce seems to be aware. Savonarola in his view ought not to have forbidden his followers to have recourse to arms, for had he urged them to use force while yet there was time, he might have done what he willed with Florence. The criticism is justified if we take the short-sighted view

and look exclusively to worldly renown. But this, too, has its disadvantages, as Machiavelli points out in his Introduction to the *History of Florence*, where he blames historians for 'having forgotten how many there have been who, lacking opportunity to win renown by praiseworthy deeds, have sought to become famous by deeds that were shameful', and for having overlooked the fact 'that matters relating to rule and government, since they possess a greatness in themselves, howsoever they may be handled and with whatsoever end undertaken, seem always to bring men more honour than blame.' (Cp. the chapter entitled 'The modern idea of Fame' in Burckhardt's *Civilisation of the Renaissance in Italy*, II. 3). Incidentally, to state that Christianity teaches that man's *'summum bonum'* consists in 'humility, abnegation, and contempt for mundane things' is inaccurate: they are but means to the end.

10. In this and in the following paragraphs (7 and 8), Machiavelli probably has in mind the *de Regimine Principum* of St. Thomas, and hence proceeds to qualify his previous statements. For though St. Thomas teaches that *mundanus honor et gloria non sunt sufficiens praemium regis* (I.7), and that a *regnum ordinari debet ad beatitudinem consequendam principaliter* (I.15), he also lays great stress on the natural virtues, especially in cap. 1 and cap. 14, and his continuator maintains that the *dominium Romanum fuit a Deo provisum propter zelum patris* (III.4), and that the *Romani meruerunt dominium propter leges sanctissimas quas tradiderunt,* which is Machiavelli's own thesis. Moreover, St. Thomas himself writes in I.4: *naturale etiam est ut homines sub timore nutriti, in servilem degenerent animum, et pusillanimes fiant ad omne virile opus et strenuum; quod experimento patet in provinciis quae diu sub tyrannis fuerunt.*

11. With this passage doubtless in mind Machiavelli now goes on to admit that he may after all be wrong. The real cause of man's pusillanimity, his *laissez-faire* attitude, and his failure to esteem liberty, lies not in Christianity, but, as St. Thomas claims, in the domination exercised for so many centuries alike over cities and over peoples by that very empire which he has taken, and continues to take, as the outstanding example of how a state which desires to expand, should be governed.

12. The reference is to X.31.10–14, where Livy says: 'There were still going on the Samnite wars of which we have spoken continuously throughout the fourth book and which were now in their forty-sixth year, reckoning from the consulate of M. Valerius and A. Cornelius, who first carried war into Samnium. I shall not describe here the slaughter which both sides suffered during this long period or the labours they underwent, which, hard as they were, were in no wise able to daunt them. During the last year ... they and their allies had been defeated by four armies led by four Roman generals, and they had lost their most distinguished commander. Their allies, the Etruscans, the Umbrians, and the Gauls were in the same plight as they were; nor could they rely either on their own strength or on that of others. Yet they did not withdraw from the war; for they had not yet grown so weary of defending liberty unsuccessfully that they preferred to surrender rather than aim at victory.' The First Samnite war is said to have occurred in 343–341, the second lasted from 327 to 314; it is now 298. Hence the war is in its forty-sixth year. L. Papirius Cursor several times commanded Roman armies against the Samnites during the second Samnite war and was awarded several triumphs. His son, who bore the same name, became consul in 293 during the third Samnite war, and gained more than one victory over them (X.38–42). The Samnites and the Sabines became subject to Rome in 290 B.C.

13. Note that the equality of which Machiavelli often speaks by no means precludes either the ownership of property or the handing of it on to children. It is also compatible with competitive industry and trading.

14. See *The Prince*, c. 9, 'De Principatu civili'.

15. XXIII.42, which gives the speech to which Machiavelli refers. This was in 215 B.C., when Marcellus was holding Nola and ravaging the countryside. Hannibal's help was again invoked by the populace of Nola in 214 (XXIV.13.8).

For the bearing of this chapter on the *de Regimine Principum* of Aquinas see *Sources B.8*, xii–xvii.

3. Rome became a Great City by ruining the Cities round about her, and by granting Foreigners Easy Access to her Honours

1. Livy I.30.1 'Crescit interea Roma Albae ruinis'. The quotation is in Latin only. For the war between Alba and Rome cp. Livy I.22–30.

2. Livy I.44.2. Rome's sixth king was Servius Tullius, who in A.W. Bk. I, 278b; F.20, is said to have trained bodies of troops for the defence of Rome.

3. Cp. D. I.4.4; 5.3–4 and 6 *passim*; and see Index *sub* 'Plebs, conflict of, with the senate'.

4. Cp. Plutarch's 'Lycurgus', n. 27.

5. Seneca says the Spartans could pay debts either in gold or in leather bearing an official stamp (*de Beneficiis* V.14); and Xenophon that Lycurgus, to discourage trading, introduced a coinage so bulky that it took a wagon to transport the equivalent of 10 minae (*Lacedaemonian Politia*, vii.5). But this coinage Plutarch says was of iron (*Lycurgus*, 9; and cp. Polybius VI.49).

6. Note that Machiavelli is here treating politics as a branch of natural science, as he does in the Preface to Book I.

7. Cp. Polybius VI.50 and D. I.6.7 and n. 8.

4. Republics have adopted Three Methods of Expansion

1. Livy's words in V.33.7.   2. *ib. Hadriaticum mare ab Hadria, Tuscorum colonia.*

3. Livy V.33–4. Gauls under Bellovesus and Sigovesus, nephews of Ambigatus, king of the Biturigians, swarmed into Italy during the reign of Tarquinius Priscus. As reasons Livy assigns both the attractions of Tuscany, and overcrowding in the fertile country in which the invaders lived. (Cp. D. II.8.2.) For an account of the Gauls or Celts, see C.A.H. VII, c. 2. The country lying between Faesulae and Arretium, two of the towns mentioned by Machiavelli, was one of the most fertile in Italy, rich in corn and cattle and all kinds of wealth, says Livy (XXII.3.3).

4. Livy mentions an Etruscan priest-king who was elected by the suffrages of twelve peoples (V.1.5), but does not give their names.

5. If a confederation of states is to become powerful and to expand, it must, in Machiavelli's view, have a central authority, and so be dominated by a power which is greater than, and controls, the rest, as was the case with the British empire

while in process of being formed, and as is the case with the empire which Russia is at present forming. A large confederation, based on equality, will not, in his opinion, work, for reasons which he now proceeds to give. Hence the idea of a world-wide confederation, based on equality, is entirely foreign to his thought.

6. Cp. Livy XXXII.32–4. This curious conference in which Philip V of Macedon speaks from a ship and Flamininus, the Roman consul, from the shore, in the presence of kings, ambassadors, and the Aetolian praetor, Phaeneas, took place near Nicaea on the shore of the gulf of Malea in 197 B.C., after Flamininus' victory at Elatea. Alexander, who speaks on behalf of the Aetolians, accuses Philip of using unfair methods (*ib.* 33); at which Philip gets annoyed, and brings the charges which Machiavelli mentions. (*ib.* 34.)

7. The reference is probably to D. II.18.9.

8. Livy says that the Etruscans were more devoted to religion than any other peoples, and that they excelled in the 'ceremonial art' (V.1.6). For the influence exercised by the Etruscans on the religion and culture of Rome, see C.A.H. VII, pp. 383–7. It is highly probable that Rome's later kings were Etruscans, and that the account given in the opening paragraph of this chapter of their early origin is substantially correct.

9. Cp. Livy V.33.7–10 on the extent of Tuscany prior to its conquest.

With this discourse compare *The Prince,* cap. 4, in which Machiavelli discusses why the Kingdom of Darius, conquered by Alexander, did not rebel against his successors; and also cap. 5, where we are told that there are three methods of dealing with a conquered people used to its own laws: (1) to ruin it; (2) to reside there; and (3) to let it live under its own laws, but with a friendly oligarchy ruling it and tribute to be paid.

5. Changes of Religion and of Language, together with such Misfortunes as Floods or Pestilences, obliterate the Records of the Past

1. The reference is probably to Aristotle who, in opposition to Plato, held this view. (Cp. *Metaphysics* XII.6.)

2. Toward the close of the fourth century A.D., numerous edicts were issued by Theodosius, Arcadius and Honorius proscribing pagan sacrifices and ordering the destruction of pagan temples, and though by a later edict (dated 20 August, 399) it was ordered that the buildings were to be preserved as public monuments once they had been stripped of unlawful ornaments, much destruction was done. In 423 Theodosius II renewed the anti-pagan legislation of his predecessors, but replaced the death penalty for offering pagan sacrifices by banishment and confiscation of goods, and forbade the ill-treatment of inoffensive pagans. The temples were to be converted into churches. A list of the principal temples destroyed between 386 and 404 will be found in Fliche and Martin's *Histoire de l'Église*, vol. 4, c. 1. On the other hand, there is no evidence to show that the popes played a prominent part in the campaign of destruction, and Italy suffered much less from it than did other countries. Moreover, Machiavelli says nothing of what was done to preserve pagan monuments and classical writings, alike in Byzantium, in Italy, France,

Spain, England and Ireland; of the libraries and episcopal palaces in which ancient manuscripts were treasured and studied; or of the long survival of paganism, which was still so strong in 410 A.D. that Augustine thought it worth while to write his *City of God* in order to answer the charges which pagans were bringing against Christianity. He forgets, too, that most of the Christian Fathers wrote not in Latin, but in Greek, and that in Church law both languages were used.

3. Gregory the Great (d. 604) had, it is true, but little use for classical learning, and wrote to Desiderius, Bishop of Vienne, reproving him for having instructed youths in classical lore. Later writers say that he tried to suppress the works of Cicero, burnt the books of Livy, and set the Palatine library on fire lest it should interfere with the study of the Scriptures; but they are writing centuries later. The last statement, for instance, is made first by John of Salisbury (d. 1180) in his *Polycraticus* (II.26; VIII.19). Moreover, in 613, only nine years after Gregory's death, Columban founded at Bobbio in northern Italy a monastery which became a treasury of classical learning and in the tenth century contained 666 manuscripts. Incidentally, Jonas, the monk who wrote his life, quotes both Virgil and Livy. (Cp. *A History of Classical Scholarship* by J. E. Sandys, c. 24.)

4. Diodorus Siculus wrote in the first decade of the Christian era a history of the world from its creation to the death of Julius Caesar in forty books, of which books 1 to 5 and 11 to 20 have survived, together with fragments of the others. He tells us in his Preface that he had spent thirty years travelling about collecting records in preparation for his work, which he wrote in Greek and called *Bibliothecae*. A Latin translation was available in Machiavelli's day, but the complete Greek edition was not published until 1559. We are also told in the Preface that the period covered by the work is 1,138 years, exclusive of events which happened prior to the Trojan war for which, as he says, he has to rely on traditions preserved by the Egyptians and others, which to the Greeks are but fables. (I.4 and 5; and for further use of Diodorus Siculus, see TABLE XIII, A.4.)

5. Cp. Polybius VI.5: 'To what are we to assign the beginning of civil societies, and how are we to ascertain their origin? As often as the generations of man perished either by floods, pestilences, or the sterility of the earth, as we are told has happened and it is reasonable to suppose will happen again, there perished everything mortal man has discovered about what used to be done, together with all the arts.' Cp. also Aristotle, *Politics* II.8, 1269a, 3 *sq.*: 'Again, men in general desire the good . . . but the primaeval inhabitants, whether they were born of the earth or were the survivors of some destruction, may be supposed to have been no better than ordinary foolish people amongst ourselves; such, anyhow, is the tradition.' Cp. also Plato, *Timaeus* 23, and *Laws* 676–7.

6. Note the analogy here drawn between the political and the natural order, and the similarity between Machiavelli's doctrine and that of Malthus.

7. Cp. D. II.4.6.

6. How the Romans proceeded in the waging of War

1. Cp. Polybius III.4. 'The end of a policy should not be . . . simply to conquer others and to bring all into subjection. Nor does any man of sense go to war with his neighbours for the mere purpose of mastering his opponents; nor go to sea for the mere sake of the voyage; nor engage in professions and trades for the mere sake

of learning them. In all these cases what is sought is the pleasure, honour, or profit, which accrues from such employments.'

2. *'corte e grosse'*, literally, short and big. The French equivalent in those days was *'courte et grosse'*, *'grosse'* in the sense of *'puissante'*, in which sense it is still used in the expression *'les gros bataillons'*. Machiavelli is talking of, and indeed, recommending, what we now call a *'Blitzkrieg'*.

3. For the confiscation of land, see Livy II.31.4 and X.1.3. A colony sent out to Narnia to guard the Umbrian frontier is mentioned in X.10.5. Cicero calls such colonies *'propugnacula imperii'*—outposts of empire (*De Lege Agraria* II.27). Of them Professor Last writes in C.A.H. Vol. VII: 'The impression given by Livy, Dionysius, and Velleius is that in some cases at least, even in the fifth century, Rome posted small bodies of her own citizens in places of strategic value, and that these garrisons retained their Roman citizenship as much as did the inhabitants of the so-called maritime colonies of which Antium was the first. And this impression is strengthened by the way in which certain of these earlier foundations finally emerge into the full light of history as *coloniae civium Romanorum* without any clear evidence being preserved to show that their status had been changed' (p. 541). Of the next century Tenney Frank says: 'The so-called Latin colony continued to be the chief device for garrisoning strategic points; including the original colonies of the Latin league there were some twenty-eight of these. The method adopted was to confiscate a portion of arable territory which was fertile enough to attract settlers at points which needed protection and possessed a strong site readily fortified. The colonists would serve as a garrison in time of need and were also liable to army service in the league forces at times when they could safely be called from home' (C.A.H. VII, p. 659).

On colonies, cp. also D. I.1.4, D. II.19.2; P. 3, Burd 187, E.18–19 and H.F. II.1–2.

4. The Aequi, for instance, attacked the colony at Sora in 302, and the dictator, Caius Junius Bubulcus, was sent out to chastise them (X.1.7–9). Lucius Lucretius Flavius had also been sent out to recover Vitellia, which had been taken by the Aequi in 393 B.C. (V.29.3–5).

5. This was not the ostensible reason, as Livy points out in IV.60 (cp. D. I.51 and n. 1); but that it was the real reason is made clear in the speech Appius Claudius delivers to the Senate in 403, where he upbraids the plebs for grumbling at the length of the siege of Veii, urging that, since they are now getting paid for their services to the state and are paid for a year's service, they ought not to expect to get off with six months (V.4.6–7; cp. V.10). On the importance of this step Professor Last writes: 'The provision of pay . . . is a departure of the deepest meaning. It is the first step of many taken by Rome towards turning an army characteristic of a typical city-state into the army of an imperial people. A citizen-militia, whose members might reasonably be expected to serve for nothing, was enough to carry on the brief border warfare in which city-states were wont to settle their accounts; but the purposes of an empire called for longer and more continuous service than this. Longer service could only be had if the troops were paid; and there is much plausibility in the view of tradition that it was the protracted siege of Veii which first forced Rome to provide her soldiers with more regular and immediate recompense than a share of the booty when victory had been won' (C.A.H. VII, p. 513).

6. When the dictator, Marcus Furius Camillus, saw that the spoils from Veii

would come to more than had been obtained in all previous wars taken together, he wrote to the Senate to know what to do with it. Some urged that whoever wanted should go to Veii and help himself. Others, and amongst them Appius Claudius, deprecated this extravagance, and suggested that the spoils should be deposited in the public treasury, whence it could be drawn upon to pay the troops, when required. The senate referred the matter to the plebs, who chose the first alternative (V.21). A proposal to put the spoils in the public treasury was defeated again after the Etruscan campaign of 388, for the soldiers seized them (VI.4.11). But from this time on it seems to have become the custom for spoils to be handed over to the treasury—'*publicari praedam*'—provided neither the troops nor private persons got hold of them first.

7. Cp. X.46. Papirius after defeating the Samnites brought back an immense sum of money in silver and copper, none of which was given to the troops but all lodged in the treasury. Carvilius, who followed him, gave some of the money he had acquired to the troops, but most went to the treasury and was spent on buildings.

In A.W. Bk. V (B.332–3; F.II.107–8) Fabrizio calls attention to the fact that wars now impoverish both the victors and the vanquished. This is due, he says, to allowing the troops to retain the spoils of war instead of handing them to the public treasury. The Romans allowed only a portion of the spoil to be distributed amongst the troops.

In regard to the payment of troops, Fabrizio in A.W. Bk. I (B.281; F.24–5) recommends that they should be paid only when on active service or engaged in military exercises in the case of the militia. That he himself and other officers (*capi*) should have been paid when not actually engaged in military service Machiavelli regards as an abuse (*ib.* B.274a; F.13).

Machiavelli does not return to the question of the advantages of a *Blitzkrieg* in *The Art of War*, but in the last paragraph of Book VI Fabrizio deprecates the carrying on of war in winter, and to this mistake ascribes the defeat of the French on the Garigliano in 1503.

7. How much Land the Romans gave to their Colonists

1. The Italian equivalent of 'three *jugera* and seven *unciae*' is missing both in the 1929 edition, which I am using, and in the Filadelfia edition of 1786. There is also a discrepancy between the text of Livy which Machiavelli cites and the text in Müller's edition, which reads: '*Agri Veientani septena jugera plebi dividerentur*' (V.30.8). Farnworth, however, in his translation gives in a footnote an alternative reading '*terna jugera et septunces diviserant*'. Commenting on the accepted text Professor Last says: 'Diodorus suggests four *jugera* as the normal grant, and this is probable. A figure so high as seven is perhaps more appropriate to the third century' (C.A.H. VII, p. 538). Moreover, the colonists who were subsequently sent out to Sutricum in 385 only got 2½ *jugera*, at which they grumbled, and those sent to Anxur in 328 only got two. Hence Machiavelli is probably right in reading 3 *jugera*, 7 *unciae* (= a little more than two acres), and is certainly right in saying that colonists got but a small portion of land. Moreover, as Professor Last points out, there was probably 'enough land left over as an *Ager Publicus* of the Roman people' (p. 540). It was, in fact, customary to assign half the land of a colony to the *Ager Publicus*.

8. The Causes which lead Peoples to quit their own Country and to inundate the Lands of Others

1. Cp. D. II.4 for Roman and Tuscan methods, and also D. II.6 for Roman.

2. The war with Jugurtha, king of Numidia, took place in 112–106 B.C. In his last chapter (c. 114) Sallust says: 'During the same period the Roman generals, Quintus Caepio and Gaius Manlius were defeated in a battle with the Gauls, and all Italy trembled with panic. From that time down to our own the Romans have held that, though all others have succumbed to their valour, with the Gauls the fight was for survival, not for glory'—'*alia omnia virtuti suae prona esse, cum Gallis pro salute non pro gloria certari*'. Farnworth, however, gives another version (Vol. II, p. 192), which accords better with the Italian text of the edition I am using: '*cum ceteris gentibus a populo Romano de imperio tantum fuisse dimicatum, cum Gallis, de singulorum hominum salute,*' where the contrast is between '*imperium*' and '*salus*' as in the text.

3. Cp. P. 3 on 'Mixed Principalities', where we are told that in the case of a country which is of the same race or has the same language as the invader, it suffices to destroy the family of the prince who was ruling there, as happened in France in the case of Britanny, Burgundy, Gascony and Normandy (E.17).

4. Cp. II.4.2. 5. Cp. II.4.2 and Livy V.33.2. 6. Livy V.34.2–4.

7. Of the second Gallic war, 226–222 B.C., Livy's account is missing, though it is mentioned in *Periocha* XX. Polybius, however, gives us an account of it in II.23–34. During the first campaign the Gauls won a great victory to the north of Clusium, but in 225 got caught between the forces of Lucius Aemilius and Gaius Atilius who had landed at Pisa (cp. D. II.1.3). The enemy lost 50,000 troops, of whom 40,000 were slain and the rest taken prisoner. Further victories were gained in 223 over the Insubrae, who had 50,000 troops under arms and far outnumbered the Romans. It was a most formidable invasion, says Polybius, and constituted a very grave danger. For the obstinacy of the battles fought and the number slain, the war was second to none in history, but for strategy it was contemptible (II.31, 35). For the site of the battle of Telamon, see II.1, n. 2.

8. Rumours that a host comprising some 300,000 fighting men, mostly Teutons and Cimbri, who were probably Celts, were gathered with their families on the Swiss side of the Alps, began to circulate in 113 B.C. Between 107 and 105 four consular armies were defeated. (Cp. D. II.12.9 and n. 13.) The barbarians were expected to cross the Alps at any moment, and Marius was appointed consul in four successive years, 104–1. It was not, however, until 102 B.C. that the invasion came. Meanwhile Marius had been training his troops, and when he met the Gauls at Aquae Sextiae they were caught between the main army and forces under Claudius Marcellus, who cut off their retreat. According to Orosius (V.16) and Livy (*Epit.* 68) 200,000 were slain and 80,000 taken prisoners.

9. Procopius, the Byzantine historian, became secretary to Belisarius in A.D. 527, and accompanied him during his campaigns in Asia, Africa, and Italy. The quotation is from Bk. II, c. 10 of his *de Bello Vandalico*, and is given in Latin: *Nos, Maurusii, qui fugimus a facie Jesu latronis filii Navae.* It is taken from a passage which in the Latin edition of 1509 bears the marginal heading: *de Maurorum origine,*

but is inexact. Procopius says that when *Jesu filius Navae* (Joshua) succeeded Moses he proceeded to reduce the inhabitants of Palestine to obedience. At that time all the sea-coast from Sidon up to the confines of Egypt was called Phoenicia, and was under a single prince. The land was occupied by several nations, both strong and numerous, Gergesites, Jebusites, and others whose names are given in the books of the Hebrews (*Joshua* 3.10 *sq.*). These peoples being unable to resist the forces of this foreign commander, withdrew into Egypt, but as they found no vacant land, they were obliged to retire into Africa, where they occupied many cities right up to the pillars of Hercules. They rebuilt the town of Tingis in Numidia, where near a large fountain are two columns of white stone on which is engraved this inscription in the Phoenician language and letters: *Nos a facie fugimus Jesu praedonis filii Navae.* Procopius is aware that the *Maurusii* are held to be indigenous, but denies this. They allowed other Phoenician immigrants under Dido to build Carthage and by them were driven further afield. Then came the Romans who ordered them to settle in the extreme parts of Africa. Livy mentions the *Maurusii* in XXII.49, who 'then occupied the farthest coasts hard upon the ocean over against Gades'. It was to them that Syphax fled with some Numidian horsemen in 214 B.C.

10. For an account of how the Trojans came to Italy and made terms with their neighbours, see Livy I.1. For an account of how Dido, the Phoenician princess, built Carthage and lived there harmoniously with her neighbours, see Procopius *loc. cit.* and Justin XVIII.4. *Massilia* (Marseilles) was founded by the Phocaeans *circa* 600 B.C. They were received in a friendly manner by Arganthonius and the Tartessians, who were already settled there (cp. Herodotus I, 163). Dido is also mentioned in P. 17 (E.134).

11. Scythia is the old name of the land which lies between the Carpathians and the Don. From the third century onwards the tribes which occupied it were continually making inroads into the Roman Empire. For an account of these invasions and those from Germany in the third century A.D., see Flavius Blondus, *Hist. Rom.*, Bks. I and II; and cp. the chapter entitled 'The Invasions of Peoples from the Rhine to the Black Sea' in C.A.H. XII.5. Orosius, writing just after Rome had been sacked by the Goths in 410, tells how for a time the Alani, the Huns, and the Goths who came from Scythia, were held in check by Theodosius the Great, 346–395 (VII.34.5; and for a further reference to these invasions see D. II.30.4 and n. 6). They ceased in the tenth century partly because the original source whence the invading hordes came was for the time being exhausted, and partly because, when the empire was revived under Otto I, who was crowned in Rome by John XXII in 962, the Slavs and the Magyars who had settled in Poland and Hungary still retained their warlike character (in spite of their having become Christians), and thus formed a barrier against any further invasions. The Tartars, to whom Machiavelli now refers, was a term first applied collectively to the Mongols, Tartars and Turks who ravaged Eastern Europe under the leadership of Jenghiz Khan, 1202–27. Then came the Ottoman Turks, who in the fourteenth century got as far as Cracow and Moscow and in the fifteenth took Constantinople in 1453 and then conquered the Balkans. It was against them that the Poles and the Hungarians were continually fighting, with varying but sometimes notable success, under Ladislas of Poland and Hunyadi of Hungary, who in 1455 defeated Mohammed II at Belgrade and thus saved Hungary for eighty years, though the Balkans were irretrievably lost.

9. What Causes commonly give rise to Wars between Different Powers?

1. Livy VII.19.4; 29.2; 30.4.
2. VII.29.3. 3. VII.31.7. 4. VII.31.2–3. 5. VII.31.4–7.
6. Livy, *Periocha* XVI. 7. XXI.5.2–3.
8. Capua, an Etruscan city, formerly called Volturnum, was taken by the Samnites in 423, and an attempt made by the Romans to drive the Samnites out, ended in failure (IV.37–40). When the Capuan league—i.e. the Campanians, was attacked by the Samnites in 343, after their futile attempt to defend the Sidicines, they had to choose between surrender to the Samnites and surrender to Rome. They chose the latter. (VII.30–1; cp. D. II.10.9 and D. II.11.1 and n. 1).
9. Cp. *History of Florence* II.24–37. In 1311 the rulers of Florence asked Robert of Naples for assistance against the Emperor and the Ghibellines, and 'failing to obtain it on the score of friendship, gave up the city to him for five years' (24). Florence was at war in 1313–15 with Uguccione, Lord of Pisa and of Lucca. King Robert's representative, Count Novello, failed to help Florence and was expelled. He was succeeded by Count Guido of Battifolle, and the king's lordship was extended for three years (25). In 1316 Castruccio Castracani became Lord of Pisa and Lucca and raided Florentine territory. The war went on until 1325, when the Florentines were defeated at Altopascio, and again appealed to king Robert of Naples. He sent the Duke of Athens to Florence, and in 1326 replaced him by his own son, the Duke of Calabria. Duke Charles held Castruccio in check for some time (30), but on his departure Florence lost Pistoia, which was taken by Castruccio shortly before his death in 1328. (Cp. D. II.12.8 for subsequent events. Cp. also Machiavelli's *Life of Castruccio Castracani*, though this is far from reliable as Villari points out in Vol. II, 302 *sq.*)

10. Money is not the Sinews of War, as it is commonly supposed to be

1. This is one of several Machiavellian maxims which Bacon uses in his treatise 'Of the true Greatness of the Kingdom of Great Britain' (Works, Vol. VII, pp. 47–64), where in discussing the 'second immoderate opinion' that 'too much is ascribed to treasure and riches' in the balancing of greatness, he not only cites this theorem of Machiavelli, but also Solon's 'memorable censure of Croesus'. The theory that 'Money was the sinews of war', was first taken, he says, from a speech of Mutianus, the lieutenant of Vespasian. But what he said was '*pecuniae sunt nervi belli civilis*' (*ib.* pp. 55–6). Cicero also says of civil war '*primum nervos belli pecuniam infinitam*' (*Phil.* 5.3.5), but not of war in general. A more general statement is, however, ascribed to Cerialis by Tacitus: 'The tranquillity of nations cannot be preserved without armies; armies cannot exist without pay; pay cannot be provided without tribute' (*Hist.* IV.74). And Thucydides ascribes to Archidamus the statement: 'War requires money no less than arms, for it is by money that arms avail' (VI.34).

2. Tommasini (I. p. 143, n. 1) and Plinio Carli (*Le Opere Maggiori di N.M.;* Le Monnier, Florence, 1948, p. 185, n. 10) deny that Quintus Curtius maintains that *money is the sinews of war*. This is open to question, for in his *de Rebus Gestis Alexandri Magni* not only is there frequent mention of the importance of *pecunia* in connection with war, but of the war in which Agis took part he says that it was being waged *ab opulentissimis Europae Asiaeque regibus in spem totius orbis occupandae,* and that it was its *magnitudo* that moved the Greeks to join in (IV.6). Moreover, in the Index to Quintus Curtius' work translated by John Digby and published in London in 1714 appear the words 'Money the Sinews of War'. The reference is to Book I, as reconstructed by Freinshem. It deals with the life of Philip II and with the early life of Alexander. Of Philip we are told on p. 46 that 'he would frequently brag that all things were penetrable by Money, and that he made use of it himself as often as of his Arms' (*Verum quum ipse pecuniae omnia penetrabilia jactaret, eaque haud minus saepe quam armis uteretur*). We are then told on p. 51 that to Alexander, at the age of twenty, 'the Nerve of great Actions, Money, was wanting' (*Etiam nervus gerendarum rerum pecunia defecerat*). The passage which Machiavelli is using in § 2, is, however, lacking in all the Delphine editions, and also in all the editions which were available in Machiavelli's day, of which I have examined at least eight. But in all of them save one there is a gap before the description of the battle between Agis III and Antipater with which Book VI opens, and there already existed numerous reconstructions. Hence it may well be on one of these that Machiavelli's statement is based. It is none the less historically inaccurate. For the battle in which Agis was slain took place near Megalopolis in 331 B.C., and Alexander did not die until 323 B.C. (Cp. for an account of Agis's campaign, C.A.H. VI.14.3, pp. 444-5). This agrees with what Quintus Curtius says, 'The Lacedaemonians were all pardoned except the authors of the rebellion, and the war was finished before Alexander defeated Darius at Arbela' (October 331 A.D.). Nor did Sparta take part in the subsequent rising provoked by the return of the exiles, of which the leadership was taken by Athens.

3. Of Persia we are told in Curtius's reconstructed Second Book that its kings trusted to the reputation their ancestors had acquired and to riches, rather than to strength and bravery, and consequently 'found their gold ineffectually opposed to the power of Alexander' (c. 1). Of Darius III, king of Persia (336-330), with whose defeat at Arbela the empire came to an end, we are told that he had 5,000 talents of gold for his pillow, and 3,000 talents of silver for his footstool, placed in repositories under the head and foot of his bed, and yet the son of Philip, who was comparatively poor, ventured to attack him (*ib.*). Cp. Darius's speech to his troops in V. c. 1, where he says that Alexander's soldiers have now no thought but of enriching themselves with immense spoils, and adds that it is necessary to 'make wars with steel, not with gold' (*ferro geri bella, non auro*).

4. Greece became subject to Rome after the victories of Q. Caecilius Metellus in 148 B.C., and the taking and destruction of Corinth by L. Mummius Achaicus in 146. The triumph which the latter celebrated in 145 was one of the richest and most magnificent that Rome had ever seen.

5. Charles the Bold, Duke of Burgundy, ruled not only Burgundy, but also Franche Comté, the Netherlands, and Flanders, and was one of the most wealthy princes in Europe. Yet he was beaten by the Swiss confederation near Grandson in March 1476; near Berne in June 1476, where some ten thousand Burgundians

were slaughtered; and finally at Nancy in October, where he was killed. (Cp. D. III.10.7.)

6. In 1516 Francesco Maria della Rovere was summoned to Rome by Leo X to answer various charges, such as his refusal to join Lorenzo de' Medici against the French for which he had accepted pay, and complicity in the murder of Alidosi in the time of Julius II. On his failing to appear he was deprived of Urbino, which was given to Lorenzo. In February 1517, though without money, artillery or provisions, he recovered Urbino and held it for eight months until 17 September, when for lack of troops and of funds he had to surrender. Guicciardini (*St. d'I.* XIII.8. p. 41) says that the war cost the Pope 800,000 ducats. The papal finances never recovered from this loss.

7. The story told of Croesus, the last king of Lydia (560–546 B.C.) in § 4 differs both in question and answer from the well-known story which Herodotus tells in I.30–3, and which Plutarch copies in his *Life of Solon* (27). The story which Machiavelli is using—and which Bacon uses in his essay on 'The true Greatness of the Kingdom of Britain' in which he endorses Machiavelli's thesis—is taken from the conversation between Solon and Croesus which Lucian relates in his '*Charon*' (12). Having got Croesus to admit that to protect is better than to be protected, Solon asks whether it is swords of gold or swords of steel that are to be used; and, having got the correct answer, infers from it that 'steel is better than gold'.

8. This incident is related by Justin in his *Historiae Philippicae* XXV, cc. 1 and 2. Ptolemy Ceraunus, the son of Ptolemy, king of Egypt, assassinated Seleucus, one of Alexander's generals, then king of Macedonia, in 280, and seized the throne, but was defeated and then murdered by the Gauls under Belgius, whose embassy he had haughtily turned down. Brennus, another Gallic leader, then in Greece, hears of this, and sends an embassy to Antigonus Gonatus, who with his father, Demetrius, had been expelled from Macedonia in 287, but on the death of Ptolemy Ceraunus had come to terms with his rival, Antiochus, son of Seleucus, and regained the throne in 277. Antigonus gave a banquet to the Gallic representatives, and showed them his gold and silver, elephants and ships (XXV. i.5–6); with the result that the Gauls under Brennus returned to Macedonia in force, occupied the enemy's camp, and, having taken away what they found there, returned to the shore (*ablatis quae invenerant ad littus convertuntur—ib.* 2.6). Hence Antigonus was despoiled, but he did not lose his kingdom, for he pursued the Gauls, inflicted on them a disastrous defeat (*ib.* 2.7), and continued to reign until he was eighty years of age.

9. After the battle of Agnadello in 1509; cp. D. I.53.3 and n. 4 and III.31.3.

10. Note that Machiavelli now proceeds to deal with the 'negative instance' he has cited in § 2.

11. C. Claudius Nero in 207 B.C. with his fellow consul, M. Livius, intercepted Hasdrubal, who was attempting to join Hannibal. Hasdrubal, putting his trust in the tried valour of his troops, thought there was a chance of winning and gave battle on the banks of the Metaurus in the March of Ancona (Livy XXVII.48.5–9), where he was defeated and slain (cp. D. III.17). The force of Machiavelli's argument is, however, not borne out by what Hannibal did in 212, when he was caught by Nero in a defile near Tarragona, and kept up parleys in the daytime while at night his troops escaped (XXVI.17).

12. Cp. Pericles' speech in Thucydides I.141–2, in which he urges the Athenians

not to yield to the demands of the Lacaedemonians and promises them victory, since 'our resources are equal to theirs' and 'they have no wealth either public or private', so that 'their greatest difficulty will be want of money, which they can only provide slowly, and war waits for no man'. The speech was delivered in 432 B.C., just prior to the outbreak of war.

13. Cp. Livy IX.17, 3–4.

14. Cp. Livy VII.30 for the speech in which the Campanians offer to surrender, and 31.4 for the actual surrender of 'the Campanian people, and the city of Capua, their lands, the temples of the gods, all things divine and human, into your jurisdiction and that of the Roman people'. The Campanians were first beaten in the territory of the Sidicines to whose assistance they had gone (29.5), and then in the plain between Capua and Tifata (29.7–8). Cp. D. II.9 n. 8; and D. II.11.1 and n. 1.

Guicciardini *in loc.* points out that those who claim that money provides the sinews of war, do not mean that money suffices or that it is more necessary than troops. All they mean is that without money to provide arms, munitions, provisions, and to pay the troops, war is impossible; though doubtless those who have their own troops need less money than those who employ mercenaries.

In A.W. Bk. VII (B.363b; F.156) Machiavelli expresses his opinion more moderately. 'Men, steel, money and provisions are the sinews of war, but of these four the two first are most necessary, for men and steel will always find money and provisions.'

11. It is not a Wise Course to make an Alliance with a Ruler whose Reputation is greater than his Strength

1. In 354 B.C. Rome made an alliance with the Samnites, but, ten years later, fresh Samnite tribes arrived and began to raid the territory of the Sidicines, to whom their neighbours, the Campanians, sent help, but were worsted in battle by the Samnites (VII.29.3–4); for, says Livy: '*Campani magis nomen in auxilium Sidicinorum, quam vires ad praesidium attulerunt*' (29.5—the Teubner edition reads: '*Campani magis nomen ad praesidium sociorum quam vires attulissent*'). Both this quotation and the phrase '*magis nomen quam praesidium*', twice repeated, are given in Latin in the text. The Campanians appealed to Rome, surrendered themselves unconditionally to the Roman power (cp. D. II.9.1, 4 and n. 8 and D. II.10.8 and n. 14), and four years later, in 339, were granted the rights of citizenship. Capua was their principal city, in size second only to Rome.

2. The attempt of Sixtus IV to reduce the ecclesiastical fiefs which had become independent, led to conflict with Florence which had formed an alliance with Niccolò Vitelli. Lorenzo de' Medici renewed the treaty of alliance with Milan and Venice for twenty-five years, and the Pope formed an alliance with Ferdinand of Naples. In 1478 Sixtus IV placed Florence under an interdict on the ground that the Archbishop of Pisa had been imprisoned, and that other priests, guilty or innocent, who had taken part in the Pazzi conspiracy, had been massacred, and the House of God had been violated. The interdict was ignored, and priests forced to say mass. Papal forces under the Duke of Calabria took several towns and laid siege

to Castellina. The Duke of Milan sent some help, but the Venetians said it was a private quarrel and did nothing. The Duke of Ferrara who was in command of the Florentine forces went home, and Genoa revolted against Milan. Ambassadors from the Emperor, the King of France and the King of Hungary came to Florence *en route* for Rome and tried to restore peace. When these negotiations broke down, Florence sent ambassadors to the King of France, Louis XI, in the hope of 'sheltering themselves under the reputation of an alliance with that prince'. The Venetians were at last induced to send cavalry under Count Carlo, who gained some successes but then died. Jacopo Guicciardini won a victory near Lake Trasimene 'in the very place where Hannibal the Carthaginian formerly gave the Romans so memorable a defeat'. But the Marquis of Ferrara and the Marquis of Mantua came to blows over the division of the spoils, and the former retired for the second time. This threw the Florentine forces into confusion, and when the Duke of Calabria attacked them at Poggibonzi, they were completely routed, lost their baggage and artillery, and, 'behaving like poltroons, fled at the turning of a horse's head or tail' (November 1479). The passages in inverted commas will be found in the *History of Florence* (VIII.10–18), where a full account of this war, which ended in Lorenzo de' Medici going to Rome and to Naples to sue for peace, is given. The Pope, says Machiavelli, 'having failed to secure in Florence the change of government he desired, decided to effect by force what he had been unable to obtain by conspiracy' (VIII.10); whereby 'he showed that he was a wolf, not a shepherd' (VIII.11). This invasion of Florentine territory accounts in part for the animosity which Machiavelli displays against the Papacy. It should be noted, however, that it was not the Pope but the Florentines who in this case appealed for help to a foreigner (cp. D. I.12.7).

3. This incident occurred in 320 B.C. (cp. Livy IX.14) after the capitulation at the Caudine Forks in 321 B.C. The Greek maritime city of Tarentum had long been jealous of Rome's growing power and another Greek city, Palaeopolis, had in 327 fallen out with Roman settlers in Campania and appealed to the Samnites, who had occupied the city. This led to the second Samnite war of 327–290 B.C. After Rome's reverse in 321, Tarentum sent legates in the hope of preventing a renewal of the war (Livy IX.14.1). Papirius resented the intervention of a people 'who were unable to control their own domestic seditions and discords' (IX.14.5). Hence the Samnites, preferring 'deception' to 'contempt', formed an alliance with the Tarentines, which they did not keep; with the result that Tarentum had to come to terms with Rome (Cp. C.A.H. VII.18, p. 584 *sq.*; and 20, p. 641 *sq.*).

Cp. Tacitus, *Annals* XIII.19: '*Nihil rerum mortalium tam instabile ac fluxum est quam fama potentiae non sua vi mixtae*',—cited at the end of P. 13, E.112.

12. Whether it is better, when threatened with Attack, to assume the Offensive or to await the Outbreak of War

1. Herodotus tells this story of the alternatives which the queen of the Messagetae put before Cyrus, King of Persia, and of the advice given him by Croesus, the Lydian king, then a prisoner whom Cyrus had taken as one of his counsellors (I.205–7). According to Herodotus, Cyrus followed the advice of Croesus. His

weaker forces he left behind, but they sufficed to defeat a third of the army of the Messagetae under Spargapises, the Queen's son, who was taken prisoner. Tomyris retired, and Cyrus pursued her, but in a battle, 'the most obstinate ever fought between barbarians' (I.214), his army was cut to pieces, and he was slain in 529 B.C. Croesus's advice, therefore, led to disastrous results. Tomyris is mentioned in A.W. Bk. VI. B.351a; F.136.

2. Livy XXXIV.60. 135 B.C., when Cyrus was about to invade Europe.

3. After Agathocles had been defeated at Himera in Sicily by the Carthaginian general, Hamilcar, he carried the war into Africa and inflicted several defeats on the Carthaginians in 310 B.C. Scipio in his speech to the senate in 205 B.C. mentions the 'rashness of Agathocles who, ignoring the war in Sicily, crossed over to Africa'. (Livy XXVIII.43.20). Cp. also P. 8, where Machiavelli follows Justin XXII (see Burd p. 231).

4. Scipio had done much the same thing himself; for, while war was still being waged between Rome and Carthage in both Italy and Spain, he invaded Africa in 204 B.C., defeated Hasdrubal and Syphax, and thus forced the Carthaginians to recall Hannibal from Italy.

5. The Athenians invaded Sicily in the seventeenth year of the Peloponnesian war, i.e. in 415 B.C., and after three campaigns were utterly defeated by Gylippus, the Syracusan general. Both Demosthenes and Nicias surrendered, the whole of the Athenian forces were either slaughtered or taken prisoners, the Syracusans joined with the Spartans in dismembering the Athenian empire, and the decline of Athens set in. (Cp. Thucydides VII.82–87.)

6. The Fable of Antaeus, the Libyan giant, son of Poseidon and Ge, is told by Juvenal, III.89; Ovid, *Ibis* 397; Diodorus IV.17, and many others.

7. Ferdinand I ruled Naples from 1458 to 1494, the year in which Charles VIII invaded Italy. He died on 25 January and was succeeded by Alphonso, who sent his son, Ferdinand, to the Romagna and a fleet under his brother, Frederick, to Genoa, where he was defeated by Louis d'Orleans on 8 September at Rapallo. Meanwhile in February there had been a revolt in Naples, and Alphonso resigned in favour of his son, Ferdinand, who, deserted by his allies, returned to Naples, from which he fled to Sicily the day before the French entered Naples on 22 February 1495. During the years 1494–6 Naples had five kings: Ferdinand I; Alfonso II; Charles VIII; Ferdinand II; Frederick.

8. Cp. D. I.23 and D. I.22.2.

9. In classing France as ill-equipped and unprepared for war in its own territory, Machiavelli is probably thinking of the failure of the French forces at the battle of the Spurs and at Terouanne, when Henry VIII invaded the country in 1513 (cp. I.21.2 and n. 2); or perhaps of the report he had himself received during his second legation to France in 1504, when he was told that Louis XII had few troops and these scattered, and that his treasury was exhausted (Cp. Villari I, p. 368.)

10. The war waged by Castruccio Castracani on Florence in 1325 is described in the *History of Florence* II.29–30, where we are told that Castruccio 'for many months rode and ravaged at will, with none to oppose him', so that the Florentines were 'at last driven to take Charles, Duke of Calabria, son of King Robert, as their Lord'. (Cp. D. II.9.4 and n. 9.) The subsequent war against Giovanni Visconti, Lord and Archbishop of Milan, in 1351–3, is mentioned in H.F. II.42 & III.2, but

we are given no details. Anyhow, Florence did not succeed in depriving Giovanni Visconti of his state, for he remained Lord of Milan till his death in 1354.

11. Machiavelli now discusses the 'negative instance' cited in § 2.

12. The Romans, after their three defeats at Trebia, Lake Trasimene, and Cannae in 218–216 B.C., made an astonishing recovery, but in 225 B.C. can hardly have had 1,800,000 men under arms to meet the Gallic threat of invasion. Polybius, who gives a detailed list of the Roman and allied forces available for the war with Hannibal in 218, puts the number at 926,000, i.e. at about half the number Machiavelli gives for 225 B.C. Anyhow, they routed the Gauls in three successive battles, at one of which, near Telamon, 40,000 were slain and 10,000 taken prisoners. (Cp. D. II.1.3 and n. 2; and D. II.8.2 and n. 7; Polybius II.24).

13. The Romans were routed by the Cimbri at Arausio, near Avignon, in 105 B.C., this being the fifth army which Rome had sent against them without success; yet when, in 102 B.C., hordes of invading Cimbri swept down into Italy, they were routed by the Romans at Campii Raudii between Turin and Milan in 101 B.C.—Q. Lutatius Catulus, who served as consul in this campaign is mentioned in A.W. Bk. V, B.335b; F.111–12. (Cp. also D. II.8.2.)

14. The Swiss were routed at Marignano, near Milan, by the French on 13 September 1515, and were forced to abandon Italy. 20,000 Swiss were engaged in this battle. Yet, when invaded, the Swiss had almost invariably been successful, e.g., at Schwyz in 1315 against Leopold of Bavaria, at Sempach in 1386 when Leopold III was slain, and twice in 1476 when invaded by Charles the Bold, who was killed in fighting the Swiss at Nancy in 1477. (Cp. D. II.10.3 and III.10.7.)

Cp. on taking the offensive or defensive in battle D. III.45, and cp. A.W. Bk. IV, 324a *sq.* and F.92–5.

Guicciardini *in loc.* objects that there are many points which Machiavelli has failed to consider; e.g. whether one's people are faithful or inclined to rebellion; whether towns are strong or weak; whether at home one has funds sufficient to sustain a long campaign; the strength of the enemy in his own country and abroad. It is one thing to say: I am carrying the war into the enemy's country; and another to say: I am relying on my own for food, and meeting the enemy abroad, as Ferrando did. To say 'I am beginning the war in his country before he has begun to attack me' is not the same thing as to say: 'I already have war in my own territory, but, to get the enemy to leave it, I am beginning to make war in his', as Scipio and Agathocles did, and as the Florentines often did in their wars with the Visconti. If one's own forces are weaker than those of the enemy it is impossible to make war in his country: hence in that case one should fight in one's own (which is what Machiavelli says in § 8, though it would seem that Agathocles' forces were weaker). 'The Romans always sought to make war in the enemy's country when they could; nor am I impressed by what the writer says about what would have happened to the Romans had they suffered three successive defeats abroad, for it would have been impossible for them to bring up two fresh armies immediately after their first defeat.'

Guicciardini's main point is that so much depends upon circumstances that it is impossible to formulate a general rule, and his argument here is sound. What he says about the impossibility of suffering three successive defeats abroad, however, will not hold, for Roman armies were defeated by the Cimbri under M. Junius Silanus in 109, under L. Cassius Longinus in 107, and under Q. Servilius Caepo and Cn. Mallius Maximus in 105. Machiavelli is aware of this, and hence in speaking of what would have happened to Rome had she suffered three successive defeats in Gaul is careful to add 'had they taken place in the same space of time'.

13. Men rise from a Low to a Great Position by Means rather of Fraud than of Force

1. Cp. P. 7, where Machiavelli says (towards the end) that no one who 'wants to make himself secure in a new principality against enemies, to win for himself friends, and to conquer either by force or by fraud'. . . can do better than take Caesar Borgia as his example. The terms used in this passage are the same as those which occur in the heading of this chapter '*o per forza o per fraude.*' Cp. also the famous passage at the beginning of P. 18 in which Machiavelli recommends to a prince the policy of the Fox and the Lion, 'for the lion cannot defend himself against snares nor the fox defend himself against wolves. Hence it is necessary to be a wolf in order to discover the snares, and a lion in order to terrify the wolves'. To rule by means of laws is the property of man, but man being what he is, this does not suffice. The ruler must also emulate the animals, and the two to choose are the lion on account of his ferocity and the fox on account of his subtlety. One must be prepared not only to use violence towards one's enemies, but also to deceive them and to break one's word, should this be in the interests of the state or of its government.—Cp. also D. I.18.4 (and note 6); also D. III.41; and H.F. III.13, where a plebeian remarks: 'If you note how men make their way in the world you will see that all who attain to great wealth and power, reach them by fraud or force, and, after attaining them, whether by deceit or violence, cloak the deformity of their acquisition under some decent disguise'. (Cp. also Guicciardini's comments at end of notes.)

2. The Philip of Macedon to whom Machiavelli here refers is Philip II (360–36) the father of Alexander, of whom he says in P. 12 that 'after the death of Epaminondas, he became commander of the Thebans, and, when victorious, deprived them of their liberty' (cp. Justin VIII.3). When mentioning Philip V, he speaks of him as Philip, the father of Perseus (cp. D. III.10; III.37). Philip II spent his youth in comparative obscurity in Thebes, but, when his brother was killed, escaped to Macedonia in 360 B.C., and became regent for his nephew, Amyntas, whose throne he soon usurped. Within a year, though surrounded by enemies, he had by bribery and other means made his position secure. He secured Athenian neutrality by leading the Athenians to believe he would restore to them Amphipolis, but when he had taken it, he declined to hand it over on the ground that they had not helped him. He was as skilled in the use of pretexts to secure alliances or to stave off hostilities as he was victorious in the field; hence his empire was built both on force and fraud (cp. D. I.26, n. 3.)

3. The same thing may be said of Agathocles, the son of a potter who became tyrant of Syracuse toward the close of the fourth century B.C., and who is taken by Machiavelli in *The Prince*, c. 8, as the type of a ruler who obtained his principality by wickedness (*per sceleratezza*). It was, however, for cruelty, rather than for fraud, that Agathocles became notorious. Machiavelli mentions but one instance of fraud, the ruse by which he got the principal citizens of Syracuse into his power and

murdered them, but adds that he also 'deceived his friends and broke his word'. This he certainly did. He promised, for instance, that he would respect the liberties of Syracuse, and then ruled it tyrannically and murdered several thousands of its citizens. To obtain money for his expedition to Africa when Syracuse was being besieged after his defeat at Himera, he promised to allow those who wished to avoid the siege, to leave the city, and then sent troops to murder and plunder them.

4. The story of Cyrus, founder of the Persian empire, as told by Xenophon in his *Cyropaedeia*, scarce bears out the theorem in support of which Machiavelli adduces it. Cyrus was the grandson of Astyages, who succeeded his father as king of Media in 594 B.C., and died *circa* 560, when, according to Xenophon, he was succeeded by his son Cyaxares II. If we accept Herodotus' story of Cyrus having been brought up by a peasant, he was in a sense of humble origin, but of this Xenophon says nothing. In I.6.27 his father tells him that, if he wishes to succeed, he must be 'full of wiles, a dissembler, crafty, deceitful, and a thief', but it is only against his enemies that he is to resort to deceit. It is Herodotus who explains how by deceit he stirred up a revolt against Astyages and thus became king of Media in 559 B.C. According to Xenophon Astyages was succeeded by his son, Cyaxares, under whom Cyrus served as a general. Having obtained Cyaxares' consent to lead an expedition against the king of Armenia who had failed to pay the promised tribute, he approached the territories of the enemy under the guise of going hunting; but, before attacking him, he sent a messenger to demand that the tribute be paid and to warn the king that he was in the neighbourhood with an armed force; 'thinking it more friendly', says Xenophon, 'to act thus rather than to march upon him without previous notice' (II.4.32). This can scarce be classed under the head of deceit. Nor, when friction arose between Cyrus and his uncle, who became jealous of Cyrus's successes to which he had contributed but little save in supplying him with troops and with funds, does Xenophon say that Cyrus acted either deceitfully or disloyally. He was accused of disloyalty in that he had led off most of the troops, while Cyaxares lay drunk, but for this he had good ground and Cyaxares is satisfied with his answer (IV.5.8-34).

5. Giovanni Visconti, Lord of Milan, died in 1354, leaving three nephews: Bernabo, who ruled Milan from 1354 to 1385; Galeazzo, who ruled Pavia from 1354 to 1378; and Matteo, who was murdered by the other two. Gian Galeazzo Sforza (the Galeazzo of the text) succeeded his father at Pavia in 1378, and murdered his uncle, Bernabo, in 1385, when he was created first Duke of Milan by the Emperor, Wenceslaus.

6. Cp. D. II.9.

7. The Samnite defeats were at Mount Glaurus and Suessela in 343 during the first Samnite war (Livy VII.33, 36, 37; for effect on Latins see 38.1).

8. Cp. D. II.9.2 and Livy VIII.2-3.

9. '*Nam etiam sub umbra foederis aequi servitutem pati possumus.*' Livy VIII.4.2, cited in Latin. In support of his contention that rulers must of necessity use fraud, if they wish to succeed, Machiavelli now cites the actions of the Romans themselves, and supports it by a statement put into the mouth of an enemy who is urging his people to make war on Rome. Such a statement is valueless unless it can be shown that the Romans *had* been using the policy of the Fox in their dealings with the Latins. There had been a treaty between Rome and the Latin League, known as the '*foedus Cassianum*', for which the traditional date is 496 B.C. Booty was to be shared

between the allies, and the generalissimo was to be chosen alternatively from the Romans and the Latins. Actually in the wars which followed the generalissimo was almost invariably a Roman, which was technically a breach of the treaty and meant that the prestige for victories went mainly to Rome. On the other hand, the Latins profited by the skill of the Roman generals and there was no attempt on Rome's part to govern her allies or to interfere with their laws and customs. Nor was there apparently any resentment until the Gallic invasion of 390 B.C., and Rome's temporary collapse. It then became apparent, says Livy, that 'Rome's allies looked upon her not only with hatred but contempt' (VI.2.4), and, from this time on, the Latins frequently helped her enemies, e.g. the Volsci in 389 (VI.2.3); Antium in 386 (*ib.* 6.4–5; 7.1–9); the Volsci again in 385 (*ib.* 12.6); and, when in 377 Antium came to terms, the Latins were so enraged that they burnt Satricum (*ib.* 33.4). All this was a violation, if not of the letter, at any rate of the spirit of the treaty with Rome, and against it the Romans more than once protested. Then, when in 358 there was a threat of a further Gallic invasion, the Latins asked for a renewal of the treaty and of their own accord sent troops to help Rome (VII.12.7); yet, in spite of this, they received in 349 a legation from Antium which had come for the express purpose of stirring them up to make war on Rome (VII.27.5). It was, then, not the Romans, but the Latins who were unfaithful to the treaty between Rome and Latium, as Livy points out in the closing words of Book VII (42.8). By its terms there was nothing to prevent the Latins going to war with whomsoever they pleased (VII.2.13); and the Romans respected their right so to do, as in the present case when they declined to help their allies, the Samnites, on whom the Latins made war in 341. There had been no '*deditio*' but only a '*foedus*' between the two peoples, and, except in the matter of the impracticable condition that generals should be appointed alternately from the two peoples, the Romans had loyally observed the treaty and had in no wise infringed the autonomy of Latium. Machiavelli, therefore, so far as Rome is concerned, has failed to make out his case. When the Romans gave their word, they usually kept it, and in consequence other peoples trusted them. Results, therefore—and it is only by results that political actions are to be judged according to Machiavelli—proved in their case that it pays to keep one's word. Nor were the successes of Cyrus due to the use of fraud; while Agathocles, who did use both violence and fraud, aroused such opposition that the soldiers murdered his sons, and after his death his regime collapsed. It is true that Philip II, the outstanding historical instance of the use of duplicity, was successful, and that Alexander was still more successful, yet in the end Macedonia succumbed to Rome. Moreover, since bribery was the chief kind of fraud practised by Alexander, and for this he collected huge funds, if his success justifies the theorem that fraud is essential to a rising man, it also justifies the theorem of Quintus Curtius that '*nervus gerendarum rerum pecunia est*' (cp. D. II.10, n. 2). That temporary success may be due to fraud is obvious, but the question at issue here is whether a greatness that endures can be secured by fraud, and this is certainly not proved by Machiavelli's argument.

Guicciardini *in loc.* writes: 'If the writer means by fraud any artifice (*astuzia*) or dissimulation the use of which does not involve guile (*dolo*), his conclusion may be true, i.e. force alone, I do not say never—which would be too precise—but very rarely leads men from low to great fortune. But if by fraud he means fraud properly so called, i.e. breach of faith or other guileful procedure, I think it will be found that there are many who have acquired very great kingdoms and empires without fraud. For instance, Alexander the Great and Caesar, who from private citizens rose to such greatness by using devices other than fraud, and who always openly admitted their ambition and their desire to rule. I have not looked up Xenophon, but I think Cyrus was instructed to use prudence, industry, and reasonable simulation or dissimulation, not fraud. Nor do I call it fraud on the part of the Romans to have made pacts with the Latins which made it possible for the latter to bear patiently their *imperium*; which they did, not because they failed to recognise right from the start that the guise of a confederation was tantamount to servitude, but because the realisation of their impotence and the way they were treated, which gave no ground for despair, made them wait, I do not say until the Romans' aim became plain, which it would have been very stupid of them not to recognise from the beginning, but until the number of their men should have so increased and they should have become so expert in military matters that they could hope to meet the Romans on equal terms. It was also prudent on the part of the Romans, not a fraud, to treat the Latins well; and I think it quite true that without using such devices and prudence not only will men very rarely rise from low to high fortune, but that they will also have difficulty in maintaining their high position. But, as to fraud, it is open to question whether it is always a good means to arrive at greatness; because, though by deceit many neat strokes are often brought about, getting a name for acting fraudulently often deprives one of the chance of attaining one's ends.'

Aristotle twice refers to force and fraud in *Politics,* Book V. In c. 4 he writes: 'Revolutions are effected in two ways, by force and by fraud. Force may be applied either at the time of making the revolution or afterwards. Fraud again is of two kinds; for (1) sometimes the citizens are deceived into a change of government and afterwards held in subjection against their will' . . . and (2) 'in other cases the people are persuaded at first, and afterwards by a repetition of the persuasion, their goodwill and allegiance are retained' (1304b, 8 *sq.*). In V.10, speaking of the reasons why monarchies fall, he says that in his day men are so fond of equality that they will not voluntarily submit to a monarchy, and 'anyone who obtains power by force or fraud is thought to be a tyrant' (1313a, 5-10).

14. Men often make the Mistake of supposing that Pride is overcome by Humility

1. Livy VIII.2.12.
2. '*Tentastis patientiam negando militem: quis dubitat exarsisse eos? . . . Pertulerunt tamen hunc dolorem. . . . Exercitus nos parare adversus Samnites, foederatos suos, audierunt, nec moverunt se ab urbe. Unde haec illis tanta modestia, nisi conscientia virium, et nostrarum et suarum?*' (VIII.4.7-10—abbreviated). The words given in Latin, are taken from the speech made in 340 B.C., from which the quotation in the last chapter was also taken. From Rome's forbearance Annius infers that the Romans are afraid of the Latins' growing power, and from the fact that this led to war Machiavelli infers that this forbearance was a mistake. It may well have been, however, Rome's respect for treaties in large part that induced her to show forbearance, and in any case the jealousy of the Latins was such that war was bound to come, whether or not the Romans showed forbearance. That Machiavelli should deprecate humility is char-

acteristic. The gospel teaching on humility was one of his main grounds for preferring paganism to Christianity (Cp. D. II.2.6.)

3. Cp. P. 19, where princes are recommended to avoid things likely to make
them either hated or contemptible in the eyes of their own subjects; and P. 21 where
princes are warned that those who, to avoid present dangers, adopt a neutral policy
are generally ruined (E.180).

Guicciardini *in loc.* objects that this theorem, as Machiavelli interprets it, is scarce
compatible with what he says in D. I.33 about the need of temporising when
danger threatens. This should be done when one's forces are not equal to those of
the enemy, but not when they are equal, which would be disastrous to one's
reputation, and would make the enemy more arrogant. It was on this ground that
Pericles always urged war with the Spartans.

15. The Decisions of Weak States are always fraught with Ambiguity, and the Slowness with which they arrive at them is Harmful

1. 'Ad summam rerum nostrarum pertinere arbitror, ut cogitetis magis quid agendum nobis,
quam quid loquendum sit. Facile erit, explicatis consiliis, accommodare rebus verba.' (Livy
VIII.4.1, cited in Latin.)
This is the third in a sequence of four theorems all based on the Latin revolt of
341 B.C., and, as in the two that precede it, so here there is a quotation from the
speech of Annius Setinus to the council of the Latins. The Romans asked for
ten, not for eight, representatives to be sent (VIII.3.8). Annius's speech is given
in VIII.4.1-11. Livy's brief account of the Lavinium incident is given in
VIII.11.2-4. The defeat to which it refers was the battle near Mount Vesuvius in
340 B.C.

2. Hieronymus, king of Syracuse, was murdered in 215 B.C. (cp. II.2.4 and
n. 5). For the advice Apollonides gave to the Syracusans during the second Punic
war, see Livy XXIV.28. He also advised them to stand by an alliance which had
lasted fifty years and brought happy results, i.e. their alliance with Rome. But in
214 Syracuse threw in its lot with Carthage and was besieged by Marcellus.

3. Livy VIII.11.2-4. 'Pro paulula via magnam mercedem Romanis esse solvendam'
—not quoted in Latin.

4. On his accession to the French throne in April 1498, Louis XII assumed the
title of Duke of Milan, made an agreement with Alexander VI, and an alliance
with the Venetians, preparatory to the invasion of Italy. Ludovico Sforza, then
ruling in Milan, had favoured the Florentine claim to Pisa and helped them both
with money and troops to stave off an attack by the Venetians. Hence, when Louis
was about to invade Italy there was a party in Florence favourable to the Duke and
hostile to the French alliance. The rapid advance of the French troops and the
capture of Milan in September 1499 placed Florence in an awkward position. In
October, however, she succeeded in arranging a fresh treaty with Louis by which
he was to support her against Pisa and she was to supply him with troops and
money for the invasion of Naples. No immediate change took place in the govern-

ment of Florence, but friction with France, which continued, may have had something to do with the appointment of Soderini as Gonfalonier for life in September 1502, since he was friendly to France. It was his vacillation that led to the revolution of 1512, when the Medici were restored with Spanish help.

5. See D. I.38.

Guicciardini *in loc.* suggests that the weakness of which Machiavelli is here speaking is in prudence and skill, though lack of power may be the cause of it. Anyhow, this kind of weakness is common alike to republics and princes. But weakness arising from the number of people with whom it rests to decide a point, and to conflicting opinions, which may be due to self-interest, is peculiar to a republic, and is also very harmful. Hesitation is, therefore, strongly to be deprecated, and decisiveness to be highly praised; and in like manner neutrality and delay in taking action is to be deprecated or praised according as it is due to hesitation or to a firm resolve.

16. How far the Discipline of Troops in our Day falls short of that maintained in Days gone by

1. At the battle of Veseris, near Mount Vesuvius, and then at Trifanum in 340 (Cp. Livy VIII.3.5 for the appointment of consuls, and VIII.10–11 for the battles.)

2. Cp. the speeches of Annius in VIII.4, and of Manlius in VIII.5.

3. VIII.6.14–15.

4. The two consuls had vowed to sacrifice themselves, should their troops waver. Those of P. Decius did so, whereupon he flung himself on the enemy and was killed (VIII.9). The son of Manlius Torquatus disobeyed orders by engaging in single combat with a Latin, whom he killed. His father ordered the Lictor to kill him (*ib.* 7.8–22). It is apropos of this incident that Livy says: '*adeo nihil apud Latinos dissonum ab Romana re praeter animos erat*' (ib. 8.2).

5. *ib.* 6.14–15. 6. cp. D. I.14.4; 15.1–3. 7. Livy VIII.6.

8. The three terms, probably of Etruscan origin, are equivalent to (i) vanguard, (ii) second line, (iii) rearguard. Cp. A.W. III.B.304, F.62–3; IV.B.320b, F.87.

9. '*Res redacta est ad triarios*', Livy VIII.8.11—cited in Latin.

10. Note the quite unnecessary adjective.

11. 11 April 1512, when the combined forces of Spain, Venice and the Pope were defeated by the French (see II.17, n. 2; and cp. A.W. II, B.287, F.35).

12. 21 May 1498. The Florentine commander was Count Ranuccio, who was replaced by Paolo Vitelli after the defeat.

13. Ciriaco dal Borgo of San Sepolcro had been in command of Florentine troops during the siege of Pisa.

Cp. P. 14 on keeping the army exercised in peace time; and P. 13 on the changes introduced into the French army since the time of Charles VII.

Cp. A.W. Bk. III. B.304–10; F.62–72, on the Roman method of drawing up an army. Cp. A.W. Bk. II, B.219–303; F.54–9, on the reasons for the present decline in military discipline.

Cp. also A.W. VII., B.356a; F.145, on the decline of military discipline throughout the world, and especially in Italy, where the art is lost; and for its cause see A.W. VII, B.366, F.161–2.

In P. 24 Machiavelli laments the deplorable state of Italy, and ascribes its lack of military virtue to the fact the old order of things has gone and no one has yet been able to find a new one (P. 24, E.212–13).

17. In what Esteem Artillery should be held by Armies at the Present Time, and whether the Opinion universally held in its Regard is Sound

1. During the war waged by the Holy League which had been formed in October 1511 against France, Brescia rebelled against the French and acknowledged the suzerainty of Venice. Venetian troops occupied the city on 2 February 1512, but the citadel held out. Gaston de Foix hurried to its relief, arrived before the city on 17 February, and on the 19th sacked it with terrible destruction and slaughter. Luigi da Porto says that the reason why the cavalry had to dismount was because the ground was covered with corpses (Bk. ii, Lett. 65). The number of killed was placed at between 8,000 and 14,000.

2. The victory of the French at Ravenna occurred two months after the sack of Brescia, namely, on 11 April 1512. The French forces under Gaston de Foix comprised 19,000 French and German infantry, 1,500 lances, 1,000 archers, and artillery supplied by the Duke of Ferrara. The confederate army comprised 13,500 infantry, 1,500 mounted spearmen, 14,000 lances, artillery and fifty newly invented scythed cars, called 'carri falcati.' It was under the command of Raymondo de Cardona, the Spanish viceroy, Pedro Navarro and two Colonnas. Hemmed in between two streams, the cavalry of the confederates was decimated by artillery fire and then routed by the French infantry. The Spanish infantry retreated in good order, and, in an attack which Gaston de Foix led against it, he was killed. The confederates lost about 12,000 men, and the French 4,000. Ravenna was taken and pillaged, and other towns fell. (For a fuller account, see Villari, Vol. II. c. 14.)

3. Ludovico Pico della Mirandola and his brother, Federigo, supported by Ercole I, duke of Ferrara, drove their brother, Gian Francesco, from Mirandola in 1502. When Venice was recovering some of the towns she had lost after the battle of Agnadello in 1509, she sent a fleet up to the Po to attack Ercole d'Este in Ferrara. Papal troops under the Cardinal d'Este marched to its relief, and Ludovico, one of its officers, was the only person killed. Subsequently the fleet was destroyed by artillery. This was in December 1509. (See Guicciardini, St. d'I. VIII.14; and cp. A.W. Bk. VII, B.354; F.143.)

4. Louis d'Armagnac, Duc de Nemours, was killed at Cerignuola on 28 April 1503, together with Chandieu, the commander of the Swiss contingent. They had rashly attacked the fortified camp of the Spaniards under Fernando de Andrada, who had just won a victory at Seminara. (Cp. A.W. Bk. IV, B.319; F.85.) Gaston de Foix was killed at Ravenna in 1512. Perault, a Spanish captain in the army of the Church, was also killed by a cannon-ball while patrolling the banks of the Panaro in 1511 (St. d'I. IX.17, p. 91).

5. At Novara on 6 June 1513 the Swiss, who had neither artillery nor cavalry, defeated the French under La Trémouille and Trivulzio, whose forces were three times as strong. (Cp. D. II.18, 7 and n. 6; and on the Swiss method of drawing up forces see A.W. Bk. III, B.305a; F.63–64.)

6. Thus in February 1512 after the Spaniards had retired from Bologna, Venetian troops were surprised by the French and all their artillery was captured.

7. The Turks fully appreciated the value of artillery. For the siege of Constantinople reputed to be the most strongly fortified city in Europe, Mahomet II in 1453 had seventy heavy pieces of artillery cast and one 'super-bombard' using balls 800 pounds in weight, which required sixty oxen to draw it. Selim I (1512–20) used artillery at Chaldiran against Ismail I, the Shah of Persia, in his campaign of 1514, and put chains between the cannon in order to prevent the enemy's cavalry getting through. He also used it against the Mameluk Sultan of Egypt and Syria, whom he defeated at Aleppo in 1516, and against his successor, Tumambeg, whom he defeated at Reydanieh near Cairo in January 1517. (For Selim, see D. I.1.9; I.19.3; and for the use of artillery cp. Oman, *The Art of War in the Middle Ages*, Vol. 2, Bk. XIII, c. 2, pp. 357–91.) The term 'Sophy' refers to the Shah of Persia, and the word 'Sultan' to the Mameluk sultan; the 'Turk' is Selim. The statement that the defeat of these rulers was due to their cavalry being disorganised by the noise, is without serious foundation. In A.W. IV, B.322a, F.89, it is ascribed to the use of musketry (*scoppietti*).

Cp. *The Art of War*, III, B.310–13; F.72–7, for the use of Artillery.

18. That Infantry should be more highly esteemed than Cavalry is shown by the Authority of the Romans and by the Example of Ancient Military Practice

1. 496 B.C.—Livy II.20.10–11.

2. 216 B.C.—XXII.49.3. The quotation is given both in Latin and in Italian. Usually these quotations are only in Latin.

3. Cp. the passage in P. 12 in which Machiavelli traces the development of 'Condottieri' from the time of Alberigo da Conio (d. 1409) who collected the famous Company of St. George and fought for Urban VI at Marino in 1379. The principle guiding them, he says, has always been 'to lower the credit of the infantry so that they might increase their own. They did this because, being without estates and dependent on their own industry, a few infantry would not win for them a reputation and they could not support many; so they had to employ cavalry in such numbers that they could manage to support them and thereby acquire a reputation, with the result that in an army of twenty thousand there would be but two thousand infantry'. Machiavelli is, of course, speaking only of Italian armies, but even so, he would seem to be exaggerating, and neither in *The Prince* nor in the *Discourses* does he cite any evidence in support of his statement that the infantry sometimes numbered but one in ten. The proportion of infantry in the 'Great Company' which Fra Moriale (Walter de Montreal) took over from Werner of Urslingen *circa* 1350, was two in nine; it comprised 2,000 crossbowmen and 7,000

mounted men at arms. A century later, in 1439, there was the same proportion in the army commanded by Francesco Sforza, namely, 2,000 infantry and 7,000 horse. (Cp. Oman, *The Art of War in the Middle Ages*, Vol. 2, Bk. 12, for the use of *condottieri* and the decline of infantry in Italy; and for Sforza, cp. Burd's *Il Principe*, note 2 on p. 270.)

4. Livy IX.22.10. In 315 B.C. during the second Samnite war Sora expelled its garrison but was retaken.

5. Machiavelli in this paragraph is trying to make out a case for the superiority of infantry over cavalry, but his account of Crassus is misleading. M. Licinius Crassus Dives, the *triumvir*, took a few towns from the Parthians in 54 B.C., but in the spring of 53 Parthian cavalry cut off his supplies and at Carrhae the Roman infantry were completely overwhelmed and routed by the cavalry and mounted archers commanded by Surenas. In 39 Mark Antony sent Ventidius Bassus to deal with the Parthians, and both in 39 and 38 he was successful for he chose always to fight on high ground. Pacorus, the Parthian general, was killed at Cyrrhestica in 38. (For the career of Marcus Crassus, see Plutarch's life, and for Crassus and Mark Antony, cp. A.W. Bk. II. B.288–9; F.37.)

6. The battle of Novara, of which mention was made in II.17.9, was fought on 6 June 1513. The Swiss had occupied Milan and other cities in the neighbourhood on behalf of Massimiliano Sforza after the expulsion of the French in 1512. The Milanese were discontented under Swiss rule, which was both costly and disorderly. Louis XII had been reconciled with Venice and to recover Milan sent an army into Italy under Louis de la Trémouille and Trivulzio. The Venetians advanced. Genoa revolted and joined the French. By the end of May there remained to the Swiss only Como and Novara, in which they were being besieged. They had neither artillery nor cavalry, but had received reinforcements. On the 6th they attacked under cover of a wood, and the French, who had both cavalry and artillery, were routed, leaving eight thousand dead on the field. Without cavalry the Swiss could not pursue them, so the remains of the army got back to France, leaving their artillery and their stores behind.

7. At the battle of Marignano on 13 September 1515.

8. 255 B.C. Polybius gives an account of this battle in I.33–4. Regulus had been left in Africa to continue the war against Carthage. He defeated Hasdrubal, Bostar and Hamilcar, when the Spartan general, Xanthippus, appeared on the scene, rallied the Carthaginians' forces, and with 4,000 cavalry and 100 elephants supported by 12,000 infantry, overwhelmed the Roman infantry, of whom 30,000 were slain and only 2,000 escaped. Among the 500 prisoners taken was Regulus himself. The Carthaginians lost about 800 of their mercenaries. Polybius mentions that the Romans were afraid of the elephants, and had made special dispositions to meet them. He ascribes the victory to the one man whose brain devised the tactics whereby a vastly inferior force used its cavalry and its elephants in such a way as to crush an infantry which was supposed to be invincible. Machiavelli makes too light of this incident. (Xanthippus is mentioned in A.W. Bk. IV, B.319b; F.85.)

9. For the career of Francesco Bussone, Count of Carmagnuola, one of the most famous *condottieri* of the fifteenth century, see Burd, *Il Principe,* note 1 to page 264. He was born in 1390, fought the Swiss at Arbedo in 1422, when in the service of the Duke of Milan; declined to disband his troops in 1423, and fled to Venice; became Captain-General of the combined Venetian and Florentine forces in 1426

(cp. H.F. IV.13); won the decisive battle of the campaign on 11 October 1427; released the 2,000 Milanese prisoners he had taken to the disgust of Venice; again became Captain-General in 1431, but failed to co-operate with the fleet Venice had sent up the Po against Milan; was decoyed to Venice and executed on 5 May 1432. Cp. P. 12 (Burd 264, E. 101), A.W. Bk. II, B.286; F. 33, where we are told that, when in command of the forces of the Duke of Milan, Carmagnuola caused his troops to dismount in order to fight the Swiss infantry.

10. For an account of the battle of Arbedo, 30 June 1422, see Oman, *Hist. of the Art of War in the Middle Ages*, Vol. II, pp. 262–3. The Swiss invaded the territory of Filippo Maria Visconti with a force of between 2,000 and 4,000 men, mainly halberdiers and pikemen. Carmagnuola had a much stronger force, comprising 6,000 horse and several thousand foot. The Swiss repelled the cavalry attack, but were unable to resist the attack of the infantry when reinforced by the dismounted men-at-arms. The Swiss put their losses at 400 men. The Italian account was different. According to Machiavelli, *The Art of War*, Bk. II (B.286; F.33), the Swiss numbered 18,000 and Carmagnuola had but 6,000 horse and a small body of foot, and of the Swiss 15,000 were slain and the rest surrendered. Anyhow, Machiavelli's main point holds good: the battle was won by infantry and dismounted cavalry after the cavalry alone had proved unsuccessful.

Cp. A.W. Bk. II. B.288–94; F.37–40, for the superiority of infantry over cavalry. Cp. A.W. Bk. III, B.313b, F.16; IV, B.319b–321a; F.87–8; and D. II.17.8 on the use of elephants.

19. Acquisitions made by Republics, when not well Governed nor handled with the Virtue the Romans displayed, contribute to the Downfall, not to the Advancement, of such Republics

1. Cp. D. II.17.9; 18.7.
2. The battle in which Lucullus defeated Tigranes, king of Armenia, took place on 6 October 69 B.C., near Tigranocerta, the new capital which the king had built and to which he had sent 300,000 captives taken in Cappadocia in 76 B.C. Lucullus, instead of awaiting the king's attack, crossed the Euphrates and Tigris, and invaded Armenia. Tigranes retired to the mountains and Lucullus besieged Tigranocerta. This caused the king to return and give battle. Plutarch in his *Life of Lucullus* says Tigranes had, not 150,000 cavalry, but 150,000 infantry and 55,000 cavalry, of which 17,000 were completely clad in steel, except for their legs and thighs, at which the Romans hacked. Lucullus had 24 cohorts, comprising 10,000 men, about 3,000 horse, but only 1,000 archers and slingers as compared with the 20,000 Tigranes had. The heavy-armed cavalry were driven back on the infantry. Of the enemy 10,000 were killed and but few horsemen escaped. The Romans lost 5 killed and 100 wounded. Tigranocerta was captured, and the Greek captives sent back home. (*ib.* 24–8; cp. A.W. Bk. II, B.288a; F.35 for the battle between Tigranes and Lucullus.)

3. Cp. D. I.6.7–8 on the way in which republics should be governed if they do not propose to expand.

4. Cp. D. I.6.9, where Machiavelli points out that states, such as Sparta and Venice, which did not intend to expand, may find themselves compelled by circumstances to do so.

5. The first German emperor was Otto I, a Saxon, who was crowned emperor by John XII on 31 January 962. From this time on the Empire remained in German hands. By the Golden Bull of 1356 the electors were finally fixed. Three of the seven were ecclesiastics, namely, the archbishops of Mainz, Cologne and Trier, and four were lay princes, the King of Bohemia, the Count Palatine, the Duke of Saxony and the Margrave of Brandenburg (cp. Aquinas, *de Regimine*, III.19).

6. The first Swiss confederation was formed between the three forest cantons of Uri, Schwytz and Unterwalden in 1291. They defeated Duke Leopold of Hapsburg at Morgarten in 1315. Lucerne joined the confederation in 1319. In 1339 Bern solicited the help of the confederation against a league of princes from whom it was striving to acquire territory, and at Laupen the confederates were victorious. Zürich joined in 1351; Zug and Glarus in 1352; Bern in 1353. The confederates sought to take Sempach, which belonged to Duke Leopold the Valiant. At Sempach in July 1386 the Swiss counted 667 corpses, almost all of them great lords or of noble blood, amongst them Leopold himself. (For details of the battles, see Oman, *op. cit.* II.11.1, pp. 233 *sq.*) Fribourg fought against the confederates in this battle, but joined with them in fighting Charles the Bold who had acquired many of the Hapsburg dominions, at Granson and Morat in 1476. It became a member of the Confederation in 1481. (On the freedom of German cities cp. Aquinas, *de Regimine* IV.1.)

7. The Empire and the House of Hapsburg became 'identical' from the time of Albert V, Archduke of Austria, who was elected emperor under the title, Albert II, in 1438. On his death he was succeeded by Frederick of Styria, a distant cousin, who became Frederick III, and whose son was Maximilian.

8. Venice became mistress of the greater part of Lombardy during the dogeship of Francesco Foscari (1423–56) after the war with Filippo Maria Visconti (1412–47), when she acquired Brescia and Bergamo and extended her dominions eastward to the Adda. Florence can scarce be said to have become mistress of Tuscany in the time of Cosimo de' Medici (d. 1464), for in 1452–3, during the war with Alfonso of Naples, her territories were overrun. She may, however, be said to have 'held Tuscany' (*aveva la Toscana*) during the rule of Lorenzo the Magnificent (1469–92), of whom Machiavelli says that 'he erected among the mountains towards Bologna the stronghold of Firenzuola; while towards Siena he began to build Poggio Imperiale, which he made extremely strong. By the acquisition of Pietrasanta and Sarzana he had closed the coast road from Genoa against enemies. Moreover, by grants and subsidies he kept the Baglioni in Perugia, and the Vitelli in Città di Castello, his friends, while the government of Faenza was entirely in his hands. All which arrangements served, as it were, as strong ramparts of his city.' (H.F. VIII.36.) This was from 1487 to 1492, after which Florence again became a prey to war and civil disturbances. Venice began to look for a land empire after her struggle with Genoa and with the Turks, for she had no means of getting grain or meat except by the sea, or by purchase from neighbouring states. She overran Padua, Verona, and Vicenza in 1426–9, and then took Bergamo and Brescia,

which gave rise to the League of Cambray, and so to her downfall at Agnadello in 1510. Machiavelli's argument is that neither Venice nor Florence benefited by their conquests because they acquired only territory, not forces for its defence, since they did not absorb the inhabitants of the conquered lands or enrol them in their armies. Consequently, Venice was better off when she was but a sea-power, and Florence when she was a small city without dependencies. The old line of walls in Florence dated from 1078. The new walls were begun in 1284. Dante refers to the ancient circle of walls (*cerchia antica*) and to the simplicity and happiness of the people who dwelt therein in *Il Paradiso* XV.97–9. It is possible that Machiavelli has this passage in mind; but his argument, Guicciardini claims, is quite invalid (see below).

9. For the effect of the luxurious life of Capua on the Roman troops, see Livy VII.38–41. This occurred after its relief in 343 B.C. (Cp. D. II.20.2–3.)

10. For the effect of Capua on Hannibal's troops when they wintered there in 216 B.C., see Livy XXIII.18.10–16.

11. '*Iam tunc minime salubris militari disciplinae Capua, instrumentum omnium voluptatum, delinitos militum animos avertit a memoria patriae*' (VII.38.5, cited in Latin, but Teubner reads *delenitos* for *delinitos*).

12. '*gula et luxuria incubuit, victumque ulcisicitur orbem*'. *Satires*, VI.291–2—cited in Latin; but the text of Juvenal does not contain the words '*gula et*'.

Guicciardini makes no comment on chapters 16 to 18, so presumably he is in agreement with what Machiavelli says on the question of the decline of discipline in the army and on the relative value of infantry, artillery and cavalry. He dissents, however, in his comments on D. III.19, from the conclusions at which Machiavelli arrives. 'Who', he asks, 'can doubt that the city of Florence and the Venetian republic would have been much weaker and less powerful than they are if their territory had been restricted to narrow confines? When they acquired neighbouring cities and enlarged their jurisdiction, it was not easy for any neighbour to attack them.' Other advantages also accrued. Moreover, to be defended by hired troops is better than not to be defended at all. 'I grant that a republic which has its own troops is more powerful and more capable of making acquisitions; but I cannot admit that an unarmed republic becomes weaker the more it acquires, nor that Venice which then feared neither king nor emperor, would have been more secure without its conquests on land and sea than it is at present.' If it were true, it should be true also of princes who have not their own forces, that they become weak when they acquire dominions which is manifestly false.

20. On the Dangers which accrue to the Prince or the Republic that employs Auxiliary or Mercenary Troops

1. Cp. P. 12 and P. 13.

2. For the first battle at Mount Gaurus, see Livy VII.32–3. The minor engagement mentioned in 36.9–13 is omitted. For the other battle at Suessula called by Livy the third, see 37.4–17. For the behaviour of the troops who remained at Capua, see 38–41. The date is 343–2 B.C.

3. Cp. D. III.6.43.

4. Cp. Polybius I.7: 'The people of Rhegium, when Pyrrhus crossed to Italy

[280 B.C.], felt a double anxiety. They were dismayed at the thought of his approach and were afraid of the Carthaginians as being masters of the sea. They accordingly asked for and obtained a force to guard and support them. The garrison, four thousand in number, under the command of a Campanian named Decius Jubellius, entered the city in 280 and for a time protected it loyally. But in 279, conceiving the idea of imitating the Mamertines, and having obtained their co-operation, broke faith with the people of Rhegium, enamoured of the pleasant site and the private wealth of the citizens, and seized the city after having, in imitation of the Mamertines, first driven out some of the people and put others to the sword.' On Pyrrhus' death Fabricius retook Rhegium in 270 and sent 300 of the rebel garrison to Rome, where they were executed. (Cp. also Livy, *Epitome* XII.)

On mercenaries, cp. P. 12 and A.W. Bk. I. B.273b; F.12. Also cp. Polybius VI.52: 'In regard to military service the Romans train themselves to a much higher standard than do the Carthaginians. The former devote their whole attention to this, whereas the Carthaginians neglect altogether their infantry, though they take some slight interest in their cavalry. The reason for this is that they use foreign and mercenary troops, whereas the Romans use their own citizen troops. In this respect, therefore, the latter are more worthy of praise than the former, for the former always base the hope of their own freedom on the courage of mercenaries, whereas the Roman republic bases it on the valour of her own people and on the assistance of allies; with the result that, though at the start a grievous disaster may be incurred, the Romans soon have whole armies going again, which the Carthaginians are unable to do.'

Cp. also Isocrates, the author on whose *'Nicocles'* the Dedication of *The Prince* to Lorenzo de' Medici is based according to Ellinger (p. 13). In his *De Pace* he says of his own city of Athens in 356 B.C.:

'To such a pitch of folly have we come that, although we ourselves are in want of daily necessities, we have set ourselves to feed mercenaries, and we afflict and tax all our own allies so as to have pay for the common enemies of mankind. Such is our inferiority to our ancestors, not only to those ancestors who won glory for themselves but also to those who won hatred, that, whereas they on occasion of war judged they ought to risk their own lives for what seemed right, and this though the Acropolis was full of silver and gold, we, who are in complete penury and are many in number, none the less make use of hired battalions like the Great King.' (*De Pace*, 46-7.)

On auxiliaries, cp. P. 13.

On *condottieri* cp. D. II.18, n. 9; P. 12 (E.100-4; Burd, notes to pp. 260-9); and A.W. Bk. I, B.273b; F.12. Cp. also A.W. Bk. VII. B.364-5; F. 159-60, where in reply to the question whether it is possible to restore the ancient discipline, the answer given is that nothing is easier, provided you have your own troops. But with foreign troops it is impossible for 'what can one do with men who go about gaming, drinking, whoring, and swearing . . . swearing by God and the saints, though whether by those they adore or those they abuse I know not. . . . How can those who neglect God have any respect for men? . . .'

21. *The First Praetor the Romans sent out was to Capua, Four Hundred Years after they had first begun to make War*

1. Cp. D. II.19.2–3, 7–9.

2. The term 'praetor'—from *'prae-itor'*, leader—was at first used in order to designate the supreme leaders in the republic, i.e. the consuls. Later, within the college of praetors a distinction was made between those who led armies forth to wars, the consuls, and those who were concerned with administration and justice, the praetors of the city. The praetorship became a distinct magistracy according to Livy in 366 B.C. (VII.1.1; cp. VI.42.11).

3. The praetor exercised the functions of a *'custos urbis'*, and it was in order to exercise precisely this function that in 317 B.C. Capua asked for a praetor as 'a remedy against intestinal disorder', and L. Furius was sent there (IX.20.5; but Livy says *'praefectus'*, not 'praetor').

4. Antium asked for magistrates in the same year and the *patroni* of the colony were appointed (IX.20.10).

5. *'quod jam non solum arma, sed jura romana pollebant'* (IX.20.10, cited in Latin).

6. Genoa became subject to Filippo Visconti of Milan in 1421 (H.F. IV.3–4); but revolted in 1435 (*ib.* V.6–7). In 1456 Alfonso of Naples attacked it both by land and sea, and the Doge, Pietro Fregoso, 'fearing he might not be able to withstand the king's attack, decided to make a gift of what he could not himself hold to someone who could hold it against his enemies . . . He therefore sent envoys to Charles VII, offering him the Lordship of Genoa. Which offer Charles accepted, and sent King René's son, John of Anjou . . . to take over possession' (*ib.* VI.35). Fregoso afterwards fell out with the Duke but was killed in an attempt to expel him in 1459 (*ib.* 37). In 1464 Francesco Sforza of Milan was invested with the Lordship of Genoa by Louis XI (*ib.* VII.7); but in 1478 it rebelled and regained its independence (*ib.* VIII.13). It was now ruled by an oligarchy favourable to France and to the French claim to Naples; but in 1507, the populace, encouraged by Julius II and Maximilian, revolted, overthrew the nobles and replaced the lilies of France by the Imperial eagle (cp. D. II.24.9). Louis XII retaliated by crossing at once to Italy; whereupon Genoa surrendered at discretion. It was united to the Royal domain, the republican leaders were executed, and a French governor was installed. But in 1512 there was a further revolt, and the castle was handed over to the Genoese by the French governor in return for 10,000 ducats. The Lantern still remained in French hands, but an attempt to revictual it in 1513 was repulsed by Andrea Doria. Later in the same year Gianluigi dal Fiesco was killed by the Doge's brother, and the Fieschi, making common cause with the Adorni and France, attacked the town, expelled the Doge and murdered his brother, who was dragged through the town at the tail of a horse. Genoa then submitted to France and Antonetto Adorno was appointed Doge. But after the defeat of the French at Novara, Genoa again acquired its liberty and Ottaviano Fregoso was appointed Doge. In 1515, however, he found himself threatened alike by Francis I, who was preparing to invade Italy, and by Milan and the Swiss, so he decided to come to terms with Francis, acknowledged French suzerainty, and, on resigning his position as Doge, was appointed governor by Francis I. It is presumably to this appointment that Machiavelli here refers. (But cp. also D. II.24.9 and notes 10 and 11; and for

an account of the above incidents, see Guicciardini's *Storia d'Italia, passim*. The last incident will be found in XII. 11, pp. 345–6.)

7. When, after the departure of the Emperor Louis of Bavaria, Castruccio made himself Lord of Pisa, the 'Florentines got possession of Pistoia by an arrangement with the citizens' (H.F. II.30). This was in 1328. Castruccio then seized Pistoia and held it for a time; but it returned to the Florentine allegiance, as it did also in 1343 after having joined with other towns which had revolted against Florence (*ib*. 38.)

8. Of Florence's attempt to seize Lucca in 1437, Machiavelli says that as her forces moved towards the city they 'destroyed all the grain and other crops, burned country houses, cut down trees and vines, carried off cattle, and, in short, left nothing undone that it is usual or possible to do against an enemy' (H.F. V.11). When Carlo of Perugia was permitted to attack Siena in 1477, the Sienese, 'always ready to think evil of the Florentines, persuaded themselves that everything that had been done was done with their consent, and made endless complaints to the Pope and to the king'. The Florentines disclaimed responsibility and bade Carlo do no more, yet the Sienese 'continued full of resentment against them, thinking that to be freed from an evil by those who had first contrived it, entailed no obligation on their part,' (*ib*. VII.32). For Pisa, see Index *sub voce* 'Pisa'.

Cp. (on the point made in § 3) Aristotle, *Politics* V.11: A king 'should distribute honours himself, but punishment should be inflicted by officers and courts of law' (1315a, 6–8).

22. How frequently Erroneous are the Views Men adopt in regard to Matters of Moment

1. See D. III.16.

2. L. Numicius was one of two praetors sent by the general congress of Latin cities in 340 B.C., to suggest that the Romans and the Latins should combine to form one people on equal terms (Livy VIII.3.9–10). Numicius' rank was equivalent to that of a Roman consul. When the proposal was turned down, war broke out and the Latins were beaten at Mount Vesuvius. They fled to Minturnae, rallied there and moved on to Vescia, where Numicius urged them to re-form and to continue the war, '*in conciliis Numicius, imperator eorum, ad renovandum bellum principes excitabat*'. It was only in name that the Romans had won a victory, he said; if the youth from the Latins and the Volsci were now to fall on them, when least they expected it, the Romans would be defeated. But, instead, it was Manlius Torquatus who at Trifanum won the day (Livy VIII.11.5–12 and cp. § 5 below).

3. When Cardinal Giovanni de' Medici, then only in deacon's orders, became Leo X in March 1513, Carpi, the Emperor's ambassador in Rome, wrote: 'The Pope will act as a gentle lamb rather than a fierce lion . . . With the exception of war against the infidels, he will not be drawn into any other except under grave provocation, and when, as it were, forced to it.' (*Lettres de Louis XII*, iv. 79, cited by Pastor, *Hist. Popes* VII, pp. 27–8). This estimate of Leo's character was fully justified by the event, but it involved him in the most intricate and tortuous diplomacy. Machiavelli is undoubtedly right when he says that Leo 'wanted to restore

Italy to its former freedom', but, if this was to be done, the two main powers of which he had to get rid were not those of France and the Swiss, but those of France and Spain. What Julius II had striven with all his might to accomplish seemed to have been in part brought about. In 1512 Francesco Vettori, Machiavelli's friend, wrote that: 'the soldiers of Louis XII have vanished like mist before the sun' without having fought a single battle or defending a single town (Vettori, *Storia d'Italia*, 287, cited by Pastor in VI, p. 416). This, however, had made Spain the dominant power in Italy, for Ferdinand was not only King of Naples but in the north held Milan, Genoa, and portions of the territory of Venice. The 'deliverance of Italy from the barbarians' was celebrated in July 1512, when by the Bull of 6 July the Swiss were declared to be 'the Protectors of the liberty of the Church'. They had, however, brought to Italy only 18,000 men. Hence the real danger lay with Spain, and was intensified when, in March 1514, Louis XII signed a year's truce with Ferdinand and offered his daughter's hand to one of Ferdinand's grandsons. Against a Franco-Spanish combination Italy would be powerless. To prevent it Leo opened negotiation with Louis. A league was to be formed between Leo X, France, Venice, Florence, and Ferrara to drive the Spaniards from Italy. But in August Louis signed the Treaty of London with Henry VIII. This guaranteed Milan and Genoa to France, which was already making preparations for a fresh invasion of Italy. It was at this juncture that Leo found himself 'sailing to meet the crisis with two compasses'. While still negotiating with Louis, he signed in September a secret treaty with Ferdinand by which each party guaranteed the other security in its Italian possessions. Meanwhile, through Vettori, the Pope had sought Machiavelli's advice. It was that neutrality would be the worst policy. The victory of France was practically certain, unless Venice deserted the French alliance. Hence his best policy was to support the French (Pastor, VIII, p. 105). Florence advised him to the same effect, suggesting that he should join the Franco-Venetian alliance. On 1 January 1515, Francis I succeeded Louis XII. He renewed the alliance with Venice, and in April signed a treaty with England. By July he had assembled an army of 35,000 men, and in August he had crossed the Alps by a pass which the Swiss had left unguarded, since they did not think it possible for the French to use it (cp. D. I.28.5). The Swiss attacked him at Marignano, but were defeated and fled.

Apart from the rumour which Machiavelli mentions, there is no evidence that Leo thought it best to let the French and the Swiss fight it out, and then fall on the victor. On the contrary he had taken sides, for the Swiss were in his pay, and in July he had at last joined the League formed by the Emperor, Spain, Milan and the Swiss against Francis. Nor did Francis solicit his help. Louis XII had done so, shortly before his death, but the Pope had put him off, declaring that a war between Christian princes would be intolerable. Francis, on the other hand, had rejected the proposal made by Ludovico di Canossa on behalf of the Pope, that Leo should support him on condition that he would waive his claim to Naples, for in this he saw but an attempt on Leo's part to gain the crown for his brother, Giuliano. Hence the main point for which Machiavelli is contending in this chapter, namely, that it is a mistake to await the issue of conflict between two powers in order that both may be eliminated, one by the victor, and the other by falling on his victorious troops, may be sound, but is not borne out by the evidence adduced in the case of Francis and Leo. It is borne out only in so far as Leo, in spite of Machiavelli's advice to the contrary, waited, expecting until almost the last moment that the

French would either drop the project of invasion, or, if they went on with it, would lose. Hence his delay in joining the league against France.

Cp. P. 21 (Burd 341 and see note; E.178–9) for further remarks on the folly of remaining neutral.

23. When Events required that the Romans should pass Judgment on Subject Peoples they avoided a Middle Course

1. Contrary to the famous dictum of Aristotle that 'virtue lies in the mean,' Machiavelli holds that in many cases it lies in the extremes. Cp. D. I.6.10; 26.3 and D. III.21 and 22.

2. '*Jam Latio is status erat rerum, ut neque pacem neque bellum pati possent*' (Livy VIII.13.2, cited in Latin).

3. Cp. D. II.10, *passim*.

4. The Romans in 341 B.C. came to terms with the Samnites, but Rome's allies, the Latins, continued the war, and declined to make peace when the Romans at the request of the Samnites intervened on their behalf. (Livy, VIII.2). To the demand of the Latins that they and the Romans should become one people on equal terms, the Romans gave a negative answer (*ib.* 4 and 5). Hence war broke out, a war that was almost a civil war, because the two peoples were so much alike (*ib.* 8.2). The Romans under Titus Manlius and Publius Decius gained a victory at Mount Vesuvius in 340 (*ib.* 8.9 to 10.14). Driven from the field, the Latins sought to rally their forces but were again defeated at Trifanum (*ib.* 11.11), and in the following year the whole of Latium was subdued by Lucius Furius Camillus (*ib.* 13). The peace which the Latins ought not to have made (cp. § 1), is the renewal of their alliance with Rome in 357, when the Romans had been hard pressed by the Gauls for three years, had been at war with the Hernici for four years, and had just declared war on the Tarquinii (Livy VII.12); for the Roman dominions had at this epoch shrunk considerably and in the maritime part of Campania the frontier was but twenty-five miles from Rome. The war which they should have avoided is the war herein described, a war which occurred seventeen years later.

5. '*Dii immortales ita vos potentes hujus consilii fecerunt, ut, sit Latium an non sit, in vestra manu posuerint. Itaque pacem vobis, quod ad Latinos attinet, parare in perpetuum, vel saeviendo vel ignoscendo potestis. Vultis crudelius consulere in dedititios victosque? licet delere omne Latium. Vultis, exemplo majorum, augere rem Romanam, victos in civitatem accipiendo? materia crescendi per summam gloriam suppeditat. Certe id firmissimum imperium est, quo obedientes gaudent. Illorum igitur animos, dum expectatione stupent, seu poena seu beneficio praeoccupari oportet*' (Livy VIII.13.14–17—cited in Latin, as also are the quotations which follow).

6. On the treatment of conquered towns cp. D. II.21.1–3; 30.7; P. 5, E.39: contrast with their treatment by a tyrant in D. I.26; P. 5, E.40.

7. '*Quam poenam meritos Privernates censeret.*'—'*Eam quam merentur qui se libertate dignos censent.*'—'*Quid si poenam remittimus vobis, qualem nos pacem vobiscum habituros speremus?*'—'*Si bonam dederitis, et fidelem et perpetuam; si malam, haud diuturnam.*'—'*Se audivisse vocem et liberi et viri; nec credi posse ullum populum, aut hominem, denique in eq*

conditione cujus eum poeniteat, diutius quam necesse sit, mansurum. Ibi pacem esse fidam, ubi voluntarii pacati sint, neque eo loco ubi servitutem esse velint, fidem sperandam esse.'—'Eos demum qui nihil praeterquam de libertate cogitant, dignos esse, qui Romani fiant.' (Livy VIII.21—the date is 330 B.C.).

8. Livy IX.3. Instead of acting in accordance with the old man's advice, the Samnite commander, Pontius, when the Romans refused to admit that they were a conquered people, ordered every man in the legions that had surrendered, to be disarmed and to 'pass under the yoke', clad in but a single garment (IX.4.3). The yoke consisted of two upright spears across which was placed a third. To pass under it was the recognised symbol of servitude. The first to pass under the yoke, says Livy in IX.6, were the consuls, half naked; then each officer according to his rank, and finally the troops. Meanwhile the Samnites, carrying their arms, stood on either side, jeering at them and mocking them, while some thrust at them with their swords. Many of the Romans who resented the indignity and showed it in their looks, were wounded or killed (321 B.C.).

9. See D. III.41–42.

In *The Prince*, c. 3 (E.19) Machiavelli says of men in general that they 'ought to be either well treated or crushed'. So, too, in c. 5 (E.39), but there we are told that there are three ways of dealing with states accustomed to live under their own laws. 'The first is to ruin them, the next is to reside there in person; the third is to permit them to live under their own laws, drawing a tribute, and establishing amongst them an oligarchy so as to keep them friendly to you.' Presumably the method of 'residing in person', like that of sending out colonies, mentioned in c. 3, falls under the head of good treatment, since otherwise we must class it as ill treatment or else admit a middle course. Anyhow, in *The Prince* three ways are given, not two.

On avoiding a middle course, see Index *sub* 'Middle course'. Also compare the policies recommended by Cleon and Diodotus, respectively, in regard to the treatment of Mytilene (Thucydides III.36–48). Cleon advocated severity, Diodotus leniency. In his speech the latter says: 'We ought not to act hastily out of a mistaken reliance on the security which the penalty of death affords. Nor should we drive our rebellious subjects to despair. They must not think that there is no place for repentance, or that they may not at any moment give up their mistaken policy. Consider: at present, although a city may actually have revolted, when she becomes conscious of her weakness she will capitulate while still able to defray the cost of the war and to pay tribute for the future; but, if we are too severe, will not the citizens make better preparations, and when besieged, resist to the last, knowing that it is all the same whether they come to terms early or late? Shall not we ourselves suffer? For we shall waste money by sitting down before a city which refuses to surrender; when the place is taken it will be a mere wreck, and we shall in future lose the revenues derived from it' (III.46). (Cp. Machiavelli's remarks on the revolt of Pisa and of Arezzo in D. I.38.5–6.)

24. Fortresses in General are much more Harmful than Useful

1. Cp. *The Prince*, c. 20, which is headed: 'Whether citadels and many other devices of which princes make constant use today are or are not of any avail.' It is

mainly, however, with the other devices that Machiavelli is concerned in *The Prince*, such as whether a new prince should or should not disarm his subjects; and should or should not create factions amongst them—questions which Aristotle raises in his *Politics*, 1311a and 1313b. The answer to these and kindred questions agrees with what he says in the present discourse, and is neatly summed up in the statement that 'the prince who has more fear of his own people than of foreigners ought to build fortresses, but the prince who has more fear of foreigners than of his own people should leave them alone'. The term used for fortresses is *'fortezze'*, which in the Latin heading of P. 20 is rendered by *'arces'*. They comprise both citadels built to dominate a town and castles built to control the countryside or a port, for neither of which has Machiavelli any use. The case of the Vitelli, of Guidobaldo, Duke of Urbino, of the Bentivogli, of Francesco Sforza, and the case of Pisa, are cited both in this discourse and in *The Prince*. But in *The Prince* we have also the case of Pandolfo Petrucci of Siena who relied on those who were looked on by others with suspicion; of Pistoia which was held by factions; and of the Countess of Forli: while in the present discourse we have the Roman incidents and that of Genoa, a comparatively recent incident of which *The Prince* makes no mention. Furthermore to fortresses proper *The Prince* devotes but the concluding section of P. 20, whereas in the present discourse fortresses constitute the main topic of a very long chapter, and the question how subjects should be treated is subordinated to this issue. The reference to the Latins and to the city of Privernum, whose loyalty was secured not by means of fortresses but by the establishing of colonies and the grant of citizenship, connects it with the previous chapter. But the folly of constructing fortresses suggests to Machiavelli other mistakes made in connection with war. Hence in the next chapter he returns to Livy, Book II, and bases chapters 25 and 26 on the mistakes made in the Etruscan war therein described.—For the fidelity of the Latins see Livy VIII.20.12–21.

2. *'Spoliatis arma supersunt'*—Juvenal, *Satires* VIII.124.
'Furor arma ministrat'—Virgil, *Aeneid* I.150.
Both quotations are given in Latin.

3. Cp. D. II.17.3–4.

4. Francesco Sforza, head of one of the two chief military schools in Italy, acquired the Duchy of Milan in 1450 (H.F. VI.24), three years after the death of his father-in-law, Filippo Maria Visconti, who was Duke from 1412 to 1447. On his death in 1466 he was succeeded by his son, Galeazzo Maria, who ended his tyrannical career in 1476 by getting himself stabbed to death (H.F. VII.34). He left a boy, Gian Galeazzo, with whom the direct line came to an end, for the dukedom was usurped by his uncle, Ludovico Sforza il Moro. (Cp. A.W. Bk. I, B.270b, F.8 for Francesco Sforza and see Geneaological Table XIIb.)

5. When Louis XII invaded Italy in 1499 Ludovico Moro fled with his brother, Ascanio Sforza, to Germany; Milan was taken on 11 September by the French army, and the citadel surrendered a few days later. In 1500 Ludovico returned to Milan at the invitation of its inhabitants, but was defeated by the French near Novara, taken prisoner, and died in prison ten years later. In 1512 the French retired from Milan when 20,000 Swiss advanced, and Maximilian Sforza, the son of Ludovico Moro, became its puppet duke; but after the battle of Marignano in 1515, he failed to hold the citadel, which surrendered on 4 October, a fortnight

later, to the French. Hence to the Sforzas, who were notoriously tyrannical in their conduct, Milan's citadel proved useless against an invading army.

6. Guidobaldo da Montefeltro became Duke of Urbino in 1482. On 21 June 1502 Urbino was taken by Caesar Borgia after a rapid march, and Guidobaldo fled to Mantua. He recovered Urbino on 29 October and rased the fortresses of Gubbio and Pergola; but had again to withdraw in December when by agreement with the Orsini, Urbino was restored to Caesar Borgia. Guidobaldo retired to Venice, but returned to Urbino in 1503 on the fall of Caesar Borgia. The taking of Urbino by Caesar Borgia is mentioned in *The Art of War*, Book VII (B.359a; F.149-150). In his 'Description of the methods used by Duke Valentine' Machiavelli says that at a meeting held on 9 Oct. 1502 the Vitelli and other princes of the Romagna decided to oppose his growing power. This encouraged the men of Urbino to revolt, and they seized the fortress of St. Leo, which was held for Borgia, some of whose troops revolted when they heard of it. But the Florentines, who hated the Vitelli, sent Machiavelli to offer help and shelter to Caesar Borgia, who, having obtained troops from France, opened negotiations with the Vitelli, promising to retain them in their possessions and not to injure the Bentivogli. In return, the Vitelli promised to restore Urbino, whereupon the Duke, Guidobaldo da Montefeltro, 'again fled to Venice, having first destroyed all the fortresses in his state, because, trusting in the people, he did not wish that the fortresses, which he did not think that he could defend, should be held by the enemy since they would in that case act as a check upon his friends' (E. 223).

7. Pope Julius II entered Bologna on 11 Nov. 1506, the Bentivogli having fled. On 20 Feb. 1507 he laid the first stone of a new fortress to be built at the Porta Galiera. On leaving the city he appointed first Ferreri, then Alidosi, as legates. Both ruled badly. The Pope was again in Bologna in 1511, but on his leaving it the Bolognese revolted, Alidosi fled, and the Bentivogli were restored.

8. Niccolò Vitelli was besieged by Papal troops in the Città di Castello in 1474, but defended it successfully owing to the help sent to him by Lorenzo de' Medici (H.F. VII.31). This caused enmity between Lorenzo and Sixtus IV, who eventually succeeded in expelling the Vitelli and replacing them by Lorenzo Giustini (*ib.* VIII.15). In 1479 Niccolò, though successful in the open field, was unable to recover the city (*ib.*); but in 1482 with the aid of Florentine troops he drove out Lorenzo who was holding it in the name of the Pope (*ib.* VIII.23). In 1484 Lorenzo attempted to retake the city but was routed by the citizens who made a sally, with the result that Sixtus IV gave up and came to terms with the Vitelli (*ib.* VIII.27).

9. In 1506 a popular rising in Genoa resulted in the overthrow of the government which was in sympathy with the French, and the Genoese began to build a fortress. Commenting on this in *The Art of War*, Book VII, (B.354b; F.143-4), Machiavelli says that it is a mistake 'to make a redoubt into which to retire when the outer walls of a city are taken', for, by so doing, 'you begin to lose your reputation, and this will diminish the esteem in which your orders are held by those who have undertaken to defend you and will discourage them. Such will always be the case if you erect bastions outside the town you have to defend, for you will always lose them since it is impossible to defend small things in days when they are subject to intensive artillery fire; and their loss will be the beginning and cause of your downfall. Thus, when Genoa rebelled against King Louis of France, the Genoese

constructed some bastions on the hills in the neighbourhood, which, when they were taken—and they were quickly taken—led to the taking of the city.' Genoa was taken on 28 April 1507 by Louis XII in person, but, instead of demolishing the redoubt, he converted it into a strong fortress. In 1510 Julius II resolved to expel the French from Italy. In Genoa the Fregosi were to lead a revolt and drive the French garrison out. The resentment aroused by Papal intervention in Genoa is mentioned in a despatch written by Machiavelli from Blois on 21 July. 'Louis', he says, 'is determined to vindicate his honour even if he loses everything he possesses in Italy.' This is actually what happened after the death of Gaston de Foix at the battle of Ravenna on 11 April 1512; for the French, though victorious, forthwith began to lose their grip and were expelled from the whole of Italy, save for a few fortresses, e.g. at Genoa and Milan. In Genoa Ottaviano Fregoso was appointed Doge by the Spanish Viceroy, in preference to the former Doge Janus Fregoso, who had been responsible for the murder of Gianluigi dal Fiesco, and had been expelled (cp. D. II.21, n. 6). This on the recommendation of Leo X, to whom he promised 50,000 ducats. The siege of the fortress built on the spur of rock, called the Codefà, and often referred to as the Lantern, now began. Several times the French attempted to relieve it, but in vain. In 1514 it surrendered for want of provisions and was demolished. (Cp. Guicciardini, *St. d'I.* VII.6, p. 116 for the building of the fortress, and XII.7, p. 328 for its destruction.)

10. Machiavelli now says that Ottaviano Fregoso preferred to hold his position as ruler of Genoa (*fondare lo stato suo*) rather by means of virtue than by means of a fortress, and that he holds it still. When did he write this? Fregoso became Doge of Genoa after the battle of Novara which took place in June 1513. But in 1515, when Francis I was preparing to invade Italy, Fregoso, while protesting to Leo X that he was still loyal to the league which had been formed to keep Francis out, secretly came to terms, and in consequence, when Francis arrived, he was reinstated as the ruler of Genoa, but, instead of being its Doge, he became its governor (cp. D. II.21.4 and n. 6); and henceforth, until 1522, when the French were expelled by the Emperor, he ruled Genoa in the name of the French king. Hence it is clear that the attempt to overthrow Fregoso's government, to which Machiavelli here refers, must have taken place prior to his fall in 1522 and after he had rased the fortress in 1514. Villari, whom Burd follows, is of opinion that he refers to the attack which was made on Genoa in 1521—immediately prior to Fregoso's fall—when a small fleet sailed thither in the hope that Genoa would revolt from the French, and when it did not do so, withdrew. If so, this is the only incident subsequent to 1517 of which Machiavelli makes mention. In the Introduction, §§ 44–6, I have set forth various reasons for rejecting this interpretation. The attack to which Machiavelli, in my opinion, refers, is that made by the combined forces of the Duke of Milan, the Swiss (4,000 of them), and the Adorni and Fieschi in 1515 when news came to them that Fregoso was about to throw himself into the arms of Francis I, as he did. The army which the Duke had got together advanced to Novara, when messengers arrived from the Pope requesting them to desist.

11. Pisa and other towns were added to the dominions of Florence after the death of Ladislas, King of Naples, in 1414 (H.F. III.29). Upon Pisa depended many other fortified towns, some of which were taken by Lucca but were restored by the peace of 1433 (*ib.* IV.25). Pisa was handed over to Charles VIII in 1494 by Piero de' Medici. Charles promised to restore it to Florence, but instead its citadel was

sold to the Pisans by d' Entragues in 1496, and the long war between Florence and Pisa (1496–1509) began. On taking the city in 1509 the Florentines built a second fortress there to the great disgust of the inhabitants, many of whom left the city. (Cp. P. 20, Burd 329, E.169.)

12. Quintus Fabius Maximus, nicknamed Verrucosus because he had a wart on his upper lip, and Cunctator because he was so slow in coming to grips with the enemy, was sent during his fifth year as consul in 209 B.C. to southern Italy to recover Tarentum from Hannibal. The citadel had never fallen into the hands of Hannibal, thanks to its governor, M. Livius Macatus, to whom, according to Plutarch (*Fabius* 23), Fabius admitted that he would never have retaken the city, had Macatus not lost it in spite of his holding the citadel. Livy's account is given in XXVII.15–16; the city was taken by a joint attack in which troops from the citadel played an important part.

13. For an account of the taking of Brescia by Gaston de Foix in 1512, cp. D. II.17.4 and n. 1; D. III.44.3 and n. 3.

14. In his '*Moralia*' under 'Notable Sayings of the Lacedaemonians' Plutarch thrice cites this remark, but in neither case with reference to Athens. (i) Someone showed Agesilaus the walls of his own town which were wonderfully strong and magnificently fortified. Do they not look fine? he asked. To which the answer was: 'Yes, certainly, as a habitation for women, but not for men' (212E). (ii) Agis, when passing by the walls of Corinth, noticed how high and well built they were, and how extensive. Who are the women who dwell within them? he asked (215D). (iii) Theopompus, when shown some fine, high walls, remarked: 'It is a dwelling-place for women, is it not?' (190A).

15. The signing of the Treaty of Noyon by Francis and Charles (13 August 1516) left the Spanish troops which had been employed by Francis with the prospect of unemployment. Some 5,000 of these were induced by Francesco Maria della Rovere to join him in an attempt to recover the Duchy of Urbino from which he had been expelled by Leo X in 1516 (cp. D. II.10.3 and n. 6). In the beginning of Bk. XIII of his *Storia d'Italia* Guicciardini tells how with his army, which was without 'money, artillery, and any provisions except horses and arms', he marched straight on Urbino, ignoring all the towns of the Romagna which were in Lorenzo de' Medici's hands, and on his second approach got the governor, Giacomo Rosetto, to surrender the town. Since this occurred on 6 February 1517, and Machiavelli speaks of it as having happened 'in quite recent times', the discourse must have been written either in 1517 or not long after this.

Cp. *The Prince*, c. 20, where the question is discussed mainly from the point of view of a prince who wants to control his state. On the building of fortresses, see A.W. Bk. VII.

Guicciardini's comments on this chapter are much longer than usual. He writes: 'Antiquity ought not to be praised so much that one disparages all modern institutions which were not used by the Romans; for experience has brought to light many things which the ancients did not think of, and, since there has been an advance and a change in standpoint, what was neither appropriate nor necessary under other conditions is appropriate and necessary under one of those prevailing. Hence, because the Romans did not employ fortresses in subject cities, it does not follow that those err who build them today, for many cases occur in which to have fortresses is extremely useful alike to a prince or a tyrant in dealing with the aforesaid citizens, or to a ruler in regard to his own subjects or to an overlord in regard to foreigners. The reasons appear to me so manifest that I am surprised that there should be those who reject this view.' No doubt fortresses are useless to a prince who is beloved by his subjects, but 'considering how often the populace, even when well-treated, is unreasonable, and how eager it is for change . . . I maintain that alike to those who are able to make the people their friends and to those who cannot hope to acquire such goodwill, it is essential to base their rule to some extent on force in order to keep the populace in fear'. 'One does not disparage medicine because one hopes to avoid falling sick. . . . Fortresses, too, prevent subject-cities from thinking of rebellion unless a foreign army comes along. The case of Milan is not to the point, for its princes lost their state not because their people rebelled, but on account of a great war. . . . A fortress may also help in recovering a city, as in the case of Brescia. . . . The reason why the Romans did not use fortresses was (i) that they did not at first make other cities their subjects, but with them formed a confederation, and (ii) that they had strong forces and also colonies and that these sufficed; but they did not destroy the fortress at Tarentum nor any others which they came across. I do not deny that other means may be more useful than fortresses, but fortresses are often useful as a security against conspiracies, as a refuge in case of rebellion, and as a means of regaining lost towns.'

25. To attack a Divided City in the Hope that its Divisions will facilitate the Conquest of it is Bad Policy

1. Livy II.44.7, cited verbatim but in Italian.
2. *ib.* 43.11; 45.1; cp. D. I.36.1, and III.12.5.   3. *ib.* 45.3–4.
4. *ib.* 45.6 *sq.*; 47.8–9. Machiavelli returns to the Etruscan war of 480–474 in the next chapter, where further particulars as to its nature are given.
5. See D. II.21.6 and n. 7 (cp. D. III.27.2–4), and P. 20, E.169 on how Pistoia was held. What Machiavelli here says of the skill with which the Florentines handled the factions in Pistoia accords ill with the account he gives of the trouble in his *History of Florence.* In II.16–21 he tells us how a quarrel arose between the Neri and the Bianchi—so-called because they were descended from the black and the white wives of Messer Cancellieri—and how this dispute spread to Florence where it became so acute that the Pope was asked to intervene; which he did, but in vain, for soon 'the whole city, the populace as well as the nobles, took sides'; so that the priors, of whom Dante was one, had to 'arm the whole people and summon aid from the adjoining country'. This was in 1300, when the strife between Guelf and Ghibbeline was at its height. The next mention of Pistoia is in II.29, where we are told that Castruccio, a citizen of Lucca who had made himself master of that city, got possession also of Pistoia, and that the Florentines were unable to prevent him ravaging their lands at will. Details of the two defeats they suffered are given in Machiavelli's *Life of Castruccio Castracani.* We are then told that in 1328 the Florentines 'got possession of Pistoia by arrangement with the citizens' (cp. D. II.21.6), but that Castruccio again forced them to surrender (II.30). When in this year Castruccio died, Pistoia presumably reverted to Florence, for it is mentioned in

II.38 amongst the subject-towns that rebelled in 1343. It was certainly subject to Florence from 1351 onwards. Perhaps, however, it is not Pistoia's voluntary submission in 1328 that Machiavelli here has in mind, but the incidents which took place in his own life-time. He was sent to Pistoia several times in 1501-2, when rioting was frequent there owing to the rivalry between the Cancelliari and the Panciatichi. The Pistoians wanted to banish the Panciatichi, who were hostile to Florence, but Machiavelli wrote to them in May 1501 to say that this course was dangerous, since it would mean that the city would be full of malcontents and the surrounding territory full of suspicion. They were to re-admit the Panciatichi, unarmed, and to keep watch on them. Similar instructions were sent in September when the conflict was renewed. It would seem, then, that Florence was seeking to retain—not however, to obtain—her hold on Pistoia by supporting the weaker party, which to some extent at any rate bears out what Machiavelli here says.

6. There is no recorded instance of Florence having brought about a change in the government of Siena by the use of armed forces, in spite of the intense rivalry between these two Tuscan states to which Machiavelli refers in H.F. VII.32; VIII.16; and D. II.21.6. Revolutions were caused for the most part, as in Florence, first by rivalry between the Ghibellines and Guelfs, and then by friction between the populace, the merchant class, and the nobility, who were also inclined to form rival parties, e.g. the Talomei and the Salimbeni after the death of Henry of Luxemburg in 1313. In 1280 both Florence and Siena allowed Ghibelline exiles to return, and from 1280 to 1354 Siena was ruled by a mercantile oligarchy known as the Nine. The expulsion of the Nine and the setting up of the Twelve, who ruled from 1355 to 1369, was due to the intervention of Charles IV. There then occurred both in Siena and in Florence popular risings, which resulted in the setting up of a more popular form of government in Siena which lasted till 1385, and in Florence in the setting up of the Magistracy of the Ten of Liberty. In 1385 this popular government was replaced by an oligarchy, which had the support of the Florentine government, also oligarchic. Siena then acknowledged the suzerainty of Gian Galeazzo Visconti and rejoiced in his victory over Florence at Casalecchio in 1402. We then find Siena and Florence uniting against Ladislas of Naples, but again falling out and taking different sides in the war between Sixtus IV (supported by Naples) and Venice, Milan and Florence, which ended in 1480. Pandolfo Petrucci, who ruled Siena from 1487 to 1512 (cp. D. III.6.39), was sometimes friendly and sometimes hostile to Florence. His son, Borghese Petrucci, was expelled owing to the intervention of Leo X in 1516, and Lorenzo de' Medici was given a *condottiere* by Siena. The influence of Florence on Sienese revolutions, therefore, does not appear to have been very great, nor is it mentioned by Machiavelli in his *History of Florence*.

7. Filippo Maria Visconti, Duke of Milan (1412-47), availed himself of the divided counsels then prevailing in Florence to enlarge his dominions, thus arousing hostility in Florence, between which and himself war broke out in 1424. Though at first victorious, when Venice came to the aid of Florence the Duke was defeated at Maclodio in 1428 and Florence regained the territory she had lost (H.F. IV.4-15). When opinion was again divided as to the advisability of making war on Lucca, the Duke again intervened in 1430, helped the Lucchese, but when peace came in 1433 neither side had gained (IV.24-5). War again broke out in 1436 when Florence made an alliance with Genoa. It ended with the victory of the Florentines at Anghiari in 1440. The Duke's position had now become so serious that he sued

for peace (VI.2). During the brief interval of peace from 1433 to 1436 Florence still remained a prey to 'all the malignant humours of factions' (VI.26). The Duke, now an old man, was again at war with Florence in 1446, but in August 1447 he died.

Cp. *The Prince*, c. 20, on the use of factions. 'Factions will never be permitted in a strong principality. Such methods for enabling one more easily to manage subjects, are only useful in time of peace, but when war comes this policy proves fallacious' (Burd 330, E.169).

26. Scorn and Abuse arouse Hatred against those who indulge in them without bringing them any Advantage

1. Cobades, of the Sassanid dynasty, ruled Persia from A.D. 488 to 531, save for a few years during which he was displaced by his brother. On the Emperor Anastasius's refusal to pay a tribute that had been paid for a hundred years, Cobades declared war on Rome. He defeated the Romans and took Amida in 503; but the inroads of Huns in the North compelled him to make peace in A.D. 505, for which he was paid an indemnity of 11,000 pounds weight in gold. (Cp. Procopius, *Bell. Pers.* I.7.12–29; Ammianus Marcellinus, XIX.1, *sq.*)

2. The reference is to the Etruscan war of 480–474 B.C., mentioned in D. II.25.1, where it is used to illustrate the folly of attacking a divided city, namely Rome. It is here used again for another purpose. In Book II, 43–47 Livy tells how when in 480 B.C. Gaius Manlius and Marcus Fabius were consuls, dissensions between the citizens had spread to the troops and they declined to fight. On learning this the enemy approached their camp and jeered at them. This so incensed the Romans that they asked to be led to battle, but the consuls still hesitated; whereupon the enemy taunted them with being unable to trust their own troops. The consuls now yielded to the urgent demands of the soldiers, and a fierce fight ensued in which the consuls had the utmost difficulty in preventing their troops from running away, and one of them, Manlius, was killed. Apparently the Romans looked upon this battle as a victory, for Fabius was offered a triumph, which he refused. Anyhow, after the peace of 474 Veii and her Etruscan allies ceased to trouble the Romans for some forty years, and her position *vis-à-vis* Southern Etruria now became secure. (Cp. C.A.H. VII.15.5 for chronology.)

3. The Capuan mutiny took place in 342 B.C. When marching on Rome the mutinous legions were met by Valerius Corvus, a popular general, to whom they submitted. He induced the senate to pass laws declaring that desertion did not fall under the head of treachery, and that for it no one was to upbraid the troops either seriously or in joke—*ne cui militum fraudi secessio esset*, and *ne quis eam rem joco seriove cuiquam exprobraret* (Livy VII.41.3). Cp. D. III.6.43.

4. After the battle of Cannae in 216 B.C. eight thousand able-bodied young men from amongst the slaves, after giving their assent, were purchased and armed at the public expense (Livy XXII.57.11). They were commanded by Tiberius Sempronius Gracchus. In 214, before engaging Hanno at Beneventum, he promised to free any slave who should bring back the head of an enemy. The result was that as soon as a slave had killed a Carthaginian, he 'wasted his time in labouring to cut

off his head', which he carried about instead of a sword, so Gracchus ordered them to drop the heads and fight, promising them freedom if they won, as they did (Livy XXIV.14-15).

5. '*Nam facetiae asperae, quando nimium ex vero traxere, acrem sui memoriam reliquunt*' —cited in Latin. Cp. Tacitus, *Annals* XV.68: '*ille* [Nero] *ferociam amici metuit, saepe asperis facetiis inlusus, quae ubi multum ex vero traxere, acrem sui memoriam relinquunt.*'

27. Prudent Princes and Republics should be content with Victory, for, when they are not content with it, they usually lose

With the heading cp. H.F. IV.14 (end): 'He who is content with a moderate victory will always gain by it, whereas, those who in victory overdo things frequently lose.'

1. Livy XXIII.11-12. 2. *ib.* 12.12-13.

3. After the fate of the Persian empire had been sealed by the battle of Issus in 333 B.C., Alexander decided to conquer Phoenicia whose navy was a constant threat to his communications. Most of the cities surrendered on his approach, but Tyre held out for seven months and was not taken until the middle of 332, when it was punished by the slaughter of 8,000 of its inhabitants and the sale of 30,000 into slavery. Plutarch tells the story of the siege in his *Life of Alexander*, but does not mention the preliminary negotiations. Of them a brief account is given by Diodorus Siculus in XVII.4. But Machiavelli's source is probably Quintus Curtius, who in Book IV. cc. 7-19, tells us that Tyre sent Alexander a golden crown and provisions, but said that if he wanted to sacrifice to Hercules he must do so at Paletyron, not in Tyre itself. Rather than allow the king to enter their sea-girt city, they would prefer to stand a siege. Alexander's first attempt to build a mole to connect the mainland with the island failed. Hence, lacking a fleet and perceiving that the siege was likely to be a long one, he sent heralds, offering peace-terms; but the Tyrians threw them headlong into the sea. A second mole was destroyed in a storm, but a third attempt proved more successful in spite of the Tyrians' desperate and ingenious methods of defence; and when his fleet came up, Alexander at last succeeded in taking the town. Alexander ordered that none should be spared save those who had taken refuge in the Temple. According to Quintus Curtius, six thousand were slain within the walls, and two thousand crucified along the sea-coast. But the Sidonians, who claimed the same founder, Agenor, managed to save 15,000 by taking them on board ship.

4. After their defeat at Ravenna in April 1512, the forces of the Holy League obtained reinforcements from Switzerland and by the end of June had expelled the French from Lombardy, save for one or two fortresses. At a meeting of the League in Mantua it was decided to depose Soderini and to restore the Medici to Florence. Soderini and Machiavelli determined to resist, and to garrison Prato; but the wealthier citizens were anxious to get the Medici back. Barbarino and Campi fell to Spanish forces under Raymond of Cardona in August. The Florentine militia fled from Prato, which was mercilessly sacked on the 29th. Under pressure from a group of armed citizens Soderini resigned rather than 'bring about the ruin of

Florence' on the 31st, and on 1 September Giuliano de' Medici entered Florence, and the republican regime came to an end.

5. Cp. D. I.22.2 and D. I.23 on the danger of risking the whole of one's fortune on part of one's forces.

6. When the power of Carthage was nearing its end in 204 B.C., Scipio sailed for Africa, but, meeting with but small success, a treaty was arranged by which the Carthaginians bound themselves to evacuate Italy, and the Romans to evacuate Africa. Scipio, in violation of this treaty, attacked and defeated Syphax and Hasdrubal in the spring of 203. Hannibal was then sent for, and further negotiations were opened by the Carthaginians which Rome agreed to; but they were now much harder (Livy XXX.16). This treaty the Romans observed, and Hannibal in crossing to Africa was unmolested; but the Carthaginians now violated it by attempting to seize the Roman fleet. Hannibal on his arrival prepared to defend Carthage, but before joining battle had an interview with Scipio, of which both Livy (XXX.30–31) and Polybius (XV.6–8) give an account. The negotiations broke down, according to Livy because the Carthaginians had seized a convoy bringing provisions to Africa, according to Polybius because the Romans insisted on unconditional surrender. The result was the battle of Zama (202) in which the Carthaginians were finally routed and the war brought to a close. Note that the Hasdrubal here mentioned is not Hasdrubal, son of Hamilcar and brother of Hannibal, but Hasdrubal, son of Gisco, a Carthaginian general.

28. How Dangerous it is for a Republic or a Prince not to avenge an Injury done either to the Public or to a Private Person

1. Machiavelli here follows the story as given by Livy in V.36. The Romans refused the demand of the Gauls partly because they did not admit that the *jus gentium* applied to barbarians, partly because they thought the deed a noble one, worthy of praise rather than blame. Diodorus in XIV.113–14 says that the Gauls demanded the surrender only of the man who had killed a Gaulish chieftain, and that his father interceded for him. The date assigned to the incident is 390 B.C., the year in which Rome was sacked and burnt.

2. '*contra jus gentium*' (V.36.6). The '*Jus Gentium*' was an unwritten law which the Romans and other Latin peoples recognised as binding in their dealings one with the other and sometimes with foreign states. Thus in Livy I.14.1 Titus Tatius violates the '*jus gentium*' when he beats up the ambassadors of the Laurentes, an injustice which is avenged by the gods when he gets killed in a disturbance at Lavinium. In II.4.7 no punishment is inflicted on the ambassadors sent to Rome by the Tarquins for having joined in a conspiracy against Rome, because to do so would violate the '*jus gentium*'. In IV.17.4 the revolt of the Roman colony at Fidenae to the king of the Veientes is looked upon by Rome as a violation of the '*jus gentium*', and ambassadors are sent to enquire into the matter. Lars Tolumnius kills them, and consequently is regarded as a '*ruptor foederis humani violatorque gentium juris*' (IV.19.3). But though the *jus gentium* applies primarily to the relation of one state to another, and in particular to the sanctity of the diplomatic corps, there is a

139

passage in IV.1 which suggests that it covered a wider field, for, when it was proposed that in Rome there should be intermarriage between patricians and plebeians exception was taken to this on the ground that it would introduce confusion into the '*jus gentium*'—*confundique jura gentium rebantur* (IV.1.2); i.e. it would cause the common law obtaining amongst Latin peoples to become divergent.

3. The account Machiavelli gives of the assault on Pausanias and of the murder of Philip II of Macedon accords well with that given by Justin in IX.6, save that Machiavelli has embellished it a little. It does not accord with the story as told by Diodorus Siculus in XVI.94, for there are two Pausaniases in his account, and the murder took place on the way to the theatre. The wedding is not mentioned. There is a brief account of the murder in Plutarch's *Life of Alexander*, 9–10; and it is mentioned by Aristotle in his *Politics* V.10, 1311b, 2. The date of the murder was 336 B.C.

29. Fortune blinds Men's Minds when she does not wish them to obstruct her Designs

1. '*Adeo obcaecat animos fortuna, cum vim suam ingruentem refringi non vult*' (V.37.1). These words, quoted here in Latin, are used by Machiavelli as the heading of the chapter. In Livy the facts which Machiavelli cites in support of his theorem, which is also Livy's, are given by him in the two chapters, V.37 and 38, which follow his statement about fortune, and are apparently meant as an illustration of how fortune operates. At the end of his account Livy remarks that the Gauls were 'stupefied' by the suddenness of this miraculous victory (39.1). To 'fate', however, Livy also ascribes the action of Rome's ambassadors in taking up arms in violation of the '*jus gentium*' (36.6). The remark that no one who reads of these events would imagine that the Romans were the same people is Machiavelli's, not Livy's. Cp. also Sallust's *Catiline* 8.1: '*Sed profecto fortuna in omni re dominatur; ea res cunctas ex libidine magis quam ex vero celebrat obscuratque*'. (Cp. Introduction, § 7.)

2. See also D. I.28.3; and cp. H.F. V.11, in which into the mouths of 'the oldest and wisest citizens of Lucca' Machiavelli puts a speech which begins with the remark: 'You must know full well that actions done under necessity cannot and ought not to be either praised or blamed.'

3. The argument used in this paragraph is not taken from Livy, though it is in accordance with Livy's thought. For it was 'by fortune herself that the Gauls were led to Ardea, where Camillus was in exile, to make trial of Roman valour' (V.44.1); and it was 'both gods and men that interfered to prevent the Romans having to live as ransomed slaves' (*ib.* 49.1). Moreover, in the long speech of M. Furius Camillus, now dictator, which occupies ec. 51 to 54, Camillus urges the people to remain in Rome instead of migrating to Veii on the ground that 'not without cause did the gods and men choose this place for building a city, these most healthful hills, this convenient river, by means of which produce can be conveyed to foreign parts and maritime supplies be obtained, with the sea conveniently at hand, yet not so close as to expose it to the danger of foreign fleets, a city singularly adapted by nature to increase. . . . Can you transfer the fortune of this place to some other? The Capitol is here, and when in the Capitol a human head was found, the answer was that this place would be the head of the world and the seat of

empire' (*ib.* 54.4–7). Commenting on the events which happened after the fall of Rome, events in which Camillus played so prominent a part, Professor Homo writes in C.A.H. (Vol. VII. p. 566): 'The great figure of the epoch . . . was the conqueror of Southern Etruria, Camillus. A man of ideas and a man of action, he personified the national recovery. . . . Under his guidance the Roman army underwent a complete transformation: and when the new weapon was forged and tested, he used it to defeat in turn all the enemies of Rome, Gauls and Etruscans, Volscians, Aequi, and rebellious Latins alike.'

Cp. the chapter on Fortune in *The Prince*, c. 25.

30. Really Powerful Republics and Princes do not purchase Alliances with Money, but obtain them by means of Virtue and the Reputation of their Forces

1. '*ut Romani auro redempti non viverent*' (Livy V.49.1—cited in Latin). The reading in the Teubner text is '*Sed diique et homines prohibuere redemptos viuere Romanos*'. Famine and pestilence were causing trouble to both armies. So a truce was arranged, but the Gauls still urged the Romans to surrender. Worn out by the siege, Rome's troops also demanded either that they should surrender or that the Gauls should be bought off, and it was agreed to pay them a thousand pounds weight in gold for the nation's ransom. But the Gauls used false weights, and, when the tribune protested, his sword was thrown into the scale by Brennus, who cried: 'Woe to the vanquished!' The dictator, Camillus, then turned up with some troops, refused to recognise the compact, and expelled the Gauls from Rome (V.48–9).

2. The people of Massilia (Marseilles) are mentioned in Livy XXI.26. They sent guides to co-operate with mounted troops sent forward by Publius Cornelius Scipio when he arrived at Massilia in 218 B.C. The Aedui are mentioned in the Epitome of Book LXI as being allies of Rome, and as having in consequence had their lands ravaged by the Allobrogae (123 B.C.). Rhodes, a powerful maritime state, helped Rome considerably in her war with Antiochus, 192–190 B.C., especially at Myonnesus where the Rhodian admiral, Eudamus, destroyed a fleet of 42 ships. She was rewarded with two dependencies, Caria and Lycia, but when she claimed that the latter was a subject-state, not an ally, Rome overruled her (XXXVII.22–24; XXXVIII.39; XLIV.15). Eumenes II, king of Pergamus, on his accession in 197 B.C., maintained the alliance with Rome which his father, Attalus, had established, and by the treaty of peace made with Philip of Macedonia in 196 obtained Oreus and Eretria, two towns in Euboea (XXXIII.30, 34). He urged the Romans to make war on Antiochus, who had tried in vain to win him over, and at the battle of Magnesia in 190, commanded in person the auxiliaries he supplied (XXXV.13; XXXVI.43–5; XXXVII *passim*). Masinissa, son of Gala, king of the Massilians, was from 213 to 206 the ally of the Carthaginians, but after their defeat by Scipio, in which he shared, he sought out the Roman commander and came to terms (XXVIII.16, 35). He succeeded his father, but held the throne with difficulty and was more than once defeated by Syphax. The tide turned in his favour when Scipio landed in Africa in 204, and for the assistance he gave the Romans he was rewarded by being made king of Numidia. Four names in this list

of peoples who paid to be Rome's allies occur also in the list of Fifth Columnists in D. II.1.6, namely, the Massilians, the Aedui, Eumenes, and Masinissa.

3. Perugia and the Città di Castello are mentioned in H.F. V.30 as having been friendly to Florence in the time of Cosimo de' Medici; and in H.F. VII.31, we are told that, when war with Sixtus IV was threatening, Lorenzo renewed the alliance with Perugia; and again that, when war broke out after the Pazzi conspiracy in 1478 and both Carlo, son of Count Braccio of Perugia, and Niccolò Vitelli of the Città di Castello were driven from their estates, both were employed by Florence in the hope of recovering them. The Marquis of Ferrara and the Marquis of Mantua were also at this time in the service of Florence (H.F. VIII.14–15).

4. The Swiss were constantly employed both by Charles VIII and Louis XII in their Neapolitan wars. There were, for instance, 4,000 of them in the army that marched on Naples in 1501; in 1502 another 2,000 were sent by sea. (Guicciardini *St. d'I.* V.4, p. 19; 10, p. 47). Later on they boasted, says Guicciardini, that it was 'by their means that Charles, King of France had subverted the happy state of Italy, and that Louis, his successor, had conquered the Duchy of Milan, recovered Genoa, and overthrown the Venetians' (*St. d'I.* XI.7, p. 251). Subsequently they fell out; but in 1515 a treaty was signed at Dijon whereby Francis I bound himself to pay the Swiss annually 40,000 *livres* during his lifetime and for ten years after his death, and amongst other conditions, to keep 4,000 Swiss continually in his service. The treaty proved abortive at the moment, but was renewed in 1516.

5. Louis XI at Picquigny in 1475 agreed to pay Edward IV a pension of 50,000 gold crowns, plus a lump sum of 75,000. Charles VIII at the Peace of Étaples, November 1492, promised to pay 620,000 crowns for the help given by England to Anne of Brittany, and to pay up two years arrears of the pension agreed upon at Picquigny. Louis XII in 1514, after the battle of the Spurs, promised to increase the pension agreed upon at Étaples. In 1525 Francis I promised 100,000 crowns a year to Henry VIII. (To get the English equivalent in pounds, divide by five.)

6. As to the facts there can be no doubt. Tacitus says: 'The Germans have attacked us more often than have either the Samnites, the Carthaginians, the Spaniards, the Gauls, or the Parthians: on their German liberty they are more keen than are the Arsacids on their kingdom', i.e. the kingdom of Parthia (*Germania* 37). The emperor Macrinus was defeated and had to pay an indemnity to the Parthian king, Artabanus V, in A.D. 227. This marks the beginning of Rome's declining power in the East, for the Sassanids now replaced the Arsacids on the Parthian throne, and in 260 the emperor Valerius was captured and died in imprisonment. Rock-reliefs still survive depicting him as a suppliant asking pardon of Sapor I, the king of kings. In the West, onwards from the time of Augustus, who had a German bodyguard, Germans were employed with increasing frequency in Rome's armies. Writing of the third century A.D., Professor Alföldi says: 'Rome was glad enough to be able to deflect their hordes or secure their withdrawal by payments. These payments developed into a regular system which, under the decent cover of the old scheme of subordinate *"foederati"*, led on to the new and superior warrior-caste found in the later Germano-Roman states. As early as Caracalla the budget was seriously burdened by the annual subsidies paid to barbarian peoples' (C.A.H. XII.5.4.)

A. H. Krappe in '*Quelques Sources Grecques de Niccolò Machiavelli*', asserts that he was certainly influenced by a passage from Procopius's '*Historia Arcana*' in writing this chapter. In it Procopius speaks of 'the immense sums paid to the Huns, in order, so it was said, to make sure of their friendship'; of how, 'having accepted this, the Huns induced other tribes to invade Roman territory and ravage it so that they too might be bought off'. Of such wars, adds Procopius, 'which began with excessive grants made by the emperor, there was no end ... Many provinces were overrun and devastated five or more times; and the damage done by the Huns was done also by Medes, Saracens, Slavs, Antae, and other barbarians, as I have narrated in my previous works; but, as I said at the beginning it is worth while here to point out the cause' (*Hist. Arc.* XI.5–11). It will be noted that there is no mention in this passage either of Germans or Parthians, but this difficulty Krappe gets over by identifying the Antae with the Germans and the Medes with the Parthians, in spite of the fact that Procopius goes on immediately to mention the large sum Justinian paid to Chosroes, who was then ruling Persia and Parthia, for the sake of peace. Nor is this the only difficulty. The *Historia Arcana* was first printed in 1623, so that, if Machiavelli read it, he must have read it not only in Greek but in manuscript! He could, however, had he wished to consult Procopius, have consulted the earlier works to which Procopius in this passage refers, namely, the '*De Bello Italico adversus Gothos gesto*' which was published at Venice in 1471, and the '*De Bello Persico et Vandalico*', which was published in Rome in 1509. I am inclined, however, to think that, when Machiavelli speaks of the emperors having begun to make grants to the Parthians, Germans, and others, he is thinking of a period much earlier than the reign of Justinian, with which alone Procopius is here concerned. For in A.W. Bk. I, B.272b; F11 he mentions that the disarming of the Romans by Augustus and Tiberius had already begun.

7. Though no chapter is headed by the theorem that a prudent ruler will not keep his people unarmed, the principle is plainly regarded by Machiavelli as of the utmost importance for all states which propose to make conquests, and all states, he claims, may have to do this, even though they had no intentions of so doing at the start. (Cp. D. I.6.6.) Bound up with it are other principles such as that a conquering people should make sure of a large population (cp. D. I.6.6–9; II.3.3; II.4.3), and in consequence should admit peoples that have been beaten in battle and have surrendered, to citizenship (cp. II.3.1–2; 23.2). It also explains Machiavelli's own zeal in forming a Florentine militia. The *locus classicus* in *The Prince* occurs in P. 20, where Machiavelli writes: 'There never was a new prince who disarmed his subjects; on the contrary, when he has found them disarmed, always has he armed them; since, when they are armed, their arms become yours; those who were loyal thus have means to maintain their loyalty, and, instead of being mere subjects, become your partisans.' Cp. A.W. Book I on the disarming of the Roman people by Augustus and Tiberius (B.272b; F.11) and of the French (*ib.* B.278; F.20.)

8. Since the reference is to an incident which took place 'but a few years ago', it cannot be to the Venetian defeat at Agnadello, in 1509, but must be to their defeat by the Spanish viceroy at Vicenza in 1513. The situation prior to the battle, when Venice saw neighbouring towns in flames, palaces destroyed, and cannon firing close to the city's walls, and the subsequent battle in which Venice lost 400 men at arms and 4,000 foot, are vividly described by Guicciardini in Book XI, cap. 15, of his *Storia d'Italia*.

9. The invasion of France by Henry VIII and the siege of Teruanne in 1513 are described by Guicciardini in the opening of his XIIth Book. He points out how Louis XII, with a negligence that was typically French, had failed to provide adequate forces to meet the invaders, and consequently decided to avoid battle 'lest, if he should be defeated, the whole of France would manifestly be in danger'. Hence Teruanne surrendered after a siege of fifty days, and when Maximilian arrived at the English camp, near where he had in his youth routed the army of Louis XI, the English paid him the compliment of calling him 'commander-in-chief'. (Cp. D. I.21.2.)

10. The quotation, which is not in this case given in Latin, is from Livy XXIII.13.2: '*Bellum igitur, inquit, tam integrum habemus, quam habuimus, qua die Hannibal in Italiam est transgressus.*' The answer Hanno got to his question bears out Machiavelli's contention that Rome had devised a successful means of bringing neighbouring peoples under her dominion in such a way as to secure their unswerving loyalty in the future. (Cp. D. II.23 and 24.1–2.) Hanno, called by Appian 'the Great', was the leader of the aristocratic party in Carthage which was opposed to the war in Italy. He is not to be confused with the Hanno mentioned in D. III.6.38 and 40.

Cp. on the use of money for such purposes Cicero's sarcastic remark in the *De Officiis* II.xv: 'But those who make a point of being beneficent and liberal, i.e. are efficient and take pains about it, will first have more people to collaborate in their kindly acts, the more people they benefit; and then, when beneficence becomes a habit, will be more ready and practised in deserving well of many people. Well did Philip write to Alexander in a certain letter, accusing him of trying to get the good-will of the Macedonians by largesse: "What the mischief induced you to entertain the hope that those would be loyal to you whom you had corrupted with money?"'

31. How Dangerous it is to put Confidence in Refugees

1. Alexander, the uncle of Alexander the Great, was made king of Epirus by Philip of Macedon who in 336 B.C., gave him his daughter, Cleopatra, in marriage, and at the marriage feast was assassinated by Pausanias. In 332 Alexander came to Italy, Livy tells us in VIII.3, and his expedition, had it been successful, would have proved dangerous to Rome. He was successful at first, in spite of the fact that the Samnites joined the Lucanians against him, and with Rome he came to terms (VIII.17.6–9). After his victory he sent some 300 distinguished Lucanian families to Epirus, but kept with him some two hundred Lucanians who had been banished from their country. These men, anxious to get home, made a pact with their own people to hand over Alexander alive or dead, on condition that they were allowed to return. In 326 Alexander held three hills near Pandosia. Two of them were taken by the enemy, and his troops there put to the sword before he could come to their rescue on account of the flooded country. In endeavouring to cross a river, he was killed by one of the exiles who were acting as guides, and thus was verified the oracle of Jupiter Dodoneus, which had been made to him when he accepted the invitation of the people of Tarentum to come to Italy (VIII.24).

2. In 426 B.C. or thereabouts, for the date is by no means certain, Themistocles went into voluntary exile, and eventually sought refuge with the king of Persia.

The name of the king was certainly not Darius I who had died in 485 and had been succeeded by Xerxes. Thucydides says that Xerxes was already dead and that Themistocles wrote to his son, Artaxerxes, who succeeded in 465, and to whom Themistocles promised to render further services in a year's time. Meanwhile he learned Persian so that he could explain matters in person (I.137-8). When in 449 the Athenians sent an expedition to Cyprus to help Amyrtaeus, who was in revolt against Artaxerxes, he was called upon to fulfil his promise (Plutarch, *Themistocles* n. 31). Thucydides says 'a sickness put an end to his life, although some say that he poisoned himself because he could not fulfil what he had promised to the King' (I.138). Plutarch says neither resentment against Athens nor the honours he had received could induce him to tarnish his fame by fighting against his own kinsmen and that in consequence he poisoned himself, so some say (*ib.* n. 31). Plutarch also says that according to many authorities Xerxes was still ruling when Themistocles went to Persia (*ib.* n. 27), though he prefers the chronology of Thucydides. Diodorus Siculus says he went to Persia seven years earlier, i.e. in the time of Xerxes, circa 471 (XI.56). Anyhow, Darius I was dead, and though Artaxerxes had a brother called Darius, whom he killed because he thought he had murdered Xerxes, it can scarce be this Darius to whom Machiavelli is referring.

32. On the various Methods used by the Romans in taking Towns

1. Cp. Livy X.53.1: '*Prima luce ad moenia omnibus copiis admotis corona cinxit urbem.*' This was at Cominium, which was taken by Roman forces under Carvilius in 293 B.C. Cp. also XXIII.44.3: '*Itaque coronam oppidum circumdedit, ut simul in omni parte moenia adgrederetur.*' Hannibal had tried to get Nola to surrender. On its refusing, he surrounded or 'crowned it'; but the Romans made a sortie, and a fierce battle ensued which might have ended in a Roman victory if rain had not stopped the fight. (Cp. A.W. Bk. VII, 358b, F.149.) The phrase '*aggredi urbem corona*' is cited in Latin.

2. Cp. Livy XXVI.42-6. 'New Carthage' was surrounded in part by the Roman fleet, in part by the army, and was assaulted by both in conjunction under Scipio (210 B.C.); but at first '*scalis et corona capi urbem non posse*'.

3. Marcus Furius Camillus having been appointed dictator to restore discipline among the troops besieging Veii who had begun to panic owing to a rumour that the Falisci and the Capenates had gained a victory and were about to attack them, stopped all skirmishing and prepared for the final stage of the siege (396 B.C.). 'Of all the works constructed,' says Livy, 'by far the greatest and most laborious was a mine to be carried right into the enemy's citadel. To prevent interruption, and lest continued labour underground should exhaust his men, Camillus divided the engineers into six sections, working six hours each in rotation, so that there was no relaxation night or day until they got through to the citadel' (V.19.10-11). (Cp. D. II.13.2 and n. 2 for other incidents in this siege.)

4. During the final stage of the war with Carthage Scipio twice laid siege to Utica, a port of the coast of Africa, and both times in vain. On the first occasion he besieged it for forty days with siege-implements brought over from Italy, but in vain: on the approach of Hasdrubal and Syphax he was forced to retire (Livy

XXIX.34–5). In the next year, 203 B.C., he made another attempt, this time attacking the city both by sea and by land; but again the approach of Hasdrubal and Syphax forced him to desist, and on this occasion to join battle with them. On their being defeated, most of the towns in the neighbourhood surrendered, including Utica itself (XXX.3.5–8 and cp. A.W. VII.3, 5–8; F.150).

5. The dates of the four sieges were 406–396 B.C. for Veii; 212 Capua; 146 Carthage; and 63 for the siege of Jerusalem by Pompey.

6. Palaeopolis was the old city of Naples, the site of which Livy says was near to that of the new city, Neapolis (VIII.22). The inhabitants were Greeks who had moved thither from Cumae. During the pestilence of 328 they gave trouble to the Campanians, and on their refusing to make reparation Rome declared war. Quintus Publius Philo, who was in command, took up a position between the old and the new city, but was recalled when war broke out with the Samnites. Meanwhile the siege went on. Succour from Tarentum and from the Samnites failed to arrive, and within the city troops from Samnium and Nola were arousing discontent. Charilaus then went to Philo (who presumably has resumed command) and offered to surrender the city. Nymphius, who was in the conspiracy, then induced the Greek garrison to go to the shore that they might put to sea and harass the neighbouring coast, whereupon the troops from Nola fled. The city was then handed over and the Samnites returned home naked and ashamed. An alternative account which says the city was betrayed by the Samnites, is, says Livy, far less plausible than that the Neapolitans of their own accord returned to the Roman allegiance (Livy VIII.22–3, 25–6).

7. Aratus of Sicyon (271–203 B.C.) is chiefly conspicuous as the statesman who aimed at unifying the whole of Greece, and might perhaps have succeeded had it not been for Philip V of Macedon. Of him in his *Life of Aratus* Plutarch says that 'he resorted to open warfare without courage and with little confidence, but in stealing advantages and secretly managing cities and tyrants was most successful. He did, indeed, win many unexpected successes in which he displayed courage, but there were just as many opportunities which he lost through over-caution. For it is not only in certain wild beasts that vision is strong by night but wholly blind in the day-time ... but there are also men whose cleverness and wisdom is apt to blunder in operations carried out in the open and proclaimed to all, but who regain their courage when confronting hidden and secret enterprises' (*ib.* 10). Thus, when at the age of seven Aratus's father was slain and he fled to the house of his aunt, Soso, it was by night that she sent him secretly to Argos (*ib.* 2); and by night that he got back into Sicyon in spite of the barking dogs, expelled the tyrant, Nicocles, and restored eighty exiles (*ib.* 4–9). It was also by night that, when he had become general of the Achaean League, he led an expedition secretly to Corinth, took the citadel which Antigonus had seized, and thus induced Corinth to join the League (*ib.* 16–23).

8. For Capua see D. II.9.4 and n. 8; 10.8; 11.2; 32.7. It surrendered in 343 B.C. For the Rhodians see D. II.30.3 and n. 2—they became the allies of Rome toward the close of Rome's war with Perseus, the last king of Macedon, having in vain tried to reconcile the two powers at the request of Perseus in 268; but it was not until two years later that Rome admitted Rhodes as a formal ally. For the assistance given by the Massilians to Rome in her war with Carthage, see D. II.1.6 and n. 8; 30.3 and n. 2. During the second Punic war they were Rome's allies. In 154 B.C. they were

forced to ask Rome to send an army to help them against the Gauls. Opimius was sent and won the first Roman victory in Transalpine Gaul. In the war with Viriathus (149–140) the Romans were again and again defeated. In 139 they laid siege to Numantia, which was taken by P. Scipio in 134, and destroyed. In the following year Rome's supremacy was acknowledged throughout Spain.

9. If the 450 years be reckoned from the foundation of the republic in 509 B.C. it brings us down to 59 B.C. the year in which Caesar obtained his first consulate, and the process of transforming the republic into a principality definitely set in.

10. Cp. D. II.6.5 and D. II.9.3.

Cp. *The Art of War*, Book VII, for sieges, and VII.B.358b; F.149 for the expression 'aggredi urbem corona'.

33. The Romans gave to Army Commanders Discretionary Powers

1. The right of the senate to be consulted in regard to peace and war obtained even in the times of the kings, for in I.49 it is mentioned by Livy amongst the customs which were abrogated by Tullius Superbus, who 'bellum, pacem, foedera, societates per se ipse cum quibus voluit, injussu populi ac senatus, fecit deremitque'. The suggestion here is that the people also had to be consulted, and this is borne out in IV.58.8 sq., where we are told that the military tribunes were instructed to propose to the people that war on Veii should at once be declared, but that the objections raised were so strong that a decision was put off. Machiavelli, however, is concerned in this chapter only with the powers of the senate *vis-à-vis* the consuls and other army commanders, and in their regard it is clear that the senate reserved to itself only the right to decide when and with whom a war should begin, and when and on what terms it should be brought to a close. Incidentally it also decided, before sending him out, to which field of operations a consul or army commander should be assigned, and, on his return, whether or not he should be awarded a triumph, though this he might refuse, as some did, e.g. Marcus Fabius after the battle in which G. Manlius was killed (cp. D. II.26, n. 2).

2. The story of Rome's advance into central and northern Etruria through the Ciminian forest in 310 B.C. is told by Livy in IX.35–6. Having relieved Sutrium to which the Etruscans had laid siege, Quintus Fabius Maximus pursued them as far as the Ciminian forest, which was then looked upon by Rome as impassable. The consul's brother, who could speak Tuscan, went forward, dressed as a peasant, to explore it, and was courteously received by the Camertines of Umbria. On his return the consul advanced, engaged the enemy who had sought refuge in the forest, climbed the Ciminian hill, and on beholding the rich expanse of country that lay before him, proceeded forthwith to plunder it. It was at this juncture that, on returning to camp, the consul found five messengers awaiting him with orders forbidding him to attempt to traverse the forest. But they were too late, and returned home with news that the deed had been done and a victory gained.

3. Cp. D. I.31.1.

NOTES ON BOOK THREE

1. In Order that a Religious Institution or a Commonwealth should long survive it is essential that it should frequently be Restored to its Start

1. The word *'principio'* which occurs in the phrase *'ritirarla verso il suo principio'* and recurs in a similar context either in the singular or the plural throughout the chapter, is derived from the Latin word *'principium'* which may mean either a temporal beginning or a beginning or source or origin in the logical sense. Since it is clear from §§ 2 and 4 that what Machiavelli has in mind is the original constitution which determines the character of a republic, a kingdom, or a religious institution, *'principio'* might be translated either by 'principle' or by 'start'. I have used 'start' because Machiavelli's point is that constitutions usually have some good in them at the start, alike in the case of churches, kingdoms, and republics, but in course of time this gets neglected, misinterpreted, abused, and, when this happens, institutions become corrupt. It is important, therefore, from time to time to remind the communities concerned of what they were like at the start, and by this means to restore them to their pristine vigour; otherwise decadence will set in. This return to the primitive was the basic demand of the reformers, Luther and others, who were Machiavelli's contemporaries, though he says nothing about them, for at the time at which he is writing the reformation had scarce begun. The claim which he makes in this discourse, and which he applies not only to political but to religious organisations, is, therefore, identical with theirs; but with a difference. For (i) it is a basic postulate in Machiavelli's theory that political institutions must be adapted to the times, which are continually changing (D. III.9); (ii) he has already warned us in D. I.37 that laws may become out of date and unsuited to new conditions, and that in this case it is futile and dangerous to seek to enforce them; and (iii) though his ideal is a constitution framed by one man and perfect from the start (D. I.9), he admits that the constitution of the state which he takes as his model for all that wish to expand, was not perfect at the start but had to be modified as time went on and circumstances altered (D. I.2.1; I.5.5; and I.6). It is in the light of these and other passages, therefore, that the present discourse should be read.

2. *Quod quotidie aggregatur aliquid, quod quandoque indiget curatione.* A medical saying cited in bad Latin of the type one finds in thirteenth-century translations from Greek

or Arabic writers. It is probably taken from a medical work by Avicenna, but I cannot trace it.

3. '*contra jus gentium*', see D. II.28.1, for an account of these incidents, which are given by Livy in V.36; and for the phrase '*contra jus gentium*' which occurs in V.36.6. For its meaning, see D. II.28, n. 2.

4. For the spontaneous revival of religion which took place after the occupation of Rome by the Gauls in 390 B.C., see Livy V.39–41, and for the decree of the senate ordering the temples to be restored, expiation to be made for neglect of divine warnings, and a college to be established in honour of Jupiter, see V.50.

5. Note the conjunction of 'virtue' (*virtù*) with 'goodness' (*bontà*)—political worth and moral worth, but political worth in the sense not of mere efficiency, but of efficiency in the interests of the state.

6. To the strong body of troops at Veii 'a head was wanting', and, with the consent of all, Camillus was sent for, but not until the senate at Rome had been consulted, and a decree had been passed recalling him from exile and appointing him dictator (V.46.6–10).

7. Spurius Maelius, an equestrian profiteer, during the famine in 440 procured corn from Etruria at his own expense, and thus was enabled not only to keep the price so high that men were dying of starvation, but to distribute it as largesse with a view to winning popular support and to introducing political innovations. When it was realised that he was aiming at making himself king, Lucius Quintius Cincinnatus, then an old man, was appointed dictator. When Maelius was summoned to take his trial he collected some of his adherents, but was slain by Ahala Servilius, who had been sent to arrest him; for which deed the latter was commended by Cincinnatus, since it had saved the republic (IV.13–14).

8. Manlius Capitolinus, who had saved the capitol in 390, was condemned to death for exciting the plebs to violence in 384 (cp. D. I.24.4 and 58.1). Manlius Torquatus's son was executed by his father's orders in 340 for having disobeyed his commands (cp. D. II.16.2). Papirius Cursor wanted to prosecute Fabius for having fought a battle against his orders in 326, during the second Samnite war (cp. D. I.31.3). For the treatment of Scipio Africanus and his brother, Lucius, see D. I.29.6 and n. 8.

9. In 1433 Cosimo de' Medici was banished from Florence, but in the next year, a supporter of his, Niccolò di Cocco was appointed Gonfalonier and with him eight priors, all partisans of Cosimo, who was recalled from exile (H.F. IV.30–3). From this time on to their expulsion by Charles VIII in 1494, the Medici maintained their ascendancy over Florence. The subsequent passage presumably refers to the treatment meted out by Cosimo's supporters to their opponents. Niccolò di Cocco threw his predecessor, Donato Velluti into prison, whereupon the party opposed to Cosimo took up arms, though actual conflict was averted by the intervention of Pope Eugenius, then residing as an exile in Florence. No sooner, however, had Cosimo's party secured themselves in power than they banished all the leaders of the opposite party (*ib.* 33), just as they, when in power, had banished Cosimo. The seditious talk next referred to, is doubtless connected with the plans of Piero de' Medici (who succeeded Lorenzo in 1492) to increase his personal power, which led to his being detested by all parties. The return of Florence to its 'basic principle', i.e. to a genuinely republican form of government, took place on his expulsion in 1494.

10. For Horatius Cocles and Mucius Scaevola see Livy II.10–13, and cp. D. II.3, nn. 3, 4. Livy mentions C. Fabricius Luscinus in Book XIII of which we only have an epitome. In it we are told that, 'having been sent to Pyrrhus to redeem the prisoners [captured near Heraclea in 280 B.C.], he was tempted by the king to desert his country, but in vain; and the prisoners were returned without ransom', (cp. D. III.20.2). Plutarch in his *Life of Pyrrhus* (20 *sq.*) gives a fuller account of Fabricius' doings and character. He was no less unperturbed by an elephant hidden behind a curtain than he was by Pyrrhus's offer of gold. P. Decius Mus the Elder was consul in 340 with T. Manlius Torquatus, and sacrificed his life in order to encourage his troops in the battle of Mount Vesuvius, 340 B.C. (cp. D. II.16.1–2 and D. III.39.3; Livy VIII.8–10); his son, also P. Decius Mus, did the same thing at the battle of Sentinum in 295 B.C., when he was consul for the fourth time with his old colleague, Fabius Maximus, and the Gauls were defeated (Livy X.26–9; and D. III.45.1–2). M. Atilius Regulus defeated the Carthaginians in Africa in 256 during the First Punic War, but in the following year was defeated and captured by Xanthippus (cp. D. II.18.7 *and n.* 8). His request to be allowed to return to his farm is mentioned in D. III.25.3 as a late instance of the poverty practised by Roman generals. In 250 the Carthaginians sued for peace and sent Regulus, then a prisoner, to negotiate it. He insisted on returning to Carthage and, according to tradition, was cruelly put to death. (Cp. Livy, *Periocha*, XVIII; Horace, *Carm.* III.5; and C.A.H. VII. p. 689.)

11. M. Porcius Cato the Censor died in 149 B.C. His great-grandson, M. Porcius Cato the Younger (95–46) entered public life as military tribune in 67 B.C., eighty-two years later. Plutarch has written a life of each of them, and in that of the younger Cato describes how he sought in vain to check the growing abuses in civil administration—the peculations of civil servants, the ignoring of debts, the use of bribery and armed retainers at elections; how he strove to thwart the ambitions of Caesar, Pompey and Crassus, and in particular how he foresaw that the prolongation of military commissions (to which Machiavelli calls attention in D. III.24) would lead to the establishment of a tyranny in Rome; how he warned Pompey what to expect if he allowed Caesar's power to increase; and how, when Caesar was about to enter Rome, he left it with Pompey, and on Pompey's defeat, killed himself rather than owe his life to Caesar.

12. For the activities of the Franciscans and Dominicans (founded in the thirteenth century) in the time of Machiavelli, see Pastor, *Hist. Popes* V, Intro. III, p. 175 *sq.*; and for the scepticism of the age, see Buckhardt's *Civilisation of the Renaissance in Italy*, Part VI, cc. 3–5. What Machiavelli says about the threat of divine punishment encouraging, rather than discouraging, sceptical prelates in their evil doing, though open to question, is of a piece with what he says elsewhere about the futility of unarmed prophets (see P. 6, E.48–9; and cp. D. III.30.4).

13. The *Curia Regis*, which used originally to travel about with the King of France, was divided by Louis IX into three parts: (i) the '*Conseil du Roi*' (Privy Council); (ii) the '*Chambre des Comptes*' (Exchequer); and (iii) the '*Parlement*' (Judiciary). Philip IV divided the '*Parlement*' into three courts: (i) the '*Chambres des Requêtes*'—a court of first instance which dealt with minor cases; (ii) the '*Chambre des Enquêtes*'—a court of appeal; and (iii) the '*Grand Chambre*', which dealt with the more important cases and appeals. These courts sat in Paris, but, in addition, there was the States-General, which tenants-in-chief attended in person, and to which

the clergy and the towns sent representatives. It met first in 1302, and again in 1308 and 1316; in short, whenever in time of crisis the king saw fit to consult the representatives of his people. Sometimes it criticised the king's action, as in 1356 when it demanded that its own representatives should collect and administer the taxes. In 1439 it passed the 'Ordonnance sur la Gendarmerie', which sanctioned the king's having a standing army. It was summoned only once by Louis XI, but in its place he established provincial Estates and local Parlements in many large towns. When it met again in 1484 the nobles, the clergy and the third estate alike protested against the abuses that had grown up during the regency of Anne of Beaujeu (1483–91). Hence, when Machiavelli speaks of the laws of France being maintained and the king's action being condemned by the 'parlements' of France, notably that of Paris, it is probably of all these courts and assemblies that he is thinking. Moreover, it was the States-General, rather than the Parlements, that strengthened the king's hand and enabled him to reduce the powers of the nobles. (Cp. P. 19, Burd 315, E.153.)

14. Machiavelli returns to the two alternatives mentioned at the outset. In Rome's case reforms were for the most part brought about by the pressure of external events, wars or the danger of wars. This is undesirable; a return to the basic principles on which a state has been founded should be brought about internally in the natural course of events, and, if possible, provided for by the constitution.

15. Cp. D. III.4 and 5 for kings who did things with a view to promoting, as they thought, their own interests; and see Aquinas, *de Regimine*, III.16, on the influence of Rome's great men.

2. That it is a Very Good Notion at Times to pretend to be a Fool

1. Tarquin the Proud, Rome's last king, sent his two sons to enquire of the oracle at Delphi why he had been seeing serpents. They were accompanied by L. Junius Brutus, the king's nephew, 'a man of very different calibre from what he pretended to be' (Livy I.56.7). For, on hearing that his uncle had put his own brother and other prominent citizens to death, 'he deliberately simulated stupidity, allowed the king to seize both himself and his property', and so behaved that 'the king should have no ground to fear him, and that of his fortune there should be nothing left which the king could covet, that in thus becoming contemptible, he might be safe' (*ib.* 7–8). Livy, it is true, does not explicitly state that in so doing Brutus had in mind the liberating of Rome, but he does suggest this, for he adds that, 'he did not refuse the cognomen "Brutus", so that beneath this name the man who was to free the Roman people concealed his intention and awaited a suitable opportunity' (*ib.* 8). The companions of Brutus looked upon him as a joke, and to this he played up. For when the king's sons were told by the oracle that 'he should enjoy sovereign power who first kissed his mother', Brutus stumbled and fell so that he might kiss his mother, the earth (*ib.* 10–12). The story of Lucretia, who had been outraged by the king, sending for her father and her husband and two trustworthy friends, one of whom was Brutus, who withdrew the dagger with which Lucretia had killed herself, and called those present to expel Lucius Tarquin and all his brood, is told in cc. 58–9.

2. Note that Machiavelli prefers conduct which is open and above board to

subterfuge, provided it is possible by such conduct to attain the good end one has in view; i.e. whenever practicable, not only should the end be good, but also the means.

3. Note the implied rejection of the Aristotelian maxim that virtue lies in the mean. It is one of the two extremes that must here be chosen, not the middle course.

3. When Liberty has been newly acquired it is Necessary in Order to maintain it to 'Kill the Sons of Brutus'

1. Livy II.5.5–20. 'Their punishment was the more remarkable because the consulship imposed on the father the office of punishing his children, and to him who should not have been a spectator, fortune assigned the task of exacting the punishment.' (*ib.* 5.5.)

2 For the 'Sons of Brutus' see D. I.16.4, 10 and n. 2 and D. III.1.5; 5.4; 6.14.

3. For Soderini see D. I.7.6 and n. 5; I.52.2 and n. 3.

4. A Prince cannot Live Securely in a Principality whilst those are Alive who have been despoiled of it

1. For the incidents related in this chapter Machiavelli relies on Livy, Book I. For the means taken by Tarquinius Priscus to obtain the throne, see c. 35. Of his juridical right Livy merely says that he became king with the consent of the Roman people (35.6). For the indignation of the sons of his predecessor, Ancus, whose guardian he had been, see c. 40.

2. For the means taken by Servius Tullius, son-in-law to Tarquinius Priscus, to obtain the throne, see I.41. In order to placate the sons of his predecessor, whom he had dispossessed, he gave to each of them a daughter in marriage (I.42), but was none the less murdered by one of them.

3. Cp. P. 7 at the end, where the same thing is said of '*personaggi grandi*' as is said here of '*potenti*', namely, 'He who believes that new benefits will cause great personages to forget old injuries is deceived'. The reference in P. 7 is to Caesar Borgia, who hoped to secure the goodwill of Julius II. Cp. the quotation from Tacitus in D. I.29.1: 'one is more inclined to repay injuries than benefits'.

4. The elder son of Tarquinius Priscus was murdered by his brother, Lucius, at the instigation of the former's wife, Tullia, whom he then married. On her ambition to become queen, see Livy I.47, and on the murder of Servius Tullius, see I.48, Lucius then succeeds as Tarquinius Superbus.

Cp. *The Prince*, cap. 4, where Machiavelli says that if in a conquered province the family of the Prince be eliminated, there is nothing to fear. For comments on this and the preceding chapter, and for further details as to the murders committed by Rome's kings, see Introduction, XI, §§ 119 *sq*. Cicero refers both to the murder of Remus and to Brutus having deprived his colleague, Collatinus, of his imperium in *De Officiis*, III.x (n. 40). The murder of Remus, though it seemed to Romulus to be expedient, was morally wrong, he says, since Romulus threw to the winds brotherly affection; but the depriving Collatinus of the office of consul was both expedient and morally right, since it was to the interest of the state that the memory of the Tarquins should be removed, and hence should have been approved by Collatinus himself, '*Itaque utilitas valuit propter honestatem; sine qua ne utilitas quidem esse potuisset.*' But note that the '*honestas*' here depends solely on its being in the interests of the state that Collatinus should lose his position.

5. What it is that causes a Hereditary Prince to lose his Kingdom

1. After the murder of his wife, his brother, and of Servius Tullius, Lucius Tarquinius was left without a rival. He then killed the principal senators (Livy I.49.1), and having thus obtained the throne purely by force, says Livy, he placed no reliance on the goodwill of his subjects, but surrounded himself with a body-guard, and sought to make himself secure by terror. He himself administered justice in capital cases. He dropped the custom of consulting the senate, and made war and peace as he pleased (I.49.2 *sq.*). In order to perpetuate his memory by erecting a temple to Jupiter, he employed both Etruscans and his own people, and then set them to work on the circus and on the public sewers (56.1–3). Then came the assault on Lucretia (58), which, conjoined with the king's arrogance and the degradation of his people, who had become labourers and stone-cutters instead of warriors (59.9), led to the revolt organised by Brutus and Collatinus (59–60).

2. Of Timoleon of Corinth, who (after killing his brother who was seeking to set up a tyranny there) was sent to liberate Sicily in 344 B.C., Plutarch, in his *Life of Timoleon,* says: 'His love of his country was remarkable, and so was his mildness of disposition, except that he had a hatred of tyrants and of wicked men' (n. 3). Having expelled Dionysius from Syracuse, he proceeded to liberate city after city, in each of which he set up a democratic form of government. Though actually the ruler of Sicily, which consulted him on all important matters, 'he spent most of his time in the country', says Plutarch, 'with his wife and children whom he had sent for from Corinth, for he never returned home' (n. 36). Even when in his old age he became blind, the citizens still continued to consult him, and brought all strangers to see the deliverer of Syracuse (n. 38). He died in 337 B.C., 'having performed,' says Plutarch, 'greater things than any Grecian of his time' (n. 37). But from this view, which is that of the historian Timaeus, Polybius dissents. 'Timoleon,' he says, 'far from having accomplished any action of first-rate importance, never even undertook one. The one expedition he carried out took him no further than from Corinth to Syracuse', and to compare one 'whose glory was gained in such a mere saucer of a place as Sicily', with the most illustrious heroes, is ridiculous. (Polybius XII.23, but this part of Polybius's work was not available in Latin in Machiavelli's lifetime).

3. In regard to Aratus, Plutarch, who wrote his life, and Polybius, who says much of him in Books II, IV and V, are agreed. It was he who by his diplomacy expelled numerous tyrants from the cities of Greece, or induced them to resign, between 251 and 245, when he became *strategos* of the Achaean League, which he persuaded most of the cities to join. His policy, says Polybius, 'was directed to one single end: to expel the Macedonians from the Peloponnese, to depose the tyrants, and to establish in each state the common freedom which their ancestors had

enjoyed before them' (II.43). 'No one surpassed him in the moderation he showed in political contests, or in his power of attaching friends and gaining allies; in intrigue, stratagem and laying plots against a foe, and in bringing them to a successful termination by personal endurance and courage, he was pre-eminent' (IV.8). 'I have written his life,' says Plutarch to Polycrates, 'that your sons may form themselves on the noble examples set by their own family' (*Aratus, n.* 2). When in 345 B.C. Syracuse appealed to her mother-city, Corinth, for help against Carthage, Timoleon was sent and within fifty days of his landing Nicetas was defeated and Dionysius surrendered. Reinforcements were obtained in spite of the blockade, which was withdrawn in 343. Timoleon then expelled the petty tyrants from Sicilian towns, and in 339 Carthage made peace.

4. Of Timoleon Cornelius Nepos says that 'as soon as possible he resigned his command and spent the rest of his life as a private citizen. Nor did he do this unskilfully, for whereas other kings relied on their *imperium,* he held sway by his benevolence' (III.4–5). Though without office, so popular was he with the Sicilians, says Plutarch (*Timoleon,* n. 35), that 'no war seemed concluded, no law enacted, no land divided, no political regulation properly made, unless he revised and retouched it'. With the Achaeans it was customary for the *strategos* to resign at the end of his year's office, and this Aratus, who was chosen as *strategos* seventeen times (Plutarch, *Aratus,* 53), used to do; as he probably did also when he was appointed '*strategos autokrator*' in 225 (*ib.* 41), for, though he appears to have held this office for more than a year, he was probably re-elected. (Cp. C.A.H. VII, p. 758 and note 3, p. 863.)

Cp. *The Prince,* cap. 2, on Hereditary Principalities, in which also there is mention of the need to respect ancient institutions. Cp. also Aristotle, *Politics,* V.10: 'Kingly rule is little affected by external causes, and is, therefore, lasting: it is generally destroyed from within. And there are two ways in which the destruction may come about: (1) when the members of the royal family quarrel among themselves [the case discussed in D. III.4], and (2) when kings attempt to administer the state too much after the fashion of a tyranny and to extend their authority contrary to the law' [cp. § 2]. 'There are now no monarchies', he adds, 'for, in our day men are more on an equality, and no one is so immeasurably superior to others as to represent adequately the greatness and dignity of the office' [cp. D. I.55 and III.8]. He also agrees with what M. says in P. 19 about hatred and contempt, for in the same passage he writes: 'In hereditary monarchies a further cause of destruction is the fact that kings often fall into contempt, and, although not possessing tyrannical but only royal power, are apt to outrage others. Their overthrow is then easily effected, for there is an end to the king when his subjects do not want to have him' (V.10, 1312*b*, 38–1313*a*, 15).

6. On Conspiracies

1. The remark that 'anyone can conspire against a prince', if taken in conjunction with the fact that 'more princes have lost their lives and their states in this way than in any other', suggests a possible reason for the extraordinary length of this chapter. It is three times the length of the next longest chapter, D. II.24, and is eight times

the length of the average chapter. In *The Prince*, too, the chapter in which conspiracies are discussed, P. 19, is twice as long as any other chapter. In the earlier chapters of *The Prince*, Machiavelli discusses how a principality may be obtained *pari passu* with the question how a principality can be maintained. In the *Discourses* he has already discussed how a republic can be maintained once liberty has been acquired, and in D. I.16–18 has laid great stress on the difficulty of maintaining liberty in a state that has been more or less servile. But as to how tyranny is to be abolished and liberty acquired he has thus far said nothing except *en passant*, e.g. in the chapter on Tyranny (D. I.10), in which he points out how many of the Roman emperors were assassinated. One way in which to get rid of a tyrant—and this the more honourable way—is by open rebellion or open war (D. III.2.2); but this is not the way in which tyrants have normally been removed in point of fact. Hence the need to discuss alike from the conspirator's, and from the ruler's, point of view the problem which conspiracies in all their aspects and all their stages present. That conspiracies have been many, but few successful is pointed out in P. 19 (Burd 312, E.151).

In Book V of his *Politics*, which is concerned with the causes of transitions from one form of government to another, Aristotle lays no less stress than does Machiavelli on the importance of conspiracies, and has at least as much, if not more, to say about them. But, though they agree to some extent, as indeed they must since they are discussing similar situations, there is no trace of dependence. Machiavelli, for instance, does not expressly mention in this chapter the demand for equality, or factions, or personal quarrels, or conflict between the aristocratic and democratic factors in a state, as amongst the causes of conspiracy, as Aristotle does in V, cc. 1 and 2. Nor does he refer to political clubs and rivalry between men of different nationalities in one and the same state (c. 6, 1035b and c. 3, 1303a). Nor yet are the instances cited by Machiavelli from Greek history the same as those cited by Aristotle except in the case of Phalaris, Dionysius, and Pisistratus. Conversely the long discussion on the organising, management, and consequences of plots is lacking in Aristotle. For the dependence of P. 19 on Aristotle, see Burd, note on pp. 310–11.

The importance of conspiracies was recognised, then, long before Machiavelli's day, but in his day they were of frequent occurrence, especially in Italy, and in the age that follows were to become of scarce less frequent occurrence in England. A leader writer in *The Times Literary Supplement* for 25 November 1944 writes: 'The history of the seventeenth and late sixteenth centuries . . . is pre-eminently the era of plots; and plots which are conceived in secret tend to finish in darkness also. The Babington Plot, the Ridolphi Plot, the Main Plot and the Bye Plot, the Gunpowder and Popish Plots, the Meal Tub Plot and the Rye House Plot—the very names carry the intonation of mysterious romance. The reason why they should be specially abundant in the Tudor and Stuart reigns is evident enough; for plots are the natural reaction of the discontented to despotic rule, as was observed by the most eminent living despot as recently as 20 July' (*T.L.S.*, 25 Nov. 1944, p. 571).

2. Cp. *Taciti Historiarum* IV.8 in the speech of Marcellus in the senate, where he, Marcellus, apropos of Vespasian, says: '*Se meminisse temporum quibus natus sit, quam civitatis formam patres avique instituerint; ulteriora mirari, praesentia sequi; bonos imperatores voto expetere, qualescunque tolerare.*' With this paragraph compare the opening remarks in P. 3, where Machiavelli says that 'those who take up arms in the hope of bettering

themselves deceive themselves and afterwards find that they have gone from bad to worse'. (Cp. Aquinas, *de Regimine* I.6.)

3. On the taking of towns by 'furtive violence' cp. D. II.32.5–6.

4. See P. 19 on how to avoid being despised and hated, and P. 17 on whether it is better to be loved or feared; also P. 16, last par. and P. 20 last par. Cp. D. II.24.2–4.

5. Cp. the opening paragraphs of P. 19, where we are told that conspiracies against princes who have the goodwill of their subjects are rare, and that, where this is the case, 'it is impossible that anyone should be so rash as to conspire'. (E.150, 152; cp. also D. II.24.3–4.)

6. On the folly of using threats, cp. D. II.26.1 and I.44.

7. In P. 17 we are told that a prince must 'take life only on proper justification and for manifest cause', and that he must be yet more careful about seizing the property of others, 'since men forget more quickly the death of their father than the loss of their patrimony' (E.135). Similarly in P. 19 (E.149) Machiavelli says that nothing makes a prince more hated than the violation of the property and the women of his subjects, and that if he leaves their property and their honour alone, most men will be content. Cp. above § 4 and Aristotle, *Politics*, V.11, 1315a, 28 *sq*.

8. For Pausanias and Philip of Macedon see § 7 and cp. D. II.28.3 and n. 3. Aristotle mentions the conspiracy of Pausanias as one due to an insult in *Pol.* V.10, 1311b, 2.

9. In his *History of Florence* VIII.35, Machiavelli says that after the retirement of the Duke of Calabria at the end of 1478, commotions in Siena were very frequent but that at length victory lay with the nobles, 'amongst whom Pandolfo and Jacopo Petrucci obtained supreme authority, becoming, the one by his prudence, the other by his courage, almost princes in that city.' The two Petrucci returned from exile in 1487. Jacopo died in 1497, and on his death Pandolfo became in fact but not in name 'prince' of Siena, and is thus spoken of in P. 20 and P. 22 without qualification. (Cp. below, § 34 and n. 50 for the attempt of the Belanti to assassinate him; and § 39 and n. 60 for the ruse by which he acquired power.)

10. Cp. *Hist. Florence* VIII.2. Giovanni de Pazzi—nephew of Jacopo, head of the Pazzi family, who on account of his wealth and high birth had been made a knight by the people—'had married the daughter of Giovanni Buonromei, a very wealthy citizen, whose property, on his death without male children, should have gone to his daughter. Carlo, Buonromei's nephew, however, seized a portion of his property, and, when the case was tried, a decree was made whereby the wife of Giovanni de Pazzi was despoiled of her father's inheritance and it went to Carlo. This wrong the Pazzi knew well was wholly the doing of the Medici. In fact, Giuliano de' Medici often reproached his brother, Lorenzo, saying he feared lest, in grasping too much, they might lose all.' (For further mention of the Pazzi conspiracy in this chapter, see §§ 13, 28, 30, 32.)

11. For the reasons which induced Brutus and Cassius to murder Caesar, see Plutarch's *Brutus*, 8–10. Plutarch denies that it was on his own private account that Cassius hated Caesar. He had from the outset displayed hatred against 'the whole race of tyrants', and it was for this reason that he induced Brutus to join him in abolishing 'a tyranny that was becoming daily more manifest'. (Cp. also D. I.10.4 and n. 9.)

Phalaris, tyrant of Acragas (Agrigentum), 570–554 B.C., was killed, says Cicero, not as the result of a plot, nor yet by a few, but as the result of an attack in which the whole of the people of Agrigentum joined. He exemplifies the effect of hatred, induced by fear, against which no power, however great, can stand (*De Officiis* II.vii.)

Dionysius the Elder, ruler of Syracuse from 405 to 367, is mentioned by Cicero in the same passage as a further example of the powerlessness of tyrants, who have aroused the resentment of their people. 'Owing to his cruelties,' says Cicero, 'he was tortured by fear, and was so afraid of getting his hair cut by a barber that he used to singe it himself with a piece of burning charcoal.' A story in Plutarch (*Dion* 6) says his physicians gave him a sleeping draught from which he never recovered. Cicero says merely that he was killed by the few. Aristotle cites the attack on Dionysius as a case of contempt evoked by bad rule (*Pol.* V.10, 1312a, 4–8), and mentions Phalaris as one who acquired a tyranny by holding high office (*ib.* 1310b, 28). The reference may, however, be to Dionysius II (cp. D. I.10, n. 5).

12. '*Ad generum Cereris sine caede et vulnere pauci*
    Descendunt reges, et sicca morte tiranni.'

                                (Juvenal, *Satires* X.112–13, cited in Latin).
And compare Machiavelli's remark about the nemesis that befalls tyrants with the *De Officiis, loc. cit.* Having quoted Ennius' saying, '*Quem metuunt oderunt; quem quisque odit, perisse expetit*', Cicero remarks: 'Nor is it alone the death of the tyrant against whom an oppressed city has risen in arms, that shows how great a pest the hatred of men becomes, but the death in like manner of all tyrants, there being scarce any who escape such a death. For fear affords but a poor guarantee of survival, whereas benevolence can be relied upon, even in perpetuity.'

13. See § 5, and D. II.28.3. The details of the assassination of Philip II of Macedon by Pausanias in 336 B.C., given in this paragraph, are all to be found in Justin IX.6, but are not given either in Plutarch's *Alexander* (9–10), or by Diodorus Siculus in XVI.93–4.

14. For details of this attempt on the life of Ferdinand of Aragon, see Prescott's *Ferdinand and Isabella*, c. XVIII. On 7 December 1492 Ferdinand had been presiding at a court which dealt with suits brought by the poorer classes, and was descending the stairs when he was attacked by a poor peasant, aged sixty, who turned out to be insane. The dagger struck the gold chain the king wore round his neck, and this saved his life, but a bone in the neck was fractured and for a week he was dangerously ill. The rumour of the attempted murder spread through the city, and, though the king desired to pardon the lunatic, the populace insisted on his dying a traitor's death.

15. Selim I (1512–20) is 'the present Turk' (cp. D. I.1.9; 19.3; and D. II.17.10). His father was Bajazet (Bayacid) II, 1481–1512, who was forced to resign in his son's favour, and a month later died of poison. The attempt to assassinate Bajazet took place after his failure to take Belgrade in June 1492 on his leaving Monastir. The assassin was killed by the guards.

16. Cp. Aristotle, *Politics* V.10, 1311a, 15 *sq.*, in which he says that plots against tyrants are almost always contrived by notables; and cp. V.11, 1315a, 8, where he warns princes against making one person great.

17. Perennis, having got rid of his colleague, Paternus, encouraged the emperor in his debaucheries, and meanwhile ruled the state, supported by the Praetorian guard until A.D. 185, when he was accused of planning a *coup d'état*, and

was handed over to some troops then marching on the city by whom he was murdered (cp. C.A.H. XI, pp. 381–2). For the conspiracy of Plautianus, see notes 30 and 43 to §§ 21 and 31. For the means by which Sejanus acquired power —his control of the Praetorian Guard, the appointment of his father as governor of Egypt, his appointment of consuls, the statues erected to him in Rome, the emperor's retirement to Capreae, the elimination of rivals, including Drusus, the emperor's son—see Tacitus, *Annals,* Book IV, 1–3, 6–12, 17, 39–41, 54, 59–60, 74. In the end, Tiberius becomes suspicious, and sends a letter to the Senate, which orders the imprisonment of Sejanus, and on 18 October, A.D. 31, he is put to death (V.6–8). As to his guilt, and in particular whether he conspired against the emperor's life, there is some doubt, for which see Furneaux's edition of the *Annals*, Introduction, c. 8, pp. 150–1.

18. Jacopo d'Appiano (d. 1398) was driven into exile by Gian Galeazzo Visconti together with Piero Gambacorti, Lord of Pisa. On their return Jacopo was made chancellor and sought to get Gambacorti to desert the alliance with Florence and support the Visconti. Gambacorti refused, so on 21 October 1392 Jacopo went to his house, seized his two sons, and, having called Gambacorti down, killed him and became Lord of Pisa in his stead.

19. When the war which Ferdinand, King of Naples, had been waging with his barons was brought to an end in 1487 by the intervention of Ferdinand of Aragon, the Spanish king, we are told in *The History of Florence* VIII. 32, that 'the King was reconciled with the barons, but put to death Jacopo Coppola and Antonello of Aversa with his sons, as having, during the war, revealed his secrets to the Pope'. Coppola, Count of Sarno, was financial adviser to the crown and had amassed considerable wealth. When Ferdinand returned to Naples in 1484, his son, Alfonso, urged him to apply pressure to Coppola and other barons. On the arrest of the Count of Montorio and the heirs of the Duke of Ascoli, the barons revolted, led by Coppola and Petrucci, the Secretary of State, and appealed for assistance to Innocent IV. In October 1485 Petrucci and Coppola offered to come to terms, and the Peace of Miglionico, nicknamed Mal Consiglio, was signed. Ferdinand undertook to pardon the barons; but in May 1487 most of them, including Petrucci and Coppola, were executed, their estates confiscated, and the few that escaped fled to Venice. The extremely brief mention made of Coppola in *The History of Florence* would none the less seem to suggest that Machiavelli had by this time revised his opinion of Coppola's importance.

20. Cp. P. 17, where princes are warned that 'friendships may be purchased instead of being won by greatness and nobility of mind, but they are not reliable, and there come times when they cannot be counted on. For men think less of offending one who has made himself beloved than one who has made himself feared, since it is a sense of obligation that holds fast the bonds of love, and this, owing to men being so wicked, fades away whenever there is a chance of personal gain; whereas fear is sustained by the dread of punishment, and this never lets you down' (E.135). Hence, though a prince ought to aim at being thought merciful, he 'should not mind the reproach of cruelty, for to be cruel in a few cases is more merciful than, by excess of mercy, to permit disorders to arise, from which follow murder and robbery' (E.133). On the danger of conferring too much power on one individual cp. Aristotle, *Politics*, V.11: 'All monarchs take the precaution of not

making one man great, but, if two or more, they look sharply one after the other' (1315a, 8–10).

21. A list of some twenty of the conspirators is given in Tacitus' *Annals*, XV.49–50: they include tribunes, poets, a consul-designate, senators, knights, and officers. Cp. C.A.H. X, p. 729 where it is reckoned that after the discovery of the plot, 19 persons were executed, 13 banished, and 4 tribunes cashiered. This plot is mentioned again in §§ 15, 20 and 22. A list of the principal conspirators concerned in the plot to kill Lorenzo and Giuliano de' Medici in 1478 is given by Machiavelli himself in H.F. VIII.3–7. It includes not only the Pazzi and their friends in Florence, but people in Rome and exiles who had been banished from Perugia.

22. See Livy II.4.5–7 for the dinner-party at which a slave heard the conspirators discussing their plans to restore the Tarquins.

23. The source would seem to be Quintus Curtius, 'De Rebus gestis Alexandri Magni,' Book VI. For in c. 7 we are told that Dymnus told his boy friend, Nicomachus, of the conspiracy, besought him to join, and threatened to kill him if he revealed the plot, which was to be carried out in three days' time; and that Nicomachus told his brother, Cebalinus, about it, who in turn tried to warn Alexander. Actually he did not warn the king personally at first, nor does Philotas' name appear in the list of the conspirators which was given by Dymnus to Nicomachus. This, however, is explained in the sequel, which is told in the rest of the book, cc. 8–11. Philotas was the person whom the conspirators intended to put in place of Alexander. Hence, when Cebalinus tells Philotas of the plot, he says nothing about it to Alexander, and Cebalinus has to find another friend of the king through whom to make his communication. The king then sends for Cebalinus, who confirms what has been said, and eventually Philotas confesses and is put to death. The date is 330 B.C. Machiavelli summarises quite a long story in a very few words; but for *Cebalino* has written *Ciballino*.

24. For the story of Scaevinus and his rusty old dagger, and of Milichus being told to prepare bandages, see Tacitus, *Annals* XV, c. 54, and for the arrest and the conflicting statements, c. 55. The date was A.D. 65.

25. An account of the discovery of the conspiracy against Hieronymus of Syracuse by a soldier's servant, a lad of the same age as Hieronymus, and of Theodotus' refusal to disclose the names of the conspirators, is given by Livy in XXIV.5. Wherefore, since Machiavelli expressly cites Titus Livy as his authority, he must have known Book XXIV. The date was 215 B.C. Machiavelli writes *Teodoro* for *Teodoto*.

26. Aristotimus, tyrant of Elaea, a city of Epirus, situate at the mouth of the Acheron, was murdered during the civil wars which arose in Greece after the death of Pyrrhus in 272 B.C. Pausanias merely says that Cylon liberated the Elaeans, having slain the tyrant with his own hands after he had taken refuge in the temple of Zeus (VI.14.11). Plutarch in his '*Mulierum Virtutes*', 253A–B, supplies further details: Cylon joined in the plot, but the person who organised it was Hellanicus, an old man who had lost two sons, and it was Thrasybulus and Lambadus who actually killed the tyrant. Neither of these authors mentions Nelematus, nor yet does Justin, who in XXVI.1 gives an account of the conspiracy which corresponds in all respects, save this, to that given by Machiavelli. Aristotimus, having got hold of a city in Epirus (*Epirotum urbs*), perpetrated numerous

atrocities, especially on some Aetolian exiles, whom he had promised to release. Hellanicus, their *'princeps'*, an old man who had lost his children, got together some friends in his house, locked the doors, and threatened to hand them over unless they killed Aristotimus, since he could not do it himself. This put an end to their hesitation, and, *'honestiorem viam eligentes'*, they swore to do as he wished. Hence, for Nelematus, who is mentioned again in § 26 as 'Nelematus of Epirus', we must read 'Hellanicus', and it was not in Epirus proper but in the neighbouring district of Aetolia that Hellanicus held dominion.

27. In contrast with the above, Machiavelli's account of the next conspiracy, that of Otanes in 521 B.C. against the Magus who was posing as Smerdis, corresponds in every detail with the account given of the incident by Herodotus in III.70–78 save that Herodotus' account is very much longer. Machiavelli has written *Ortano*: it should be *Otano*.

28. In view of the mention of Titus Livy in § 30 as the authority for what is there related of the killing of Nabis by Alexamenes, it is to be presumed that Livy is the authority also for this passage. True, in our present text the number of troops the Aetolians sent with Alexamenes is 30 horse, selected from young knights, and 1,000 foot, not 200 (XXXV.35.4), but otherwise the two accounts agree. The praetor, Damocritus, warned the troops not to speculate on their future movements, but to obey blindly the orders given. They joined up with the army Nabis commanded, as if they were going to fight with it; and of the commission entrusted to him Alexamenes said nothing to his men until the moment for action arrived. Livy XXXV.35, 16–17. (192 B.C.)

29. For this further incident in the conspiracy of Piso we go back to Tacitus' *Annals*, in which for Piso's qualifications see XV.48. After the arrest of Epicharis, 'the conspirators resolved to hurry on the assassination in Piso's beautiful villa at Baiae, which was a favourite resort of Nero's, and to which he would often go to bathe and dine without escort or any state belonging to his rank' (*ib.* 52). Hence Machiavelli's remarks on what might have happened had this plan been carried out. But Piso would not consent to such a breach of hospitality (cp. § 15).

30. For the conspiracy of Plautianus against the emperor, Septimius Severus (193–211), described in this paragraph, mentioned in § 9, and referred to again in § 31, Machiavelli relies upon Herodian, as he himself indicates in § 31; not upon Dion Cassius, who was in Rome at the time and also gives us an account of these events. Plautianus was a fellow-townsman of the emperor, and, like Sejanus in the time of Tiberius, had acquired almost unlimited power. Dion Cassius thinks the story of the plot was fabricated by Antoninus (Caracalla), in order to get rid of an all-powerful rival. For the 'too many benefits' conferred on Plautianus, see Herodian III.34, and for the commissioning of Saturninus to commit the murder and his request for something in writing—a *'libellum'*—see III.38. On the discovery of the plot, Plautianus was sent for and executed—in A.D. 205. (III.39–42).

31. For the betrayal of Epicharis by the captain of triremes to whom she had communicated the plot to murder the emperor Nero, and for her steadfastness, see Tacitus, *Annals*, XV.51.

32. For the conspiracy of Laetus and Eclectus against the emperor Commodus in A.D. 192, Machiavelli relies on Herodian, not on Dion Cassius. For (i) the story of Laetus and Eclectus given in this paragraph is not mentioned by Dion Cassius, and (ii) the poison mentioned in § 41 was not, according to Dion, administered

in a drink, but in meat—in *carnibus bovinis*; whereas Machiavelli's account here and in § 41 tallies with Herodian's in his *'De imperio Romanorum Imperatorum post Marcum'* I.52–5. (Cp. also P. 19 on Commodus, and C.A.H. XI.9.7.)

33. Machiavelli's account of Macrinus' conspiracy in § 25 summarises neatly the long and detailed account of it given by Herodian in IV.22–24. Caracalla's suspiciousness, his fondness for consulting astrologers, his letter to Maternianus and Maternianus' reply stating that Macrinus is conspiring against him, the intercepting of the letter which the emperor receives with others just as he is getting into a chariot and so hands them over to Macrinus to deal with, Macrinus' fear lest a second letter be sent, his choice of Martialis as the murderer, and the deed itself, performed on 8 April A.D. 217, while the emperor is halting during a journey and has got down from his horse, are all mentioned in Herodian's account.

34. See § 19 above, but for 'Nelematus' read 'Hellanicus'—cp. note 26 above.

35. On the folly of using threats, see § 4 above.

36. For the change of plan in the Pazzi conspiracy, see H.F. VIII.5. The conspirators from Rome travelled in the train of Raffaello di Riario, Archbishop of Pisa and Cardinal of St. George, whom the Pazzi had invited for this express purpose. Their first plan was to kill Lorenzo and Giuliano at their villa in Fiesole, but, 'whether by accident or purposely, Giuliano did not come'. The next plan was to kill them at a banquet to be held on Sunday, 26 April, 'but word being brought to Francesco [de Pazzi] on Sunday at daybreak that Giuliano was not coming to the banquet, the chief conspirators again assembled, and decided that there should be no further delay, for as the plot was known to many, it could not long escape discovery. So it was settled to kill the brothers in the cathedral Church of Santa Reparata.' To this plan Giovambattista da Montesecco, who was to have killed Lorenzo, objected, 'saying he durst not add sacrilege to treachery', so 'the business had to be committed to Messer Antonio da Volterra and the priest, Stefano, neither of whom, by nature or by habit, was fitted for such an attempt', with the result they muddled it, and Lorenzo got off with a slight wound in the throat. (See below, §§ 30 and 32.)

37. For the story of the failure to kill Marius in 88 B.C., see Plutarch's *'Caius Marius'*, nn. 37–40. Marius took shelter with an old man in the neighbourhood of Minturnae, in Campania, whither he had fled; but was caught and handed over to the magistrates of Minturnae, who sent him under guard to the house of a woman, Fannia, who was supposed to be his enemy, but in fact befriended him. It was decided to put him to death, but as no citizen would undertake to do this, a soldier, whom some say was a Gaul and others a Cimbrian, was despatched, sword in hand, to kill him. But on entering the darkened chamber, he saw light flashing from Marius's eyes and heard a solemn voice say, 'Dost thou dare kill Marius?' Whereupon he threw down his sword and fled, saying he could not do the deed; and the citizens, repenting, sent Marius away by ship, for it would be a disgrace, they thought, to 'put to death the preserver of Italy'. On the impression made by the majesty of a prince, cp. P. 19 (Burd 312, E.151).

38. Neither Thucydides nor any other of the authorities cited by Pauly-Wissowa mentions the conspiracy against Sitalces to which Machiavelli here refers (*vide sub* 'Sitalkes'). Hence 'Sitalces' is probably a mistake for 'Cypselus', so called because his mother, Labda, hid him in a trunk when the Bacchiadae came to kill him. For they had been before to Petra, and Labda had given them the child, which they had

passed round, but, when the child smiled on the first of the ten conspirators, pity restrained him from killing it, and he passed it on. So did they all, and then, having returned it to its mother, attacked each other with mutual recriminations for not having killed it. The two stories correspond, save that the conspirators only returned once, and were not punished until Cypselus grew up, became tyrant of Corinth, and banished or killed his opponents or deprived them of their property (Herodotus V.92).

39. Alfonso d'Este succeeded his father, Ercole I, as Duke of Ferrara in 1505. In the following year a conspiracy was formed by Ferrante and Giulio, illegitimate sons of Ercole I, to depose him. It failed and the two brothers were imprisoned for life (cp. Guicciardini, *St. d'I.* VII.4, p. 284).

40. '*Collegit et ipse animum confusum tantae cogitatione rei*' (Livy XXXV.35.18, cited in Latin). For the events leading up to this, see § 19 above and n. 28.

41. When Verus, coadjutor of the emperor Marcus, died in 169, his widow, Anna Lucilla Augusta, daughter of Marcus, was given in marriage to Claudius Pompeianus, formerly governor of Pannonia, and now the emperor's chief adviser. When Marcus Aurelius was succeeded by his son, Commodus, in 180, who married Crispina, Lucilla was relegated to a subordinate position, and, becoming jealous, availed herself of the resentment Commodus had aroused amongst the senators to form a conspiracy to displace him in favour of her own son. The accounts given by Dion Cassius (LXII.4), Aelius Lampridius (*Hist. Augustae Scriptores*, Commodus 4), and Herodian (I.20-3) agree as to the place in which the murder was attempted—a dark passage leading to the theatre—and as to the cause of its failure—the warning given when the assassin brandished his dagger and said 'The senate sends you this'; and again as to Lucilla's being the prime mover. They differ, however, in regard to the assassin. Dion Cassius and Lampridius say that it was Claudius Pompeianus, Lucilla's husband, who attempted the murder; whereas Herodian says Lucilla persuaded a young man, Quintianus by name, impetuous and daring, and a member of the Senate, to take a dagger and await a suitable opportunity to slay Commodus, which he eventually attempted in a dark place leading to the theatre, drawing his dagger and saying in a loud voice that it was sent by the senate, but taking so long over it that he failed to wound the emperor and was caught by his bodyguard. Hence it would seem to be Herodian's account that Machiavelli is following, though the words used by Quintianus are given by Herodian in *oratio obliqua*.

42. Machiavelli does not mention the words used by Antonio de Volterra in the account he gives of this conspiracy in *The History of Florence* VIII.6; nor does Guicciardini mention them in his *Storia Fiorentina*, c. 4. They are, however, mentioned by a contemporary writer, Parenti, cited by Pastor. (*Hist. Popes* IV, p. 309 n.) Moreover, as Machiavelli was nine years old when the events took place on Easter Sunday in 1478, he would have heard the details even if he was not present in the cathedral. (Cp. above §§ 5, 13, 28 and 30.)

43. The instructions given to Saturninus by Plautianus were that he should pretend to have some grave secret to impart to the emperor, Severus, and, having thus gained access to his apartments, should kill 'the old man and also his son [Antoninus], each in his own apartment'; and it was precisely the difficulty of killing two people '*diversis habitantes cubiculis*', that, according to Herodian (III.38), led him to betray the plot instead of carrying it out. (Cp. §§ 9, 21 and n. 30.)

The Italian in Barbèra's edition is *'abitanti in diversi paesi'* (in different countries), whereas Herodian says 'in different rooms'. Hence it is better to read with the Filadelfia edition *'in diversi luoghi.'*

44. If for 'Diocles' we read 'Hipparchus', what Machiavelli here says agrees with the account given by Thucydides in VI.54–9 of the plot formed by Harmodius and Aristogiton against the sons of Pisistratus in 514 B.C. Hippias, the elder son, escaped, but Hipparchus was killed, and the result was that 'to the people [of Athens] at large the tyranny simply became more oppressive, and Hippias, after his brother's death living in great fear, slew many of the citizens' (VI.59—with which compare what Machiavelli says below about 'those who survive becoming more insupportable and more bitter'). The mistake, however, is not Machiavelli's, but is due to Justin, who in II.9 says that 'after Pisistratus's death, Diocles, one of his sons, was killed by the brother of a girl he had outraged', and that 'another of his sons, Hippias by name', then took over his father's government, and took care that no one concerned in the conspiracy should survive.

45. The conspiracy of Chion and Leonides against Clearchus, who had put sixty senators to death (D. I.16.7 and n. 6) and committed other atrocities is described by Justin in XVI.5.1–11. He mentions that two conspirators were disciples of Plato, but says that 'they did not succeed in liberating their country, for Satyrus, the brother of Clearchus, carried on the tyranny in the same way, and for many years the people of Heraclea were subject to the tyranny of his successors' (*ib.* 17–18). The date is 353 B.C.

46. Cp. H.F. VIII.6, and note 36 above.

47. For the persecutions which followed these conspiracies, see for Athens note 44 above; for Heraclea note 45; and for the revenge taken by Lorenzo de' Medici, H.F. VIII.9, where we are told that there were many executions, that the streets were strewn with corpses, and that Jacopo de Pazzi, the head of the family, after being executed, and twice disinterred, was trailed naked through the streets by the halter with which he had been strangled, and then thrown into the flooded Arno. Francesco Salviati, Archbishop of Pisa, who was cognisant of the plot, was also hanged. For the reactions of Sixtus IV to the murder and to the vengeance of Lorenzo, see Pastor, *Hist. Popes IV*, c. 7, pp. 313–19.

48. Plutarch's account of the liberation of Thebes by Pelopidas confirms what Machiavelli says about the difficulty of the undertaking and about the part played by Charon. It was at Charon's house in Thebes that the twelve conspirators assembled in the winter of 379 B.C., and Charon, when the polymarks sent for him, lulled their suspicions. Nor was this the only moment at which the plot almost miscarried, for Hipposthenidas, when he heard the conspirators were coming, sent a messenger to tell them to wait awhile, but did not deliver it since he could not find the bridle of his horse; and Archias got a second message containing details of the plot, but was too drunk to read it. According to Plutarch, however, it was not Charon, but Phillidas, who had got himself appointed counsellor to the polymarks, plied them with wine, and used every endeavour to keep their minds off the subject of the plot to which he was privy. Nor does Plutarch speak of ten tyrants; he mentions by name only the polymarks, Archias and Philip, who gave the dinner-party; Leontidas and Hypates; and three harmosts, two of whom were executed and one fined. Nor, though Plutarch remarks that it is not easy to find other cases in which so few men, and these destitute, overcame so many who were more powerful, by courage and

sagacity, he claims that there is a parallel in Thrasybulus' case, and so like it that the Greeks called the two cases 'sisters' (*Pelopidas* 7–13).

49. For the events which perturbed the conspirators who were about to murder Julius Caesar, see Plutarch's *'Brutus'*, nn. 14–16.

50. During 1495–6 Florence was at war with Siena, from whom she hoped to recover Montepulciano. The brothers, Giacoppo and Pandolfo Petrucci, were then 'the principal citizens in Siena' and in 1497 they supplied Piero de' Medici with arms that he might force his way into Florence (Guicciardini, *St. d'I.* III.13). In this year Giacoppo died, and in 1498 Pandolfo, who 'by ingenuity and artifice had arrogated to himself great authority' (*St. d'I.* IV.3, p. 314), was in favour of coming to terms with Florence, but was opposed by his father-in-law, Niccolò Borghese, and by the Belanti out of jealousy and by the people at large because they disliked Florence. However, Pandolfo got his way, and after signing a truce for five years with Florence, his power was such that he procured the condemnation of his father-in-law for having opposed him (*St. d'I.* IV.3). The Belanti were now in grave danger and a plot was formed to kill Pandolfo. Machiavelli mentions two Belanti in connection with this plot: Luzio Belanti, who had married Pandolfo's daughter whom later on Pandolfo took away from him (cp. § 6), and Julio Belanti, in whose house the conspiracy was hatched, and who, on its failure, was driven with his family from Siena (§ 34). Guicciardini does not mention this conspiracy, but he does say that Pandolfo, having failed to get his way by peaceful methods, called in some friends from the country, with whose help he maintained peace in Siena and saved himself from tumults. He then made a truce with Florence for five years, and, having had his father-in-law put to death for opposing it, struck such terror into his opponents that they allowed him to rule as an autocrat (*loc. cit.*). For Pandolfo Petrucci, cp. §§ 5 and 39 and notes 9 and 60. The Filadelfia text reads *Giulio* for *Luzio* both here and in § 5. Luzio is not mentioned.

51. i.e. owing to the difficulty of killing more than one tyrant at one and the same time (see § 31 above, and cp. III.4).

52. A long account of the conspiracy formed by Giovanni Andrea da Lampagnano to kill Galeazzo Maria Sforza, who by his licentiousness and cruelty had made himself hated in Milan, is given in *The History of Florence* VII.34–5. It took place on Christmas Day, 1476, in the church of San Stephano. After the murder Giovanni Andrea fled, but got entangled in the dresses of some women who were squatting on the ground, and was killed by a moor. Carlo Visconti was slain by the bystanders, and Girolamo Olgiato was subsequently arrested by the police and executed. The failure of the conspiracy in this passage is ascribed not to the vengeance of the Sforzas who survived, but to the fact that those whom the conspirators hoped would follow and defend them did neither. From it Machiavelli draws two lessons: (i) princes should make themselves so loved that none who would slay them can escape, and (ii) it is vain to expect a disaffected multitude to second conspirators in time of peril (*ib.* end of § 35).

53. An account of the murder of Count Girolamo Riario of Forli by Francesco d'Orso in 1488 will be found in *The History of Florence* VIII.34. Francesco's life had been threatened and he lived in constant fear, so after supper in May he sought an interview with the count, killed him and also some members of the town guard, whereupon the people, who hated Girolamo, rose and sacked the palace, making the Countess Caterina and her children prisoners. The trick by which the Countess

recovered the capital is there related, but without the sordid detail mentioned in this paragraph (§ 35), and we are told that, on resuming the reins of government, she avenged her husband's death with unsparing cruelty. Girolamo Riario was the son of Sixtus IV, and Caterina was the daughter of Galeazzo Maria Sforza, murdered in 1488. On recovering the citadel, she waited for help from Milan, and so recovered her state. (Cp. P. 20, last paragraph; and A.W. Bk. VII, B.354–5; F.144.)

54. See P. 19 on the security of princes who gain the goodwill of the populace; see also Index *sub* 'Populace, good-will of' and 'vengeance of'—also cp. P. 19, E.150–1; and cp. Burd, 310, n. 10 on Conspiracies.

55. Cp. Plutarch's *Caesar* 69.2: Caesar's guardian genius, 'whose help he had enjoyed through life, followed him even after death as an avenger of his murder, driving and tracking down his slayers over every land and sea until not one of them was left, but even those who in any way whatsoever either put hand to the deed or took part in the plot were punished'. For the attitude of the people and for details as to the death of Brutus and Cassius, see Plutarch's *Brutus*. When Brutus and his fellow conspirators, with blood-stained hands, displayed their daggers, the people were terrified, but when Cinna began to revile Caesar they 'broke into a rage and abused Cinna so bitterly that the conspirators withdrew again to the Capitol' (18.6). When during the funeral oration Antony displayed the blood-stained robe of Caesar and pointed to the holes the daggers had made, a riot ensued: some cried out to kill the murderers, and, when the body had been burnt, 'the crowd seized half-burnt brands and ran round the houses of Caesar's slayers to set them on fire' (20.3–4). Brutus and Cassius escaped, made their way to Greece and then to Asia, where they gathered not only a great treasure, but an army and a fleet. Misfortune, however, dogged their steps, and Brutus, sleepless, began to see visions of an avenging genius. In their first battle with Antony and Octavian in 42 B.C., they were victorious, but at Campi Philippi in the same year both of them were nervous and made blunders. Cassius was beaten by Antony; and Brutus, thinking Cassius victorious, did not go to his aid; while Cassius, thinking Brutus dead, and mistaking a relieving force for enemies, committed suicide (42.4; 43.5–7). At sea Brutus's fleet was also victorious, but 'Heaven, wishing to remove from the scene the only man who stood in the way of him who was capable of ruling alone, kept from Brutus the knowledge of this good fortune' (47.4). He fought a battle, which he ought to have won, but some of his troops deserted to the enemy, the rest lost heart, he was surrounded, and perished by throwing himself on his own sword (49.2–4; 52.4).

56. Cp. Sallust's *'Bellum Catilinarium'*, c. 31, for Catiline's speech to the Senate before his flight from Rome in 63 B.C. He had ordered Marcius and Cethegus to go early to Cicero's house to kill him, but Fulvia warned Cicero in time, and he summoned the senate, which Catiline attended to make his defence, but, says Plutarch, 'no one would sit with him and all moved away from the bench where he was'. Lentulus remained in Rome when Catiline fled, but the letters he sent by the Allobrogian ambassadors to Catiline and the Gauls were intercepted, and he was arrested (Plutarch's *'Cicero'*, 16–19).

57. The story of the attempt of Hanno, *'princeps Carthaginiensium'*, to poison the senate at a banquet given in his house, and then to seize supreme power, is told by Justin (XXI.4). Forewarned by servants, the senators declined Hanno's invitation

to the marriage feast of his daughter; but, lest their knowledge of his design might cause more trouble than the design itself, they were content to decree that all should observe moderation in the amount spent on marriage feasts (*ib*. 4.4–5). Poison, presumably, was somewhat expensive. The date is *circa* 350 B.C.

58. Caesar had with him but 300 horse and 5,000 legionaries when in 49 B.C. he seized Ariminium and then marched on Rome (Plutarch's *Caesar* 32.1), but the panic caused in the city was so great that Pompey and the senators fled, and within sixty days Caesar, without bloodshed, became master of all Italy (35.2). Of the troops which Agathocles got together for his attack on Syracuse, Justin gives one account and Diodorus another, but it is certain that, as Justin says (XXII.1.16), he twice made up his mind to get control of Syracuse and was twice exiled, and that, in order to get back, he used armed forces both in 322 B.C. and in 317 B.C. (cp. C.A.H. VII.19.1). The Cleomenes here referred to is presumably Cleomenes III, for it was after his decisive victory over Aratus and the Achaean League at Ladoceia in 225 B.C. that he returned to Athens and killed the ephors mentioned in D. I.9.5 and D. I.18.7.

59. The story of Pisistratus' ruse is told by Plutarch in his *Life of Solon*, n. 30.

60. Cp. H.F. VIII.35, where Machiavelli says that commotions were frequent in Siena from 1478 onwards and that 'now the people and now the nobles got the upper hand, until at last victory remained with the nobles, among whom Pandolfo and Giacoppo Petrucci obtained supreme authority'. They returned from exile in 1487. But it was not until after the death of his brother in 1497 and the crushing of all opposition in 1498 (cp. note 50 above and Guicciardini, *St. d'I*. IV.3) that Pandolfo ruled supreme in Siena. In P. 20 Machiavelli says that Pandolfo ruled his state more by those who were distrusted than by others, and in P. 22 he is commended for having chosen so clever a man as Antonio da Venafro for his secretary. On 18 January 1503 pressure was brought to bear on the Sienese by Caesar Borgia and Pandolfo was expelled, though the citizens would have 'preferred to bear with the tyranny of a fellow citizen rather than to become subject to a foreign yoke' (*St. d'I*. V.12, p. 62). On his leaving the city disturbances broke out, and at the suggestion of the Florentines, backed by orders from Louis XII, Pandolfo was recalled. This, says Guicciardini, pleased his friends, 'who took up arms the night before he arrived, and thus overawed those who were opposed to him' (*ib*. p. 65). It was he who eventually restored Montepulciano to Florence shortly before his death, which occurred on 12 May 1512. (Cp. above notes 9 and 50.)

61. Catiline marched out of Rome with 300 well-armed men, and the ensigns of a magistrate (Plutarch's *Cicero* 16). He then joined Manlius, got together an army of 20,000, and went round the cities trying to get them to revolt (*ib*.). When news came of the suppression of this, 'the greatest conspiracy that had ever taken place in Rome', many of his followers deserted him, and, 'giving Antony battle with the troops that remained to him, he was slain' (*ib*. 22). Actually it was by M. Petreius that the legions of Rome were commanded in the early days of 62 when Catiline and some 3,000 of his adherents perished on the field. Antony with another army held aloof (Sallust, *Bell. Cat.* 59).

For Hanno, see Justin (XXI.4.6–8), who says not only that Hanno armed 20,000 slaves (*servi*), but also that he got help from Africa and the Moorish king, and that, having been beaten with rods, his eyes dug out and his arms and legs broken, he was crucified in public, and that his sons and relatives, even the innocent, were put to the torture (*supplicio traduntur*), to prevent any member of that abominable house from either repeating the crime or avenging Hanno's death (*circa* 350 B.C.).

62. After the defeat of the Persians at Plataea in 479 B.C., Athens attacked Thebes and forced her to hand over those who had induced her to fight with the Persians against Greece. Whereupon the Boeotian cities revolted. But 'Sparta, being anxious to obtain the help of Thebes in her war with Athens, came to the help of the Thebans in order that she might regain her imperium over the Boeotians' (Justin III.6.10).

63. See above, §§ 1–5 and 11, and cp. D. III.4 and D. III.5.2.

64. See above, note 32. Herodian says the poison was administered in a drink, whereas Dion Cassius says it was administered in the meat which Commodus ate. Both state that the emperor was violently sick, and threw up the poison, and that in consequence the conspirators had to send someone to strangle him. Both say that he was strangled by 'a strong young man', called Narcissus (who, according to Dion Cassius, was an athlete) and that the person who administered the poison was Marcia, the emperor's mistress, formerly the mistress of Quadratus who had joined in the conspiracy of his cousin Lucilla and had been executed in 192. (Cp. Herodian I.17.8 *sq.* with Dion Cassius LXXII.22 *Commodus* XVIII.)

65. Livy VII.38–41. Caius Marcius Rutilus, the new consul, thought that, in order to frustrate the plot of the legions to seize Capua, the 'best course was to prolong their hope of executing their project, whenever they should feel inclined, so he spread a rumour that they would be wintering in the same towns the next year' (38.9). He then found various excuses for sending the more troublesome of the men back to Rome, where they were detained by the other consul under various pretexts. When this separation of the troops was realised by the men, they decided to take immediate action, and to force Titus Quinctius to become their general (39). But when confronted with another Roman army under Marcus Valerius Corvus they opened negotiations, and after he had harangued them, agreed to submit to the dictator (40–1). The date is 342 B.C. For *Rutilo* Machiavelli has written *Rutilio*. See Index *sub* 'Capua' for other references to this conspiracy.

66. For the first appointment of Walter de Brienne, Duke of Athens, as governor of Florence representing Charles, Duke of Calabria, who in 1325 had been invited to become its lord, see H.F. II.30. This episode ended when the Duke of Calabria died in 1326, but in 1342 the Duke of Athens was again invited to Florence to act as 'Captain' of her forces, which had been worsted in the war with Pisa, and on this occasion, with the aid of a section of the nobility, he set up a tyranny, against which the Priors protested in vain (*ib.* 33–5). Three conspiracies were then formed, and on the arrest of Antonio Adimari, riots broke out on 26 July 1343. A conflict took place in the market-place in which the supporters of the duke were defeated, and, after the mob had glutted its fury, the duke was induced to retire and to renounce all his rights over Florence (*ib.* 36–7).

67. The account given of the revolt of Arezzo in 1501–2 by Guicciardini in *St. d'I.* V.8 agrees in substance with Machiavelli's account. Trusting in the goodwill of the citizens and in the authority of Florence, Guglielmo de Pazzi arrested two (not one) of the conspirators who had been egged on by Vitellozzo to stir up a revolt. Whereupon the populace rose in the name of liberty, seized the town, save

for the citadel to which Cosimo, the bishop and the commissioner's son, had fled; sent for Vitellozzo who was annoyed that the rising had taken place before the appointed time, but came with some troops; and within a fortnight the citadel had surrendered for want of provisions, and eight of its occupants were held as prisoners.

68. For the arrangement between Callippus and Dion, that the former should pretend to be a conspirator, see Plutarch's *Dion* (54). In the end Dion grew suspicious, and Callippus sent some Zacynthians who, having failed to strangle him, procured a sword and cut his throat (*ib.* 57). Callippus then became tyrant of Syracuse—in 353 B.C.

It was Francesco Brunelleschi who told the Duke of Athens of the conspiracy that had been formed against him, but we are not told in *The History of Florence* that he was put to death (cp. II.36 *sq.*).

7. How it comes about that Changes from Liberty to Servitude and from Servitude to Liberty sometimes occur without Bloodshed and sometimes abound in it

1. For the expulsion of the Tarquins, see Index under 'Tarquins', and for the expulsion of the Medici, see Index under 'Medici'. Livy I.59–60 and II.1–2.

8. He who would transform a Republic should take Due Note of the Governed

1. Cp. D. I.34.4 and D. III.6.37.   2. Livy II.41—485 B.C.

3. For the honours bestowed on Marcus Furius Camillus and the jealousy it aroused in Marcus Manlius Capitolinus, see Livy VI.11. For the tumults he raised and his consequent arrest, see VI.14–16. Many people on such occasions wore mourning and let their hair grow long, and a dejected crowd presented itself at the prison (16.4); but at his trial in 384 B.C. no one did so, 'a circumstance that had never occurred before' (20.1–3). He was condemned by the people to be thrown from the Tarpeian rock—a sentence which excited the horror of his judges (20.10–12).

4. '*Hunc exitum habuit vir, nisi in libera civitate natus esset, memorabilis*'—Livy VI.20.14. Machiavelli's comments on this paragraph correspond closely with Livy's. The quotation is in Latin.

5. See next chapter, D. III.9.

6. The death of Manlius Capitolinus took place in 384 B.C., when Rome had scarce begun her conquest of neighbouring tribes and her constitution was still in a state of flux. The supremacy of Marius gave place to that of Sulla three hundred years later, in 88 B.C., when Rome had conquered the world. Her aristocratic and wealthy classes had now become exceedingly corrupt and licentious, and lorded it over an impoverished and discontented populace, burdened with debt and for ever clamouring for its remission. Moreover, at the close of the Social or Italian war, vast numbers of non-Romans received the full rights of citizenship with the result that Rome ceased to be a city-state dominating Italy, and became the capital of an

Italian state in which all the peoples of Italy shared. It at the same time lay at the mercy of the huge armies which had to be raised for foreign wars, and consequently of their commanders, of which Marius was one and his rival, Sulla, another. It was, in fact, under Sulla that in 88 B.C. a Roman army for the first time took Rome, thus enabling Sulla to gain control of the state and of its policy—for the time being; for on his going abroad to fight Mithridates, Marius returned and established a reign of terror, only to be defeated and slain by Sulla on his return in 83 B.C.

7. Note the oft-recurring terminology derived from the Scholastic doctrine of matter and form. Natural forms are educed from the potentiality of matter by the action of a natural cause; the forms devised by human art are 'impressed' on matter by human agency, and in like manner political forms are impressed on the people of a city or a state.

8. Machiavelli calls attention to the shortness of life in the opening paragraph of D. III.1. In consequence of it, it is impossible for anyone during his lifetime either thoroughly to reform a corrupt state (cp. D. I.17.5 and D. III.1.7) or thoroughly to corrupt a state that is sound. Successive generations of men of the same type are required in both cases. Cp. P. 11 (E.93), where the difficulty of overcoming factions is ascribed to the short lives of the popes.

9. Cp. the opening discourse of this book, esp. § 7.

See on the need of appropriate 'material', *The Prince*, cap. 6, Burd. 209, E.47.

Cp. Plutarch's *'Praecepta gerendae reipublicae'*, 3 (799 B and C): 'Statesmen must apply themselves to the understanding of the character of the citizens . . . for, if the statesman himself attempt to produce a change in the character and nature of the people, he will not easily succeed, nor is it safe, but it is a matter that demands a long space of time and great power.' . . . Not that the statesman should 'imitate the character of his people,' but that 'he should understand it and employ for each type those means by which it can be brought under his control. For ignorance of their character leads to no less serious mistakes and failures in constitutional states than it does in the friendships of kings.' Cp. also the *de Regimine Principum* IV.8.

9. That it behoves one to adapt Oneself to the Times if one wants to enjoy Continued Good Fortune

1. The tactics pursued by Quintus Fabius Maximus Cunctator, to whom the senate gave discretionary powers on Hannibal's arrival in Italy and the defeat at Lake Trasimene in 217 B.C. (XXII.11.1–3), are described by Livy in XXII.12 and 18. Though he never let the enemy out of his sight, he persistently avoided an engagement (12.8 and 18.6). After the defeat at Cannae, for which he was in no wise responsible, he succeeded in quieting the populace, and by means of scouts made frequent efforts to discover what the enemy was about. His behaviour was scarce less cautious during the campaign in 215. He raided the lands of the Campanians and thus forced them to send troops from Capua into the field, whereupon he retired so that the crops might grow, and when they were ready, he seized them and, having thus obtained provisions, retired into winter quarters (XXIII.46.9–48.2).

2. The speech in which Q. Fabius Maximus advised against the proposed expedition to Africa in 205 B.C., is given in Livy XXVIII.40. He objects to any undue haste partly because of his natural inclination to act cautiously, which he still holds to be the prudent course though his critics ascribe it to cowardice and sloth, partly because of the jealousy and quarrels which the eagerness of consuls to seek glory is likely to evoke.

3. For Soderini's failure to adapt himself to changed circumstances, see D. I.7.6 and n. 5; I.52.2 and n. 3; III.3.2–3; and cp. Guicciardini, *Storia Fiorentina*, c. 28.

4. For the impetuosity of Julius II, see D. I.27; P. 25; and Guicciardini's sketch of his character in *St. d'I.* XI.8, and cp. VI.5, pp. 107–8, where we are told that even his enemy, Alexander VI, admitted that his word could be trusted.

5. On the difficulty of changing one's character, see D. I.18.5.

6. Cp. D. I.18.5; 49.2–3; and D. III.1.5–10.

Ellinger assigns a passage in Isocrates' '*Archidamus*' (written *circa* 362 B.C.) as a possible source for this chapter. Sparta had been defeated at Mantinea, but the death of Epaminondas had to a large extent neutralised the effect of the Theban victory. Sparta's allies urged that she should recognise the independence of Messene on the ground that it would be better to surrender part of her territory to her enemies rather than to run further risks (n. 13)—the very advice on which Machiavelli says that Venice should have acted when confronted by the League of Cambray (D. I.53.3). The party in Sparta who wanted peace on these terms argued that 'sensible peoples should not adopt the same attitude when things are going well as when they are going badly, but should always adapt their decisions to present circumstances, and follow the course of events, and should not contemplate what lies beyond their power. Nor should they in such circumstances seek what is absolutely right, but what is expedient' (n. 34). To which Archidamus replies: 'I agree with them in regard to the other points, but no one will persuade me that anything is more serviceable than to do what is right' (n. 35). And in like manner he advised against recognising the independence of Messene,—advice which the Spartans followed.

Cp. the speech of the Corinthians in Thucydides I.71: 'Your [Spartan] ways, as compared with theirs [the ways of the Athenians] are old-fashioned. And, as in arts, so also in politics, the new must always prevail over the old. In settled times the traditions of government should be observed; but when circumstances are changing and men are compelled to meet them, much originality is required.'

Cp. also Cornelius Nepos' description of Alcibiades: '*quum tempus posceret laboriosus, patiens, liberalis, splendidus, non minus in vita quam victu: affabilis, blandus, temporibus callidissime inserviens*' (Alcibiades I.3).

10. *That a General cannot avoid an Engagement if the Enemy is determined to force him to it at All Costs*

1. '*Cneus Sulpitius dictator adversus Gallos bellum trahebat, nolens se fortunae committere adversus hostem quem tempus deteriorem in dies, et locus alienus, faceret*' (Livy VII.12.11; quoted in Latin). The reading in the Teubner text is: '*dictatori neutiquam placebat, quando nulla cogeret res, fortunae se committere adversus hostem, quem tempus*

deteriorem in dies faceret, locis alienis sine preparato commeatu, sine firmo munimento moran-tem . . . The date is 358 B.C. (cp. A.W. Bk. IV, B.321, F.88).

2. See D. II. Pref. 7; II.16; 18.9; 19.1–2 and D. III.27.4.   3. D. II.12.

4. Cp. Livy XXII.18. On being worsted in an encounter with some Spanish troops on the hills, 'Fabius moved camp and, traversing the pass, occupied a strong and elevated position above Allifae'. Then, when Hannibal made a feint as if to march on Rome, 'Fabius marched along the hills, keeping in between the enemy's forces and the city of Rome, neither refusing nor offering battle'.

5. Philip, the father of Perseus, i.e. Philip V, so called to distinguish him from Philip II, the father of Alexander. In the spring of 198 B.C. he established himself in a strong position near the pass of Antigoneia which commanded the route into Macedonia. From it the consul, P. Villius Tappulus, was unable to dislodge him; but T. Quintius Flamininus, who replaced him, was informed of another pass which enabled him to get into the rear of the Macedonian army, which he defeated (Livy XXXII.11–12). Epeirus now submitted, and Philip retreated into Thessaly, whither Flamininus followed him. Philip adopted the scorched-earth policy, destroying towns as he retreated, and as Flamininus also ravaged the country, it suffered from both. Thessaly was now invaded from three sides. Euboea, Locris and Phocis were overrun, and the position of Philip became so desperate that he opened negotiations for peace, but the terms offered were so severe that Philip declined to accept them. Other provinces formerly subject to Macedonia, including the Pelo-ponnese, submitted to Rome. The war ended in June 197 with the defeat of Philip at Cynoscephelae in Thessaly, whither he had gone to collect fresh recruits (XXXIII.7–10).

6. Gaius Sulpicius Peticus was appointed dictator in 358 B.C. to repel a Gallic invasion. Like Fabius Maximus the Dilatory, he saw no need to join battle so long as time and the situation were daily impairing the enemy's strength (see quotation at opening of chapter). Hence he forbade his soldiers to fight, eager as they were to do so. They complained that they had been given a general 'who thought that if he did nothing victory would fly down from heaven into his lap'. Mutiny threat-ened. The Gauls jeered at the Romans for refusing to fight; so Peticus eventually joined battle and the Gauls were routed (VII.12–15).

7. The quotation—part of that given in the opening words of the chapter—is in Latin.

8. For Scipio's invasion of Africa, see D. I.53.8 and n. 12; II.12.3 and n. 4; 32.4; III.9.3 and n. 2.

9. Whether Hannibal might not have defeated Fabius, had he shown a little more energy, is open to question, but neither he nor the Gauls were in a position similar to that of Scipio, who had conquered most of Africa, had a base close at hand, and abundant supplies.

10. Morat was the second of the three defeats suffered by Charles the Bold at the hands of the Swiss, whose territory he invaded in March 1476. He was defeated at Granson, and in June of the same year suffered a still more disastrous defeat at Morat (cp. D. II.10.3 and n. 5). For the battle of Novara (1513), in which the French troops sent by Louis XII under La Trémouille and Trivulzio to conquer Milan were defeated by the Swiss, see D. II.17.9 and n. 5; 18.7 and n. 7.

Cp. on the impossibility of avoiding battle A.W. Bk. IV, B.325–6, F.94–5.

11. That he who has to deal with several Foes, even though he be Weaker than they are, can actually Win, provided he can sustain their First Attack

1. On the function of the tribunes of the plebs and their hostility to the patricians, see D. I.3–6; 37.2; 39.3; and see Index *sub* 'Tribunes'.

2. Cp. D. I.2.4, 14; and D. III.1.2; also D. I.6.6 for the impossibility of remedying one inconvenience without introducing another.

3. See Livy VI.37–42. After the tyranny of the Decemvirate the Valerio-Horatian legislation of 449 B.C. restored the sanctity of the tribunes of the plebs, of whom there were normally ten, any one of whom might protest and appeal to the people against the action of any of the others. The plebs, egged on by the tribunes, next demanded admission to the office of consul. This the patricians averted by agreeing to the appointment of tribunes with consular power, to which office plebeians were eligible. But in 377 the tribunes, C. Licinius and L. Sextius, again proposed that one of the two consuls should be a plebeian, and with it conjoined another yet more popular proposal concerning the payment of interest on debts (VI.35). The passing of these laws the patricians prevented by appearing with their followers at elections and preventing the laws being read (*ib.*). But for nine successive years these two tribunes were re-elected. Then in 368 a friendly dictator was appointed in the person of Publius Manlius, who appointed a plebeian as his Master of Horse. Supported by the dictator, Licinius and Sextius now declared that, if re-elected, they intended to submit to the people *en bloc* their proposal that there should be a plebeian consul, together with measures concerning the payment of debts and land reform (VI.38–9). This meant that they proposed to ignore the protests of other tribunes who were favourable to the patricians and who thus far, by exercising their right of *provocatio*, had prevented the laws being submitted to the people. Against this Appius Claudius Crassus, grandson of the Decemvir, protested in a long speech, declaring that it was like forcing people either to take poison with their food or to abstain from food altogether (VI.40–1). He succeeded in postponing the measure, but in 367 the recalcitrant tribunes were re-elected for the tenth time, and the Licinian legislation was passed, together with a measure requiring that of the keepers of the oracles (*decemviri sacris faciendis*) five should be plebeians. Many of the plebeians were wealthy men. Hence the effect of this legislation was to make it possible for men to be elected to the highest offices in the state, not on account of their merits or their birth, but on account of their wealth. To this point Machiavelli returns in D. III.16; but his present point is that, just as the patricians, in spite of their declining power, succeeded in holding up the Licinian legislation for ten years by dividing the enemy's forces, i.e. the tribunes, so a weaker power may gain a victory if only it can resist the first attack and then succeed in breaking up a hostile confederation. Since, however, the patricians were ultimately defeated, this argument from analogy has not much force.

4. In December 1482 Sixtus IV formed an alliance with Naples, Milan and Florence, guaranteeing to the Duke of Ferrara possession of his estates, and envoys were sent urging Venice to relinquish those she had taken. Venice, indignant that the Pope had changed sides, refused, and was placed under an interdict in May

1483. Meanwhile, Ercole d'Este, Federigo Gonzaga, Marquess of Mantua, and Giovanni Bentivoglio of Bologna had joined the '*lega santissima*', and the Venetian treasury was exhausted and her arsenals empty. It was then, says Commines, that 'Duke Ludovico came to the aid of their honour and credit, and everyone again got his own, except the poor Duke of Ferrara, who had been drawn into the war by his father-in-law in part and in part of his own doing, and was now obliged to surrender the Polesina to the Venetians. It is said that the affair brought Duke Ludovico in 60,000 ducats.' (*Memoirs, VII.3*). Peace was made on 7 August 1484 by the Treaty of Bagnolo. To Sixtus IV, who was on his death-bed, it seemed to be so dishonourable a peace that he refused to confirm it. (For the subsequent events see n. 6 below, and cp. D. I.53.3 and n. 4.)

5. Eleven years later, on 31 March 1495, alarmed at French successes, the Emperor Maximilian, Ferdinand and Isabella of Spain, Pope Alexander VI, and Ludovico il Moro of Milan joined with Venice in forming a holy league against France, known as the League of Venice. The confederates pledged themselves for twenty-five years to defend each other's dominions against all attacks by foreign powers. This forced Charles VIII to hasten back from Naples, but before the year was out Ludovico of Milan had signed a separate peace with Charles at Vercelli on 9 October. The other confederates were not parties to this treaty, and when in 1496 Charles began to make preparations for a fresh invasion of Italy, Henry VIII was induced to join the League as a non-belligerent, on 15 July. This did not satisfy Ferdinand of Spain, who in October opened negotiations with Charles VIII, with whom he signed a truce on 25 February 1497. This led to the final break-up of the League. The emperor withdrew his troops from Italy. Venice formed an alliance with Louis XII in April 1498, and in August a treaty of peace between Ferdinand and Louis XII was signed at Marcoussis.

6. The League of Cambray, which was formed against Venice in December 1508, comprised the Emperor, Louis XII, Julius II, Ferdinand of Aragon, the Dukes of Savoy and Ferrara and the Marquess of Mantua. The Venetians were routed by the French at Agnadello on 14 May 1509 (cp. D. I.53.3 and D. II.10.6). In February 1510 peace was signed between Venice and Julius II, who by the end of the year was acting in concert with Venice against France, the Emperor and Ferrara. Ferdinand of Aragon he detached from the League by investing him with the Kingdom of Naples in July.

12. *That a Prudent General should make it absolutely necessary for his own Troops to fight, but should avoid forcing the Enemy to do so*

1. See Index *sub* 'Necessity' and cp. D. III.11.1. The moral philosopher is probably Aquinas who in the *de Regimine Principum*, I.1, says that in place of the instruments with which animals are endowed, man has *ratio, per quam sibi haec omnia officio manuum posset praeparare;* that this makes it necessary for him to live in society; and that *hoc etiam evidentissime declaratur per hoc quod est proprium hominis locutione uti.* Aristotle says the same thing, but less concisely in *Politics* I.2.

2. Though this chapter is not based on any particular incident cited by Livy, it may well have been suggested by the 'obstinacy' displayed by the troops under

Sulpicius, when he declined to let them join battle with the Gauls (cp. D. III.10, n. 6), or again by the stubborn resistance offered to the Romans by the cities which were subject to Philip, whose exploits are described in D. III.10.3. But cp. also, especially for § 2, the passage cited from Thucydides III.40, given at the end of D. II.23.

3. Florence's immediate neighbours, Arezzo, Prato, Volterra, and Pisa, though subject to her jurisdiction, were ever ready to revolt, and to regain Pisa she had to fight from 1496 to 1509. Siena in the south and Lucca in the north-west, were independent republics, and with them she was frequently at war. Of Venice's neighbours, Padua, the nearest, was ruled by the Carraras till taken by Venice in 1405. Ferrara to the South was ruled by a duke, and Bologna was subject sometimes to the Bentivoglio, sometimes to the Visconti of Milan, and sometimes to the Papacy. To the West Vicenza was a republic till taken by Venice in 1405, Este was a dukedom, Verona was ruled by the della Scala till 1389, when it passed into the hands of the Sforzas, while Brescia, still further to the West, was held by the della Scala till 1421, when it became subject to Milan, and in 1426 to Venice, as did all the towns just mentioned. (Cp. *de Regimine Principum* IV.8.)

4. The reference is plainly to the fall of the republic in 1512 and the return of the Medici. The undertaking was that they should return as private citizens. Giuliano entered on 1 September; the treaty with the Spanish viceroy was signed on the 3rd; and on the 6th a *Practica* was convoked to devise the new constitution. This constitution lasted for ten days. On 16 September, Cardinal de' Medici entered Florence; a riot ensued; and, urged on by the Medici, the mob demanded a *Parlamento*. When it met, the Consiglio Grande was abolished; the Gonfalonier was appointed for only two months, and to the Signoria and Colleges appointments were made as the Medici nominated.

5. Plutarch in his *Life of Marcus Crassus*, the triumvir, tells us how he was deceived in the war with Orodes, king of Parthia, first by the king of Armenia and then by Ariamnes, an Arabian chieftain, both of whom assured him that the Parthians were incapable of putting up any strenuous resistance; with the result that he attempted to march through Mesopotamia, where he was defeated in 53 B.C. by Surenas, the Parthian general. The Roman troops urged Crassus to seek refuge in flight (27). This he attempted and with the remnants of his army got as far as Sinnaca (29). Surenas then offered to allow the Romans to retire, at which 'the troops were enraptured', and when Crassus hesitated, they urged him to go and meet Surenas, and under threats compelled him to do so (30). At the meeting Crassus was treacherously slain, and in the slaughter that followed 20,000 Romans were killed and 10,000 made prisoners (31).

6. '*Justum est bellum quibus necessarium, et pia arma quibus (nulla) nisi in armis spes est.*' (Livy IX.1.10, cited in Latin—321 B.C., during the second Samnite war. Machiavelli omits the word '*nulla*'.)

7. Livy II.47.1–9, 480 B.C. Cp. D. I.36.1 and II.25.1.

8. '*Ite mecum; non murus nec vallum, armati armatis obstant; virtute pares, quae ultimum et maximum telum est, necessitate superiores estis*' (Livy IV.28.5, cited in Latin—431 B.C.).

9. '*ultimum et maximum telum*'. (IV.28.5, cited in Latin).

10. Cp. Livy V.21.13—*Dictator praecones edicere jubet ut ab inermi abstineatur. Is finis sanguinis fuit.*

Cp. A.W. Bk. VI, B.349–51; F.133–4.

13. Which is it best to trust, a Good General with a Weak Army or a Good Army with a Weak General?

1. The story of Coriolanus is told in II.40, but the remark Machiavelli mentions occurs in II.39.2, where Livy says that the generals selected by the Volsci for the war with Rome, by the common consent of all the peoples concerned, were Attius Tullus and Cnaeus Marcius, a Roman exile in whom their chief hope was placed; and this hope he by no means disappointed, so that it is clearly seen that the Romans were stronger in their generals than they were in their army,—'*ut facile appareret ducibus validiorem quam exercitu rem Romanam esse*'. Coriolanus' full name was Cnaeus Marcius Coriolanus (cp. A.W. Bk. VI, 349b; F.133).

2. After the defeat of Syphax by Carthage in 212 B.C., the two Scipios had to face a powerful army under Hasdrubal Mago and Hasdrubal Gigo. Though reinforced by 20,000 mercenaries, both Publius and Cnaeus were defeated and slain, one in the field and the other in his camp. Lucius Marcius and T. Fonteius rallied the remnants of the Roman legions, who held their own until C. Claudius Nero arrived with reinforcements (Livy XXV.36–9).

3. '*quia ibat ad exercitum sine duce*' refers to the battle of Ilerda in 49 B.C., and '*vado ad ducem sine exercitu*' to the battle of Pharsalus in Thessaly in 48 B.C. Both quotations are in Latin. Cp. Suetonius, *Julius Caesar*, 34: '*Hos [Consules Pompeiusque] frustra per omnes moras exitu prohibere conatus, Romam iter convertit [Caesar]: appelatisque de Republica patribus validissimas Pompeii copias, quae sub tribus legatis, M. Petreio et L. Afranio et M. Varrone, in Hispania erant, invasit, professus ante inter suos 'ire se ad exercitum sine duce, et inde reversurum ad ducem sine exercitu*'. Ellinger gives this as the source in '*Die Antiken Quellen der Staatslehre Machiavelli's,*' p. 60.

4. L. Licinius Lucullus, who was to gain such striking victories over Mithradates in the war which broke out in 74 B.C., obtained his command largely owing to the high opinion Sulla had had of his abilities, but in part owing to the influence of the notorious Braecia, and her friend, Cethegus. Since he had served under Sulla in the Social war and had had command of a small fleet during the siege of Athens, he was not wholly without experience. Nor is Machiavelli's statement that it was the army that made of him a good general compatible with the account Plutarch gives of that army in his *Life of Lucullus*; for not only had the troops 'long been corrupted by luxury and avarice', but they had murdered Flaccus, their consul and commander, and were thoroughly out of hand, though otherwise brave and experienced soldiers (*n.* 7). Plutarch ascribes Lucullus' success in handling them to the fact that 'in him they had found a real commander, whereas before they had been induced to serve by the electioneering device of holding out to them pleasant prospects' (*ib.*). It may well be, then, that in this passage Machiavelli is following Appian, who gives an account of Lucullus' successes in the second war against Mithridates (74 B.C.—cp. *Bell. Mith.* 71 in Mendelssohn's edition), but says nothing of his previous exploits except in connection with the fleet in c. 51, where he also states that Flaccus, who was sent by the Marian party against Mithridates, was inexperienced in war, so much so that another general, Fibria, had to be sent with him. Quite possibly, therefore, Machiavelli is confusing Lucullus with the inexperienced Flaccus.

5. So hard pressed was Rome after her defeat at Cannae that in 215 the dictator,

Marcus Junius, and Titus Sempronius Gracchus, his master of horse, enlisted 8,000 able-bodied young men from amongst the slaves who were willing to serve (XXII.57.11). In 215 Gracchus marched with an army of slaves from Luceria to Casilinum to join with the consul, Quintus Fabius, in his attack on that town, which was taken largely owing to the bravery of the slaves to whom Gracchus had promised freedom if they won (XXIV.14–16). Cp. D. II.26.5; III.38.2.

6. For the arming of the populace by Pelopidas and Epaminondas, see D. I.21.3 and n. 3.

7. Already before Alexander's death in 323 generals and governors of provinces had begun to display arrogance, avarice and injustice. In fact, the whole empire, says Plutarch, 'was in commotion and ripe for rebellion' (*Alexander* 68). On his death, Alexander's remark that 'the Macedonians would never stand being governed by a woman' (*ib.*) was verified, for the infantry under Meleager revolted, and chose as king, Arrhidaeus, the illegitimate son of Philip II, rather than the child soon to be born of a barbarian woman, Roxane. (Cp. Diodorus XVIII.9 *sq.* for further details and subsequent events.)

8. Roman legions revolted several times during the civil war of 49 to 36 B.C. (i) Plutarch mentions a revolt amongst the tired legions sent to Brundisium in 48 with a view to their crossing to Greece with Caesar, but when they found Caesar gone they repented. (*Caesar*, n. 37.) (ii) Suetonius mentions a mutiny of the 9th legion at Placentia in 49, and of the 10th near Rome in 47, but both quickly repented, on the second occasion as soon as Caesar addressed them as '*Quirites*' instead of as '*Milites*' (*Julius Caesar*, 69–70). A more important revolt occurred at the end of the civil wars in 36 B.C. after the surrender of Sextus Pompeius at Messana. Lepidus allowed his fourteen legions to join with the eight Sextian legions in plundering the town and ordered Octavian to leave Italy. But the legions soon deserted Lepidus, who was deprived of his position as triumvir by Octavian. Livy mentions this revolt in Epitome CXXXI, the date being 33 B.C., and it is almost certainly this that Machiavelli has in mind.

14. What Effects are produced by the appearance of New Inventions in the course of a Battle and by the hearing of Strange Cries?

1. See Livy II.64.6. T. Quintius Barbatus Capitolinus, during the war with the Volsci in 469–468 B.C., finding that the Romans were outnumbered and were likely to give way, made use of a '*salubre mendacium*', crying '*Fugere hostes ab cornu altero*', and thus '*Impetu facto, dum se putant vincere, vicere.*' Cp. D. III.40 for what Machiavelli has to say on the use of such 'frauds' in warfare; and Livy III.70 for another case in which one wing gave way and was saved from disaster mainly by the efforts of this Quintius.

2. A substantially similar account of the failure of the Oddi to recover Perugia from the Baglioni in 1495 is given by Guicciardini in *St. d'I.* III.2, pp. 215–17. The Baglioni supported the Guelfs. After repulsing the Ghibelline faction, they were not content with slaughtering numbers of those who had fled, says Guicciardini, but 'hanged many more in Perugia with that cruelty which partisans are wont

to exercise towards one another'. Note that the 'few years' (*pochi anni*) which elapsed between this incident and the writing of this discourse, must have been at least eighteen, for Machiavelli can scarce have written it before 1513 at the earliest.

3. See Livy VII.14.6–10. Caius Sulpicius Peticus, seeing that the enemy's position in 358 B.C. was steadily deteriorating, was reluctant to engage them in battle (cp. D. III.10.1), but was forced to do so by the eagerness of his troops. Hence, since his army was numerically weaker than that of the Gauls, he devised the strategem (*ars aliqua*) which Machiavelli describes. (Cp. A.W. Bk. IV, B.321, F.88).

4. See Diodorus Siculus II.16 for this incident. Diodorus accepts as historical the legends related by Ctesias, according to whom Semiramis was the foundress of the Assyrian empire of Nineveh. In the early legends of Indo-European Armenia the goddess Ishtar, who was worshipped in Nineveh *circa* 1000 B.C., as the Queen of the Gods (cp. C.A.H. III.1.1), was introduced into the Armenian pantheon under the name of Semiramis or Saris (cp. C.A.H. III.8.4.)

5. See Livy IV.33. Mamercus Aemilius in 426 B.C. was in command of the Roman army which was posted some 1,500 paces from Fidenae with the Tiber on its left and mountains on its right. As soon as the battle began, it was attacked by an immense multitude of Gauls armed merely with firebrands. The dictator, seeing that the battle looked more like a conflagration than a fight and that his left wing was giving way, shouted: 'Are you going to be vanquished by smoke, to be driven from the field by an unarmed enemy like a swarm of bees?' 'Put the flames out with your swords, or seize the brands and hurl them back.'

6. '*Suis flammis delete Fidenas, quas vestris beneficiis placare non potuistis*' (Livy IV.33.5 —cited in Latin).

Cp. A.W. Bks. IV, B.321 *sq.*, F.88 *sq.* on new inventions; and Bk. VII, B.356a, F.146, on new French inventions.

15. That at the Head of an Army there should be One, not Several, Commanders, and that to have a Plurality is a Nuisance

1. '*Tres tribuni potestate consulari documento fuere, quam plurium imperium bello inutile esset; tendendo ad sua quisque consilia, cum alii aliud videretur, aperuerunt ad occasionem locum hosti*' (IV.31.2, cited in Latin). Machiavelli's account follows that given in this chapter. The Veientes had raided Roman territory, and in the raid some youths from Fidenae were said to have taken part (*ib.* 30.4–5). Rome appointed four tribunes with consular power, but they gave contradictory orders, and the people of Rome insisted on the appointment of a dictator. Mamercus Aemilius was nominated by one of the tribunes, Aulus Cornelius, in spite of its being customary for a dictator to be nominated only by a consul. Aulus Cornelius became his master of horse, and the engagement took place which Machiavelli has already described in D. III.14.5–6.

2. Guicciardini in his account of the siege of Pisa in 1500 (*Storia Fiorentina* c. 21) mentions the sending of G. B. Ridolfi and Luca degli Albizzi as commissaries

to the army which was being sent to Pisa in June 1500, the disorderly conduct of the troops, the quarrels of the Gascons and Swiss mercenaries with the commissioners about their pay, the departure of Ridolfi on plea of sickness, the withdrawal of the Gascons, and the seizure of Albizzi by the Swiss; but of the quarrel between the two men, and of Albizzi's change of conduct, he says nothing. Machiavelli, however, was secretary to the commissaries, accompanied them on their march, and wrote daily reports to the Signoria. For a fuller account of the incident and of the documents concerning it, see Villari, I, pp. 269–74. Cp. also D. I.38.5.

3. '*Saluberrimum in administratione magnarum rerum est, summum imperii apud unum esse*' (Livy III.70.1, cited in Latin). The Quintius here mentioned is T. Quintius Barbatus Capitolinus (cp. D. III.14.1), who had been elected consul for the fourth time, with Agrippa Furius as his colleague (*ib.* 66.1), for the war with the Aequi and Volsci in 446 B.C. Agrippa resigned his command in favour of his colleague, but the remark is made by Livy, not by Agrippa.

Cp. A.W. Bk. I, B.272, F.10, and II, B.300, F.36 on unity of command.

16. Genuine Virtue counts in Difficult Times, but, when Things are going well, it is rather to those whose Popularity is due to Wealth or Parentage that Men look

1. See Thucydides, Book VI, 8–24. First we have the vote in favour of sending an expedition to Sicily under Nicias, based on untrue statements made by the envoys from Egesta as to the money lying there (8); then Nicias's long speech objecting to the expedition (9–14), a few words about the ambitious motives of Alcibiades (15), followed by his speech in favour of the undertaking (16–19), and by Nicias's acceptance of the position of commander-in-chief, since he sees that the Athenians are determined on war (19–23). The date is 415 B.C. (Cp. also D. I.53.7.)

2. On keeping the citizens poor, but the state rich, see D. I.37.3; II.19.2; and III.25.

3. Cp. D. II.1.3, where we are told that after Rome's victories over various peoples, and finally her victory over Antiochus, there was no power in the world that could resist her.

4. L. Aemilius Paulus, surnamed Macedonicus on account of his victory over the Macedonians at Pydna in 168, is selected by Plutarch as an outstanding example of a Roman citizen who scorned the usual methods by which people win popularity and gain appointments, since he held that such honours should follow on bravery, justice, and honesty, virtues in which he soon surpassed all his contemporaries (*Aemilius Paulus*, 2). Sextus Aurelius Victor in his *De Viris Illustribus Urbis Romanae* 56, states that he applied three times for the office of consul, but without success, before being appointed consul for the war with the Ligurians. Plutarch, on the other hand, says that it was after the 'memorable actions' of this his first consulate that he applied again and was turned down (*Paulus Aemilius*, 6). It is possible that Plutarch is wrong in placing this incident after the consulate in 182 when Paulus defeated the Ligurians in Spain, and that he should have placed it after the first expedition to Spain in 191, when Paulus distinguished himself as praetor in what

was practically a proconsulship (*ib.* 4); but anyhow, between his first consulship proper in 182 and his yet more distinguished consulship, when as an old man he defeated Perseus and earned for himself the surname '*Macedonicus*', no less than thirteen years elapsed during which Paulus was living in retirement, for his second consulship did not begin until 168.

5. There is a life of Antonio Giacomini Tebalducci by Jacopo Nardi, a contemporary writer. He is also mentioned by Guicciardini in his *Storia Fiorentina* (c. 23 last paragraph) as a man chosen to be the Florentine commissary in 1502 on account of his reputation as a soldier, his valour, his devotion to the people and his indifference to the great men of the city. In May 1502 Vitellozzo and the Orsini were advancing on the Val di Chiana, Maximilian was demanding from Florence huge sums of money for his coronation, the French alliance was also proving costly, the Pisans had assumed the offensive and Caesar Borgia was marching to their aid with a view to making Pisa an independent state with himself as its Duke and another Borgia as Archbishop (cp. Villari, I, p. 290). It was at this juncture that Giacomini was appointed commissary-general and was given charge of the Florentine troops then encamped before Pisa who were to march through the Val di Chiana in the hope of suppressing the rebellion. He was again appointed commissary when the war with Pisa was renewed in 1503 and in May he received a letter from the Ten, signed by Machiavelli, congratulating him on refusing to treat with the Pisans who were growing afraid of the siege operations then in progress. He was commissary again in 1504, but resigned in September, ostensibly on the ground of ill health, but in reality because he disapproved of Soderini's scheme for diverting the course of the Arno. In 1505 after his victory at San Vincenti, he was sent to Pisa, but the Florentines were twice repulsed, and for this, rightly or wrongly, Giacomini was held to be responsible (cp. D. I.53, 9–10 and n. 13). Hence during the last stage of the siege, 1508–9, Giacomini was passed over, and in his place were appointed three commissioners, Niccolò Capponi, Antonio da Filicaia and Alamanno Salviati.

6. Pisa surrendered unconditionally on 31 May 1509, and the Florentine troops entered the city on 8 June. It might, Machiavelli suggests, have been forced to surrender unconditionally in 1508, when it was already hard pressed, had Giacomini been in charge of the operations; in which case Florence would not have had to pay Louis XII 100,000 ducats, Ferdinand 50,000, and 25,000 to be distributed by Georges d'Amboise, for permission to carry on. The agreement to pay these sums was signed in March 1509, but the demand for payment had been made in 1508.

7. On the need of citizens having such virtues see D. III.47.

17. *That to a Person to whom Offence has been given, no Administrative Post of Importance should subsequently be assigned*

1. When in the winter of 208–207 B.C. Rome was threatened with another invasion by the Carthaginians under Hasdrubal, who was preparing to cross the Alps, C. Claudius Nero and M. Livius Salinator were chosen as consuls. Livius

went north to Narnia on the Flaminian Way and then marched to Sena Gallica on the east coast so as to prevent Hasdrubal marching down the coast road to join Hannibal in the south. Nero with another consular army marched south so as to prevent any attempt on the part of Hannibal to move northwards. The messengers bringing news of Hasdrubal's movements for which he was anxiously waiting, were intercepted, and, on learning this, Nero marched rapidly north to join forces with the other consul, Livius, now at Sena Gallica. (Cp. D. II.10.7 and n. 11; and C.A.H. VIII.4.3.)

2. An account of the earlier expedition of Claudius Nero, who with the two legions he had commanded at Capua in 212 B.C., was sent by sea to Spain where he allowed Hasdrubal to escape his clutches, is given by Livy in XXVI.17. Thus far Machiavelli's account of these two incidents in the career of Claudius Nero agrees with the account which Livy gives of them, save that no mention is made of Nero's being reproached either by the senate or by the people for allowing himself to be deceived. He was, however, forthwith replaced by Publius Cornelius Scipio, son of the Scipio who had fallen in Spain, to whom supreme command of the forces in Spain was given in spite of his being but a young man.

3. So wedded is Machiavelli to the principle laid down in D. I.23, that it is a mistake to risk one's all on a part of one's forces (cp. D. I.22.2 and D. II.12.7), that he misses altogether the significance of Nero's forced march with part of his forces to join the other consul. For (i) Rome had twenty-three legions in the field at this moment, of which seven were in the south, watching Hannibal, one at Capua, two garrisoning Tarentum, two under Fulvius Flaccus operating against Hannibal, and the two under Nero from which he selected the troops (6,000 infantry and 1,000 cavalry) with which to support Livius, so that in the south, there remained ample forces to cope with any move that Hannibal might make; and (ii) the crucial battle, as Nero saw, was obviously going to be fought in the north where Livius was confronted with an army comprising 30,000 troops under Hasdrubal, who was determined to force a passage. Nero's manœuvre was in fact one of the greatest episodes in the second Punic war, and was completely successful, for in the valley of the Metaurus Hasdrubal's forces were completely routed and Hasdrubal himself was killed, and with this defeat the last hope the Carthaginians had of breaking Rome's hold on Italy came to an end (cp. C.A.H. VIII, p. 95). On the other hand, Nero's 'audax iter' did cause the greatest alarm in Rome, where it seemed to many that the camp in the south had been left 'sine viribus, sine imperio, sine auspicio', and that it lay at Hannibal's mercy (Livy XXVII.44.4; but cp. also 50.9–11).

4. Nero's answer to these objections has been recorded by Livy in c. 45. He claims that he has done the right thing, and assures his troops that they are about to gain a great victory, but of his experience in Spain and of the resentment he felt on account of the treatment meted out to him, he says nothing at all. There is, in fact, in this passage a confusion between the two consuls (see Guicciardini's comment). It was Livius Salinator, not Claudius Nero, who was disgruntled. Livius had been consul some twelve years earlier, had won a victory of no small moment over the Illyrians, and had been awarded a triumph; but had been found guilty and fined for distributing the spoils unjustly, and 'had borne this disgrace so badly that he had gone to live in the country and for many years had avoided the city and the society of his fellow-men' (Livy XXVII.34.4). When he was invited again to become consul, he 'rated the fathers' for the injustice they had done him. 'If he was a good man,

why had they condemned him? If they thought he had behaved badly in his previous consulate, why offer him the office again?' (*ib.* 12–13). He accepted office reluctantly, the more so in that he looked upon Nero as one of those who had been 'contemptuous of his misfortune'. 'Why should we be reconciled?' he asked. 'We shall fight the better if we fear our actions are being watched' (*ib.* 35.7–8). It is, moreover, not to Nero, who had been elected because '*longe ante alios eminebat*' (XXVII.34.1), but to Livius Salinator that Livy ascribes the cynical remark mentioned in this paragraph. Why such a hurry? asked Quintus Fabius before the battle. Because, replied Livius, 'from the enemy I shall either obtain great glory or a well-deserved, if dishonest, joy at the sight of the citizens' defeat' (XXVII.40.9).

5. Machiavelli may be right in maintaining that it is foolish to entrust a disgruntled citizen with a high administrative post. The evidence he here cites, however, does not bear out this contention, but the contrary. For, though one of the two generals had a grievance, both behaved with the utmost loyalty, bravery and devotion in their service of the state on their being appointed consuls on this, one of the most critical moments in Rome's history.

Guicciardini *in loc.* remarks: 'Much more has a prince to abstain from commissioning a person he has injured than has a republic, for one who has been injured by a prince recognises that all his injuries are due to him, whereas one who has been injured by a republic recognises that the injury inflicted on him has been done by some individual or else by a magistrate acting in the name of the city, and by attacking the city he can hardly avenge himself. Moreover, he who seeks the ruin of his country injures his parents, friends, his own affairs and himself, and incurs infamy, which does not happen if he seeks vengeance on a prince; and it is easier to destroy a prince than a republic.'

'What is said in the Discourse about Claudius Nero is too absurd to be believed . . . and the speech which the writer ascribes to him was not his speech but that of Salinator.' And that Salinator ever thought of betraying his country is disproved by his own actions, for he refused the consulate until it was forced on him by leading citizens.

In the Giunta edition of the *Discorsi* the confusion which occurs in this chapter between Livius Salinator and Claudius Nero was corrected, and the chapter rewritten—it has been alleged by Machiavelli himself; but this is incorrect, for the edition in question contains a note to the effect that it was not Machiavelli who wrote the amended chapter. Moreover, in subsequent editions the mistake reappears, since they follow Machiavelli's manuscript. In A.W. Bk. VI, B.348a; F.131, all that Machiavelli says is that Claudius Nero, in lessening the army facing Hannibal, did so secretly in order to help a friend, and that to leave tents standing, flags flying, camp-fires burning, and guards posted, is the proper course in such a case to pursue.

18. Nothing becomes a General more than to anticipate the Enemy's Plans

1. There are two lists of the sayings of Epaminondas, one in Plutarch's *Moralia* in the *Apophthegmata*, the other in the *Epaminondas* of Cornelius Nepos, IV.5–6, but neither contains this particular aphorism. There is, however, in Plutarch's *Apoph*-

thegmata a passage which runs: '*Chabrias dicebat optimum hunc esse imperatorem qui maxime cognitas habeat res hostium.*' Hence it may well be that it is this statement that Machiavelli has in mind, and that he has ascribed it wrongly to Epaminondas instead of to Chabrias (see Plutarch, *Opera*, ed. Reiske, Vol. VI, p. 710). Chabrias, a famous Athenian general, fought against Agesilaus in 378 B.C., and was killed at the siege of Chios in 357. His life was written by Cornelius Nepos.

2. Cp. Plutarch's *Brutus*, 42–3. At the battle of Philippi in 42 B.C., between Octavius Caesar and Antony on the one hand and Brutus and Cassius on the other, the left wing under Cassius was thrown into disorder and knew nothing of what had happened on the right, though in fact Brutus had routed the enemy. 'The want of knowing this', says Plutarch, 'was their undoing. Brutus neglected to relieve Cassius, thinking that, like himself, he had been victorious, and Cassius did not expect relief from Brutus, thinking that Brutus, like himself, had been overcome' (42). Hence he caused himself to be slain by his freedman, Pindarus, and his body was found severed from his head (43). Cp. D. III.6, n. 55.

3. The battle fought between Francis I and the Swiss at Santa Cecilia in Lombardy is the battle which we now called 'Marignano'. There are two other discourses in which Machiavelli refers to it, namely, D. II.18.7 and D. II.22.2–3, but in neither of them does he give the battle a name. Nor does Guicciardini in the long account he gives of this battle in *St. d'I.* XII.15. Guicciardini says that on the eve of the battle Francis moved his camp from Marignano to San Donato, three miles from Milan, where the Swiss troops lay. The Swiss, urged on by Cardinal Schinner, marched out of Milan the same evening, drew up in order of battle and at night made a fierce attack on the French camp which lasted four hours and resulted in the capture of 15 cannon. Messengers were despatched to announce a Swiss victory (which, incidentally, reached Rome where the victory was celebrated). During the night there was a tacit truce, and the French army re-formed. At sunrise the Swiss again attacked, but d'Alviano came up with reinforcements from Lodi and the Venetians also arrived. Hence the Swiss were forced to retreat, which they did in good order, though on both days they had suffered very heavy losses. Moreover, there were two companies, Guicciardini tells us, who had spent the night in a villa which was burnt by a troop of Venetian horse. Hence of these companies it is certainly true that their ignorance of what had happened proved to be their undoing. And doubtless there were others, for the battlefield covered a wide area which included alike San Donato, Santa Cecilia, and Marignano itself.

4. Guicciardini says that the combined Papal and Imperial army was at Piacenza, and that before the battle it had, after considerable discussion, crossed the Po, but had withdrawn when it found that Lodi had been occupied by d'Alviano's troops (*St. d'I.* XII.15).

5. See Livy IV.37–8 for an account of the battle fought by Aulus Sempronius Atratinus against the Volsci in 423; 38–9 for the exploits of Tempanius; and 40–1 for the subsequent enquiry into the conduct of Sempronius. Machiavelli has written 'Aequi' of whom there is no mention in IV, 37–41. He should have written 'Volsci'. The Aequi lay to the east of Rome, the Volsci to the south-east, with the Hernici in between.

6. For Guicciardini's account of the incidents described in § 4, see *St. d'I.* IV.3, p. 316. The date was 1498.

19. Whether in controlling the Masses Considerateness is more Necessary than Punishment

1. See Livy II.55–60. The immediate cause of the trouble in 472–471 B.C. between the nobles and the plebs was the refusal of Volero Publilius, a centurion, to serve as a common soldier. When about to be flogged, he appealed first to the tribunes and then to the people, with the result that the lictors were maltreated (55). The plebs elected him as tribune and the senate appointed as consul Appius Claudius, the son of Appius, who was both hated by, and hated the plebs, with Titus Quintius Barbatus Capitolinus as his colleague (56). Quintius saved the situation by having his colleague forcibly removed from the forum (56–7). Claudius was then sent to fight the Volsci, and behaved so harshly toward the troops that they obeyed him but slowly and he could do nothing with them (58), and the army was at length put to flight (59). Quintius, on the other hand, was cordial in his treatment of the troops, who obeyed him readily, so that the Aequi were afraid to engage them (60).

2. '*In multitudine regenda plus poena quam obsequium valet.*' Though the statement is given in Latin it does not occur in the works of Tacitus and in the only passage in which he compares '*obsequium*' with '*poena*' he says just the opposite. This passage occurs in the *Annals* III.55.5, and runs: '*Obsequium inde in principem et aemulandi amor validior quam poena ex legibus et metus*'—'Hence subservience toward a prince and the desire to emulate him counts for more than penalties imposed by laws and fear.' Though in a note to Guicciardini's commentary we are told that the quotation Machiavelli gives represents the '*nota sentenza*' of Tacitus, there can be but little doubt that it is from this passage in Tacitus that the supposed quotation is derived, and that in consequence both are wrong. All those I have consulted on the matter are agreed about this. But, if the reference be to *Annals, Book III*, we obtain a clue to the date at which the discourse was written, for the first four books of the *Annals* were not published until 1515.

3. For the efficiency of Titus Manlius Imperiosus Torquatus see D. I.11.2. D. II.16.1–2; 23.1. For his severity see D. III.22, and cp. III.1.5.

4. Cp. the chapter on Cruelty and Clemency in *The Prince* (c. 17). Cp. also D. III.6.4–5, and the remarks on Antoninus, Commodus, and Maximinus in P. 19. The reference is presumably to P. 17, but the doctrine of the two chapters at first sight seems to be scarcely consistent. Both assert that a ruler 'ought to inspire fear in such a way that, if he does not win love, he avoids hatred' (P. 17, E.135); and that to avoid hatred he must abstain from seizing the property of citizens (*ib.*, and cp. Aristotle, *Politics* V.11, 1315a, 28 *sq.*). Again, with the statement in P. 17 that 'reasons for taking life are difficult to find and soon lapse' agrees the statement that 'no prince is keen on shedding blood, unless driven to it'; and the statement in P. 17 that 'pretexts for taking away property are never wanting to the prince who has begun to live by robbery' is in accord with the supposition of D. III.19 that some princes are given to pillage. But whereas in P. 17 we were told that reasons for taking life seldom occur, in D. III.19 we are told that 'in connection with pillage, neither the occasion nor the desire to shed blood is ever lacking'. The discrepancy, however, disappears if we bear in mind that in both chapters Machia-

velli is contrasting the law-abiding prince who avoids both pillage and bloodshed, except when driven to it, with the licentious prince who is given to pillage and in consequence also to the shedding of blood. A like contrast will be found in Seneca's 'De Clementia', where he sets the true prince, 'who bears no stain and has never shed his compatriot's blood', over against the tyrant, who delights in shedding blood. Tyrants and kings, he says, 'are alike in mere outward show of fortune and extent of power', but 'tyrants are cruel to serve their pleasure', whereas kings are cruel 'only for a reason and of necessity, for kings kill only when induced to do so for the good of the state' (I.11–12). Clemency, Seneca says, 'makes rulers not only more honoured, but also more secure; is at the same time the glory of sovereign power and its surest protection'. The tyrant, on the other hand, is 'hated because he is feared, and wishes to be feared because he is hated, not knowing what frenzy is engendered when hatred grows too great' (ib.).

There is also a discrepancy between the contention in D. III.19 that it is better to secure the loyalty of troops by treating them with consideration rather than harshness, and the statement in P. 17 that 'when a prince is with his army, and has under his command a multitude of troops, it is altogether necessary for him to care nothing should he get a name for cruelty, for without it he could never keep his army together and ready for action'. Nor is it possible to reconcile these two statements, for in P. 17 Machiavelli goes on to blame Scipio for his excessive forbearance, which, had he remained in command, would in time have destroyed both his fame and his glory (E.137), whereas in D. III.21 he treats the conduct of Scipio and Hannibal as but alternative ways of producing the same effect.

Guicciardini *in loc.* remarks that neither unmitigated severity nor unmitigated good nature (*umanità*) or graciousness (*piacevolezza*) is of any use to a ruler, but when combined in the right proportion they are most valuable. This, however, rarely happens, since in nature there is always some imperfection. Moreover, whether it is better to be more severe than gracious (as Tacitus is alleged to have said), or more gracious than severe will depend upon whether one's subjects are 'so noble and generous that they yield more readily to graciousness than to fear, or, on the contrary, are so dour that they cannot be moved by gentleness, but have to be subdued and broken by asperity. Nor can it be doubted but that there is need thus to accommodate oneself to their condition. Apropos of which Frederick Barbarossa, a most excellent prince, who, though born in Germany, had long experience of Italy, said that the two first nations in the world, second to none and full of many virtues, were the Germans and the Italians; but that to rule them demanded different methods, for the Teutons were arrogant, insolent, and of such a type that were you to use gentleness they would ascribe it rather to fear than to good nature; whereas the Italians were more tractable, more affable, and of such a nature that they would treat asperity with contempt rather than be afraid of it. Hence with the latter it was necessary sometimes to pardon delinquencies and to show kindness; but with the former to punish them severely since otherwise they would become yet more insolent.'

A distinction must also be made, says Guicciardini, between one who rules in his own right and one who acts as the minister of another. For a prince has need of the very special goodwill of his people if he is to keep his state. If he be but a minister, he should in dealing with an army appeal to love rather than fear, since he needs the goodwill of the troops, but in governing a city should instil a certain amount of terror, since his office is but temporary and it is the prince who requires its goodwill.

20. A Single Act of Common Decency made a Greater Impression on the Falisci than did all the Forces of Rome

1. Cp. Livy V.27 for the episode of the treacherous Faliscan schoolmaster. 'There are laws of war as well as of peace', says Camillus; 'we have learned to wage them no less justly than bravely' (27.6). The incident occurred during the siege of Falerii in 394 B.C. by Marcus Furius Camillus, for whom see Index *sub* 'Camillus', (Cp. C.A.H. VII.15.7, p. 516.)

2. Cp. Livy, *Periocha* XIII for the mission of C. Fabricius Luscinus to Pyrrhus in 278 B.C. The letter sent by C. Fabricius and Q. Aemilius, Roman consuls, to King Pyrrhus, informing him of the conspiracy is given by Plutarch in his *'Pyrrhus'*, 21. (Cp. also Cicero, *de Officiis* I.xiii, n. 40; and D. III.21.4.)

3. The taking of New Carthage by P. Cornelius Scipio Africanus Major in 210 B.C. is related by Livy in XXVI.46, and the restoration of his wife to Allucius, a native chieftain in XXVI.50. (Cp. for Scipio, D. III.3.21 and see Index.)

4. See P. 19 for the virtues which peoples expect their ˈprinces to display.

5. The biographers of princes on whom Machiavelli mostly relies are Plutarch; for Alexander, Quintus Curtius; for the Roman emperors, Herodian; and for Cyrus, Xenophon. A famous work giving rules for the conduct of princes was written by one of his contemporaries, namely, Baldassare Castiglione (1478–1529), who wrote *'Il Cortegiano'* (The Courtier). It was written in .1514, published by Aldus in Venice in 1528, and translated into English in 1565. (For other works on Princes, see Gilbert, *Machiavelli's 'Prince' and its Forerunners*, Introduction.)

6. Cp. Xenophon's *'Cyropaedeia'*. For his early character and popularity, see I.4; for his generosity and magnanimity, III.1.41–2; for the honours shown him, III.3.2; for his method of government, VII.5.72 *sq.*, VIII.1–2 and 6. For his alleged deceitfulness, see D. II.13.1 and n. 4.

21. How it comes about that Hannibal, whose Procedure differed radically from Scipio's, yet produced the same Effect in Italy as Scipio did in Spain

1. See previous chapter, where it is implied that an army when handled with consideration is more likely to win than one that is handled harshly, and similarly that a city if treated with consideration, is more likely to surrender. Hannibal's treatment alike of his men and of the places he conquered proved equally successful. Hence the same effect may be produced by opposite lines of conduct. This topic is discussed in the next chapter, and again in *The Prince* cp. P. 17 where the question is whether it is better to be clement or cruel, to be loved or to be feared, and P. 19, where it is laid down that anyhow one must avoid being either hated or despised, consequences which the over-cruel prince and the over-clement prince, respectively,

inevitably bring about. The general principle underlying all these theorems is that similar effects may be produced by dissimilar, and even contrary, causes.

2. For the effect produced by Scipio's conduct in Spain, cp. Livy XXVII.20.5: 'It was clear to Hasdrubal and Mago that alike in public and private the minds of all [the Spaniards] were overwhelmed by the benefits Scipio had conferred, and that there would be no end to the transference of their allegiance until every Spanish soldier had either been removed to the remote parts of Spain [which were still loyal] or transferred to Gaul.' (Cp. also A.W. Bk.VI, D.352a; F.137.) For Hannibal's character compare Livy XXI.4.6–9 with Polybius IX.22, 24–6. Having described his coolness, his tirelessness and his bravery, Livy says: 'These great virtues in the man were counterbalanced by monstrous vices, inhuman cruelty, a worse than Punic perfidy. Wholly false and irreligious, he had no fear of God, no regard for an oath, no scruples.' This, however, as Polybius points out, may not be the real Hannibal, but Hannibal as the Romans saw him. On the situation after the battle of Cannae in 216 B.C., Livy remarks that 'Hannibal was master of Apulia, of Samnium, of nearly the whole of Italy' (XXII.54.10). It is, however, an exaggeration to say that 'all the Italian cities revolted to Hannibal'. Cp. Hanno's speech to the Carthaginian senate, mentioned in D. II.30.6: 'The fight at Cannae, you say, was almost the destruction of the Roman empire, and all Italy is admitted to be in revolt. Has any nation of Latin race revolted to us? Has a single man of the five-and-thirty Roman tribes deserted to Hannibal?' (XXIII.12.15–16). Machiavelli himself, in fact, calls attention in § 4 to the fact that Naples and other towns remained loyal. (Cp. Polybius X.33.)

3. See D. I.37.1 and P. 3, opening paragraph, on the desire for change. And for the means to win popular favour see Index *sub* 'Populace, on playing up to the'.

4. See P. 17 on whether it is better to be loved or feared; also, on the danger incurred when fear becomes excessive, see D. I.45.4; and P. 19 on the avoiding of hatred and contempt.

5. Cp. D. I.6.6 on the inevitability of meeting with inconveniences whatever course be adopted.

6. Cp. D. I.6.10 and D. III.2.3 on the impossibility of adopting a middle course; and for its inadvisability see Index *sub* 'Inconveniences'.

7. See Livy XXVIII.24–9 for the mutinies which broke out when Scipio fell ill, and 32–4 for the measures Scipio took to suppress the revolt of Mandonius and Indibilis.

8. On the mutual hatred of the Romans and Carthaginians see Livy XXI.1. For the suicide of Hannibal see Livy XXXIX.51; and for the attempt to poison Pyrrhus, see D. III.20.2 and n. 2.

9. On the army with which Hannibal invaded Italy, see Livy XXI.21, and for his address to his troops when Italy came in sight, *ib.* 43–4.

10. Note that Machiavelli does not claim that the alleged conduct of Hannibal was praiseworthy; he claims merely that it was successful; which it was for the time being, but not in the long run.

Cp. *The Prince*, chapter 17, on 'Cruelty and Clemency and whether it is better to be loved or feared'; especially the concluding paragraph in which Scipio is severely criticised for his 'too great forbearance' and Hannibal is praised for having by severity kept together a heterogeneous army. (See D. III.19, n. 4.)

22. How the Severity of Manlius Torquatus and the Sociability of Valerius Corvinus won for Each the same Degree of Fame

1. T. Manlius Imperiosus Torquatus, the son of L. Manlius Capitolinus Imperiosus, was twice dictator; in 353 B.C., when he won a victory over the Etruscans, and in 349, during the war with Veii. In 320, according to the *Fasti,* he became dictator for the third time, but Livy does not mention this. He was also consul three times, in 347, 344, and 340.

M. Valerius Corvus, or Corvinus, was consul no less than six times between 348 and 300 B.C., and was only twenty-three when he first obtained this rank, though, like Manlius, he had already won fame by fighting with a gigantic Gaul, if indeed the story is to be credited. He was dictator twice, in 343, and in 301 when he was seventy years of age; was interrex in 332 and 330, and held curule office twenty-one times.

Machiavelli's remark that in triumphs the two men were equal is scarce accurate. Valerius celebrated four triumphs, the first in 346 when 4,000 prisoners in chains preceded his chariot (VII.27.8); the second in 343 after his victories at Cumae and Suessula (VII.38.3); the third in 335 (VIII.16.11); and the fourth in 301 after his victory over the Etruscans at the age of seventy (X.6.11). Manlius Imperiosus Torquatus, according to the *Fasti Triumphales,* obtained only one triumph, i.e. in 340, owing to his victory over the Latins, Campanians, and Sidicines. Livy mentions none, but Diodorus mentions this one in XVI.90.

2. '*Manliana imperia*' (VIII.7.22), and for his severity see VII.4-5.

3. VII.4, when he was banished by his father who became dictator in 363 B.C.

4. The fight with the gigantic Gaul took place in 361 B.C., with the consul's permission. It was then that Manlius acquired the name 'Torquatus', owing to his having taken a necklace from the man he slew (VII.10).

5. When in 362 Manlius's father was accused of tyrannical conduct and cruelty during his dictatorship and of having even banished his own son from house and home although he was innocent, this same son threatened the tribune with death if he did not withdraw the accusation (VII.5).

6. '*Injussu tuo adversus hostem nunquam pugnabo, non si certam victoriam videam*' (VII.10.2, cited in Latin).

7. See Aristotle, *Politics* III.15, 1286b. 27 *sq.*; and cp. the comments in Aquinas, *Politicorum, III, Lect. xiv* (last paragraph), 'A king should have more power than the many have collectively, otherwise he would be unable to punish them.'

8. See D. III.1.5 and cp. III.17.2 on the impossibility of realising the requisite conditions.

9. See D. III.21.3-4.   10. Cp. D. III.20.3 and D. II.13.1.

11. '*Non alias militi familiarior dux fuit, inter infimos milites omnia haud gravate munia obeundo. In ludo praeterea militari, cum velocitatis viriumque inter se aequales certamina ineunt, comiter facilis vincere ac vinci vultu eodem; nec quemquam aspernari parem qui se offerret; factis benignus pro re; dictis haud minus libertatis alienae, quam suae dignitatis memor; et (quo nihil popularius est) quibus artibus petierat magistratus, iisdem gerebat*' (VII.33.1-4, cited in Latin).

12. VIII.7-8.   13. VIII.10.8.

14. Conjoined with his efficiency as a general, this justifies Machiavelli in calling Manlius 'politically virtuous' according to the meaning he assigns to this word, for both he and Valerius laboured not in their own interests but for the common good.

15. P. Valerius Publicola replaced Tarquinius Collatinus, who with Brutus was Rome's first consul, in 509 B.C. (Livy II.2). He defeated the Veii and Tarquinii, and was suspected of aiming at kingly power owing to the house he had built on the Caelian hill (*ib.* 6–7, cp. D. I.28.3 and n. 5). He acquired the surname 'Publicola'—friend of the people—on account of the 'Valerian laws' which made it treason to aim at kingship and granted a right of appeal to the people (*ib.* 8). He was again consul in 508 and 507, and was elected for the fourth time in 504, when he gained a second triumph by defeating the Sabines (*ib.* 11, 15–16). Valerius Corvinus, or Corvus, belonged to the same *gens,* but lived a century and a half later.

16. Cp. the *Cyropaedeia* IV.2.34 *sq.* and V.1.19 for Cyrus' treatment of his allies; IV.4 for his treatment of prisoners; V.3.46–50 for his intimacy with his officers and troops; and V.4.24 for his treatment of those who had come over to his side.

17. Many commentators think that the 'gentleman' referred to in this obscure passage is Vettor Pisani, the Venetian admiral who in 1380 destroyed the fleet of Genoa and put an end to her sea power. (Cp. Tommassini, Vol. II, pp. 162–3, n. 3, and Plinio Carli, *Le Opere Maggiori di N. Machiavelli,* 3rd Ed., p. 213.) Vettor Pisani (1324–80) was defeated at sea by Luciano Doria on 5 May 1379 and only six galleys escaped. On Whitsunday the enemy appeared off San Nicolo di Lido, and Pisani, together with his colleague Steno, was indicted before the Senate, which was jealous of his popularity with both sailors and populace. The advocates urged the death-penalty, but in the end Pisani was sentenced to six months' imprisonment and to loss of office for five years. Trieste fell and then Chioggia, and Venice was reduced to such straits that in 1384 she ordered the destruction of all records of her plight. Under the new admiral, Giustiniani, the sailors refused to fight, and joined with the populace in demanding the release of Pisani. On 19 August the senate yielded and Pisani was released. He bade the excited mob which surged around him, 'Be silent and pray to Saint Mark.' He then took command of the fleet, drove the Genoese from every port which they had occupied and completely destroyed their fleet. But in 1380 he died while still at sea, and there were rumours of foul play.

Hence if it be the tumult which arose in 1379 that Machiavelli has in mind, his account of the incident is more garbled than is his account of any other incident mentioned in the *Discourses.* Pisani did quell a disturbance, but it was not due to a quarrel between sailors and the populace, nor was it on this account that Pisani was imprisoned, nor yet is there any doubt as to whether the penalty inflicted was imprisonment or death. It is also surprising that Machiavelli should have forgotten the name of the greatest admiral that Venice ever had. Hence, until someone discovers in the annals of ancient Venice a passage similar to that which Machiavelli appears to be citing—and no one has thus far found the passage—I prefer to suspend judgment as to who the gentleman was.

See Guicciardini's comments in his *Considerazione sul* II.19, which agrees with what Machiavelli here says. Cp. also A.W. Book VII.8.363a; F.156, where Machiavelli says that when in camp fear and punishment is to be used, but in the field the hope of reward.

23. Upon what Account Camillus was banished from Rome

1. '*Ejus virtutem milites oderant, et mirabantur*' (V.26.8, cited in Latin). The reading in the Teubner text is: '*praeda ad quaestores redacta cum magna militum ira; sed severitate imperii victi eandem virtutem et oderant et mirabantur*'.

2. The three reasons for the hatred which Furius Camillus incurred are mentioned by Livy in V.23, but rather as facts than as reasons for hatred, except in the case of the chariot with four white horses. This was thought to be unbecoming not merely in a citizen, but in a human being (*ib.* 23.5), and by the populace was looked upon as an outrage since Camillus seemed to be emulating Jupiter and the Sun (*ib.* 23.6). We are also told that the contribution of a tenth part of their booty which all were expected to make as an offering to Apollo, tended to alienate the minds of the plebs from Camillus (*ib.* 23.11). All Livy says, however, of the cause of Camillus' banishment (*ib.* 32.7) and of the heavy fine imposed is that it was connected with the booty taken at Veii. When it occurred we are not told. His banishment is mentioned in connection with incidents which happened five years later in 391 B.C.

3. Cp. *The Prince,* cap. 16, last paragraph, and cap. 19, opening paragraphs. Burd says that this remark appears to have been determined by Sallust, *Bell. Jug.* iii: '*frustra autem niti neque aliud se fatigando nisi odium quaerere, extremae dementiae est*'— 'to strive in vain and to expect nothing but hatred as the result of one's labour is sheer madness' (Burd's '*Il Principe*', note on page 290). Cp. D. I.60.2.

24. The Prolongation of Military Commands made Rome a Servile State

1. See D. I.37.

2. Livy III.21—460 B.C. For the influence exercised by Lucius Quintius Cincinnatus; see also III.19, 20.

3. Livy VIII.26. Two unprecedented events, Livy says, occurred in 326 B.C. Publilius Philo was granted a triumph after the expiration of his year of office, and his office was prolonged, a thing that had never occurred before.

4. See D. I.37.6–7 and nn. 9, 10, and for Caesar see Index *sub voce*.

5. Note the inconveniences each alternative entails: if quick conquests, then prolonged commissions and ultimately servitude; if no prolonged commission, then slow conquests.

In *The Art of War* Machiavelli speaks of the change from a well-ordered state to one in which important citizens employ armed forces to break laws, despoil provinces, and to tyrannise over their country; with the result that the common soldier breaks his oath, ceases to respect the senate, and lends his support to tyranny (A.W. Bk. I, B.271.a–b, F.9; B.272–3, F.10 *sq.*). In place of the old custom in which the common soldier and his general alike returned to his ordinary avocations after a war, we now have standing armies in time of peace as well as in time of war, and it was precisely this that led to the downfall of the republic of Rome and the setting up of a tyranny under the Caesars (*ib.*). The change came about at the time of the Gracchi (B272a, F.10).

Guicciardini *in loc.* agrees that the prolongation of military commands provided an opportunity for obtaining control of the republic; but points out that 'the principal cause of the trouble was corruption in the city, which was given to avarice, luxury, and had so far departed from its ancient customs that in it there were sanguinary conflicts which always bring about tyranny in free peoples. Hence the ease with which citizens and soldiers were so corrupted that a Catiline who had no military command and no armies could hope to get control of the republic. Hence the plotting of the powerful to divide military commands and armies between them. Hence the irregular prolonging of military commands, such as Caesar's, which was due neither to the needs of the republic, nor to the exigencies of war, nor to the admiration evoked by his virtue, but to the plot to get control of the republic in which Pompey and Crassus joined. . . . Sulla's command had not been prolonged when he first came to blows with Marius. Its cause was the split between the nobility and the plebs, for, since the plebs had Marius as its head, the nobility were forced to look for one. Whence I infer that, when Rome was not corrupt, the prolongation of military commands and the continuing of the consulate, which often took place in difficult times, was useful and sound; but that, when a city is corrupt, civil conflicts break out and the seeds of tyrannies are sown even if there be no prolongation of military commands. The conclusion to be drawn is, therefore, that, even if there had been no prolongation, there would not have been lacking a Caesar or somebody else to get control of the republic, nor yet either the design or the power to effect it by other means.'

N.B. The only chapters in Book III on which Guicciardini comments are chapters 17, 19 and 24.

25. Concerning the Poverty of Cincinnatus and of many other Roman Citizens

1. See D. I.37.3 *sq.*, II.19.2, and III.16.3 on the need of making some provision for keeping citizens poor.

2. See D. I.37.

3. '*Operae pretium est audire, qui omnia prae divitiis humana spernunt, neque honori magno locum, neque virtuti putant esse, nisi effusae affluant opes*' (III.26.7; cited in Latin). This war with the Aequi took place in 458 B.C. (cp. A.W. Bk. V, B.336b, F.113).

4. III.29.2.   5. *ib.*   6. III.27.1.   7. III.26.8.

8. Marcus Atilius Regulus, victor in the battle fought with Hasdrubal, Bostar and Hamilcar in 256 B.C.; defeated and captured in 255; imprisoned for five years, when he was allowed to go on a peace mission to Rome. As this failed, he returned voluntarily to Carthage, and was brutally murdered. His request to be allowed to return home in 256 to look after the little farm on which he lived is mentioned by Livy in Epitome XVIII and by Valerius Maximus IV.4.6 (Cp. D. III.1.7, and A.W. Bk. I, B.271b; F.9.)

9. For Paulus Aemilius, see D. III.16.4 and n. 4. The story of his giving a silver cup of five pounds weight to his son-in-law, Aelius Tubero, is told by Plutarch in his *Paulus Aemilius*, 28. After his victory over Perseus in 168 B.C., he reserved for

himself none of the immense quantity of silver and gold found in the royal palaces, but handed it to the quaestors to be put in the public treasury. Tubero was one of the sixteen relatives who lived with him and were supported by his small farm, and the cup, says Plutarch, acquired by virtue and honour, is said to have been the first piece of silver his family possessed. Neither the men nor the women in his family used vessels of silver or gold. On the other hand, Aemilius Paulus cannot have been a very poor man, for he employed masters to teach his children grammar, logic, rhetoric, sculpture, and painting, and others to teach them to break in horses and dogs, and to train them in riding and hunting (6). Moreover, from the loot acquired from the palaces of Perseus he did reserve to himself the king's library for the sake of his sons who were men of letters (28). We must not suppose, then, that when Machiavelli speaks of poverty, he means extreme poverty or is opposed to the acquisition and enjoyment of property. On the contrary, he expressly states that this is essential to a well-run state (see D. II.2.10).

10. Valerius Maximus is almost certainly the source for this discourse, for he cites in the chapter entitled *De Paupertate laudata* (IV, c. 4) as examples of poverty all three of the persons mentioned by Machiavelli, namely, Quintius Cincinnatus, (Marcus) Atilius Regulus, and Paulus Aemilius. Plutarch also has a short treatise entitled *De Cupiditate Divitiarum* in his *Moralia,* and there is a paragraph in which he discusses poverty in *Aristides and Cato compared* (n. 4). There is also a passage in praise of poverty in Xenophon's *Convivium, IV.29 sq.*

26. How Women have brought about the Downfall of States

1. Cp. Livy IV.9 and 10 for the riots in Ardea which occurred in 443 B.C.
2. For Lucrezia and the Tarquins, see D. III.2.1 and 5.1 and Livy I.58–9.
3. For Virginia and the Decemviri, see D. I.40.8; 57.3; and Livy III.44 sq.
4. See D. III.6.4–5; and cp. Aristotle, *Politics* V.10, 1311a, 33–b, 23; also V.11, 1314b, 24, where he says 'The insolence of women has ruined many tyrannies'.

27. How Unity may be restored to a Divided City, and how mistaken are those who hold that to retain Possession of Cities one must needs keep them divided

1. On the folly of attacking a divided city, and how best to deal with it see D. II.25; and on the folly of using factions to hold it, see P. 20. (Burd 329 and note; E.169.)

2. Livy IV.10.6.—The ringleaders were killed by the consul.

3. For the incidents related in this paragraph (§ 2), cp. P. 17, opening paragraph; also see Guicciardini, *Storia Fiorentina* c. 22 and c. 24 (pp. 269–71), and Villari I, c. 4. Pistoia was subject to Florence. The Cancellieri were favourable to the republican régime then obtaining in Florence, whereas the Panciàtichi supported the Medici, then in exile. The whole city and its surroundings had long been divided between these two sections of the nobility, says Guicciardini, both of which, but especially the Cancellieri, were much impoverished after 1494. When disturb-

ances broke out in January 1501 Florence intervened, adherents of both parties were imprisoned in Florence, but it was decided that the rest should return to Pistoia and that if they caused any further trouble they should be heavily fined. This was on the advice of Machiavelli, who acted throughout as the agent of Florence and urged that it would be dangerous to keep the Cancellieri in Pistoia and shut the Panciatichi out to roam the countryside. But in October 1501, and in January 1502, fresh rioting broke out and Florence again had to intervene. It is this trouble that Machiavelli is speaking of when he says that fifteen years ago the Panciatichi were divided against the Cancellieri and tumults were the result. Hence this discourse was written, presumably either in 1516 or in 1517. Machiavelli's letters and his report on the disturbances are still extant. (Cp. *Op.* P.M. V.411 and VI.288).

4. For the futility of fortresses, see P. 20, where the sentence: 'It was necessary to hold Pistoia by factions and Pisa by fortresses' recurs (Burd 329 and see note, E.169). Cp. also D. II.24 and see Index *sub* 'Fortresses'.

5. Flavio Biondo—better known as Flavius or Flavius Blondus Forliviensis— (1392–1463), was papal Secretary of State from the time of Eugenius IV to Pius II. He accompanied Eugenius IV on his visit to Bologna, Ferrara and Florence, of which, therefore, he had first-hand knowledge. He wrote ten books entitled '*Romae Triumphantis*', three entitled '*Romae Illustratae*', and a work on the history of Italy from the time of Honorius and Arcadius down to his own times, entitled '*Historiae decades tres*' (see Table XIII. A.17). The words cited are taken from the latter work (see the Basle edition of *Flav. Blondii Hist.* published in 1559, dec. ii. *lib.* 9, p. 337).

6. The events referred to in this paragraph (§ 6) are described at great length by Guicciardini in his *Storia Fiorentina* cc. 24–6, and more briefly in his *Storia d'Italia* V.8–9 (cp. Villari, I, c. 4). The fall of Arezzo and the revolt of the Val di Chiana and other places, which followed in May, were both brought about by Vitellozzo, acting in conjunction with Pandolfo Petrucci, Gian Pagolo Baglione, and the Orsini. Their aim was to restore Piero de Medici to Florence, and ostensibly they had the support of Caesar Borgia, who was following with a strong force. Florence appealed to Louis XII, who responded by peremptorily forbidding an attack on Florence and promising to send troops to her aid. Meanwhile Arezzo had fallen (cp. D. I.2.2; 38.6; II.23.3, III.6.44), and Valentino had seized Urbino, whither Machiavelli was sent to listen to the threats of the Duke to form an independent state with Pisa as its capital (cp. D. III.16 n. 5). But with the arrival of Imbault in July, Vitellozzo at once withdrew from Arezzo and the neighbouring towns. These he handed over to Imbault, who declined to pass them on to Florence, and in consequence was replaced by Messer de Lant (or Lanques), who carried out the agreement made by the French king. Machiavelli's reports on the 'Legation to Duke Valentino', 'the Legation to Arezzo', and 'on the Rebellion of the Val di Chiana and Arezzo' are all extant. (Cp. *Op.* P.M. IV.65–257; Detmold III.241–80 for Duke Valentino; and *Op.* P.M. III.360 *sq.* for Arezzo; and *Op.* P.M. III.365 *sq.* for the Val di Chiana.)

7. The arms of Florence, consisting of a lily and a lion, were known as the Marzocco. Hence those who proclaimed themselves to be partisans of the Marzocco consisted of those inhabitants of towns subject to Florence who were loyal in their allegiance. Monsieur de Lanques is astonished that Florence should have tolerated such a state of affairs, for to a Frenchman at this epoch the existence of a royal party and an anti-royal party in France was unthinkable.

Machiavelli referred to Aristotle's doctrine on divided cities in a letter to Vettori given by Ellinger on p. 62. Vettori replied on 26 August 1513 that he could not recollect the doctrine. Actually *Politics*, Book V, is almost wholly concerned with the divisions which arise in cities between different parties, especially the rich and the poor. Thus in V.9 we are told that 'to make two of a city' by fostering quarrels between the rich and poor is a mistake common to both oligarchies and democracies (1310a, 2–5). So, too, tyrants are given to sowing quarrels among citizens and embroiling friends with friends, the populace with the notables, and the rich with one another, and regard this as one of the arts by which a city is to be held. (V.11, 1313b, 16–18.)

28. That a Strict Watch should be kept on the Doings of Citizens since under cover of Good Works there often arises the Beginning of Tyranny

1. Livy IV.13–16. Maelius' misdoings were at length reported by Lucius Minucius, the prefect of the markets in 439 B.C., whereon the consuls were blamed for not having reported the matter before, and Lucius Minucius was appointed dictator, 'that there might be someone competent to deal with such great power' (*ib.* 13.12). Cp. D. III.1.5.

Cp. Aristotle, *Politics* V.8, 1308b, 20 *sq.* 'Since innovations creep in through the private life of individuals, there ought to be a magistracy which will have an eye to those whose life is not in harmony with the government, whether oligarchy or democracy or any other. And for a like reason increase of prosperity in any part of the state should be carefully watched.' Cp. D. I.46.3 where Machiavelli says there should be an institution for this purpose and promises to discuss it, but does not do so in this chapter, though it is the obvious place.

29. That the Faults of Peoples are due to Princes

1. The heading, which runs '*Che gli peccati de' popoli nascono dai principi*', might be translated 'That the faults of the populace are due to their rulers', but I have translated it more literally since in the example given it is princes proper, not rulers in general, that are involved, and, though the stress is on the populace, the nobility also may ape the bad manners of their princes. The view here expressed is in accord with what Machiavelli says elsewhere about the virtues of the populace; cp. D. I.58, where they are compared with those of a prince, and his oft-repeated declaration that it is essential to all rulers to secure their good-will, and that once it be secured they can be relied upon. (See Index *sub* 'Populace'). Note, too, the implication that men are prone not merely to evil, but also to good, and that which is brought out will depend largely upon the way in which they are treated.

2. Cp. the account of the Romagna and of the princes who ruled it in P. 7. Cp. also P. 17, where we are told that: 'Caesar Borgia was accounted cruel; yet his cruelty reconciled the Romagna, kept it united, and restored to it peace and loyalty. Hence, if one ponders the matter well, it will be seen that Borgia had a

much higher sense of his duty (*stato molto più pietoso*) than the people of Florence who, to avoid the reproach of cruelty, suffered Pistoia to be destroyed.' To say that Pistoia was destroyed is an exaggeration, but it was certainly reduced to a sorry state by the long-continued factions which Florence failed to suppress (cp. D. III.27.2, 4–5 and n. 3. For a list of the barons with whom Caesar Borgia came in conflict during his three campaigns, see Burd, pp. 218–19, n. 15).

3. The seizure of the golden bowl which was being conveyed to Delphi by pirates and its restoration by Timasitheus is told by Livy in V.28.1–5.

4. '*Timasitheus multitudinem religione implevit, quae semper regenti est similis*' (V.28.4, cited in Latin.)

5. '*E quel che fa'l signor, fanno poi molti;*
   Chè nel signor son tutti gli occhi volti.'

See '*Rappresentazione di S. Giovanni e Paolo*' in the *Opere di Lorenzo d'Magnifico, Bari*, 1914, 2,100. The reference is given by A. H. Gilbert in 'Machiavelli's *Prince* and its Forerunners', 1938, p. 44.

Cp. on the topic of this chapter, Cicero, *de Legibus III, xiv*, cited in Table XIII. A, *sub* Cicero.

30. (i) It is necessary for a Citizen who proposes to use his Authority to do any Good Work in a Republic, first to extinguish all Envy; and (ii) what Provisions are to be made for the Defence of a City which the Enemy is about to attack

1. '*Nec quicquam de majestate sua detractum credebant, quod majestati ejus concessissent*' (VI.6.7, cited in Latin); and for the account of what happened in 389 B.C., see VI.6.6–7.

2. The above particulars are given in Camillus' speech (*ib.* 6.12–15).

3. '*Nec quicquam,*' etc.

4. On the need for removing rivals see D. I.16.4–5, 7; D. III.3 and 4. This Machiavelli holds to be essential alike in the case of rival claimants to a throne, and a rival party seeking by violence to overthrow a government. It should be noted however (i) that the rivals here in question are persons who would prefer to see their country ruined rather than fail to obtain their ends, i.e. they are ready to become traitors; (ii) that it is only in their case that Machiavelli here claims that their extermination is necessary; and (iii) that the alternative method, described in § 2, supposes that all parties are prepared to unite for the common good owing to some grave danger, and hence that in such a case they are not prepared to sacrifice their country to attain their own ends.

5. Cp. *Exodus* xxxii.25–8. Moses having received the law on Mount Sinai descends from the mountain only to find that the Israelites have fallen into idolatry and are worshipping a golden calf. Standing at the entrance to their camp, he bids those who are on the Lord's side come to him. The sons of Levi gather round him and are ordered to slay every man his brother, his companion and his neighbour;

'and there fell of the people that day about three thousand men'. On previous occasions when the people had murmured against him, Moses had shown them remarkable consideration. Cp. for instance, Exodus xiv. 10 *sq.*

6. There were those in Savonarola's day who accused him of inciting the people to riot, and it is possible to put this interpretation upon the sermons he preached, especially on the 'Renovation Sermon' which he preached on 13 January 1495 (cp. Villari's *Life and Times of Savonarola*, II.7, pp. 331–5). But his followers did not thus understand him. Nor can there be the least doubt but that they interpreted him aright. The wrath which was to descend upon Florence and Italy and upon the princes of the Church was the wrath of God, not the wrath of an angry people rising against their rulers in any movement which he was to lead. There was but one occasion on which Savonarola urged that violent measures should be taken. It occurred in 1496 when there was grave danger of the Medici being restored by force of arms. On that occasion, crucifix in hand, he exhorted the city to put to death all who sought to re-establish a tyranny in Florence. 'One must treat these men as the Romans treated those who sought to recall the Tarquins . . . Cut off his head, were he even the chief and head of thy house; cut off his head' (Villari, *op. cit.* III.1, pp. 369–70). It was, however, the magistrates, not the mob, who were thus to vindicate 'justice'. Neither in his *Storia Fiorentina* (c. 12, pp. 123 *sq.*), nor in his *Storia d'Italia* which contains two references to Savonarola in Book II (c. 2, p. 130; c. 7, p. 155) and five in Book III (c. 8, p. 258; c. 10, p. 267; c. 13, pp. 283, 287; c. 15, pp. 295–8), does Guicciardini suggest that Savonarola incited his followers to violence. (Cp. also D. I.11.6 and n. 14; D. I.45.2 and n. 6; D. I.56.1 and n. 1.)

7. For Soderini, see D. I.7.6 and n. 5; D. I.52.2 and n. 3; D. III.3.2–3.

8. Cp. also Polybius I.35.

9. This does not mean that the populace should not be armed. On the contrary, Machiavelli urges that for purposes of defence they should be armed, but in an orderly way. (Cp. D. I.6; D. II.20 and II.30.4; and A.W. Bk. I, B.277b, F. 18.)

31. Strong Republics and Outstanding Men retain their Equanimity and their Dignity under all Circumstances

1. '*Nec mihi dictatura animos fecit, nec exilium ademit*' (Livy VI.7.5 cited in Latin).

2. The preceding defeats being on the Ticinus in 218 and at Lake Trasimene in 217.

3. Cp. XXII.57.9–12.

4. Cp. the speech of Marcus Junius, the representative of the prisoners in XXII.59, and Manlius Torquatus' reply in XXII.60.

5. Cp. XXII.61.13–15.

6. For Hanno's speech, see Livy XXIII.12, and cp. D. II.30.6.

7. For the peace-terms proposed by Antiochus after the naval battle at Myonnesus in 191 B.C., see Livy XXXVII.35, and for the king's reaction see c. 36, 9.

8. For the mission Antiochus sent to Scipio after his defeat at Magnesia in 190, see Livy XXXVII.45.

9. '*Quod Romani, si vincuntur, non minuuntur animis; nec si vincunt, insolescere solent.*' Cited in Latin, but not taken from Livy, though similar words occur in Scipio's reply to the ambassadors from Antiochus: '*animos, qui nostrae mentis sunt, eosdem in*

omni fortuna gessimus gerimusque, neque eos secundae res extulerunt nec adversae minuerunt' (Livy XXXVII.45.11–12; from which the heading of the discourse would seem to have been taken).

10. On the aspirations of Venice toward sovereignty in Italy, see A.W. Bk. I, B.277–8, F.19, where Machiavelli says that Venice might have set up a new monarchy had she trained and employed her own troops instead of using *condottieri,* such as the Duke of Mantua. Cp. also Guicciardini, *St. d'I.,* Bk. I.1, p. 5, on their desire for sovereignty; IV.14, p. 392, on their subservience to Louis XII in 1500; and on their subsequent defiance of him when ready for war in 1509, see VIII.11, pp. 266–7; on their refusal to give up Faenza to Julius II in 1503 when fortune favoured them, see VI.13, pp. 149–50; on the affront offered to Julius in 1508 and on the opinions expressed of him in the Venetian senate, see Book VIII.1. On the change from arrogance to subservience to Julius, cp. Pastor, *Hist. Popes* VI, pp. 308 and 316. Cp. also H.F. I.29.

11. On the partial defeat of the Venetians by d'Alviano at Vailà on 14 May 1509, see Guicciardini, *St. d'I.* VIII.4; and with the panic it caused in Venice compare the brief summary given by Machiavelli with the long account Guicciardini gives in Book VIII.5. They were prepared, says Guicciardini, 'to reconcile themselves on any terms whatsoever with the Pope, the King of the Romans, and with the Catholic King [of Spain]', but not with the King of France, whom they mistrusted (*ib.*, p. 274).

12. Though the defeat at Vailà was but partial, it was followed by further vigorous attacks by the French, backed by the Swiss, so that, says Guicciardini, 'in fifteen days the King had made himself master of all that part of the Milanese which had been allotted to him at Cambray' (*ib.* p. 275). In the Romagna the towns seized by Venice were attacked by papal troops under Francesco da Castel del Rio, Cardinal of Pavia (pp. 275–6); and 'every day new enemies to the republic arose' (p. 277), amongst them the Duke of Ferrara and the Marquis of Mantua, who recovered their possessions (*ib.*), with the result that the Venetians thought it best to withdraw from Padua, Verona, and other towns which owed allegiance to the Emperor (p. 278). Whether the Venetians could have done much to stem the tide which was flowing so strongly against them, is open to question. Formidable armies were arrayed against them, but it is clear from the obsequious tone of the speech which Guicciardini ascribes to the Venetian ambassador when addressing the Emperor, that Venice was in a state of panic, and that, as the ambassador said, 'all her ancient valour and determination seemed to have vanished, and all her noble ardour and thirst for glory in war to have been extinguished' (pp. 279–81). For contemporary letters dealing with the situation from the Venetian standpoint, see the '*Diaries of Marino Sanuto*' for the month of May 1509, especially n. 120 *sq.* in Volume VIII, p. 247 *sq.* Cp. also D. I.53.3; D. II.10.6; and P. 20 (Burd 330, E.169.)

13. On the need of military discipline, see Index *sub* 'Military discipline', and cp. P. 12 (Burd 253, E. 97), where we are told that 'the chief foundation of all states, new as well as old or composite, are good laws and good armies; and, since there cannot be good laws where the state is not well-armed, it follows that where states are well-armed, they have good laws'.

14. See D. III.30.1, 5–6; and supra, § 1.

15. '*Quod quisque didicit, aut consuevit, faciet*' (Livy VI.7.6, cited in Latin).

Cp. Polybius VI.1: 'The true test of a perfect man is his power of bearing with spirit and dignity violent changes of fortune.'

And on the importance of education, see Aristotle, *Politics*, Book VIII, and the passage in V.9, cited in D. II.2, n. 7.

32. *What Means some have adopted to prevent a Peace*

1. See Livy VI.21. During the war with the Volsci in 386-5 the Romans found amongst the prisoners they had taken, troops from Velitrae and Circei, which were Roman colonies (VI.13.8, and cp. 12.6). There had been a revolt, but it was not until 383 that the Romans decided to repress it (*ib.* 21.3). Whereupon those responsible for the revolt dissuaded the colonies from sending an embassy to make terms with Rome, and induced the plebs to make a raid on Roman territory (*ib.* 21.6-8). This fresh attack, says Livy, put an end to all hope of peace (*ib.* 8).

2. A long account of the 'Mercenary or Libyan War' is to be found in Polybius I.65-88. After the 'longest, most continuous, and most severely contested war known to us in history' (63), i.e. the first Punic war, a treaty was signed in 242 whereby the Carthaginians engaged to evacuate the whole of Sicily (62). In consequence the motley crowd of mercenaries whom the Carthaginians had been using in Sicily were sent to Sicca, where, for lack of something better to do, they began calculating the amount of pay due to them and the compensation to which they thought themselves entitled (66). The natural result followed. There was a revolt, instigated by a runaway slave, Spendius, and by a Libyan called Mathos, who were elected leaders of the insurgents (69). The Carthaginians, having sent various members of the senate to treat with the insurgents, at length sent to them Gesco, a popular general (68). But when they demanded their pay, Gesco refused to produce it, telling the men to go and ask Mathos for it. Enraged at this, they arrested Gesco and the Carthaginians who were with him; and 'Mathos and Spendius, thinking that the speediest way in which to secure an outbreak of war, was for the men to commit some outrage' . . . sent them to plunder the Carthaginian baggage, manacled Gesco, and treated him with violence and insolence (70). Forced contributions from neighbouring towns provided them with abundant funds (72). Hanno, who was in command of Libya, having failed to repress the revolt was replaced by Hamilcar Barcas (75), who by his leniency looked like winning over many of the Libyans, so, to prevent this, Spendius seized Gesco and about seven hundred of his fellow prisoners, cut off their hands and other extremities, broke their legs, and threw them, still alive, into a trench (80). The rebels then 'passed a decree, which they encouraged each other to observe, to put every Carthaginian whom they caught to death with torture . . . This decree they carried out precisely and persistently' (81).

The two accounts tally in all respects save two. The name of the general whom the Carthaginians sent as ambassador to pacify the rebels was Gesco according to Polybius, whereas Machiavelli says Hasdrubal. And in Polybius' account the returning soldiers who took part in the revolt came from Sicily, not from Sicily and Sardinia. There was a revolt amongst the Sardinian troops to whom the disaffection had spread from Africa, but it took place in Sardinia itself, which for the time being the Carthaginians lost. In spite of these two discrepancies there can be little doubt that it is Polybius' account that Machiavelli is using. The shorter account of the Mercenary war given by Diodorus in what remains of his twenty-fifth book does not comprise anything like all the points which Machiavelli mentions, and his main point—the use of an outrage in order to ensure that war should come about —is not mentioned at all. Nor yet can Machiavelli have been using the yet shorter account of the incident given by Appian in his *Libyca*, c. 5. Appian, incidentally, gives the name of the ambassador as Gesco, whereas Diodorus merely says that the Carthaginians sent a herald. The mistake as to the name may well have been due to a mistake in the early Latin text of Polybius which Machiavelli was using, though it is given correctly in later editions. It is just possible, too, that the mistake about Sardinia is due to the same cause, though it would seem to be more likely that Machiavelli has slipped up here, as he sometimes does, though very rarely.

Cp. A.W. Bk. I, B.270, F.7-8, on the trouble caused by troops when disbanded.

33. To win a Battle it is essential to inspire the Army with Confidence both in itself and in its General

1. Cp. D. III.38, for a further discussion of what a general must do to inspire his troops with confidence in himself. Machiavelli passes on here to discuss how to inspire confidence in victory.

2. On the use of auspices, cp. D. I.14.

3. Cp. D. I.14.4, where Claudius Pulcher is called Appius Pulcher, his full name being Appius Claudius Pulcher.

4. '*Eludant nunc licet religiones. Quid enim interest, si pulli non pascentur, si ex cavea tardius exiverint, si occinuerit avis? Parva sunt haec, sed parva ista non contemnendo, majores nostri maximam hanc republicam fecerunt*' (VI.41.8, cited in Latin). The Appius Claudius who made this speech in 368 B.C., in reply to the proposal that the Licinian-Sextian laws should be passed *en bloc* (cp. D. III.11.1 and n. 3), was the grandson of the Decemvir. His surname was Crassus.

5. See Livy VI.28-9, and cp. D. II.29.1 for the defeat on the Allia.

6. '*Vides tu, fortuna illos fretos ad Alliam consedisse; at tu, fretus armis animisque, invade mediam aciem*' (VI.29.1-2, cited in Latin). The dictator was Titus Quintius Cincinnatus, and the date 380 B.C.

7. '*Militum etiam sine rectore, stabilis virtus tutata est*' (VI.30.6, cited in Latin). The dictator had been replaced by six military tribunes, amongst them Publius and Caius Manlius to whom the war with the Volsci was committed by arrangement with the others (*ib.* 30.1-3). Machiavelli wrongly says 'consuls'. Date 379 B.C.

8. Livy IX.37. The war in 310 B.C. had spread from Etruria to Umbria, and the Roman troops under Fabius Maximus Rullianus were advancing on Sutrium. Fabius had to restrain their eagerness. He ordered them to take their meal, and then addressed them, telling them that the Etruscans were not to be compared with the Samnites, nor so numerous, and that 'beside this, he had a secret weapon, about which they would know in good time, but meanwhile it was best to be silent' (*ib.* 37.6).

Cp. A.W. Bk. VII, B.362b, F.158, on inspiring the troops with confidence; also *ib.* Bk. IV, Fabrizio's concluding speech.

34. What Kind of Reputation or Gossip or Opinion causes the Populace to begin to favour a Particular Citizen; and whether the Populace appoints to Offices with Greater Prudence than does a Prince

1. See D. I.11.2 and D. III.22.2.

2. He threatened the tribune with death unless his father got off. Livy VII.5.3–5 and cp. D. I.11.2.

3. See D. I.58.7 and cp. D. I.5. For the way the prince chooses advisers see P. 22 and 23. He, like the populace, takes note of the company a man keeps (see § 5, and cp. P. 22, opening paragraph).

4. See Index *sub* 'Manlius Imperiosus Torquatus, Titus', for the various incidents.

5. See Livy XXI.46 for the story of Publius Cornelius Scipio's rescue of his father, who was wounded during the battle on the Ticinus; XXII.53 for the oath he forced those to take who were conspiring to leave Rome; and XXVI.50 for the story of the damsel he restored to her parents and to her fiancé, Allucius. And for Machiavelli's references to these incidents see Index *sub* 'Scipio'.

6. Cp. Plutarch's remarks on the use of slogans in public oratory—*Praecepta gerendae reipublicae*, 6 (803 A). Mussolini took Machiavelli's advice so much to heart that he used to placard towns and villages with notices in letters three feet high announcing that '*Mussolini ha sempre ragione*'—'Mussolini is always right'.

7. Appius Claudius, the Decemvir, is the outstanding instance of a sudden change of character, but thus suddenly to change is bad policy; cp. D. I.41, and D. I.40.2; 42.1.

8. The speech is given in XXIV.8. Titus Otacilius had been nominated but not elected.

Cp. Guicciardini's remarks on D. I.47.

Plutarch in his '*Praecepta gerendae reipublicae*' remarks that 'the masses are the more ready to accept a beginner because they are so palled and surfeited with those to whom they are accustomed, just as spectators at a show are glad to get a new performer' (10, 804 D.).

Cp. P. 21 on how a prince should gain renown; P. 22 on the Secretaries of Princes; and P. 23 on Flatterers.

35. What Dangers are run by one who takes the Lead in advising some Course of Action; and how much greater are the Dangers incurred when the Course of Action is Unusual

1. There is no chapter either in the *Discourses* or in *The Prince* in which Machiavelli discusses the question how best to handle a new enterprise involving many persons. True, the setting up of a civil principality involves many people and many

conflicting interests, but P. 9, which deals with this topic, has presumably already been written, and in any case no mention is made of the difficulty arising from the fact that many people must needs be concerned in such an enterprise. There is therefore at least one chapter of the *Discourses* which Machiavelli intended to write but did not write—which lends some colour to the claim that his work is unfinished.

2. The term 'bashaw'—*Bascià*—is the old English word for 'pasha', and the term 'Sophy'—*Sofi*—is the old English term used to denote the ruler of Persia.

3. Guicciardini gives an account of the invasion of Persia by Selim I in 1514-16, and of his subsequent conquest of Syria and Egypt in *St. d'I.* XIII.9, but treats it from the standpoint of the danger threatening Christendom by Selim's growing power. He states that after taking Tavriz, the capital, Selim retired, largely owing to the scarcity of supplies, and that on his return he punished many of his soldiers for having mutinied. He does not, however, mention the person who counselled him to undertake this expedition, or his subsequent fate. Syria was invaded in 1516 and Cairo taken in 1517. (For Selim see D. I.1.9 and 19.3; D. II.17.10 and D. III.6.7.)

4. For the appointment of the first plebeian consul, see Livy VI.42.9 and VII.1. Machiavelli omits his name, though Livy gives it. It was Lucius Sextius, who, together with Licinius, had long striven to obtain this concession from the patricians. The granting of it in 366 put an end to the expedient of appointing military tribunes with consular power in lieu of consuls. The first plebeian consul to conduct a war under his own auspices was Lucius Genucius (VII.6.8). Commenting on his defeat by the Hernici, Livy says the state was anxious, and that, when it fell out that Genucius got caught in an ambush by a superior force, and was routed and killed, the patricians were by no means so grieved at the public disaster as they were elated at the unsuccessful leadership of the plebeian consul (*ib.* 9-10). Cp. the remark Machiavelli makes at the end of § 4 and the story of Claudius Nero in III.17.1.

5. This incident is not mentioned in Livy's account of the battle of Pydna, fought on 22 June 168 B.C. (Livy XLIV.41-6). Plutarch, however, in his *Life of Paulus Aemilius* (23), who won it, tells us how Perseus 'on entering Pella during the night killed with his dagger two of his treasurers, Euctus and Eulaeus, who, while waiting on him, complained of some of his actions and provoked him by their untimely and critical remarks'.

36. Reasons why the French have been, and still are, looked upon in the Beginning of a Battle as more than Men, and afterwards as less than Women

1. In the heading Machiavelli speaks of '*i franciosi*', a term which includes both the Gauls and the people who were known to him, as they are known to us, as 'the French'. With what he says of their behaviour in battle compare what Guicciardini writes in *St. d'I.* Bk. II, c. 11, p. 187, where he tells us that the common people had grown disused to arms and lost their warlike spirit owing to their having been disarmed by their kings, weaned from the love of military exercises, and encouraged to devote themselves to trade. Hence 'the French could not trust their own infantry,

which fought timorously, unless supported by a strong body of Swiss'. What Machiavelli says of the French is explained by the fact that they still had excellent cavalry, but these when backed by their own infantry could not withstand the enemy's counter-attacks. Oddly enough, much the same thing is said of them by the Byzantine emperor who wrote a work entitled 'Tactica'. It is ascribed to Leo XI (A.D. 886–911), but may have been written not by the 'philosopher-king' but by Leo III, the Isaurian (A.D. 680–740). 'The Franks and Lombards are bold and daring to excess', says Leo. In fact, 'so formidable is the charge of the Frankish chivalry with their broadsword, lance, and shield, that it is best to decline a pitched battle with them till you have put all the chances on your own side. You should take advantage of their indiscipline and disorder; whether fighting on foot or on horseback, they charge in dense, unwieldy masses, which cannot manoeuvre, because they have neither organisation nor drill. . . . Hence they readily fall into confusion if suddenly attacked in flank and rear—a thing easy to accomplish as they are utterly careless and neglect the use of pickets and vedettes and the proper surveying of the countryside.' (Cited from *Const.* XVIII, by Oman in his *Art of War in the Middle Ages*, Vol. I, p. 204.)

2. Livy VII.10. The credibility of the Gallic invasion of 367 and the legend of Titus Manlius and the Gaul is questioned by modern historians (C.A.H. VII. pp. 526, 572), and Livy himself thinks the incident occurred six years later, namely in 361 (cp. VII.9–10 with VI.42.5–6). For other references to the slaying of the Gaul, see Index *sub* 'Manlius Imperiosus Torquatus, Titus'.

3. Livy X.28.4. The Latin, which is not quoted here, expresses the opinion Fabius Maximus had formed of the Gauls: *'persuasum erat duci . . . Gallorum quidem etiam corpora intolerantissima laboris atque aestus fluere primaque eorum proelia plus quam virorum, postrema minus quam feminarum esse'* from which comes the heading of the discourse.

4. Livy frequently refers to the fury of the Gauls' first onslaught and their subsequent slackness, and contrasts it with the Romans' dogged perseverance; e.g. V.39.1; 49.5; VI.42.7–8; VII.11.1 and 12.10. Cp. also Polybius II.35.

5. Lucius Papirius Cursor, who is angry with Q. Fabius Maximus Rullianus for having fought a battle contrary to his orders and gained a victory at which Rome was rejoicing, points out in his speech what would be the consequence of encouraging the slackness and indiscipline which Papirius' conduct exemplified. The quotation, which is in Latin, is as follows: *'Nemo hominum, nemo Deorum, verecundiam habeat; non edicta imperatorum, non auspicia observentur; sine commeatu vagi milites in pacato, in hostico errent; immemores sacramenti, licentia sola se ubi velint exauctorent; infrequentia deserant signa; neque conveniatur ad edictum, nec discernantur, interdiu nocte; aequo iniquo loco, jussu injussu imperatoris pugnent; et non signa, non ordines servent; latrocinii modo, caeca et fortuita, pro sollemni et sacrata militia sit'* (Livy VIII.34.8–10).

Cp. Machiavelli's short treatise 'On the Nature of the French' (Barbèra 730–1; Detmold IV.419–20).

37. Whether Skirmishes are Necessary before a Battle, and how, if one decides to do without them, the Presence of Fresh Enemy Troops is to be discovered

1. See Index *sub* 'Good'.

2. '*Tanti ea dimicatio ad universi belli eventum momenti fuit, ut Gallorum exercitus, relictis trepide castris, in Tiburtem agrum, mox in Companiam transierit*' (VII.11.1; cited in Latin). For the intimate connection of evil with good, cp. D. I.2.24 on the inherent malignity of good governments, and see Index *sub* 'Inconveniences' and the impossibility of avoiding them.

3. See D. I.23 and cp. D. II.12.7–9.

4. '*Ne eos novum bellum, ne novus hostis terreret*' (VII.32.5; cited in Latin)—343 B.C.

5. Cp. D. I.23 on passes, and D. II.24 and 32 on towns.

6. Cp. n. 2 above: *tanti ea dimicatio ad universi belli eventum momenti fuit;* and see n. 10 below.

7. Philip V not only laid waste the territory surrounding Athens after his failure to take the city in 200 B.C. (Livy XXXI.14.10 and 26.1), but, when in 198 Flamininus first took Epeirus and then advanced into Thessaly, Philip in his retreat deliberately destroyed the towns and ravaged the countryside (Livy XXXII.13).

8. The plight in which the Romans found themselves after Cannae is described in the reply given to envoys sent by loyal Campanians. There was nothing Rome could do. Her legions, her cavalry, her arms, her standards, her horses, her supplies, had all been destroyed. The Campanians are exhorted to fight in the common cause, but must look to themselves (XXIII.5).

9. See Plutarch, who in his *Life of Marius* supplies all the data which Machiavelli uses in this paragraph (§ 6). The Cimbri are described in n. 11, where we are told that they had routed many reputable armies employed to guard Transalpine Gaul (cp. D. II.8.2). Hence Rome became alarmed and appointed Marius consul for the third time in 103 B.C., and for the fourth time in 102 (nn. 13–14). The Cimbri, who had been joined by the Teutons and the Ambrones, divided their forces, and the latter went to engage Marius. Marius refused to join battle owing to their incredible numbers and the fierceness of their battle-cries. Instead, he ordered his troops 'to mount guard upon the ramparts in turns, so that they might grow accustomed to the forbidding appearance of the enemy . . . and become acquainted with their arms and the way they used them. Thus, what was at first terrible, by being looked upon would in time become of small account. For he was of opinion that to objects of terror novelty adds a fictitious glamour, the terror of which is removed by familiarity' (n. 16; cp. D. III.14). 'When the daily sight had lessened the terror of his troops', Marius joined battle and the enemy's army of between 100,000 and 200,000 was wiped out at Aquae Sextiae in 102 B.C. (Cp. A.W. Bk. V, B.335b, F.111–12.) In the next year they invaded Italy and were again defeated by Marius at Campi Raudii (101 B.C.).

10. '*Qui ob rem parvi ponderis trepidi, in Tiburtem agrum et in Campaniam transierunt*' (Livy VII.11.1: cited in Latin. But the first phrase is not given by Teubner, nor does it occur in the passage cited in n. 2.)

Cp. A.W. Bk. VII, B.363a, F.156, on the use of *piccole zuffe*.

38. What ought to be done by a General so that his Army may have Confidence in him

1. See D. III.37.6.

2. '*Tum etiam intueri, cujus ductu auspicioque ineunda pugna sit, utrum, qui audiendus dumtaxat magnificus adhortator sit, verbis tantum ferox, operum militarium expers, an qui et ipse tela tractare, procedere ante signa, versari media in mole pugnae sciat. Facta mea, non dicta, vos, milites, sequi volo; nec disciplinam modo, sed exemplum etiam a me petere, qui hac dextra mihi tres consulatus, summamque laudem peperi*' (VII.32.10–12; cited in Latin).

3. i.e. in D. III.37.2.

4. For Gracchus who raised an army of slaves see D. II.26.5 (Livy XXII.57), and for the victory he won with them see D. II.26, n. 4 (Livy XXIV.14–15). For Epaminondas and the new army he raised in Thebes and led to victory see D. I.21.3 and n. 4; and D. III.13.3.

5. For use of sham fights, see D. II.17.8.

6. Cp. the Lacaedemonian saying, quoted in D. I.21.3, that warriors are born wherever men are born, and cp. P. 14.

Cp. A.W. Bk. IV, end, F.96 on how to inspire confidence.

39. That a General ought to be acquainted with the Lie of the Land

1. See the speech Cyrus makes to his officers after supper on the eve of the battle with the king of Armenia. (Xenophon, *Cyropaedeia* II.4.22–9; and cp. also his treatise '*de Venatione*', of both of which Latin translations were extant in Machiavelli's day.) Platina also says of hunting: *ea enim bellicae arti persimilis est* (*Principis Diatuposis* 3.2).

2. '*Vides tu, Aule Corneli, cacumen illud supra hostem? Arx illa est spei salutisque nostrae, si eam (quoniam caeci reliquere Samnites) impigre capimus*' (Livy VII.34.4; cited in Latin). The date is 343 B.C., when the first Samnite war broke out.

3. '*Publius Decius tribunus militum, conspicit unum editum in saltu collem, imminentem hostium castris, aditu arduum impedito agmini, expeditis haud difficilem*' (ib. 34.3; cited in Latin). This P. Decius Mus was the father of the P. Decius Mus mentioned in D. III.45.1–2 (cp. D. III.1.7 and D. II.16.1–2).

4. '*Ite mecum, ut, dum lucis aliquid superest, quibus locis hostes praesidia ponant, qua pateat hinc exitus, exploremus. Haec omnia sagulo militari amictus ne ducem circumire hostes notarent, perlustravit*' (ib. 34.14–15; cited in Latin).

Cp. A.W. Bk. V, B.334–6, F.109–13, and P.14 (Burd 278, E. 116–17).

40. That it is a Glorious Thing to use Fraud in the Conduct of a War

1. This discourse and the two which follow it form a set, the purpose of which is to justify, on grounds of expediency in the interests of the state, actions commonly

regarded as dishonourable. In this discourse the use of 'fraud' is justified on the ground that everybody recognises that it is legitimate, and even 'glorious', to use it in time of war. In the next chapter the principle is extended so as to cover any 'dishonourable' action performed in time of emergency when the state is in peril. To confirm this, in the third chapter appeal is made to the commonly accepted principle of moralists that promises elicited by force are not binding. The term 'fraud' (*la fraude*) is here used in the same sense as it is used in the famous passage in P. 18, in which we are told that it is one of the two means which every prince must be prepared to use, the other being 'force'. It should be noted, however, that, whereas in P. 18 Machiavelli includes under 'fraud' failure to keep one's promises or to abide by one's pledged word, in this chapter he expressly excludes this case. Nor does he even claim that breaches of contract on the part of a state or a prince are useful, except in rare circumstances. The term '*fraud*' for which '*astuzia*' is frequently substituted, covers any piece of trickery or sharp practice.

With this compare what St. Thomas says in his *Summa Theologica*, II,II.40, art. 3. The article is entitled: 'Whether it is lawful in warfare to use snares' (*uti insidiis*). 'Snares and frauds', he says, 'would seem to be, like lying, a breach of faith'. 'But against this is what Augustine says in QQ *super Joshua*, VI.q.10: "When a just war has been undertaken the question whether it is waged openly or by means of snares is irrelevant from the standpoint of justice."' 'Hence my answer is that snares are used to deceive the enemy; and that there are two ways in which anyone may be deceived by the deeds or words of another person. One way consists in making a false statement or in failing to keep a promise. This way is always unlawful; nor "ought one in this way to deceive an enemy, for in war there are rights and agreements which should be kept even with the enemy", as Ambrose says in his *De Officiis* I.29. The other way in which a person may be deceived by our words or deeds is when we fail to explain to him our intention or to make our meaning clear (*ei propositum aut intellectum non aperimus*); and this we are never bound to do, for in religious doctrine many things have to be kept secret especially from the infidel lest he should make mock of them. . . . Much more, therefore, should the plans we are making for an attack on an enemy be kept secret from him. Hence on the concealing of plans lest they reach the enemy great stress is laid in military treatises, e.g. in the *Strategemata Francorum* of Sextus Julius Frontinus, I.1. Such concealment of plans falls under the head of snares, which it is lawful to use in a just war. Nor are such snares rightly called frauds; nor yet do they contravene justice or imply a disordered will, for one's will would be disordered were one to will to conceal none of one's affairs from other people.'

Judged by this criterion the ruse used against Fabius Maximus would be quite legitimate, but the lie which Pontius, the Samnite, ordered the shepherds to tell, would not be legitimate, for he was giving false information, since '*quod facit aliquis per alium, facit per se*'.

2. Hannibal classed himself as the third greatest general that had lived up to his own day, the other two being Alexander and Pyrrhus. When asked by Scipio where he would have placed himself 'if you had beaten me', he answers 'First' (Livy XXXV.14; Plutarch, '*Flamininus*', 21). He is recognised not only by Polybius and Plutarch, but also by Livy, as one of the world's greatest strategists, and as being particularly partial to ruses or snares of which a notable and partially successful instance is his use of oxen with torches attached to their horns in order to induce

the enemy to abandon the pass they were guarding (Plutarch, *Fabius Maximus* 6; Livy XXII.17; Polybius III.92-4; and see § 2 in the text). But, as Plutarch points out, Hannibal also made mistakes, not only on this occasion when he chose guides who led him astray owing to his pronouncing the word '*Casilinum*' as if it were '*Casinum*', but also in not marching on Rome after his victory at Cannae, so that Barcas was moved to say: 'You know how to gain a victory, Hannibal, but not how to profit by it' (*ib.* 17; cp. Livy XXII.51, where for 'Barcas' we have 'Mahar-bal'). Nor were his ruses by any means always successful. 'Marcellus in his fifth consulate was, indeed, drawn into his snares and killed by an ambuscade [in 208 B.C.], but though he tried all his wiles and arts against Fabius, only once did he get him to make a slight mistake', namely, when he forged letters from the inhabitants of Metapontus offering to surrender the city, and Fabius would have gone there had not the auspices been unfavourable (*ib.* 19). Cornelius Nepos in his short *Life of Hannibal* says, apropos of the war with Eumenes II, king of Pergamus, that, 'since he could not fight with arms, he fought with snares'. This consisted in throwing serpents into the enemy's ships, which they took as a joke until they found out what they were, when they put back to port (XXIII, cc. 10-11). Oddly enough in his short chapter 'On Stratagems' (VII.4) Valerius Maximus mentions Hannibal not as a strategist, but as one who, together with his brother, Hasdrubal, was deceived by the strategy of Claudius Nero and Livius Salinator. (Cp. D. II.10.7 and D. III.17; and cp. also Cicero, *de Officiis* I.xxix.108).

3. See for the fraudulent methods of Philip II of Macedon D. I.26.2; 59.8; and D. II.13.1. And for the statement 'may win an empire but not glory' see P. 8 (Burd 233, E. 69).

4. The Perugian lake is Lake Trasimene, where the Romans were defeated in 217 B.C. Between the lake and the Cortonian mountains there was a gap—'*velut ad idipsum de industria relicto spatium*' (XXII.4.2). As the Romans were passing through, the Carthaginians fell on them and the slaughter lasted three days. A further account of the battle and of the skill with which Hannibal played on the weakness of his opponent's character is given by Polybius in III.81-5.

5. See note 2 above for the references to Livy, Polybius and Plutarch. After the battle of Lake Trasimene Hannibal marched south to Campania. He then decided to march north again to look for winter quarters. Fabius, who held Casilinum, was blocking the direct route, so he decided to go by another route, but was misled by his guides and found himself approaching the narrow defile which the Romans were holding. By driving the oxen with their flaming head-gear up the mountains on either side, he caused the Roman guard to think they were surrounded, and in consequence they fled and Hannibal got safely through the pass.

6. The ruse by which the Samnites induced the Roman army to go to the rescue of the Lucerians, their choice of the shorter route which led through the Caudine Forks, the nature of the country and of the ambush in which they were caught, are fully described by Livy in IX.2.

7. '*Quae, neque amicos parat, neque inimicos tollit*' (IX.3.12, cited in Latin). It was on this ground that Gaius Pontius rejected the '*media via*' which his father proposed.

8. See D. II.23; and Index *sub* 'Middle Course'.

Cp. A.W. Bk. IV, B.322 *sq.*, F.88-93; and Bk. VII, B.349 *sq.*, F.132-9, on the use of stratagems in war. Cp. also the remarks made by Brasidas in addressing

the Spartans before his last battle: 'The greatest reputation is gained by those stratagems in which a man deceives his enemies most completely, and does his friends
most service' (Thucydides V.9).

41. That one's Country should be defended whether it entail Ignominy or Glory, and that it is Good to defend it in any way whatsoever

1. In spite of the fact that the Roman army in the Caudine Forks lay at the
mercy of the Samnites and was destitute of all means of subsistence the consuls sent
envoys to ask for peace on equal terms, declaring that otherwise they preferred to
fight (IX.1-2). Pontius replied that, 'since even though defeated and at his mercy
they failed to realise what had befallen them, he would send them, unarmed and
clad in a single garment, under the yoke; but that the peace-terms between victors
and vanquished should be as between equals; and that, provided they retired from
Samnite territory and withdrew their colonies, Roman and Samnite should live
on terms of equality each under his own laws' (*ib.* 4.3-4). To pass voluntarily
under the yoke, however, i.e. to pass between two spears crossed by a third spear,
was an accepted symbol whereby those who passed under the yoke became entirely
subject to those who had caused them to do so. Hence the Romans were confronted
with an apparent contradiction which they had to solve as best they could.

2. The speech in which Lentulus, the Roman consul, proposes that his troops
should accept the conditions laid down is taken from Livy (IX.4), but the Latin
is not cited. Having spoken of the fortifications and of the people of Rome, Lentulus
says: '*Produntur ea omnia deleto hoc exercitu ... dedendo ad necem patriam deserimus et
prodimus ... ea caritas patriae est, ut tam ignominia eam quam morte nostra, si opus sit,
servemus. Subeatur ergo ista, quantacumque est, indignitas et pareatur necessitati, quam ne
di quidem superant*' (*ib.* 4.12-16). All that Lentulus has said is that 'for love of one's
country, one should be ready to suffer, if need be, alike ignominy and death', and
that since, if his army were annihilated, it would be the end of Rome, no alternative
remained but to submit to whatever indignity the Samnites chose to inflict.

3. Note the inference which Machiavelli draws from this speech of Lentulus. It is
that one should be prepared not merely to suffer ignominy and death for the sake of
one's country, but that, if its safety is really at stake, one should use any means, just
or unjust, kind or cruel, in order to save it and should set all other considerations
aside. No statement quite so sweeping as this is to be found even in *The Prince*. Yet
it follows logically from the principle that the end justifies the means. For, if in the
political sphere the supreme end which all right-minded statesmen seek be the
well-being and security of the community as a whole, and this well-being and
security be in peril, then on the general principle, laid down in D. I.9.2, that
actions are good if their effects be good, any action is justifiable if we have good
reason to think that it will save the state in time of peril, even the use of atomic
bombs, even the killing of unarmed citizens and children, even, it may be, con-
centration camps and the atrocities perpetrated therein, provided always that they
conduce to the safety of the state.

It is not, however, thus that Machiavelli argues. He relies not on deduction, but
on induction, and as usual cites examples in confirmation of the maxim which

heads the chapter. What we have then to ask is whether the examples cited do or do not bear out Machiavelli's contention. In the case of Lentulus the answer is most emphatically in the negative. Lentulus neither claims nor suggests that 'it is good to defend one's country in any way whatsoever, just or unjust'. All he claims is that he was right in himself submitting, and in causing his army to submit, under constraint, to a shameful and degrading ceremony in order to save the lives of his men, which were essential to the safety of his country. The ceremony might be, and by the Samnites was, interpreted to mean that the whole Roman people had become their subjects. But, as Livy points out, the action of Lentulus and his army was not a treaty between the two peoples. A treaty between the two peoples could only be made with their consent, and the Romans had not consented, nor had the consul authority to conclude a treaty. Nor were the customary formalities observed. The Caudine peace, in short, was an agreement for which 'the consuls, legates, quaestors, military tribunes, whose names are still extant', says Livy, alone were responsible (Livy IX.5). Hence the question of justice or injustice thus far does not arise.

4. In further support of the theorem which heads this chapter, Machiavelli cites the attitude of the French toward their monarch. The final decision in all matters of policy rested with the king, and it was held to be disloyal to criticise him. The king, it was said, can do no wrong. This saying, however, does not mean that the king is *'legibus solutus'*, i.e. is bound by no laws. The theory that the king was *'supra jus et contra jus et extra jus'* had indeed begun to find favour in France, but what the exponents of this theory meant, in France as amongst the Citra Montani, was that the king, as the source of all legislative and judicial authority, was not bound by any positive law or amenable to any *parlement* or court. They did not mean that he could do as he liked in regard to the natural law, by which he was bound in precisely the same way as any of his subjects. Philip de Commines, describing the attitude of the French people toward their monarch says: 'I have heard courtiers remark that the king takes what he wills, but I have never heard the king himself say so. No doubt in saying this they showed their devotion to their master, but either they misunderstood his real interests or else they did not know what they were talking about' (*Memoirs* V.19).

I have used in order to indicate the topic Machiavelli is discussing in these three chapters (40–2) the famous dictum of Cicero, *'Salus populi, suprema lex'* (*De Legibus* III.3.8), for it seems to say more or less what Machiavelli is saying, namely, that in politics the highest law and the supreme criterion by which all political conduct should be judged is the security of the state. This, however, is not what Cicero meant. He admits that there is a distinction between what is honourable and becoming in man and what is useful to him in life, i.e. between what he calls *'honestas et decus'* and the *'commoda vitae'*, material things and the capacity to use them; and that between what is honourable and what is expedient there may seem to be conflict. In fact, he adds, 'men have slipped into the habit of distinguishing what is honourable from what is expedient in such a way that what is honourable has come to mean what is not expedient and what is expedient what is dishonourable; than which there could be no doctrine more pernicious to human life.' (*De Officiis*, II.iii.9). Hence the maxim *'Salus populi, suprema lex'* does not mean for Cicero that moral obligation is to be subordinated to expediency in affairs of state. Nor did the Romans hold this, for Livy makes it quite plain that they recognised a '*jus gentium*' which was higher than any man-made law, a law to which all civilised peoples were subject and with which all treaties and all public enactments must conform if they were to be binding in conscience. The question of consequences is relevant, and, if they were likely to prove disastrous, the Romans, like other peoples, sought ways and means of evading the law, as Machiavelli proceeds to point out in the next chapter. But they did not deny that the law was binding, and still less did they affirm that any means, just or unjust, might be used in order to save the state when its situation was perilous. Hence Machiavelli has by no means proved his case. All he has done is to adduce a Roman incident and to cite a saying current in France upon both of which he has put a false interpretation.

42. *That Promises extracted by Force ought not to be kept*

1. The speech made by the consul who was mainly responsible for the surrender at the Caudine Forks is given by Livy in IX.8–9. The main points he makes are (i) that he was responsible for the undertaking he had given to the Samnites (*ib.* 8.4); (ii) that, since in doing this, he had not been acting under the orders of the Roman people, they were not bound by his promise, 'except in regard to surrendering our bodies to the Samnites' (*ib.* 8.5); hence (iii), if this were done, there would be nothing to prevent Rome engaging in a further war with the Samnites, and to do so would be an offence neither against religion nor against justice (*ib.* 8.6). In his second speech Postumius again emphasises his main point, which is that the Roman people were not responsible for what their consuls and other officers had done; and it is on this ground that eventually those responsible for the surrender (inclusive of the tribunes, who had resigned on this account) were handed over to the Samnites (*ib.* 9–10). He does not, be it noted, argue that the agreement had been extracted by force. Hence the incident, after all, is not really *ad rem*. The Samnites, moreover, declined to accept the surrender on the ground that the Roman people were responsible for what their agents had done, and that, if there was to be a surrender, it ought to be a surrender of the whole army, which should return to the position which had occasioned the surrender (*ib.* 11),—a point that had already been raised by one of the tribunes (*ib.* 8.14). The remark with which this paragraph concludes is taken almost verbatim from Livy IX.12.3: '*ut clariorem inter Romanos deditio Postumium quam Pontium incruenta victoria inter Samnites faceret*'— where the '*deditio*' (which Machiavelli renders by '*per avere perduto*') refers to his offer to return to the Samnites as a slave (cp. IX.11.1). The whole incident makes it clear that the Romans were anxious to do the right thing, and that the only point which troubled them was whether they were not in conscience bound to surrender their whole army. A plainer case of their respect for the '*jus gentium*' it would be difficult to find.

2. That forced contracts are not binding—*non ligant foedera facta metu*—was the commonly accepted doctrine both amongst canonists and moralists in Machiavelli's day, as it is now. Thus, St. Thomas says that 'the obligation a man incurs by a promise made to someone else is nullified by force (*per coactionem*), since he who uses force deserves that the promise made to him should not be kept' (*Summa Theologica*, II, II.q.89, a.7, ad. 3). Hence to the statement which heads this chapter no exception can be taken, save that it would seem to be chiefly on the ground that everybody keeps doing it, that Machiavelli maintains it is the proper thing to do.

3. The further point which Machiavelli makes in § 2, that princes no longer stand by their promises when the reason which induced them to make them no longer holds good, is also akin to a point which St. Thomas raises in II, II.q.110, a.3, ad. 5. To break a promise falls for St. Thomas under the head of lying (*menda-cium*) since it is to falsify one's word. If, however, St. Thomas argues, 'he who makes a promise intends to do what he promises he does not lie, since he does not say anything contrary to what he has in mind. But if he does not do what he promises, he seems to act dishonourably in that he changes his mind. There are, however, two grounds which excuse him in this: first if he promised what was manifestly unlawful, since in making such a promise he sinned and in changing his intention does well. Secondly, if the conditions have changed affecting the persons concerned and their affairs (*si sunt mutatae conditiones personarum et negotiorum*); for, as Seneca says in "*De Beneficiis*" IV.34 and 35, in order that a man should be bound to do what he has promised, it is requisite that everything should remain unchanged: since otherwise he neither lied when he made the promise since he did not promise what he had in mind with the aforesaid conditions in view; nor in failing to fulfil his promise is he acting disloyally, since the conditions no longer hold good.'

It is to some such case as this that Machiavelli presumably refers when he says that princes break their promises 'when the reasons which caused them to make such promises no longer hold good'; but the condition as thus stated will cover the case in which it ceases to be to the interest of a prince to keep his promises, and to break a promise on this ground St. Thomas would not admit to be justifiable. There is, however, a passage in Cicero's *De Officiis* which Machiavelli may have had in mind. In it Cicero says: 'A given promise or agreement may turn out in such a way that its performance would prove detrimental either to the person to whom the promise has been made or to the person who made it. . . . Promises are, therefore, not to be kept if the keeping of them is to prove harmful to those to whom you have made them; and if the fulfilment of the promise should do more harm to you than good to him to whom you have made it, it is no violation of moral duty to give the greater good precedence over the lesser good' (I.x, n. 32). E.g. If you have promised to support a friend in court and your son falls ill you are excused.

Furthermore, 'promises are not binding which are extorted by intimidation, or which we make when misled by false pretences' (n. 32). 'Injustice also arises through an over subtle or, it may be, fraudulent interpretation of the law . . . and through an interpretation of this kind a great deal of wrong is done in transactions between states' (*ib.*). E.g. a general agrees to a truce of thirty days, and then raids the enemy during the nights. 'Sharp practice is under all circumstances to be avoided.'

4. For the question whether it is 'praiseworthy or not', i.e. right or wrong, to break promises we are referred to *The Prince*, where in chapter 18 we are told that, since amongst princes there are so many wolves about, 'a wise lord neither can, nor ought he to keep faith when his doing so may be turned against him and the reasons which led him to make the promise have ceased to exist. Not that this precept would hold if men were wholly good, but, since they are bad and will not keep faith with you, you are not bound to keep it with them' (E.142).

On this sweeping generalisation which obliterates all distinction between legitimate and illegitimate grounds for failing to keep a promise, and on the consequences of adopting the policy Machiavelli recommends, I have made some remarks in the Introduction (XI, §§ 113-18). Here it suffices to point out that once a state begins to look for grounds on which to evade its obligations, the transition from legitimate to illegitimate grounds is easy, and is illustrated by the incident on which this chapter is based. When it had been decided in Rome that the agreement Postumius had made with the Samnite commander did not bind the Roman people, he returned to the Samnite camp and surrendered himself as a prisoner. Having done so, he declared himself to be now a Samnite, struck the Roman consul, and thus provided the Romans with a '*casus belli*' (Livy IX.11.11).

Cp. P. 18 on the way in which princes should keep faith.

43. That Men who are born in the same Country display throughout the Ages much the same Characteristics

1. The principles here enunciated are basic alike to Machiavelli's method and to his theory of politics. Hence, in a logical reconstruction of his theory, the theorem that (i) man's passions and basic appetites remain fundamentally the same throughout the ages, will appear amongst the postulates upon which the whole of his theory rests. But if the springs of human action be the same, it follows that (ii) there will be a genuine resemblance between what takes place in the sphere of human activities in different places and in different times throughout the world's history. Hence the possibility of generalisation, and, if we accept the principle that 'similar causes in similar circumstances give rise to similar effects', the possibility of forecasting what will happen in the political order given a certain political situation, just as we can forecast in the natural order what will happen given a certain physical situation. This parallelism Machiavelli recognises (cp. his Preface to Book I, § 3 and n. 3). But, though human nature remains fundamentally the same in its basic appetites, they are, as he points out in the Preface to Book II, § 3, liable to change as we grow older, and again are subject to the control exercised by education and by laws, a point which he now proceeds to consider.

2. As Machiavelli reminds us again and again, the effect of education, custom, and law is to modify man's appetites and to mould them in accordance with a certain pattern. This does not destroy the possibility of inference based on what is past; for human appetites, as thus modified, tend to perpetuate themselves, and so to become more or less constant in particular peoples, and even in particular families (cp. D. III.46). It is this point, which also is basic to his theory, that in this discourse he seeks to establish by citing the example of the French.

3. For the characteristics here ascribed to the French and German peoples it would be difficult to find confirmatory evidence. The fierceness of the French in battle is mentioned in D. III.36, and there are frequent references to the double-dealing and avarice of the French kings (see Index *sub* 'Charles VIII', 'Louis XII', and 'Francis I'; and compare the five-point indictment of Louis XII's Italian policy in P. 3). Double-dealing, however, can hardly be said to have characterised the French people.

4. The treaty by which Charles VIII promised to restore Pisa to the Florentines was part of the general treaty signed with Florence on 25 November 1494. The text is given in Burchard's *Diarium* II, App. 25, and is cited by Burd in his

Historical Abstract, p. 94. The city, inclusive of the citadel and town, was to remain in the king's hands during his Neapolitan campaign. The *'dominium'* and the *'fructus'*, however, was still to remain with Florence, as previously; and as soon as the campaign was over, the aforesaid *'regia majestas'* was to be restored to Florence. Commines in his *Memoirs*, VIII.21, admits that d'Entragues in handing Pisa back to the Pisans and in selling other towns committed a gross breach of faith.

5. There is only a brief reference to this war between Florence and Gian Galeazzo Visconti in *The History of Florence* III.25. When the war broke out in 1390 things had at first gone well with Florence, thanks to Sir John Hawkwood, then in Florence's employ. But after his death Gian Galeazzo overran the whole of north Italy and had already prepared the crown wherewith he was to be crowned king of Italy as soon as Florence had surrendered. Florence appealed to Rupert, king of the Romans. The first sum was to be paid him at once, and the second after four months' warfare. He came to Italy but was worsted outside Brescia on 14 October 1401, and after this did nothing except haggle for the remainder of his pay. On his returning to Germany the Florentines were defeated at Casalecchio, and Bologna surrendered, but on 3 September 1402 the Duke died unexpectedly and Florence was saved.

6. Livy X.10, the traditional date being 300 B.C. The Etruscans were preparing for war when there was a serious invasion of Gauls. The Etruscans, who had plenty of money, sought to enlist them as allies for the war with Rome. The price was settled and paid, but when called upon to march, the Gauls claimed they had been paid merely for not raiding Etruscan lands (10.6–10). And the Etruscans preferred to make war alone rather than to employ such savages.

Cp. Guicciardini's comments on D. III.19, for characteristics of the Germans and Italians which Frederick Barbarossa noted and which would seem to have endured.

44. Results are often obtained by Impetuosity and Daring which could never have been obtained by Ordinary Methods

1. *'rebellasse, quod pax servientibus gravior, quam liberis bellum esset'.* (Livy X.16.5; cited in Latin). The Samnite war broke out afresh in 298 B.C. The pro-Samnite Lucanians were forced to give hostages for their good behaviour; and the Samnites were defeated near Bovianum. They were again defeated by Q. Fabius Rullianus and P. Decius Mus in 297 (X.14), and the Apulians who had tried to join them, also suffered a defeat (X.15). It is at this juncture that the Samnites are said to have failed to secure peace on reasonable terms and consequently to have appealed to the Etruscans, whose territory they were forced to enter as they retired before the advancing forces of Rome. Not only Livy, but Polybius also in II.19, states that the Etruscans joined them, and that it was with their combined forces that Rome had to deal. See also Polybius II.20.

2. An account of the taking of Bologna in 1506 has been given in D. I.27.1 and is referred to again in D. II.24.7. According to Guicciardini *St. d'I.* Bk. VII, c. 3, Louis XII was annoyed with the Baglioni who had failed to support him on the Garigliano after having been paid 14,000 ducats. Hence he at once promised to send troops, but, when it came to the point, hesitated for fear of offend-

ing Venice. Venice demanded Faenza in return for her neutrality, which the Pope was reluctant to grant. Florence alone responded to his appeal. (For further particulars see Pastor, *Hist. Popes* VI, Bk. II, c. 3.)

3. For the taking of Brescia by Monsieur de Foix in 1512 see D. II.17.4 and D. II.24.12. The decision to go *via* the territory of Francesco Gonzaga, Marquess of Mantua and Standard-bearer of the Church, without giving him time to refuse is mentioned by Guicciardini in *St. d'I.* Bk. X, c. 10, where a full account of the march and of the taking of the city will be found. *En route* de Foix encountered Gian Pagolo Baglione with a strong force and also some Venetian light horse, both of which he routed, and within nine days from the time he left Bologna was before the walls of Brescia.

45. Whether it is the Better Course in Battle to await the Enemy's Attack and, having held it, to take the Offensive, or to make on the Enemy a Furious Onslaught at the Start

1. With this theorem compare D. II.12, which is headed 'Whether it is better, when threatened with attack, to assume the offensive or to await the outbreak of war'—a connected but by no means identical question. Cp. also the remarks on sieges (including that of Brescia) in D. II.17.3 and 6; and D. III.10 on the possibility of avoiding an engagement.

2. The story of the death of Publius Decius Mus the Younger in the decisive battle which the Romans fought against the combined forces of the Samnites, the Gauls, and—according to Livy—also the Etruscans and the Umbrians at Sentinum in 295 B.C., is told in X.28–9. When he saw his jaded troops giving way, Decius spurred forward his horse into the thickest of the fight and was killed. The situation was saved by Quintus Fabius Maximus Rullianus who sent troops to support the wing Decius had commanded, advanced slowly to attack the right, and sent cavalry to fall on the flanks and to cut off the enemy's retreat (X.29). On this single incident Machiavelli bases the important military theorem which heads the chapter, though doubtless he had in mind also the notorious impetuosity of the French.

Cp. also on this topic A.W. Bk. IV, B.324a. *sq.*, F.92–95; and cp. D. II.12.

46. How it comes about that in a City a Family retains for a Long Time the same Customs

1. The interposition at this juncture of a theorem which is a particular case of D. III.43, and takes us back to Book IX in Livy, may have been suggested by the mention of Quintus Fabius and his slow methods in the preceding discourse, for his cognomen was Maximus and he belonged to the same family as his more illustrious descendant, Fabius Maximus Cunctator, who was the mainstay of the republic in the critical years which followed the defeat at Lake Trasimene in 217.

2. Cp. IX.33.3, where Livy says that Appius Claudius, the censor, came of a family which seemed fated to be the opponents of the tribunes and of the plebs.

This is borne out by the previous history. The first Appius Claudius to be mentioned, Sabinus Regillensis, supported the patricians so vigorously, when consul in 495, that disturbances were the result (Livy II.21 and 23). In 471 his son took the same line, with the result that there were even more serious disturbances and discontent amongst the troops (II.56–7; 58.4–9). His grandson, Appius Claudius Crassus, was the decemvir who behaved first as a demagogue and then became a tyrant (see D. I.35 and 40–4). The grandson of this Appius is described as a man 'trained from his youth to oppose the plebs' (Livy V.2.13–14). It was he who got a measure passed enabling any one tribune to veto the proceedings of the rest. The censor, mentioned in the text, Appius Claudius Caecus, was his grandson, and the date was 310 B.C.

3. For the refusal of Appius Claudius Caecus to resign the censorship, see Livy IX.33.4. It can scarce be said that the trivial arguments he used in order to defend his action (*ib.* 33.9) betray arrogance, but both he and his family are accused of arrogance in the speech of Publius Sempronius, which follows in IX.34.

47. That a Good Citizen out of Love for his Country ought to ignore Personal Affronts

1. Papirius had quarrelled with Q. Fabius in 325 B.C., because Fabius had disobeyed his orders and engaged in battle with the Samnites, whom he defeated near Imbrivium. Fifteen years later, in 310 B.C., occurred the incident Machiavelli describes. Livy gives an account of it in IX.38, and expressly mentions Fabius's '*obstinatum silentium*' and the '*insignis dolor*' which he displayed. The consul's name was C. Marcius Rutilus Allifas. Machiavelli put this maxim in practice when for his country's sake he became Curator of the Walls in 1526.

48. When an Enemy is seen to be making a Big Mistake, it should be assumed that it is but an Artifice

1. The dictator, Marcus Valerius Maximus, had gone to Rome in 302 B.C. to renew the auspices, but had already returned when this incident took place (X.4.3). It was toward a Roman outpost (*praesidium*) near a burnt-out town that the pseudo-herdsmen drove their cattle, only to be discovered by the scouts sent out by Cn. Fulvius, since their accent was much too polished for herdsmen (X.4.7–12). It was, moreover, the dictator who attacked them, since the force commanded by Fulvius was too small to cope with them (*ib.* 4.12 and 5). Machiavelli has confused the ambush mentioned in X.3.4 as having occurred while the dictator was in Rome, and the ambush described in X.4.

2. Livy V.39.1–3, the reference being to the fall of Rome in 390 B.C. (cp. D. II.29.1).

3. A slightly different version of this incident is given by Guicciardini in *St. d'I.* VIII.8, p. 289. It occurred when the Pisans, cut off from their allies and from all supplies, were at their last extremity in 1508–9. Some of the citizens initiated the plot according to Guicciardini, and employed Alfonso del Mutilo as their intermediary. According to Machiavelli it was the Florentines who employed him, but quite possibly he took money from both.

49. *A Republic that would preserve its Freedom, ought daily to make Fresh Provisions to this End, and what Quintus Fabius did to earn for himself the title Maximus*

1. Compare with this chapter the opening chapter of this book. The fact that the book ends on the same note on which it opens suggests that Machiavelli intended to close his work with this chapter.

2. In 331 B.C. many leading men in Rome died during a pestilence. A slave-girl said they had been poisoned by the Roman matrons. Twenty patrician ladies were found preparing drugs over a fire. They said they were not poisonous, but, on being made to eat them, they died. This led to a further investigation, as a result of which 170 matrons were condemned to death (Livy VIII.18.)

3. In 184 B.C., by order of the Senate, the praetor, Q. Naevius Matho, spent four months investigating poison cases and condemned 2,000 persons (XXXIX.41). These cases were connected with the Bacchic rites performed in Roman night-clubs. The attention of the consuls was called to their obscene and criminal character in 186 B.C. when numerous members, male and female, were executed or imprisoned, their meeting-places demolished, and their rites prohibited (XXXIX.18).

4. The sending of the disgraced legions to Sicily is mentioned by Livy in XXIII.25, but not any regulations as to their conduct. That their treatment was very severe is clear, however, from the petition sent to Rome in 212, complaining that it was worse than the treatment meted out to captives, and asking to be allowed to serve again, if only as slaves. (XXV.5–7.)

5. 'Decimatio'—the punishment of the tenth part of a disgraced army—is mentioned by Livy (in II.59.11) as having been inflicted by Appius Claudius Sabinus on the troops who threw away their arms and fled before the Aequi and Volsci in 471 B.C. Dionysius says it was customary in cases of cowardice in face of the enemy (IX.501). Polybius says that 'the tribune assembles the legion, calls the defaulters to the front, selects five or eight or twenty by lot, so that those selected shall be about a tenth of those guilty of cowardice'. These are put to death, and the rest put on barley, instead of wheat, for their rations. 'Since all are equally in danger, and by the reduced rations an example is made of the rest, the best possible means are thus taken to inspire fear for the future and to correct the mischief which has already occurred' (VI.38). For 'Decimatio' see also A.W. VI, B.344b; F.126.

6. This Quintus Fabius, surnamed Rullianus, was consul six times. It was he who, as curule aedile in 331, discovered the plot of the women to poison their husbands, and who in 325 gave battle to the Samnites in contravention of the orders of L. Papirius Cursor. Of him in 304 Livy says that 'for the sake of concord, and at the same time to prevent the elections being controlled by the lowest people, he put the whole of the large mob that used to frequent the market place into four tribes, which he called "city-tribes"; for which people were so grateful that they gave him the cognomen of "Maximus", not for the many victories he had won, but for introducing this regulation' (IX.46.15). Polybius, however, states (in III.87), that the surname was first given to his son, the Quintus Fabius who was dictator in the time of Hannibal. From Livy IX.46, X.3.4–7, and XXX.26, it would none the less seem to be quite clear that the earlier Fabius bore the title.

CHRONOLOGICAL
AND OTHER TABLES

LIST OF TABLES

217

TABLES I TO IX
CHRONOLOGICAL TABLES

Table I. Events prior to the Founding of Rome in 753 B.C.

Traditional dates. B.C.	Events	Discourses
2188	Egypt, the most ancient of ancient kingdoms	I.58.3
	— imposes on all the need to work	I.1.9
2059	Virtue flourishes in Assyria	II.Pref.5
2000	Semiramis at war with the king of India	III.14.5–6
1491	Moses leaves Egypt	I.1.6
	— eliminates the envious	III.30.4
	— founds kingdom of Israel	I.9.5
	— destroys previous inhabitants	II.8.3
	— The Moors migrate to Africa	II.8.4
1234	Theseus founds Athens	I.1.3
1180	Aeneas migrates to Italy (Livy I.1–2)	I.1.6, 11
	— forms a confederation in Italy (Livy I.1–2)	
—	Dido founds Carthage *(Justin, XVIII.6, gives the date as 825 B.C.)*	II.8.5
1055	David, king of Israel, conquers his neighbours	I.19.2
	— makes everything new	I.26.1
1015	— succeeded by Solomon, a peaceful king,	⎰I.19.3
977	but most of the kingdom is lost by Rehoboam	⎱I.19.2
884	Lycurgus founds the kingdom of Sparta	I.9.5
	— converses with God	I.11.4
	— draws up Sparta's constitution *(see Index sub 'Lycurgus')*	⎰I.2.1, 15, 17 ⎱ I.6.4
700	Virtue flourishes in Media	II.Pref.5

Table II. The Period covered by Livy's First Decad, 753–293 B.C.

For Roman incidents ordinary type has been used; for others italics.

THE SEVEN KINGS OF ROME

Traditional dates. B.C.		Livy	Discourses
753–716	Romulus builds Rome	I.6	I.1.11
	— kills Remus	I.7	I.9.1–4
	— his legislation (*See Index* sub		$\begin{cases} \text{I.2.17} \\ \text{I.11.1} \end{cases}$
	'Romulus')	I.7–8	
	— acquiesces in murder of Titus Tatius	I.14	$\begin{cases} \text{I.9.1} \\ \text{I.18.7} \end{cases}$
	— makes war on his neighbours	I.7–12, 14–15	I.19.1
715–672	Numa Pompilius, a religious and peaceful king	I.18–21	I.19.1, 5–6
	— confers with the nymph, Egeria	I.19	I.11.3–4
	— legislation	I.18–21	$\begin{cases} \text{I.1.11} \\ \text{I.11.1} \end{cases}$
680	*Conspiracy to kill Cypselus (= Sitalces)*	—	III.6.29
672–642	Tullus Hostilius, a warlike king	I.22–23	I.19.1, 5
	— the war with Alba	I.22–30	I.22.1
	— the Horatii and the Curiatii	I.24–5	I.23.1
	— Horatius kills his sister	I.26	I.24.1
	— the war with Veii	I.27–9	I.22.2
	— the ruin of Alba	I.29	II.3.1
	— uses his own people in wars	I.31	I.21.1
	— legislation	I.31	I.49.1
642–617	Ancus Martius combines peace with war	I.32.3	I.19.5
616–579	Tarquinius Priscus obtains the throne	I.35	III.4.1
	— *Bellovesus invades Italy*	V.34	II.4.2; 8.2
	— *Sigovesus invades Spain*	V.34	II.8.2
	— killed by sons of Ancus	I.40–4	III.4.1
594	*Solon draws up laws for Athens*	—	I.2.16
	— *converses with God*	—	I.11.4
	— *founds a republic*	—	I.9.5
578–535	Servius Tullius: Legislation	I.42–4	I.49.1
	— maintains 80,000 men under arms	I.44	II.3.1

Traditional dates. B.C.		*Livy*	*Discourses*
578–535	— fails to win over Tarquin's sons ⎫ — is murdered, leaving no heirs ⎭	I.46–8	⎰III.4.1–3 ⎱III.5.1, 4
561	*Pisistratus establishes a tyranny in Athens*	—	⎧III.6.39 ⎨I.2.16 ⎩I.28.2
560–546	*Croesus, King of Lydia: shows treasures to Solon*	—	II.10.4
559–529	*Cyrus conquers Armenia*	—	⎰II.13.1 ⎱III.39.1
	— *deceives Cyaxares and becomes King of the Medes*	—	II.13.1
	— *displays clemency and affability during conquests*	—	⎰III.20.3 ⎱III.22.9
	— *the war with Tomyris: Croesus's advice*	—	II.12.1
	Virtue flourishes in Persia	—	II.Pref.5
554	*Phalaris slain by the people of Agrigentum*	—	⎰ III.6.6 ⎱cp. I.10.3
550	*The Massilians form a confederation in Spain*	—	II.8.5
534–510	L. Tarquinius Superbus murders Servius Tullius	I.48	III.4.1
	— kills senators and gains throne	I.48–9	III.5.1
	— forces people to work as slaves	I.56, 59	III.5.1
	— is fooled by Junius Brutus	I.56	III.2
	— Brutus avenges Lucretia	I.58–9	III.26.2
521	*The conspiracy of Otanes against Smerdis*	—	III.6.19
514	*The Conspiracy of Harmodius (Hippias survives)*	—	III.6.32
510	Expulsion of the Tarquins (*see Index* sub '*Tarquins*'	I.58–60	⎰III.5.1 ⎱I.4.1
	The Pisistratidae expelled from Athens	—	⎧I.2.16 ⎨I.58.7 ⎩II.2.2
B.C. 509–293	THE DEVELOPMENT OF THE ROMAN REPUBLIC		
509	Brutus restores liberty to Rome	II.1	I.17.2
	Kings replaced by consuls	II.1	I.20.1
	Appearances kept up: Lictors and the Sacrificial King	II.2	I.25.2
	D. Tarquinius Collatinus, Rome's ⎫ first consul, is banished ⎭	II.2	⎰III.5.1 ⎱I.28.3
	Conspiracy to restore the Tarquins	II.3–4	⎰I.32.1 ⎱III.6.14
	The Sons of Brutus executed	II.5	⎧I.16.4 ⎨III.1.5 ⎩III.3.1
	Conflicts arise between the Patricians and the Plebs	II.7–8, 18 *sq.*	I.4

B.C.		Livy	Discourses
509	P. Valerius Publicola becomes suspect	II.7–8	$\begin{cases} \text{I.28.3} \\ \text{III.22.9} \end{cases}$
	In *Athens banishments follow the expulsion of the Pisistratidae*	—	I.28.2
	In *Athens expansion follows the expulsion of the Pisistratidae*	—	$\begin{cases} \text{I.58.7} \\ \text{II.2.2} \end{cases}$
508	In Rome expansion follows the expulsion of the Kings	—	I.58.7
	The FIRST ETRUSCAN WAR: H. Cocles defends the bridge	II.10.11	I.24.3
	— Scaevola kills Porsenna's secretary	II.12	I.24.3
	— The Senate remits the tax on salt	II.9	I.32.1
501	The FIRST LATIN WAR: The first Dictator appointed	II.18	I.33.1
496	⚔ LAKE REGILLUS	II.19–20	II.18.1
	The *Foedus Cassianum* between Rome and the Latins	II.22 (and cp. VIII.9)	II.13.3
494	The first Secession of the Plebs	II.32–3	cp. I.3.2
493–431	WARS with the VOLSCI and AEQUI	II.22 *sq.*	II.1.3
491	Coriolanus proposes to starve the Plebs	II.34	I.7.2, 4
	— is banished	II.35	I.29.6
	— leads the Volsci and defeats the Romans	II.38–40	III.13.1
486	Spurius Cassius proposes the first Agrarian Law	II.41	I.37.2
	— is condemned and put to death	II.41	III.8.1
480–474	WAR with the ETRUSCAN LEAGUE, comprising 12 cities	V.1	II.4.1–2, 6
	The Etruscans and Veientes attack divided Rome	II.43–7	II.25.1
	— insult the Romans	II.45	II.26.3
	— defeated by M. Fabius and C. Manlius	II.45	I.36.1
	The Veientes surrounded, but escape. C. Manlius killed	II.47	III.12.5
480	*Themistocles suggests the destruction of the Greek fleet*	—	I.59.7
479	⚔ PLATAEA: *Thebes defeated. The Boeotian cities revolt*	—	III.6.40
472	The Publilius riots. Troops disobey Appius Claudius	II.55–60	III.19.1
471	The practice of '*Decimatio*' introduced	II.59	III.49.3
469	Q. Barbatus Capitolinus rallies the Roman army against the Volsci	II.64	III.14.1
467	The colony at Antium: few people want to go	III.1	I.37.4

B.C.		Livy	Discourses
466	*Themistocles' advice to Darius* (sic) *leads to his suicide in 449*	—	II.31.2
463	Appeal of the Latins rejected because of pestilence	III.6	I.38.1
462	Terentillus' proposal to restrict powers of consuls	III.9	I.39.3
461	The Sybilline books consulted	III.10	I.13.3
460	Appius Herdonius seizes the Capitol	III.15–18	I.13.4
459	L. Q. Cincinnatus becomes consul declines to have consulate renewed	III.21	III.24.2
458	— leaves his farm to become dictator	III.26	III.25.2
	— resigns the dictatorship after defeating the Sabines	III.29	cp. I.34.5
451–449	THE DECEMVIRATE	III.31–54	{ I.35 I.40–5
451	The Ten appointed to draw up laws	III.33	I.35.1
	Power of the Consuls suspended	III.33	I.40.2–3
	Appius Claudius gains the ascendancy by favouring Plebs	III.35	I.40.4
450	The Ten appointed for a second year	III.34–5	{ I.35.1 I.40.4
	The nobility form a bodyguard for Appius and the Ten	III.37 } cp. III.41 }	{ I.40.7 I.42
	Appius turns against the plebs	III.36–7	{ I.40.5–6 I.41
	The war with the Sabines and Volsci (*sic*) goes badly	III.38–41	{ I.40.8 I.43
449	Valerius and Horatius oppose Appius } Virginius kills his daughter }	III.49	{ I.40.8 III.26.2
	Revolt of the troops: 20 tribunes appointed	III.50–1	I.44
	The Secession of the Plebs who demand vengeance	III.52–3	I.44
	Liberty and order restored	III.54–5	{ I.40.8 I.45.1
	Appius tried: right of appeal refused	III.56–7	I.45.1
448	M. Duillius puts an end to reign of terror	III.59	I.45.3
446	Agrippa Furius resigns his command in favour of his colleague	III.70	III.15.4
445	Institution of TRIBUNES with CONSULAR POWER	IV.6	{ I.47.1–2 I.39.3 III.1.3

B.C.		*Livy*	*Discourses*
443	Patricians continue to be elected as consuls	IV.7	I.48
	Institution of the CENSORSHIP	IV.8	I.49.1
	Period of office reduced to 18 months	IV.23–4	
442	Ardea besieged by Volsci and occupied by Rome	IV.9–10	III.26.1–2
	— those responsible for disturbances executed	IV.10	III.27.1
439	Spurius Maelius executed for cornering corn	IV.13–15	III.1.5 III.28.1
	Cincinnatus and Mento quarrel and hold up proceedings	IV.26	I.50.1
431	(※ MOUNT ALGIDUS) Defeat of Vettius Messius and the Volsci	IV.28–9	III.12.6
431–404	THE PELOPONNESIAN WAR: *Pericles' advice*	—	II.10.8
427	*The Revolt in Corcyra*	—	II.2.5
426	Revolt of the Fidenates: The tribunes quarrel; A. Cornelius appoints Mamercus Aemilius dictator, and he defeats the Fidenates	IV.31–3	III.15.1 III.14.5–6
423	Tempanius raids the camp of the *Aequi* (= Volsci)	IV.37–41	III.18.3
415	*Athens: The expedition to Sicily: Nicias advises against it*	—	III.16.1 I.53.7
413	— *The Athenians defeated by Gylippus*	—	II.12.4
408	Patricians accused of corrupt practices in elections	IV.44, 56–7	cp. I.48
405	*Dionysius the Elder, tyrant of Syracuse*	—	III.6.6
406–396	THE SIEGE OF VEII	IV.58 *sq.*	I.13.2 II.6.2
406	The introduction of military pay	IV.59–60	I.51 I.52.1 II.6.3
	The Etruscans refuse to help Veii because she has a king	V.1	II.2.1
402	Generals fined for misconduct in the war	V.12	I.31.2
398	Pestilence: only patricians chosen as tribunes	V.13–14	I.13.1
	The appeal to Delphi *re* Alban lake	V.15–16	I.13.2
398–360	*Agesilaus II, king of Sparta*	—	I.10.3
396	Camillus appointed dictator	V.19	I.13.2
	— promises immunity to civilians	V.21	III.12.7
	Veii taken by means of a sap	V.19	II.32.2

B.C.		Livy	Discourses
396	— pillaged: Juno's statue removed	V.22	I.12.4
	The triumph of Camillus	V.23	III.23.2
395	Camillus insists on fulfilment of vow	V.25 ⎫	⎰ III.23.2
	The Senate orders troops to provide a		
	tenth	V.23, 25 ⎭	⎱ I.55.1
	The proposed migration to Veii	V.24–5	I.53.1
	The Senate persuades the Plebs not to		
	go	V.51–55	I.54.3
394	Camillus takes Falerii: treatment of		
	schoolmaster	V.27	III.20.1
393	Gifts to Apollo captured by pirates	V.28	III.29.2
391	Camillus indicted and banished	V.32	⎰ I.29.6 ⎱ II.29.1, 4
	Distribution of land at Veii amongst		
	Romans	V.30	II.7
	A colony sent to Adria by the Etrus-		
	cans gives name to the sea	V.33	II.4.2
391–389	THE GALLIC INVASION AND SIEGE		
	OF ROME	V.34 *sq.*	
391	Aruns of Clusium invokes the aid of		
	the Gauls	V.33	I.7.8
	The Fabii aid the Etruscans *v.* Gauls	V.36	⎰ II.28.1 ⎱ III.1.3
390	Marcus Caedicius hears voices in the		
	Via Nova	V.32	I.56.2
	⚔ ALLIA. Rome in confusion. For-		
	tune intervenes	V.37 *sq.*	II.29.1
	The troops from Allia retreat to Veii	V.38	II.29.4
	Rome besieged. The Gauls hesitate to		
	enter	V.39	III.48.3
	Rome taken by the Gauls	V.41	⎧ II.1.3 ⎨ II.8.2 ⎩ III.1.3
	Manlius Capitolinus saves the Capitol	V.47	⎰ I.8.1 ⎱ I.24.4
	Camillus recalled from Ardea and made dictator	V.46	⎰ III.1.3 ⎱ I.29.6
	— prevents the Romans from buying off the Gauls	V.48–9	II.30.1
389	Citizens recalled from Veii	VI.4	I.57.1
	Revival of Religion in Rome	⎰ V.39–40 ⎱ V.50	III.1.3
389–380	THE WAR with the VOLSCI and ETRUSCANS	VI.2 *sq.*	II.1.3

B.C.		Livy	Discourses
389–380	The Etruscans and Latins attempt to destroy Rome		III.30.1,
	Camillus as dictator prepares for its defence	VI.6	5–6
	Appointments given to Q. Servilius, L. Quintius, Horatius and Cornelius		III.31.6
384	Manlius Capitolinus becomes jealous of Camillus	VI.11–20	I.8.1 III.8.2–3
	— starts a sedition and is condemned and executed	VI.16–20	I.24.4 I.58.1 III.1.5
	— death regretted	VI.20	I.58.1, 3
383	The revolt of Circei and Velitrae	VI.21	III.32.1
380	T. Q. Cincinnatus defeats the Praenestines on the Allia	VI.28–9	III.33.3
379	The two Manlii narrowly escape defeat by the Volsci	VI.30	III.33.3
	Pelodipidas liberates Thebes from Spartan tyranny	—	I.6.7 III.6.32
	— *and Epaminondas organise a Theban army*	—	I.21.3 III.13.3
377–367	THE LICINIAN-SEXTIAN LEGISLATION. Agrarian Law	VI.35 *sq.*	I.37.3–4
377	*Thebes rebels against Sparta*	—	II.3.3 I.6.7
371	⚔ LEUCTRA. *Epaminondas defeats the Spartans*		III.38.2
368	Patrician opposition to the laws: Appius Claudius' protest	VI.40–42	III.33.2
367	Tribunes with consular power replaced by consuls	VI.42	I.39.3
366	Consulate opened to plebs: L. Sextius first Plebeian consul	VI.42 VII.1	III.35.3 I.60.1
367	*Dionysius I of Syracuse murdered*	—	III.6.6
	Dionysius II succeeds his father	—	I.10.3
363	L. Manlius Imperiosus appointed dictator	VII.3–4	I.11.2 III.34.1
	— indicted for cruelty and defended by his son	VII.4–5	cp. III.19.2
362	Lucius Genucius, a plebeian consul, is defeated by the Hernici	VII.6	III.35.3
	⚔ MANTINEA: *Epaminondas killed; Thebes loses her freedom*	—	I.17.5
361–358	WAR WITH THE GAULS		III.22.2
361	Titus Manlius fights a Gaul and earns the name 'Torquatus'	VII.10–11	III.34.3 III.36.1

B.C.		Livy	Discourses
361	The Gauls invade Tiburtine lands and Campania	VII.11	III.37.1, 6
359–336	*Philip II King of Macedon, Methods of*	—	I.26.2
	— Frauds of	—	II.13.1
	— Untrustworthiness of	—	I.59.8
358	C. Sulpicius Peticus avoids open battle	VII.12–13	III.10.1
	and then defeats the Gauls	VII.14	III.14.4
357	*Dion returns to Syracuse and expels Dionysius II*	—	I.17.1
354	*— is murdered by Callippus*	—	III.6.45
	Clearchus, Tyrant of Heraclea, restored by, and kills, nobles	—	I.16.7
353	*— The conspiracy of Chion and Leonidas*	—	III.6.32
350	*Hanno attempts to poison the Carthaginian senate*	—	III.6.38
	— collects an army of Moors, but is defeated and crucified	—	III.6.40
348	Valerius Corvinus becomes consul at age of 23	VII.26	I.60.1
344–337	*Timoleon of Corinth rids Sicily of tyrants*	—	$\left\{\begin{array}{l} \text{I.10.3} \\ \text{I.17.1} \\ \text{III.5.3} \end{array}\right.$
343–341	THE FIRST SAMNITE WAR: Samnites attack Sidicines	VII.29–37	II.1.3
	The Campanians bring to Sidicines rather a name than help	VII.29	$\left\{\begin{array}{l} \text{II.11.1} \\ \text{II.10.8} \end{array}\right.$
343	The Campanians appeal to Rome for help	VII.29	II.9.1
	Capua and the Campanians surrender voluntarily to Rome	VII.30–31	$\left\{\begin{array}{l} \text{II.10.8} \\ \text{II.9.4} \end{array}\right.$
	Capua helps Rome to invade Samnium	VII.32	II.1.6
	Valerius Corvinus orders skirmishes to discover enemy's strength	VII.32	$\left\{\begin{array}{l} \text{III.37.3} \\ \text{III.38.1} \end{array}\right.$
	✗ MOUNT GAURUS AND SUESSULA: Samnites twice defeated	VII.32–9	$\left\{\begin{array}{l} \text{II.13.3} \\ \text{II.20.2} \end{array}\right.$
	P. Decius Mus saves the army of Cornelius	VII.34	III.39.3–4
342	REVOLT of the legions at CAPUA—due to luxurious habits	VII.38	II.19.8
	— suppressed by C. M. Rutilus	VII.38	III.6.43
	— Corvinus forbids reproaches	VII.41	II.26.4
341	Treaty of Alliance with the Samnites	VIII.2	II.1.3
340–336	THE GREAT LATIN WAR	VIII.1–15	$\left\{\begin{array}{l} \text{II.1.3} \\ \text{II.4.3} \\ \text{II.6.2} \end{array}\right.$
	Causes of the war		II.13.3–4

B.C.		Livy	Discourses
340	The Samnites complain that the Latins have attacked them	VIII.2	II.14.1
	The Campanians throw off their allegiance to Rome	VIII.2–3	II.13.3
	The Latin embassy: Annius Setinus' speech	VIII.3–4	$\begin{cases} \text{II.14.1} \\ \text{II.15.1} \end{cases}$
	T. Manlius Torquatus kills his son for disobeying him	VIII.7	$\begin{cases} \text{II.16.1–2} \\ \text{III.1.5} \\ \text{III.22.7} \end{cases}$
	— compared with Valerius Corvinus	—	III.22
	✕ MOUNT VESUVIUS (Veseris). The Latins routed	VIII.8–10	II.16.1
	Decius Mus sacrifices his life	VIII.9	$\begin{cases} \text{II.16.1–2} \\ \text{III.1.7} \end{cases}$
	The Lavinians start too late to help the Latins	VIII.11	II.15.5
339	Numicius urges the Latins to renew the war	VIII.11	II.22.1, 5
	Camillus reduces Latium	VIII.13	II.23.2
338	Latium can neither make peace nor war	VIII.13	II.23.1
	Camillus advises pardon or elimination	VIII.13–14	II.23.2
338	✕ CHAERONIA: *Philip of Macedon conquers Greece;*	—	I.9.5
337	*death of Timoleon: tyranny restored in Syracuse*	—	I.17.1
336	*Pausanias kills Philip II of Macedon*	—	$\begin{cases} \text{II.28.3} \\ \text{III.6.5, 7} \end{cases}$
336–323	*Alexander the Great*	—	I.1.9
	— succeeds Philip II of Macedon	—	I.20.2; 26.3
	— wars of	—	II.8.1
334	*— goes to Asia*	—	II.31.1
332	*— conquers Tyre*	—	II.27.3, 5
331	*— builds Alexandria to design of Deinocrates*	—	I.1.4, 10
	— ✕ Megalopolis; death of Agis III	—	II.10.2
330	*— conquers Darius*	—	II.10.3
330	*— Conspiracy of Dymnus and Philotas*	—	III.6.14
328	*— kills Cleitus*	—	I.58.3
323	*— death of*	—	$\begin{cases} \text{II.10.2, 5} \\ \text{III.13.4} \end{cases}$
333	Alexander of Epirus invited to Italy	VIII.3 ⎱	II.31.1
331	— is killed by a Lucanian exile	VIII.24 ⎰	
331	170 Roman matrons executed for attempt to poison husbands	VIII.18	III.49.1

B.C.		Livy	Discourses
330	Rome pardons the Privernates after their revolt	VIII.21	II.23.4
327–304	THE SECOND SAMNITE WAR	VIII.23 *sq.*	II.1.3
326	Q. Publius Philo's consulate prolonged	VIII.26	III.24.3
	— Palaeopolis taken by furtive violence	VIII.26	II.32.5
	The Latins and Privernates remain loyal to Rome: no fortresses used	VIII.20	II.24.1
325	Q. Fabius Maximus engages in battle against orders of Papirius Cursor, but is not punished	VIII.30 *sq.*	{ I.31.3 III.1.5
	Fabius defended by his father	VIII.33	I.31.3
	Papirius' speech on discipline	VIII.34	III.36.4
323	*Alexander's infantry revolt and choose Arrhidaeus as king*	—	III.13.4
322	*Agathocles' tyranny in Syracuse based on fraud*	—	III.6.39
	— tyranny established by armed forces	—	II.13.1
321	Samnite offer of peace rejected by Rome	IX.1	III.12.4
321	⚔ CAUDINE FORKS.		
	— The ruse of Gaius Pontius	IX.2	III.40.2
	— Gaius Pontius adopts a middle course	IX.3	{ III.40.2 II.23.6
	— The Romans pass under the yoke	IX.4–6	III.41.1
	— Rome declines to recognise the surrender	IX.8–12	III.42.1
321	Offer of alliance by Tarentum turned down	IX.14	II.11.3
317	The first Roman prefect sent to Capua	IX.20	II.21.2
	Antium models its laws on Rome	IX.20	II.21.2
315	Sora expels its garrison but is retaken	IX.22–4	II.18.5
314	Conspirators in Rome and in Capua arrested by M. Menenius	IX.26	I.5.6, 7
	The trial of M. Menenius, the Plebeian dictator		
310	Appius Claudius Caecus refuses to resign the censorship	IX.33–4	III.46.2
310	*Agathocles crosses to Africa, after defeat in Sicily*	—	II.12.3, 8
310–308	THE CONQUEST OF ETRURIA		II.1.3, 5
310	Q. Fabius Maximus penetrates the Ciminian forest	IX.35–6	II.33.2
	The Camertines form an alliance with Rome	IX.36	II.1.6

B.C.		Livy	Discourses
310	⚔ PERUSIA: Fabius Maximus exhorts his troops	IX.37	III.33.4
	Papirius Cursor nominated dictator by Fabius Maximus	IX.38	III.47
308	⚔ LAKE VADIMO		⎧ I.15.1
	Etruria conquered	IX.39, 41	⎨ II.5.5
			⎩ II.6.2
304	Q. Fabius Maximus so-called because he instituted city tribes	IX.46	III.49.5
302	Etruria revolts. Cn. Fulvius escapes an ambush	X.3	III.48.1
300	Etruria pays the Gauls for help, which is not given	X.10	III.43.4
298–290	THE THIRD SAMNITE WAR		II.1.3
297	The Samnites are defeated, invade Etruria, and obtain her help	X.14–16	III.44.1
295	⚔ SENTINUM		
	— Fabius awaits enemy's attack	X.28	III.45
	— P. Decius Mus (junior) sacrifices his life	X.28	III.1.7
293	Ovius Paccius revives a Samnite ceremony	X.38	I.15.1–2
	⚔ AQUILONIA: Papirius consults the Pullarii	X.40–1	I.14.3
290	Samnium conquered and laid waste after 46 years of war	X.31, 45	II.2.9
	The Romans 'crown' and take Cominium	X.43	cp. II.32.2
284	*Formation of the Second Achaean League*	—	II.4.1, 4

Table III. Growth of the Roman Empire
280–146 B.C.

B.C.	Events	Discourses
280–275	THE WAR WITH PYRRHUS. Pyrrhus lands in Italy ⎫	
280	The Samnites join Pyrrhus. ✕ HERACLEA. Roman ⎬	II.1.3
	defeat ⎭	
279	The revolt at Rhegium	II.20.4
	Fabricius Luscinus refuses Pyrrhus' gold	III.1.7
278	— tells Philip of plot to kill him	{III.20.2 / III.21.4}
277	*The Gauls invade Greece and despoil the King of Macedonia* ⎫	II.10.5
	Antigonus defeated by Brennus ⎭	
275	✕ BENEVENTUM. Pyrrhus, defeated,	
	returns to Epirus	II.1.3
272	*Aristotimus, an Aetolian tyrant, murdered*	III.6.19, 26
266	Rhodes becomes formally Rome's ally	{ II.32.7 / cp. II.30.3 }
264–241	THE FIRST PUNIC WAR	{II.1.3 / II.8.2}
264	The Mamertines form an alliance with Rome against ⎫	{II.1.6 / II.9.2}
	the Carthaginians, and war breaks out in Sicily ⎭	
256	M. Regulus Attilius defeats the Carthaginians in ⎫	{III.25.3 / III.1.7}
	Africa, ⎬	
	then asks leave to return to his farm ⎭	
255	M. Regulus Attilius defeated by Xanthippus, who ⎫	II.18.7
	uses elephants. He is taken prisoner ⎭	
251 *sq.*	*Aratus the Sicyonian expels tyrants*	III.5.3
	— *His nocturnal adventures*	II.32.6
250	Regulus Attilius returns as a prisoner to Carthage	cp. III.1.7
249	✕ DREPANA. Cl. Pulcher ignores the auspices and is	{ I.14.4 / III.33.2 }
	beaten	
241	Revolt of the Punic mercenaries under Spendius and	
	Matho	III.32.2
240	*Agis IV tries to restore Lycurgan constitution, but is killed by* ⎫	I.9.5
	the Ephors ⎭	
238–225	THE GALLIC WARS	{II.1.3 / II.8.2}
	Rome employs 1,800,000 troops. Defeats followed by	
	victory	II.12.9

233

B.C.	Events	Discourses
237	Cleomenes III of Sparta succeeds Leonidas, defeats Aratus at Laodicea, and kills the ephors	I.9.5 / I.18.7 / III.6.39
225	⚔ TELAMON, defeat of the Gauls	II.1.3 / II.8.2
223–222	War with Ligurians and Gauls. ⚔ CLASTIDIUM	II.1.3
220–179	Philip V of Macedon. (*See below* sub *the Macedonian wars*)	
219–201	THE SECOND PUNIC WAR. (Livy XXI–XXX)	II.1.3
219	Saguntum appeals to Rome	II.1.6
218	Gnaeus Scipio sent to Saguntum, is attacked by Hannibal	II.9.2
	Saguntum captured by Hannibal	I.59.5
	The Massilians co-operate with Cornelius Scipio in Spain	II.30.3
	Hannibal crosses the Alps	I.23.3 / I.31.1
	— thrice defeats the Romans	II.12.9
	⚔ TICINUS: The Romans await Hannibal on the Ticinus and then near Corezzo	I.23.3
	— P. Cornelius Scipio rescues his father	III.34.4
217	⚔ LAKE TRASIMENE: Hannibal's ruse	III.40.1
	Q. Fabius Maximus Cunctator appointed dictator	III.9.2–3
	— his go-slow policy saves Rome	III.10.2–4
	— policy disapproved	I.53.5
	— Hannibal eludes him	III.40.1
	M. T. Varro appointed consul and is defeated	I.53.5
	Rome's troops dismount	II.18.2
216	⚔ CANNAE M. T. Varro is not punished	I.31.3
	Hanno comments on the Roman defeat	II.30.6 / III.31.2
	— advises peace	II.27.2
	Scipio prevents a flight to Sicily	I.11.2 / III.34.9
	Pacuvius Calavius quells tumults in Capua	I.47.3
	The Campanians told to look to themselves	cp. III.37.5
	The disgraced legions sent to Sicily	III.49.2
	Hannibal winters in Capua: his troops become disaffected	II.19.8
215	T. Sempronius Gracchus enlists a slave army and assists in taking of Casilinum	III.13.3 / II.26.5 / III.38.2
	Hieronymus of Syracuse: conspiracy of Theodotus	III.6.17
	— death lamented	I.58.1
	— liberty restored	II.2.4

B.C.	Events	Discourses
193–188	Hannibal's advice to Antiochus	II.12.2, 9
	Eumenes II of Pergamus urges Rome to declare war	II.1.6
193	Antiochus send envoys to Scipio; the conditions of peace	III.31.2
192	*Nabis is killed by Alexamenes*	III.6.19, 30
190	✗ MAGNESIA. Victory of Scipio. Rome conquers Asia Minor	I.18.3 III.16.4 III.31.2
185	Rome proves ungrateful to Scipio (Cato's criticism)	I.29.6 III.1.5
184	The conspiracy of the Bacchanals.	III.49.2
183	Hannibal poisons himself (cp. P. 17)	III.21.4
182	Aemilius Paulus defeats the Ligurians; but no further office is given to him	III.16.4
168	✗ PYDNA. Aemilius Paulus defeats Perseus Perseus kills his advisers	III.16.4 III.35.5
	Aemilius Paulus remains a poor man	III.25.4
167	Greece conquered	I.18.3 II.10.3
154	The Massilians appeal to Rome for help against the Ligurians	II.1.6 II.32.7
149	Death of Cato the Elder	III.1.7
146	Siege and destruction of Carthage	II.32.4

Table IV. Decline of the Republic,
133–27 B.C.

B.C.	Events	Discourses
(215–161)	New legislation against luxury and ambition fail to prevent decline because Institutions remain unchanged	} I.18.2–5
133–121	THE TIMES OF THE GRACCHI	{ I.4.3 I.6.1
133	The revival of the Agrarian laws by T. Sempronius Gracchus leads to armed conflict	I.37.5, 9
129	M. Aquillius organises the province of Asia	I.18.3
125	The Massilians appeal to Rome for help against the	
122	Gauls (first transalpine colony founded at Aquae Sextiae)	} II.1.6
	The Aedui appeal to Rome for help against the Allobroges, who are defeated by C. Sextius Calvinus	{ II.1.6 II.30.3
121	A consul, Opimius, is appointed dictator	cp. I.34.9
112–106	THE WAR WITH JUGURTHA	II.8.1
107–101	THE GALLIC WAR: Teutons and Cimbri invade Italy and defeat the Romans four times	II.8.1–2
105	⚔ ARAUSIO: Defeat of Romans by Cimbri	II.12.9
104–78	THE TIMES OF SULLA AND MARIUS. Liberty lost	{ I.28.1 III.8.5
104–101	Marius, the leader of the plebeian party is elected consul in four successive years	I.37.6
102	⚔ AQUAE SEXTIAE. Marius defeats the Teutons	{ II.8.2
101	⚔ CAMPI RAUDII. Marius defeats the Cimbri, who had invaded Italy	} III.37.6
90–88	Sulla and Marius find troops to support them in actions contrary to the common good	III.24.3
88	The SOCIAL WAR. Marius expels Sulla, who returns to Rome with an army and expels Marius: the nobility victorious	cp. I.37.8
74	Lucullus sent out against Mithradates	III.13.3
69	⚔ TIGRANOCERTA. Lucullus routs Tigranes	II.19.1
67	M. Porcius Cato enters public life	III.1.7
	The prolongation of military commands. (Cato protests)	III.24
66–62	The conspiracy of CATILINE	I.10.4
64	— discovered; Catiline remains a senator	III.6.37

237

B.C.	Events	Discourses
62	The defeat and death of Catiline	III.6.40
63	Siege of Jerusalem	II.32.4
55	Pompey reinstates Ptolemy XI as king of Egypt	I.59.3
53	Crassus gains slight successes over the Parthians, but is defeated and slain at CARRHAE, by deceit, not force	{ II.18.6 / III.12.3
51–48	CAESAR *versus* POMPEY, who too late begins to fear him	I.33.5
	Caesar heads the Marian faction and Pompey that of Sulla	{ I.17.2 / I.37.7
49	Caesar makes himself master of Italy	III.6.39
	thus seizing what Rome's ingratitude had denied him	I.29.5
	and completing spoliation of the republic	{ I.10.9 / I.52.4
	✕ ILERDA: defeat of Pompey's army under Afranius and Petreius	III.13.2
48	✕ PHARSALUS: defeat of Pompey by Caesar	{ I.59.3 / III.13.2
	Pompey killed in Egypt by order of Ptolemy XII	I.59.3
44	The CONSPIRACY OF BRUTUS AND CASSIUS	III.6.6, 33
	— murder of Julius Caesar	{ I.17.2 / cp. I.10.4
	— the people rise against Brutus and Cassius	III.6.36
43	Antony declared an enemy of the state: Octavian sent to join the consuls at Mutina, is reconciled to Antony	I.52.3
42	✕ PHILIPPI. Victory of Antony and Octavian; death of Brutus and Cassius, who thought Brutus had lost the battle	{ III.6.36 / III.18.1
38	Mark Antony defeats the Parthians	II.18.6
36	Revolt of the Veterans (under Lepidus)	III.13.4
29	Herod executes his wife, Mariamne	I.58.3

Table V. The Rule of the Emperors,
27 B.C. to A.D. 713

(1) THE EMPERORS FROM AUGUSTUS TO MAXIMINUS, 27 B.C. TO A.D. 238

(Machiavelli in D. I.10.5 counts Julius Caesar as an emperor (see note 11). The empire is, however, more correctly held to have begun in 27 A.D., when Octavian assumed the title of Augustus. A list of the Emperors from Julius Caesar to Maximinus, classified according as they were 'good' or 'bad', will be found in D. I.10, note 11.)

	Events	Discourses
27 B.C. to A.D. 14	Augustus (or Octavian); nephew of Julius Caesar — The world enjoys a long peace. Florence founded	I.52.3 — I.1.5
A.D.		
14–37	Tiberius, conspiracy of Sejanus (A.D. 31)	III.6.9
37–41	Gaius Caligula: classed as 'bad' emperor	I.10.5
	— assassinated	I.17.2
41–54	Claudius (not mentioned)	—
54–68	Nero: assassinated	I.10.5
65	— Conspiracy of Piso	III.6.13, 20
	— — discovered owing to Scaevinus	III.6.15
	— — Epicharis denies complicity	III.6.22
68	— his murder extinguishes Caesar's stock	I.17.2
68–69	Galba: assassinated though a good emperor	I.10.6
69	Otho (not mentioned)	—
69	Vitellius: assassinated	I.10.5
69–79	Vespasian: ungrateful to Antonius Primus	I.29.3
79–81	Titus: inherits. Good Emperor	I.10.5, 6
81–96	Domitian (not mentioned)	—
96–98	Nerva: no need of a praetorian guard	I.10.5
	— heads list of adopted emperors	I.10.7
98–117	Trajan: good emperor	I.10.5
117–38	Hadrian: good emperor	I.10.5
138–61	Antoninus Pius: good emperor	I.10.5
161–80	Marcus Aurelius: good emperor (see P. 19)	I.10.5, 7
180–92	Commodus: conspiracy of Quintianus and Lucilla	III.6.30
185	— conspiracy of Perennis	III.6.9
192	— conspiracy of Laetus and Eclectus	III.6.24
	— murdered (see P. 19)	III.6.41

A.D.	Events	Discourses
192–3	Pertinax: assassinated though a good emperor (see P. 19)	I.10.6
193	Julianus (not mentioned), murdered (see P. 19)	—
193–211	Severus: wicked, yet dies in his bed (see P. 19)	I.10.6
205	— conspiracy of Plautianus	II.6.9
		21, 31
211–17	Antoninus Caracalla: killed by order of Macrinus (see P. 19)	III.6.25
217–18	Macrinus: has Caracalla murdered (see P. 19)	III.6.25
218–22	Heliogabulus (not mentioned) (see P. 19)	—
222–35	Severus Alexander (not mentioned) (see P. 19)	—
235–8	Maximinus: 26th Emperor (see P. 19)	I.10.6

(2) THE DECLINE OF THE EMPIRE, A.D. 238 TO 713

1st–4th cent.	Grants made by the Emperors to Parthians, Germans and other neighbouring peoples constitute the first step in the Empire's decline (e.g. by Caracalla and Macrinus, and by Gallus Caesar to the Goths (351 to 354)	II.30.4
4th cent.	More than 30 peoples migrate westward from Scythia	II.8.6
5th cent.	The whole of the Western Empire occupied by Goths and Vandals	II.8.2
427–530	— The Vandal Kingdom of Africa	
466–711	— The Visigothic Kingdom of Spain	
493–553	— The Ostrogothic Kingdom in Italy	
451	Venice founded as a refuge from Attila and the Huns	I.1.3
503	Cobades, King of Persia, sacks Amida	II.26.2
533–40	Belisarius wages war with the Vandals and Goths	II.8.2, 4
590–604	Gregory the Great destroys pagan records	II.5.2
656	Ragusa occupied by refugees during the Avar invasion	I.1.7
633–713	The Saracens conquer a great part of the world	II.Pref.5
633 sq.	— — — Syria	
637	— — — Jerusalem	
640	— — — Egypt	
652	— — — Persia	
663	— — — Africa	
711–13	— — — Spain and Asia Minor	

Table VI. The Middle Ages,
A.D. 768–1468

A.D.	Events	Discourses
768–814	Charles the Great, founder of the French kingdom	I.16.9
	— subjugates the Lombards and expels their king	I.12.7
	Virtue flourishes in the kingdom of the Franks	II.Pref.5
—	Florence rebuilt; follows the fortune of the party that is uppermost in Italy for 200 years	I.49.3
962	The Imperial title transferred to Germany (Otto the first German to be crowned Emperor)	II.19.4
1202–27	Tartar invasions	II.8.6
1210	St. Francis of Assisi (Rule approved by Innocent III) ⎫	III.1.8
1216	St. Dominic (Rule approved by Honorius III) ⎭	
1226–70	Louis IX: the *Conseil du Roi* divided into a Privy Council, the Exchequer, and the Parlement (judiciary)	cp. III.1.9
1250	The 'Captain' and a 'Podestà', both foreigners, appointed to try all cases involving capital punishment	I.49.4
1252–1517	The rule of the Mamelukes in Egypt	I.1.9
1291	The Swiss Confederation (Uri, Schwyz and Unterwalden—other cantons join later)	cp. II.4.1, 4–6
1296	Closure of the Great Council in Venice: it distributes all preferments	cp. I.50.3
	The Consiglio dei Rogati shares jurisdiction with the Great Council	cp. I.49.5
1310	A committee of public safety appointed in Venice after the revolt of Baiamonte Tiepolo—made permanent in 1355	I.49.5
1311	Florence appeals to Robert of Naples (1st time), and acknowledges his suzerainty for 5 years	II.9.4
1315	✕ MORTGARTEN. Leopold of Hapsburg defeated by the Swiss League, composed of the three forest cantons	cp. II.19.5
1325	Castruccio Castracani attacks Florence. Florence appeals to Robert of Naples (2nd time), who sends ⎫ first the Duke of Athens, and then his son to help ⎬ them ⎭	II.9.4 II.12.8
1328	Pistoia submits voluntarily to Florence	⎰II.21.6 ⎱II.25.2
1339	✕ LAUPEN. The Swiss league defeats a confederation of princes. Zurick, Glug, Glarus, and Bern join	II.19.4–5

241

A.D.	Events	Discourses
1342	Florence calls in Walter de Brienne, Duke of Athens to ⎫	III.6.44–5
1343	act as 'Captain'. He is overthrown and expelled ⎭	
1350 *sq.*	Growth of Condottieri: 'The Great Company' and in 1379 the Company of St. George become famous	II.18.4
1351–3	War between Florence and Giovanni Visconti of Milan	II.12.8
1356	The States-General in France demands that its officers ⎰	II.16.9
	shall be consulted *re* taxation ⎱	cp. III.1.9
1365	The Swabian League formed by Leopold, son of Charles IV	II.4.6
1379	Disturbances in Venice owing to the imprisonment of the admiral, Vettor Pisani, who on his release destroys the Genoese fleet.	cp. III.22.10
1385	Gian Galeazzo Visconti murders his uncle, Bernabo, and is created first Duke of Milan	II.13.2
1386	⚔ SEMPACH. The Swiss League defeats Leopold the Valiant	II.19.5
1390–1402	War between Florence and Gian Galeazzo Visconti: subsidies paid by Florence to the Emperor	III.43.3
1392	Piero Gambacorti of Pisa murdered by Jacopo d'Appiano	III.6.10
1405–26	Venice extends her dominions in Italy: Padua, Vincenza, Brescia taken, etc.	III.12.2
1412–47	Venice becomes mistress of Lombardy (in the dogeship of Francesco Foscari)	II.19.6
1414	Florence acquires Pisa and builds a fortress to hold it	II.24.10
1422	⚔ ARBEDO. Carmignuola defeats 16,000 Swiss, using dismounted cavalry	II.18.8
1424–40	Wars between Filippo Maria Visconti of Milan and ⎫	II.25.4
	Florence ⎭	cp. III.43.3
1433	The Otto di Guardia in Florence acquires right to inflict capital punishment	I.49.4
	Niccolò da Uzzano tries to prevent the banishment of Cosimo de' Medici	I.33.4
	Cosimo de' Medici banished	I.52.2
1434	Niccolò di Cocco becomes Gonfalonier, throws rivals ⎫	I.33.4
	into prison and recalls Cosimo ⎭	cp. III.1.6
1438	The Emperor and the Archduke of Austria become identical on the election of Albert II of Austria	II.19.5
1447	Death of Filippo Maria Visconti of Milan (cp. P. 12)	I.17.3
1455	⚔ BELGRADE. Ladislas of Poland and Hunyadi of Hungary defeat Mohammed II and hold Christendom against the Turks	II.8.6

Table VII. Events contemporary with Machiavelli's Early Life, 1469-98

(Events in Machiavelli's life are given in italics; the events referred to in the text in ordinary type; and events not mentioned, but relevant to the text, in ordinary type in brackets.)

A.D.

1469 *Birth of Niccolò Machiavelli, son of Bernardo di Niccolò and of Bartholommea Nelli (May 3)*
The rulers in this year were:

Frederick III, Emperor, 1452-93

Louis XI, King of France, 1461-83

Edward IV, King of England, 1460-83

John II, King of Aragon, 1458-79

Henry IV, King of Castile, 1454-74

Ferrando, King of Naples, 1458-94

Pope Paul II, 1464-71

Mohammed II, Sultan, 1451-81

Charles the Bold, Duke of Burgundy, 1467-77

Galeazzo Maria Sforza, Duke of Milan, 1466-76

Borso d'Este, Duke of Ferrara, 1450-71

LORENZO AND GIULIANO DE' MEDICI assume the government of Florence on the death of Piero de' Medici (3 Dec.)

1471 The Consiglio del Comune and the Consiglio del Popolare replaced by the Council of Two Hundred.

Events	Discourses
Florence continues the policy of making grants to her neighbours, e.g. Perugia	II.30.4
Under the rule of Lorenzo Florence gradually becomes mistress of Tuscany (see II.19. n. 8)	II.19.6

1471-84 SIXTUS IV (Francesco d'Albizzola della Rovere).
[The Orsini Colonnesi, and other barons, who maintain armed forces, still keep the Papacy weak (P. 11).]

1474 Sixtus IV drives Niccolò Vitelli out of Città di Castello, and builds a second fortress there   II.24.8
[Isabella, the wife of Ferdinand of Aragon, succeeds to Castile and Ferdinand to Aragon in 1478, the two kingdoms thus becoming united.]

1475 TREATY OF PICQUIGNY. Edward IV is paid 70,000 crowns to retire from France, and an annuity of 50,000   II.30.4

243

A.D.	Events	Discourses
1476	Galeazzo Maria Sforza, Duke of Milan, is murdered by Giovanni Andrea da Lampognano on Christmas Day	III.6.35
	[Bona of Savoy, regent, for the infant duke Gian Galeazzo till 1478, when LUDOVICO MORO replaced her.]	
1476-7	CHARLES, DUKE OF BURGUNDY, attacks the Swiss, who are always difficult to overcome at home,	cp. II.12.8-9
	is defeated at Granson, and then at MORAT in 1476	III.10.7
	and is finally overwhelmed and killed at Nancy in Jan. 1477	II.10.3
1477	Office of 'Captain' abolished in Florence, and the 'Podestà' abolished shortly afterwards	I.49.4
1478	The PAZZI CONSPIRACY	$\left\{\begin{array}{l}\text{III.6.5, 13,}\\\text{28, 30, 32}\end{array}\right.$
1479	SIXTUS IV, having placed Florence under an interdict, joins with Ferdinand of Naples in an attack on Florence, which appeals to France, but obtains a name rather than protection	II.11.2
	[Genoa induces Sarzana to revolt against Florence, and Lorenzo goes to Naples to arrange a truce.]	
	He surrenders the possessions of Florence in the Romagna to Ferdinand of Naples and agrees to pay the Duke of Calabria an annual tribute	cp. II.30.2
1480	[On his return he sets up the Council of Seventy and the committee of Eight—the *Otto di Pratica*]	
1481	Mohammed II, who had conquered his neighbours and built up a strong kingdom, dies, and is succeeded by BAJAZET II, who prefers peace	I.19.3
	[The Turks withdraw from Otranto]	
	Fribourg joins the Swiss confederation	II.19.4
1482	Niccolò da Castello, father of the Vitelli, recovers Città di Castello, and destroys the two fortresses which had been built by Sixtus IV (cp. P. 20)	II.24.8
	[Venice declares war on Ercole d'Este, Duke of Ferrara who is supported by Florence, Naples, and Milan (3 May).]	
1482-3	THE HOLY LEAGUE (*Lega Santissima*). 'All Italy forms a confederation against the Venetians' (23 Dec. 1482)	III.11.3
	[Sixtus IV places Venice under an interdict]	
1484	Venice induces Ludovico Moro to desert the League and arrange the peace of Bagnolo (7 Aug.), by which Venice recovers her dominions and part of Ferrara	III.11.3
1484-92	[Innocent VIII, pope (Giovanni Batista Cibò).]	
1484	Savonarola, preaching at San Geminiano in Florence, prophesies that the Church will soon be scourged and then renovated	cp. I.11.6

A.D.	Events	Discourses
1484	The barons of Naples, led by Coppola, Count of Sarno, revolt against Ferdinand of Naples and Alfonso, Duke of Calabria	III.6.10
1486	[Peace signed at Rome between Innocent VIII and Ferdinand of Naples, who promises to pay tribute and to pardon the barons]	
1487	Ferdinand breaks the treaty, refuses to pay tribute, and executes the barons, including Coppola	III.6.10
1487	PANDOLFO PETRUCCI and his brother, Jacopo, return from exile and speedily establish their supremacy in Siena (cp. P. 20, H. F. VIII.35)	III.6.39
1488	The people of FORLI rise against Count RIARIO, kill him, and take his wife and children prisoners. She recovers the citadel by a ruse, and then the town (cp. P. 20)	III.6.35
1491	[Ferdinand of Spain completes the conquest of Granada, and thus establishes his position as a 'new prince' (P. 21).]	
	[Charles VIII (1463–98) marries Anne of Brittany (6 Dec.) and the regency of Anne of Beaujeu ends.]	
1492	The Duomo in Florence is struck by a thunderbolt and Lorenzo de' Medici dies (8 Apr.)	I.56.1
	Italy at this time 'is under the dominion of the Pope, the Venetians, the King of Naples, the Duke of Milan, and the Florentines. The aim of these powers is (i) to prevent armed foreigners from entering the country, and (ii) to prevent one another from seizing more territory' (P. 11).	
	In his Lent sermons SAVONAROLA foretells the coming of Charles VIII	I.56.1
	Machiavelli finds Employment as a Government Clerk.	
	[ALEXANDER VI (1492–1503) (Rodrigo Borgia) obtains the Papacy by bribery (11 Aug.) on the death of Innocent VIII.]	
	Henry VII (1485–1509), who had supported Anne of Brittany, is bought off by the Treaty of ÉTAPLES in which Charles VIII promises to pay him 620,000 crowns and an annuity of 50,000 (3 Nov.)	cp. II.30.4
	Columbus discovers America (Oct.)	{ cp. Pref. to Bk. I
	Attempt to assassinate Ferdinand, King of Spain (7 Dec.)	III.6.7

245

A.D.	Events	Discourses
1492	Attempt to assassinate Bajazet II at Monastir	III.6.7
1493	[Alexander VI sets out to crush the Orsini, the Colonna, and other Roman barons, whose factions have long perturbed Italy (P. 7).]	
	[CHARLES VIII is urged by Ludovico Moro and Giuliano de la Rovere to lay claim to the kingdom of Naples.]	
1494	Ferdinand of Naples, before his death on 25 January, warns his son, Alfonso, to await the coming of Charles VIII, within his own domains. The advice is ignored	II.12.5
	[The French Court moves to Lyons (1 March) and assembles an army.]	
	SAVONAROLA again foretells the coming of the sword of God in his Lenten sermons on Noah's Ark, and above Arezzo armed hosts are seen fighting in the sky	I.56.1
	The populace believes that Savonarola converses with God	I.11.6
	CHARLES VIII COMES TO ITALY. ['94 is M's key date, references frequent.]	
	(Sept.) Charles crosses the Alps at Mont Genèvre, advances to Turin and Asti; is visited by Ludovico Moro; on to Pavia; interviews Gian Galeazzo Sforza, who dies shortly afterwards; on to Piacenza and Sarzana. His easy victory due to sin, as Savonarola said, but the sin was the employment of auxiliaries and mercenaries (P. 12).	cp. $\begin{cases} \text{I.56.1} \\ \text{II.16.6} \end{cases}$
	(8 Nov.) Francesco Valori returns to Florence and takes up arms against Piero de' Medici	I.7.5
	(9 Nov.) Piero flies to Bologna, and no one loses by his expulsion except himself	III.7.2
	Florence becomes a prey to conflicting factions	I.47.4
	(10 Nov.) PISA obtains her independence after being subject to Florence for 100 years (P. 5.)	$\begin{cases} \text{I.39.2;} \\ \text{II.16.6} \end{cases}$
	(17 Nov.) CHARLES enters Florence, and promises to restore Pisa on condition that Florence pays him 20,000 florins every six months	III.43.3
	[(Dec.) Charles passes *via* Siena and Viterbo, and enters Papal territory. He enters Rome on 8 Dec. in spite of Alexander's refusing him admission.]	
	(23 Dec.) The constitution of Florence is remodelled on the lines laid down by Savonarola. It comprises a *Consiglio Maggiore* (or Lower House), a *Consiglio degli Ottanta* (or Senate); the *Dieci di Libertà e Pace* (to deal with finance and war); the *Otto di Balìa* (to administer justice). Parliaments were abolished	cp. I.45.2

A.D.	Events	Discourses
1495	A law is passed, on the advice of Savonarola, allowing an appeal in cases of treason from the *Otto di Guardia e Balia* to the *Consiglio Maggiore* (15 March)	I.45.2
	Alfonso of Naples, without fighting a battle, abdicates in favour of his son, Ferdinand (3 Feb.)	II.12.5
	[Ferdinand retires *via* Capua and Naples to Sicily, as the French advance. They enter NAPLES on 22 Feb.]	
	The LEAGUE OF VENICE is formed on 31 March. In it 'the whole world (the Empire, Spain, Venice, Milan and the Papacy) conspire against France'	III.11.4
	[(12 May), Charles VIII is crowned King of Naples and Sicily.]	
	[(20 May), Charles leaves Naples in charge of the Duc de Montpensier and marches north *via* Rome, Siena and Pisa.]	
	[(6 July) ✕ FORNUOVO (Il Taro). The Italians fight badly (P. 26), and Charles crosses the Taro, and retires to Turin.]	
	(10 Oct.) The TREATY OF VERCELLI. Ludovico Moro deserts the League, allows Louis d'Orleans to escape from Novara, and forms an alliance with Charles VIII	cp. III.11.4
	(Oct.) Charles returns to France. Genoa left in charge of the Duke of Ferrara; Pisa in charge of d'Entragues, who sells Sarzana to Genoa and Pietra Santa and Mutrone to Lucca	I.39.2
	(May) Gonsalvo Ferrante of Cordova, the Great Captain, begins the re-conquest of the Kingdom of Naples on behalf of Ferdinand II	I.29.4
	[✕ SEMINARA. French victory. Gonsalvo retreats to Reggio, but by the end of the year has recovered the greater part of Calabria.]	
	The Oddi, the Ghibelline faction which has been expelled from Perugia, attempts to drive out the Baglioni, but fails	III.14.2
	d'Entragues hands the citadel of PISA over to the citizens in return for a grant to be made by Venice, Milan, Genoa, and Lucca (Jan.)	III.43.2
	[FLORENCE decides to make war on PISA]	
	[VENICE takes PISA under her protection]	
	[ALEXANDER VI employs Guidobaldo, Duke of Urbino, to crush the Orsini and Bartolommeo d'Alviano; and appoints Giovanni, Duke of Gandia, Gonfalonier of the Church. The Baglioni, della Rovere, and the Vitelli join the barons. Colonna supports the Pope. (P. 11.)]	

A.D.	Events	Discourses
1495	In Naples the Duke of Montpensier surrenders at Atella (July) and the French evacuate the kingdom	cp. I.29.4
	[Ferdinand of Naples dies (5 Oct.), and is succeeded by his uncle, FREDERICK, the fifth king Naples has had in three years.]	
	[Alexander confers the title of 'Catholic' on the King of Spain]	
	[Maximilian enters Italy at the request of Ludovico Moro and goes to help Pisa, but his fleet is destroyed and he returns home]	
	Death of Bartholommea Nelli, Machiavelli's Mother (11 Oct.)	
1497	[✠ SORIANO (26 Jan.). Papal forces defeated; Duke of Urbino a prisoner. Naples sends Gonsalvo and Prospero Colonna to help the Pope. Peace signed on 5 Feb.]	
	The King of Spain deserts the League of Venice, and signs a truce with Charles VIII by which they agree to invade Naples jointly (25 Feb.). The League breaks up	III.11.4
	The BIGI PLOT to restore the Medici fails. Five of the conspirators are refused the right to appeal, and are executed (April)	I.45.2
	[Giovanni Borgia, Duke of Gandia, is murdered in Rome (14 June).]	
	[CAESAR BORGIA abandons his ecclesiastical career, and takes the Vitelli into his pay.]	
	[SAVONAROLA is held responsible for the Bonfire of Vanities (7 Feb.)]	
	He resumes his sermons on 4 May and a riot ensues	cp. III.30.4
	[Alexander VI excommunicates him (12 May).]	
1498	[A second Burning of Vanities occurs during the Carnival.]	
	[Alexander VI threatens to place Florence under an interdict.]	
	[The Trial by Fire ends in a fiasco (6 April).]	
	The Frateschi are attacked on their way to the Cathedral (8 Apr.). Rioters attack the house of Pagalantonio Soderini, but his brother, the Bishop of Volterra, pacifies the rioters	I.54.2
	Francesco Valori heads the supporters of Savonarola. He is murdered on his way to the Signoria	cp. I.7.5
	[Savonarola and Fra Domenico are tortured, condemned and burnt in the Piazza (23 May).]	
	[LOUIS XII (1498–1515) succeeds Charles VIII as King of France (7 Apr.).]	
	✠ SAN REGOLO (21 May). The Florentines under	

A.D.	Events	Discourses
1498	Count Ranuccio are defeated owing to their cavalry falling back on the infantry	II.16.6
	On the death of his brother, Jacopo, PANDOLFO PETRUCCI becomes tyrant of Siena (cp. P. 20 and 22.)	III.6.39
	He seeks to come to terms with Florence, but is opposed by his father-in-law, Niccolò Borghese, whom he executes, Luzio and Julio Belanti conspire against him, but fail	III.6.5, 34

Table VIII. Events contemporary with Machiavelli's Period of Office, 1498–1512

The references for the Legations and Reports are to (i) the edition by Passerini and Milanesi (Op. P.M.); and (ii) to Detmold's translation in four volumes (D), with volume and page in each case. References to Barbèra's edition are indicated by Op. B, with page.

A.D.	Events	Discourses
1498	*(19 June) Machiavelli is appointed Secretary to the Signoria in place of Alessandro Braccesi*	
	(14 July) Machiavelli becomes Chancellor to the Ten of Liberty and Peace	
	(June) Florence appoints Paolo Vitelli captain-general of her forces (P. 8 and P. 12). Ottaviano Riario of Forli and Jacopo d'Appiano of Piombino also enter her service	cp. II.30.3
	[Vitelli captures Vico Pisano and Librafratta.]	
	The Venetians under Bartolommeo d'Alviano invade the Val di Lamona and take Marradi. Florence sends up fresh levies under d'Appiano and Venice withdraws (Aug.)	III.18.4
	[(26 Aug.) Fall of Lepanto. The Turks raid Venetian territory. Alexander's appeal for a Crusade in 1499 and 1500 meets with no response.]	
	[(17 Aug.) Caesar Borgia resigns the Cardinalate and is created DUKE OF VALENTINOIS by Louis XII.]	
	(18 Sept.) Louis XII receives Italian ambassadors at Étampes. Those from Florence agree that she shall remain neutral if Louis will help her to recover Pisa. Florence fails to ratify the agreement	II.15.6
	[Alexander nullifies the marriage of Louis XII with Jeanne of Artois, thereby setting him free to marry Anne of Britanny (P. 7)]	
1499	[(9 Feb.) LOUIS XII forms an alliance with VENICE for the recovery of Milan from Ludovico Moro.]	
	[(4 Mar.) The Florentine generals demand an increase of pay.]	
	(24 Mar.) Machiavelli's First Legation. He is sent to Pontedera to arrange matters with Jacopo d'Appiano of Piombino (Op. P.M. III.1–4; D. III.3–5).	

A.D.	Events	Discourses
1499	[Venice agrees to withdraw the help she is giving PISA on receipt of an indemnity.]	
	Increased taxation in Florence to meet the costs of the war. Cries of 'Down with the ten expenders'. The TEN are not reappointed in 1499, but are re-elected in 1500	I.39.2
	(June) Machiavelli's 'Discourse made to the Magistracy of Ten on Pisan Affairs' (Op. P.M. VI.284 sq.)	
	(12–25 July) 'Legation to the Countess of Forli' to arrange about the Condotta of her son, Ottaviano Riario. Ends in failure (Op. P.M. III.4 sq.; D. III.6–26; 7 Lett.)	
	[Paolo Vitelli takes Cascina (26 June), but fails to take PISA (Aug.), is arrested (30 Sept.) and executed in Florence (1 Oct.).]	
	[(Aug.) INVASION OF ITALY by the French under Trivulzio.]	
	[(6 Oct.) LOUIS XII enters Milan, and all the Princes of Northern Italy make their submission (P. 3.).]	
	[Venice acquires Cremona and the Ghiaradadda.]	
	Florence undertakes to supply Louis with money and troops for his attack on Naples. He promises to help them against PISA	II.15.6
	[CAESAR BORGIA'S FIRST CAMPAIGN. He gets troops from Louis XII and seizes IMOLA (27 Nov.), but the citadel holds out. He then takes Forli (19 Dec.), but Catarina holds out in the citadel till 12 January 1500 (P. 13 and 20).]	
1500	[(5 Feb.) Ludovico Moro recovers Milan (P. 3).]	
	(5 Apr.) Louis XII retakes Milan	III.15.3
	Ludovico Moro is taken prisoner and dies in a French prison ten years later. The citadel has been no use to him	II.24.5
	French and Swiss under Hugo de BEAUMONT are sent to help in the siege of PISA in return for 24,000 ducats a month (P. 13)	I.38.5
	Pisa offers to surrender to Beaumont. Florence sends three commissioners, of whom M. was one. They refuse to accept the conditions	I.38.5
	Luca di Antonio degli Albizzi retires, leaving Giovanni Batista Ridolfi in charge of operations. The troops mutiny and the Gascons desert	III.15.3
	(10 May) Death of Machiavelli's Father	
	(June) Commission to the Army in the field before Pisa (Op. P.M. III.37 sq.; D. III.27–39)	
	(28 July to 2 Dec.) Machiavelli's First Legation to the Court of France to explain the situation to Louis XII and obtain fresh troops (Op. P.M. III.87 sq.; D. III.40–140; 28 Lett.)	
	Machiavelli converses with the Cardinal de Rouen at Nantes (P. 3).	

A.D.	Events	Discourses
1500	[CAESAR BORGIA'S SECOND CAMPAIGN. He invades the Romagna with French troops (Sept.); takes Pesaro and Rimini, but fails to take Faenza (P. 13).]	
	[(11 Nov.) TREATY OF GRANADA, Louis XII and Ferdinand of Aragon agree to divide Naples between them (P. 3).]	
1501	(Jan.) The rivalry of the Panciatichi and Cancellieri in PISTOIA leads to bloodshed. Florence herself becomes divided, and her intervention only causes further riots in July, October and January 1502	III.27.2

*Machiavelli is sent to Pistoia in February, July and October. His
'Report on Pistoia' (Op.P.M. III.355 sq.) and 'Commission
to Pistoia' (Op.P.M. III.246 sq.)*
[CAESAR BORGIA uses the Orsini (i.e. mercenaries instead
of auxiliaries) in order to take FAENZA (25 April); is
created Duke of the Romagna, and proceeds to attack
Bologna, but is held up by orders from the French (P. 7).]
Caesar Borgia asks leave to cross Florentine territory. Florence hesitates. He advances to within 7 miles of Florence
and is made Captain-General with a salary of 36,000
ducats   I.38.3
(18 Aug.) 'The First Legation to Siena' (Op.P.M. III.358).
[SECOND INVASION OF NAPLES, d'Aubigny crosses Alps
(1 June), reaches Rome (23 June), sacks CAPUA
(24 July) (P. 26).]
[FREDERICK II of NAPLES resigns and retires to France
(6 Sept.), where he dies in 1504. GONSALVO lands at
Tropaea, and occupies Calabria (July–Sept.) on behalf
of FERDINAND, King of SPAIN (P. 21).]
[Oliverotto Euffreducci murders his uncle, Giovanni Fogliano, and makes himself Lord of FERMA (P. 8).]

1502	[Florence promises 40,000 ducats a year to Louis XII for three years, to supply 6,000 cavalry, in return for his protection (Apr.).]	
	[CAESAR BORGIA'S THIRD CAMPAIGN. Takes formal possession of Piombino in February.]	
	GIUGLIELMO DE' PAZZI sent by Florence as commissioner to the Val di Chiana; hears that the Vitelli are conspiring to take Arezzo, arrests one of the conspirators, which provokes a riot and he is taken prisoner (May)	III.6.44
	The Vitelli occupy AREZZO and the whole of the VAL di TREVERE and the VAL di CHIANA. Florence appeals to France	I.39.2 II.23.3
	Caesar Borgia takes URBINO (21 June—P. 20). Guido Ubaldo flees to Mantua.	II.24.6

A.D.	Events	Discourses

1502 *Machiavelli accompanies Piero Soderini on an Embassy to Urbino. Borgia disclaims responsibility for the Revolt of Arezzo and demands a change of Government in Florence (24 June).*

French troops under IMBAULT recover Arezzo, but Florence refuses to accept the terms laid down. Imbault accepts them and refers Florence to Louis XII (*July*) I.38.6

de LANQUES replaces Imbault and reports that in all towns some people say they belong to the Marzoccan party, i.e. are loyal to Florence III.27.6

Machiavelli is sent to arrange matters with de Lanques (14 Aug.). 'Legation to Arezzo' (Op.P.M. III.360).

Lanques hands over Arezzo (26 Aug.). Disagreement in Florence as to how the inhabitants are to be treated. Florence adopts a middle course II.23.3

Machiavelli sent to Arezzo on 11 September and 17 September. He writes his treatise: 'On How to Treat the People of the Val di Chiana after its Revolt' (Op.P.M. III.365 sq.)

FLORENCE decides to appoint a GONFALONIER FOR LIFE (26 Aug.).

PIERO SODERINI is appointed on 29 Sept. } {I.56.1 / I.2.2

(*5 Oct.*) *Machiavelli is sent to Duke Valentine at Imola, and remains with him until 20 January 1503. 'Legation to Duke Valentine' (Op.P.M. IV.1 sq.; D. III.141 sq. 52 Lett.).*

[The DIET at MAGGIONE in Perugia (9 Oct.) The Orsini call a meeting of the captains in command of Caesar Borgia's mercenaries, who are opposed to his aggrandisement and to that of the Church (P. 7).]

[✠ FOSSOMBRONE, Orsini and his fellow-conspirators victorious (17 Oct.).]

URBINO revolts against Caesar Borgia, and Guidobaldo of Montefeltro on his return razes all its fortresses (P. 20) II.24.6, 14

[Borgia obtains help from France and most of the conspirators come to terms (Nov.)]

[Urbino surrenders and Guidobaldo withdraws (8 Dec.).]

[RAMIRO D'ORCO, who had been appointed Governor to restore order in the Romagna, is arrested on 22 December and murdered on the 28th (P. 7).] cp. III.29.1

[THE SINIGAGLIA MURDERS (31 Dec.) Oliverotto da Fermo and Vitellozzo Vitelli strangled (P. 8). The Duke of Gandia and Paolo Orsini are taken prisoners and executed on 18 January, 1503.]

'Description of the manner in which Duke Valentine killed Vitellozzo Vitelli, etc.' (Printed in Everyman's Ed. p. 217 sq.)

[War breaks out between the SPANIARDS and the FRENCH in NAPLES (July). GONSALVO occupies Tarentum. D'Aubigny replaced by the Duc de Nemours.]

A.D.	Events	Discourses
1502	*Machiavelli marries Marietta di Ludovico Corsini.*	
1503	[CAESAR BORGIA INVADES TUSCANY, using his own troops. He captures Perugia and Piombino and takes Pisa under his protection; demands the expulsion of Pandolfo Petrucci from Siena. Siena raided. Petrucci goes to Lucca. Louis XII forces Borgia to desist and reinstates Pandolfo Petrucci in Siena (29 Mar.) (P. 7 and 13).]	

Machiavelli is sent to Pandolfo Petrucci in Siena (26 Apr.) to ask for an Alliance and for the Restoration of Montepulciano. 'The Second Legation to Siena' (Op. P.M. IV.294 sq.; D. III.281–2).

[Alexander VI died on 18 August.]

[PIUS III, Pope, 22 September–18 October (Francesco Todeschini).]

(23 Oct.) Machiavelli is sent to Rome where he remains till 18 December. First 'Legation to the Court of Rome.' (Op. P.M. IV.297 sq.; D. III.283 sq.; 49 Lett.).

JULIUS II, Pope (1503–13). (Giuliano della Rovere, who had protected Caesar Borgia and promised to make him Gonfalonier of the Church, is elected. Machiavelli was in Rome for the election.)

[Caesar Borgia returns to Rome, and takes refuge in the Castle of Sant' Angelo. The conquered towns revolt except in the Romagna, which waits a month (P. 7).]

[VENICE seizes Faenza and Rimini.]

[The Orsini and Colonnesi join forces with Gonsalvo in Naples.]

GONSALVO DE CORDOVA reconquers the Kingdom of Naples for Ferdinand, King of Aragon (April–December)   **I.29.4**

✠ CERIGNUOLA (28 Apr.). Duc de Nemours killed   **II.17.7**
Gonsalvo enters Naples (14 May). Louis XII prepares for a fresh invasion under La Trémouille, who resigns and is replaced by the Duke of Mantua.

✠ GARIGLIANO (28 Dec.). Gonsalvo victorious. Piero de' Medici drowned.

The French evacuate GAETA (Jan. 1504).

PISA. Antonio Giacomini in command. Takes Vico Pisano and Verruca; but further advance is prevented by La Trémouille   **cp. III.16.5**

| 1504 | *Machiavelli is sent to Lyons to ask for protection against Venice (18 Jan.). 'Second Legation to the Court of France' (Op. P.M. V.1 sq.; D. III.389 sq.; 15 Lett.)* | |

(11 Feb.) At LYONS France and Spain sign a truce for three years. Louis XII abandons the claim to Naples.

1504   The supporters of France in Naples thus have no one to
       whom to turn and many lose their estates.   I.59.5
       [Caesar Borgia resigns the Romagna to JULIUS II (13 Jan.),
       and the fortresses are handed over. He goes to Naples
       with a safe-conduct on 28 April, but is arrested by Gon-
       salvo and sent as a prisoner to Spain (20 Aug.). He
       escapes and is killed in battle at Viana (12 Mar., 1507).]
       PISA: *Machiavelli is sent to Piombino to prevent Jacopo d'Appiano
       from sending help to Pisa (Apr. 2). 'Legation to Jacopo IV of
       Appiano' (Op. P.M. V.91; D. III.445).*
       Giovan Paulo Baglione, Marcantonio Colonna and
       Jacopo Savelli are employed to serve under Antonio
       Giacomini (May), who takes Librafatta, but in Septem-
       ber is replaced by Tommasso Tosigni.   cp. III.16.5
       Florence attempts to divert the course of the Arno, but fails.
       Machiavelli writes his 'Decennale Primo', 1494–1504. (B.800–811)
       TREATY OF BLOIS (22 Sept.). Louis XII, Maximilian,
       and Philip of Burgundy, at the suggestion of Julius II,
       agree to attack VENICE, which now holds eastern Lom-
       bardy up to Crema and Cremona; Ravenna, Faenza
       and Rimini in the Romagna; and 'contemplates estab-
       lishing a monarchy in Italy similar to that of Rome'. (It
       comes to nought.)   III.31.3
1505   [⚔ PONTE CAPPELLESE, near Pisa (27 Mar.). Florentine
       defeat.]
       Antonio Giacomini appointed Commissary-General   cp. III.16.5
       *Machiavelli sent to Perugia to induce Baglione to enter the service
       of Florence, but he refuses (Apr. 9).
       'Legation to Gianpaolo Baglione', (Op. P.M. V.93 sq.;
       D. III.445 sq.)
       Machiavelli sent to arrange terms with John Francis Gonzaga,
       Marquess of Mantua, who has been appointed Captain-General
       (4 May). The Negotiations break down. 'Legation to the Mar-
       quess of Mantua' (Op. P.M. V.103 sq.; D. III.454 sq.)
       Machiavelli is sent to interview Pandolfo Petrucci who has offered
       to help Florence to recover Pisa, but the proposal falls through
       (16 July). 'Third Legation to Siena' (Op. P.M. V.109 sq.;
       D. III.457 sq.; 7 Lett.).*
       ⚔ SAN VINCENTI (17 Aug.). Bartolommeo d'Alviano,
       who has invaded Florentine territory, is defeated by
       ANTONIO GIACOMINI and ERCOLE BENTIVOGLIO   I.53.9
       At Bentivoglio's suggestion Soderini obtains leave of the
       Council of Eighty and of the Great Council for a re-
       newed attack on PISA. Giacomini is given the command.
       *Machiavelli is sent to the camp before Pisa (21 Aug.). 'Second
       Expedition to the Camp before Pisa' (Op. P.M. V.337;
       D. III.482).*

A.D.	Events	Discourses
1505	Gonsalvo sends 300 infantry to help Pisa. The attack fails (14 Sept.). Giacomini withdraws and his army is disbanded. He retires in disgrace	I.53.9–10
	[VENICE restores some towns in the Romagna to Julius II, but retains Faenza and Rimini.]	
	[Second TREATY OF BLOIS between Ferdinand and Louis XII, who resigns his claims to Naples and betrothes his niece to Ferdinand. Ferdinand promises 700,000 ducats and an amnesty to the Angevin barons in Naples.]	
	Alfonso d'Este succeeds his father as Duke of Ferrara. His brothers plot to kill him but fail	III.6.29
1506	THE FLORENTINE MILITIA. Machiavelli, supported by Soderini and Giacomini, obtains leave to enrol all citizens capable of bearing arms in a new militia (see the chapters on mercenaries)	II.20
	Machiavelli spends the first three months of 1506 on the Enrolment. Numerous reports. The Ten to N.M. on 23 January and his Report (Op. P.M. V.141–52; D. IV.3–5).	
	'Discourse on how to arm the State of Florence' (Op. P.M. VI.330 sq.)	
	'Discourse on the Ordinance and on the Florentine Militia' (Op. P.M. VI.335 sq.)	
	JULIUS II sets out with 24 cardinals to expel Giovanni Bentivoglio from Bologna (26 Aug.). He asks for troops from France and from Florence. Florence agrees conditionally	III.44.2
	Machiavelli sent to convey the answer of Florence to Julius II (27 Aug.). 'Second Legation to the Court of Rome'. (Op. P.M. V.153 sq.; D. IV.10 sq.; 40 Lett.)	
	(Dec.) The 'Nove Della Milizia' is appointed to take charge of the Militia and Machiavelli becomes its Secretary.	
	'A Provision instituting the Magistracy of the Nove della Militia' (Op. P.M. VI.339 sq.)	
	Giovanpaolo Baglione of Perugia makes his submission to Julius II at Orvieto (8 Sept.) Julius II enters Perugia (13 Sept.) Julius II enters URBINO (25 Sept.), excommunicates Bentivoglio (7 Oct.)	I.27
	Giovanni Bentivoglio surrenders BOLOGNA. Julius enters the city (11 Nov.), stays there two months, and builds a fortress there (P. 25). His impetuosity successful because it suited the times	II.24.7 III.9.5
	FERDINAND of ARAGON becomes suspicious of GONSALVO, goes to Naples (29 Oct.), and deprives him of his command	I.29.4
	[GENOA. A riot early in the year results in the expulsion	

1506 of the nobility and the setting up of a popular government of Eight Tribunes. The Genoese then seize towns
in the Riviera and refuse to surrender them to Louis XII,
who withdraws from the proposed League against Venice.]

1507 *The 'Nove della Militia' is appointed and Machiavelli becomes its*
Chancellor (10–12 Jan.). The Signoria grants Machiavelli a
Patent of Nobility (15 May).
Don Michele, formerly in the service of Caesar Borgia, is
appointed by Machiavelli to train the Militia.

The Duke of Savoy marches to the relief of Monaco
which the Genoese are besieging. GENOA surrenders,
and Louis XII enters the town (28 Apr.), and a French II.21.4
governor is appointed   II.24.9
Louis orders the construction of a fortress on the Codefà

The DIET of CONSTANCE (27 Apr.) approves MAXI-
MILIAN's plan to go to Rome to be crowned Emperor.
The Venetians refuse to allow him to pass through their
territory   cp. III.31.3

Machiavelli is sent to Siena to interview the Cardinal of Santa
Croce who is on his way to visit the Emperor on behalf of
Julius II (Aug. 10–15) 'Fourth Legation to Siena' (Op.
P.M. V.241 sq.; D. IV.76 sq.; 3 Lett.).

[The SAVONA CONFERENCE (28 June. Ferdinand returns
from Naples and meets Louis XII. They agree (i) to
attack Venice, (ii) to ask Maximilian to join them, (iii)
that a council shall be called to reform the Church and
(iv) that Pisa be restored to Florence.]

At Savona Gonsalvo dines with the kings and Louis
treats him as an equal. Ferdinand then takes him to
Spain (11 July), where he lives in comparative obscurity
till his death in 1515   I.29.4

Julius II despatches a Legate to the Emperor and Machiavelli is
sent to Siena to interview the Legate (10–15 Aug.)
Florence, having decided to play for time (cp. P. 3; D. I.33
and III.11.5), sends Francesco Vettori to the Emperor (27 June),
and in December sends Machiavelli to join Vettori and to offer
Maximilian 50,000 ducats if he will agree to protect Florence.
M. joins the Emperor at Constance and remains with him until
6 June, 1508.

1508 *(6 Jan.) Machiavelli with Maximilian at Botzen.*
(Feb.) Maximilian assumes the title of Emperor-elect.
Desultory warfare between Venice and Maximilian.
(6 June) Maximilian and Venice sign a six months' truce.
'Legation to the Emperor' (Op. P.M. V.249 sq.; D. IV.83 sq.;
14 Lett.).
'Report on the Affairs of Germany' (June 1508) (Op.
P.M. VI.313 sq.; B.740 sq.; D. IV.384 sq.).

A.D.	Events	Discourses

1508   *'Discourse on the Affairs of Germany and the Emperor' (1509)*
(Op. P.M. VI.323; D. IV.402 sq.)
'Reflections on German Affairs' (Op. P.M. VI.324 sq.;
B.740 sq.; D. IV.391 sq.)
[PISA. The new militia ravages Pisan territory, and Louis
XII threatens to send Trivulzio to help the Pisans.]
Machiavelli sent as Commissioner to the Camp before Pisa.
Letter of the Ten (16 Aug.) ordering the Militia to obey
Machiavelli (Comm. per il Dominio, Op. P.M. V.337;
D. IV.256). He receives a further commission in November
'per far fanti' (Op. P.M. V.342); and is in charge of the siege
operations—levying troops, ravaging the countryside, intensi-
fying the blockade—from July 1508 to March 1509 (Op.
P.M. V.343 sq.; D. IV.156 sq.)

(10 Dec.) The LEAGUE OF CAMBRAY is formed against
VENICE by Maximilian, Louis XII, Ferdinand of
Aragon, Julius II, the Dukes of Savoy and Ferrara,   I.53.3
and the Marquess of Mantua. Venice hesitates to re-   III.11.5
linquish any of her gains
She thus fails to divide the allies

1509   THE FALL OF PISA. *Machiavelli still Commissioner to the*
Camp before Pisa (Jan. to March). (Op. P.M. V.392 sq.)
[The Genoese fail to relieve Pisa from the blockade.]
[Louis XII gives permission for the siege to continue in
return for 100,000 ducats, 50,000 to Ferdinand, and
50,000 to Georges d'Amboise.]
Three Commissioners are sent to Pisa to form three camps,
but fail to take it. Giacomini was passed over   III.16.5
Machiavelli sent to Piombino to interview Jacopo d'Appiano who
has reported that Pisa is prepared to surrender (10 Mar.).
'Legation to the Lord of Piombino' (Op. P.M. V. 383).
[(May–June). Negotiations for surrender.]
Alfonso del Mutolo offers to let the Florentines into Pisa,
but they fail to get in   III.48.4
PISA SURRENDERS (8 June). *Machiavelli arranges the terms of*
surrender, and provides the city with food. (Op. P.M. V.413 sq.)
Florence grants the citizens full civic rights, but, instead of   II.24.1
making it an ally, builds there a second fortress (P. 20)   cp. III.27.4
VENICE: [Julius II excommunicates Venice (27 Apr.).]
✗ VAILA (or AGNADELLO), May 14. (Cp. P. 20 and 26)
The Venetians under Bartolommeo d'Alviano are   I.6.7
defeated by the French and lose all their possessions,   II.10.6
though half their troops reach Verona in safety, and she   III.31.3
still has a well-filled treasury
[France gets Bergamo and Brescia and the Lombard towns
revolt. The Emperor gets Verona, Vicenza, and Padua,
and Venice offers to become tributory to him.]

A.D.	*Events*	*Discourses*

1509   Julius II acquires Faenza, Rimini, Cervia and Ravenna,⎫
     thus 'stripping Venice of her power' in the Romagna ⎬ cp. I.12.7
[Louis XII and Julius II withdraw from the war.]

[Venice retakes Padua and forces the Emperor to retire to
     Verona. He asks Florence for financial aid, and is pro-
     mised 40,000 ducats.]

*Machiavelli sent to Mantua to pay the second instalment which
     fell due in November. He finds the Emperor gone.*
'*The Legation to Mantua on Affairs concerning the Emperor*'
     (Op. P.M.V.433 sq.; D. IV.195; 13 Lett).
During his absence an attempt is made to deprive him of his office.
A Venetian fleet attacks Ferrara in December, but is
     destroyed by artillery. During the engagement Ludo-
     vico Pico della Mirandola is killed by a cannon-ball   II.17.7
Machiavelli writes the second 'Decennale', 1504–9 (B.811 sq.)

1510   Peace signed by Julius II and Venice (24 Feb.), Julius ⎫
     having come to see that he must save Lombardy from ⎬ { III.11.5
     France   ⎭ { I.12.7

[Death of Cardinal d'Amboise, Louis XII chief adviser
     (May 25).]

[Julius signs a treaty for 5 years with 12 Swiss cantons
     (Mar. 14).]

[Sends Marcantonio Colonna to attack Genoa in conjunc-
     tion with a force from Milan and the Venetian fleet (July).
     The citizens fail to revolt, and Colonna escapes by sea.]

[Julius excommunicates Alfonso d'Este, Duke of Ferrara,
     who is continuing the war with Venice (9 Aug.), and
     sends Francesco Maria della Rovere, Duke of Urbino,
     to attack FERRARA. On 22 September the Pope enters
     Bologna in person.]

[Florence has thus far taken no part in the war with Venice,
     and Louis XII now demands of her a statement of policy.]

*Machiavelli is sent to Blois to explain matters (July). 'Third
     Legation to the Court of France' (Op. P.M. VI.2 sq.;
     D. IV.220 sq., 18 Lett. last dated 10 Sept.). 'Reflections on the
     Affairs of France' (B.731 sq.; D. IV.404 sq.). 'On the
     Nature of the French' (B.730; D.419).*

*Machiavelli is sent to Siena to break off the Truce with Petrucci
     (2 Dec.). 'Commission to Siena' (Op. P.M. VI.124;
     D. IV.278) Patent only*

*Machiavelli spent the first part of 1510 organising the Militia; in
     December he is commissioned to form a troop of cavalry. 'Com-
     missione per Il Dominio' (Op. P.M. VI.124; D. IV.277.
     Patent only).*

The pacific policy of Soderini unsuited to the times ⎫   { I.52.2
He fails to overcome envy   ⎬   { III.9.5
                                                   { III.30.4

A.D.	Events	Discourses
1510	Soderini replies to his critics before the Great Council, and defends his policy (22 Dec.)	I.7.6
	Filippo Strozzi reveals a plot to kill Soderini and restore the Medici, organised by Princivalle della Stufa	cp. I.52.2
1511	[Julius II occupies Mirandola (20 Jan.).]	

[The Duc de Chaumont dies (11 Feb.), and Gian Giacomo TRIVULZIO and GASTON DE FOIX are given command of the French forces.]

Machiavelli is sent to Siena to arrange an alliance with Pandolfo Petrucci and for the handing over of Montepulciano to Florence. (May 1) Treaty published Aug. 12.

Machiavelli is sent to arrange a Treaty with Luciano Grimaldi of Monaco (12 May). 'The Expedition to the Lord of Monaco' (Op. P.M. VI.125-9; D. IV.279. Patent only).

[The French recover Mirandola and Concordia.]

Bologna, discontented with the government of the Papal Legate Alidosi, admits the Bentivogli and Trivulzio (20 May)   II.24.7

[The Duke of Urbino murders Alidosi at Ravenna (24 May).]

[The Duke of Ferrara recovers lost towns.]

[Julius II is summoned to appear before the Concionabulum at Pisa, held with the consent of Florence (1 Sept.).]

[Julius lays Florence and Pisa under an interdict.]

Machiavelli sent to interview the Cardinals supporting the Council of Pisa at Borgo San Domino to induce them to wait (12 Sept.).

Machiavelli sent to France to interview Louis XII at Blois in order to persuade him to postpone the Council (Sept.–Oct.). 'Fourth Legation to the Court of France' (Op. P.M. VI.131 sq.; D. IV.281 sq., 4 Lett).

Machiavelli sent to Pisa to induce the Cardinals to move elsewhere (3 Nov.).

They agree to move to Milan, and Machiavelli returns to Florence (12 Nov.) 'Commission to Pisa during the time of the Council' (Op. P.M. VI.176 sq.; D. IV.297 sq., 1 Lett by M.).

Machiavelli engaged in preparing for the defence of Florence. 'Commissione per fare soldati' (Op. P.M. VI.188; D. IV.303, Patent and one Lett.).

[The HOLY LEAGUE to defend the Church and recover Ferrara is signed by Julius II, Venice, and Ferdinand of Spain on 4 Oct. Henry VIII joins on 17 Nov.]

1512	[Gaston de Foix occupies Bologna, which the League has failed to take.]	
	Brescia rebels, and is occupied by Venetian troops, but the French still hold the citadel	II.17.4
	Gaston de Foix leaves Bologna, *via* the territory of the Duke of Mantua	III.44.3
	and retakes Brescia, with help from the citadel	II.24.11-12

A.D.	*Events*	*Discourses*
1512	✕ RAVENNA (11 April). The French force the Spaniards to give battle	II.17.6
	Both sides fight in serried ranks. The French commander ⎱ Gaston de Foix, though victorious, is killed ⎰	⎰ II.16.5 ⎱ II.17.7
	The 'French are now expelled with the help of the Swiss,' who descend on Lombardy and occupy Milan (May)	I.12.7 II.22.2
	Genoa revolts, and Ottaviano Fregoso is elected its Doge	II.24.9
	[The French evacuate the Romagna; Pavia capitulates; and the Concionabulum at Pisa comes to an end.]	
	These events leave Florence with no one to whom to turn	I.59.5

*Machiavelli prepares the National Troops for War (Jan.).
'Advice concerning the Appointment of an Infantry Commander' (Op.P.M. VI.358).
Obtains the passing of a law approving a National Cavalry (30 Mar.). 'Second Provision for a Mounted Militia' (Op. P.M. VI.352; D. IV.303).*

[Pandolfo Petrucci dies (21 May), having handed over Montepulciano in August 1511.]

Machiavelli sent to Siena (4 June): and to the Val di Chiana and Montepulciano in June. 'Commission to Pisa and other places' (dated 7 May; Op. P.M. VI.189 sq.; D. IV.304 sq.; 11 Lett.).

	THE FALL OF FLORENCE. Raymond de Cardona, accompanied by Giovanni and Juliano de' Medici, enters Florentine territory and demands the deposition of SODERINI, and that the Medici return as private citizens. Florence refuses to depose SODERINI	cp. III.12.3
	Raymond de Cardona, finding that there has been no revolt in Florence, makes overtures of peace, which Florence rejects, with the result that PRATO is sacked by the Spaniards on 29 August	II.27.4
	The Palace in the Piazza is struck by lightning	I.56.1
	The enemies of SODERINI take up arms and force him to resign (31 Aug.) He flies to Siena	⎧ I.52.3 cp. ⎨ III.3.2–3 ⎪ III.9.5 ⎩ III.30.4
	Florence ruined because she had supported the French	I.59.5
	The MEDICI are restored to Florence and the constitution is changed (The Great Council and the National Militia are abolished, and the Gonfalonier is to hold office for two months only)	I.2.2

Machiavelli is deprived of all offices by five decrees (7 Nov.).
[Maximilian Sforza is appointed Duke of Milan (29 Dec.).]

	SELIM I, the present Turk (1512–20), succeeds Bajazet II, and resumes the aggressive policy of his grandfather, Mohamet II	I.19.3 III.6.7

Table IX. Events which occurred while Machiavelli was writing his *Discourses*, 1513–17

A.D.	*Events*	*Discourses*
1513	[LEO X (1513–21). Julius II dies on 20 February, and on 11 March, Giovanni, Cardinal de' Medici, is elected Pope.]	
	A Plot is formed against the Medici. Pietro Paolo Boscoli and Agostino Capponi are arrested and executed (22 Feb.). Machiavelli, after being arrested and tortured, is released. He retires to his estate at Sant' Andrea, near San Casciano, and devotes himself to writing. 'The Prince' is completed by the end of the year and the 'Discourses' are begun.	
	[Cardona seizes Parma and Piacenza on behalf of Milan.]	
	[The TREATY of BLOIS (23 Mar.). Louis XII and Venice come to terms.]	
	[The TREATY of ORTHEZ (1 Apr.). Ferdinand makes peace with Louis XII, in spite of his agreement with Henry VIII, who is preparing to attack France. This leaves Louis free to join Venice in an attack upon Milan.]	
	⚔ NOVARA (6 June). The French, who have laid siege to Novara, are forced to give battle to an army of 19,000 Swiss	III.10.7
	The Swiss, though without either artillery or cavalry, rout the French Louis withdraws from Italy	II.17.9 II.18.7
	HENRY VIII crosses to France on 30 June, and using only his own troops, defeats the French at the battle of ⚔ GUINEGATTE (The battle of the 'Spurs', 16 Aug.)	I.21.2
	Terouenne and Tournay are captured, and everyone is in trepidation lest the whole kingdom be ruined	II.30.6
	Henry returns to England on 17 Oct., Louis having agreed to increase the pension promised at Étaples (confirmed 14 Aug., 1514)	cp. II.30.4
	[Giulio de' Medici is created a cardinal (23 Sept.).]	
	[Florence is ruled nominally by a Council of 70 and a Council of 100, but in reality by Lorenzo de' Medici.]	
	[The Venetian commander, Bartolommeo d'Alviano captures Cremona, Bergamo and Brescia, but on the advance of the League's forces under Cardona, is forced to retire to Vicenza.]	

A.D.	*Events*	*Discourses*
1513	✳ VICENZA (7 Oct.). The Venetians are routed, and only because it is girt by water was Venice itself saved	II.30.6
	[The TREATY OF CORBEIL. Louis XII is reconciled with the Pope. (6 Nov.).]	
	[The Pisan cardinals are pardoned.]	
	[The Duke of Milan restores Parma and Piacenza to the Pope.]	
1514	[The National Militia are revived in Florence (19 May).]	
	[Louis XII marries Mary, Henry VIII's sister.]	
	Selim, the Great Turk, prepares to attack Syria and Egypt but is advised by a Pasha to invade Persia first	III.35.2
	✳ CHALDIRAN (23 Aug.). Defeat of Ismail I. Won by Selim in person mainly owing to his use of artillery	{ II.17.10 cp. I.30.1
1515	FRANCIS I (1515–47) succeeds Louis XII (d. 1 Jan.); proclaims himself Duke of Milan; forms an alliance with Venice; and gets together an army at Lyons for the invasion of Italy. Leo, who is anxious to preserve the freedom of Italy, declines to join him	II.22.1–2
	Fregoso, the Doge of Genoa, on learning this, acknowledges the suzerainty of Francis I, and is appointed Governor of Genoa	II.24.4
	The Duke of Milan, supported by 4,000 Swiss and the forces of the exiled Adorni, marches to attack Genoa, but at Novara is held up by despatches from Leo X	II.24.9
	Francis, avoiding passes guarded by the Swiss, crosses the Alps by the Col d'Argentière. The Swiss retire on Milan (Aug.)	I.23.5
	[Prospero Colonna is surprised and captured at Villafranca (15 Aug.).]	
	✳ SANTA CECILIA or MARIGNANO (13 Sept.). The French win after a two days battle, but the Swiss get away with half their forces	II.18.7
	News that the Swiss had won on the first day caused some of the Swiss to remain behind and get killed, and a Papal and Imperial force to advance too far and almost get captured	
	[On receipt of the news in Rome, the supposed victory was celebrated.]	
	Neither Leo nor Ferdinand, who are in alliance, dare to attack the French	II.22.3
	Maximilian Sforza, who still holds the citadel of Milan, surrenders it to the French (4 Oct.) and resigns his rights in return for a pension	II.24.5
	[Leo comes to terms with Francis, and cedes Parma and Piacenza (11 Oct.).]	
	[Leo visits Francis at Bologna, passing through Florence *en route* (30 Nov.–8 Dec.).]	

A.D.	Events	Discourses
1516	[Ferdinand of Aragon dies. Charles (afterwards Emperor) inherits all his dominions (23 Jan.).]	
	[Lorenzo de' Medici expels Francesco Maria della Rovere from Urbino (30 May), and is created Duke of Urbino and Gonfalonier of the Church.]	
	[TREATY OF NOYON (13 Aug.) between Francis I and Charles, who is to marry Louise of France and obtain Naples as her dowry.]	
	[TREATY OF FRIBURG (29 Nov.). Francis signs a pact of eternal peace with the Swiss.]	
	SELIM I expels the Mameluke Sultans from Syria and Egypt	I.1.9
	⚔ DABIK (24 Aug.), near Aleppo. Defeat of the Sultan, Khansou Ghori.	
	⚔ GAZA (28 Oct.). Defeat of the Sultan, Touman. Both victories largely due to the use of artillery	II.17.10
1517	⚔ RADANIEH (12 Jan.). Final defeat of the Sultan, Touman.	
	Francesco Maria della Rovere, the exiled Duke of Urbino, though without the 'sinews of war', collects disbanded Spanish and French troops, and, ignoring all towns *en route*, recaptures Urbino (6 Feb.)	II.10.3 II.24.14
	[LEAGUE OF CAMBRAY renewed. Maximilian, Charles, and Francis I guarantee each other security in their dominions.]	

Machiavelli during this period has (i) a correspondence with Francesco Vettori, the Florentine ambassador in Rome, 1513; Op. B.880–96; wrote in 1515–16 his 'Chapter on Ingratitude', Op. B.841–5, his 'Chapter on Fortune' Op. B.845–9, and his 'Chapter on Ambition', Op. B.849–53: and in 1517 the uncompleted poem 'L'Asino d'Oro' Op. B.817–40.

For the closing years of Machiavelli's life,
1518 to 1527, see Introduction III,
§§ 47–54.

TABLES X TO XII

GENEALOGICAL TABLES

Table X. The *'Familia Maclavellorum'*

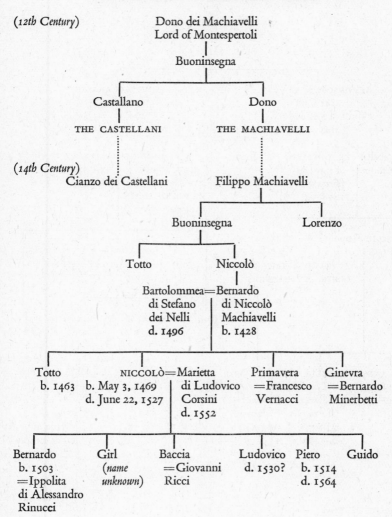

(*12th Century*) Dono dei Machiavelli
Lord of Montespertoli

Buoninsegna

Castallano   Dono

THE CASTELLANI   THE MACHIAVELLI

(*14th Century*)
Cianzo dei Castellani   Filippo Machiavelli

Buoninsegna   Lorenzo

Totto   Niccolò

Bartolommea＝Bernardo
di Stefano   di Niccolò
dei Nelli   Machiavelli
d. 1496   b. 1428

Totto   NICCOLÒ＝Marietta   Primavera   Ginevra
b. 1463   b. May 3, 1469   di Ludovico   ＝Francesco   ＝Bernardo
d. June 22, 1527   Corsini   Vernacci   Minerbetti
d. 1552

Bernardo   Girl   Baccia   Ludovico   Piero   Guido
b. 1503   (*name   ＝Giovanni   d. 1530?   b. 1514
＝Ippolita   unknown*)   Ricci   d. 1564
di Alessandro
Rinucci

Table XI. The House of Aragon and Naples

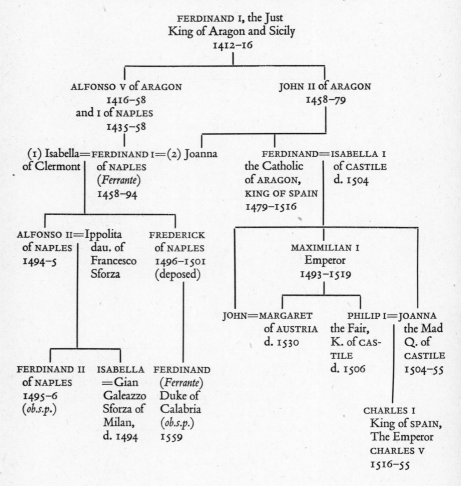

FERDINAND I, the Just
King of Aragon and Sicily
1412–16

ALFONSO V of ARAGON
1416–58
and I of NAPLES
1435–58

JOHN II of ARAGON
1458–79

(1) Isabella=FERDINAND I=(2) Joanna
of Clermont | of NAPLES
(*Ferrante*)
1458–94

FERDINAND=ISABELLA I
the Catholic | of CASTILE
of ARAGON, | d. 1504
KING OF SPAIN
1479–1516

ALFONSO II=Ippolita
of NAPLES | dau. of
1494–5 | Francesco
Sforza

FREDERICK
of NAPLES
1496–1501
(deposed)

MAXIMILIAN I
Emperor
1493–1519

JOHN=MARGARET
of AUSTRIA
d. 1530

PHILIP I=JOANNA
the Fair, | the Mad
K. of CAS- | Q. of
TILE | CASTILE
d. 1506 | 1504–55

FERDINAND II
of NAPLES
1495–6
(*ob.s.p.*)

ISABELLA
=Gian
Galeazzo
Sforza of
Milan,
d. 1494

FERDINAND
(*Ferrante*)
Duke of
Calabria
(*ob.s.p.*)
1559

CHARLES I
King of SPAIN,
The Emperor
CHARLES V
1516–55

TABLE XIII

SOURCES

Table XIII. Sources

A. Authors and Works mentioned in the Discourses

1. Livy	7. Procopius	13. Virgil
2. Aristotle	8. Q. Curtius Rufus	14. Juvenal
3. Cicero	9. Sallust	15. Dante
4. Diodorus Siculus	10. Tacitus	16. Lorenzo de' Medici
5. Herodian	11. Thucydides	17. Flavius Blondus
6. Plutarch	12. Xenophon	

B. Authors and Works not mentioned but certainly used in the 'Discourses'

1. Polybius	4. Lucian	7. Vitruvius
2. Herodotus	5. Suetonius	8. Aquinas and the
3. Justin	6. Valerius Maximus	*de Regimine Principum*

C. Authors possibly used or suggested as having been used in the 'Discourses'

1. Ammianus Marcellinus	10. Orosius
2. Appian	11. Pliny
3. Julius Caesar	12. Aemilius Probus
4. Dion Cassius	(= Cornelius Nepos)
5. Dionysius Halicarnassus	13. Seneca
6. Frontinus	14. Aurelius Victor
7. Isocrates	15. Vegetius
8. Josephus	16. Velleius Paterculus
9. Marsilius of Padua	

D. Concluding Remarks on the Sources used in the 'Discourses' and in 'The Prince'

N.B. The numbers given in parentheses, preceded by an 'E', refer to Ebert's 'General Bibliographical Dictionary', O.U.P., 1837, 4 vols.

A. AUTHORS AND WORKS MENTIONED IN THE 'DISCOURSES'

1. LIVY. Titus Livy was born at Patavium in 59 B.C. He lived for the most part in Rome and died in A.D. 17 at the age of 76. His *Annals of Rome* were divided into 'decades,' of which the 1st decade (Books I to X) survives whole and covers the period from 753 to 293 B.C. The 2nd is lost. The 3rd (XXI–XXX) covers the

period 219–201 of the Second Punic War, and survives intact. The 4th (XXXI–XL), covering the period 201–179 is also intact. Of the 5th, only Books XLI–XLV survive, but they were not discovered until 1531. The *Editio Princeps* is: LIVIUS TITUS. HISTORIAE ROMANAE, *Decades III* (scil. *Lib. 1–10, 31, 32, 34–40*) *ex recogn. J. Andreae, ep. Aleriensis. Romae. Sweynheym and Pannartz. Without date (1469), large folio. (E.12071.)*

Between 1470 and 1480 six editions of this work were printed (E.12072–7); and in 1513 there appeared another edition comprising '*quae extant decades . . . cum Lucii Flori epitome recognita, annotatt. Sabellici et familiari Ascensii explanatione*'. *Par. J. Parvus.* non. Dec. 1513, fol. (E.12084).

Machiavelli's commentary, as he tells us in the Preface, is on those books of Livy which 'have not had their continuity broken by the malignity of time', i.e. it is on the first decade. References for the incidents taken from Livy will be found in the notes and also in the Chronological Tables (Table II).

The following passages are quoted (all in Latin unless indicated by 'not L'):

Livy	Discourses	Livy	Discourses	Livy	Discourses
I.30.1	in II.3.1, 3	VI. 4.5	in I.57.1	34.8–10	in III.36.4
III. 1.7	in I.37.4 (not L)	6.7	in III.30.1	34.14–15	in III.39.3
4.9	in I.34.9	7.5	in III.31.1	38.5	in II.19.8
20.5	in I.13.4	7.6	in III.31.6	VIII. 4.1	in II.15.1
26.7	in III.25.2	20.14	in III.8.3	4.2	in II.13.3
35–37	six in I.40	20.15	in I.58.1	4.7	in II.14.1
50.16	in I.44.1 (not L)	29.1–2	in III.33.3	8.11	in II.16.3
70.1	in III.15.4	30.6	in III.33.3	11.4	in II.15.6 (not L)
IV. 6.11	in I.47.1	41.8	in III.33.2	13.2	in II.23.1
6.12	in I.47.2	VII.10.2	in III.22.2	13.14–17	in II.23.2
28.5	in III.12.6	11.1	in III.37.1, 6	21	six in II.23.4
31.2	in III.15.1	12.11	in III.10.1, 4	34.8–10	in III.36.4
33.5	in III.14.6	29.5	in II.11.1, 2	IX. 1.10	in III.12.4
V. 6.7	in III.30.1–2	32.5	in III.37.3	3.12	in III.40.3
22.5	in I.12.4	32.10–12	in III.38.1	20.10	in II.21.2
26.8	in III.23.1	32.14	in I.60	X.16.5	in III.44.1
28.4	in III.29.2	33.1–4	in III.22.6	28.4	in III.36 (title)
37.1	in II.29.2	34.3	in III.39.3	31.14	in I.15.1
49.1	in II.30.1	34.4	in III.39.3	39.12	in I.15.2

Three phrases are also cited from Livy, namely '*Jus Gentium*' in II.28.1 and III.1.3 (cp. V.36.6); '*Manliana imperia*' in III.22.1 (cp. VIII.7.22); and '*aggredi urbem corona*' in II.32.2, with which cp. XXXVII.4.10, '*corona est aggressus*' and other passages given in the note *in loc.*

The later books are frequently used for the second and third Punic wars and for other incidents. From them there are five quotations, namely, a passage from:

Livy	Discourses
XXII.49.3	in II.18.2
XXIII.13.2	in II.30.6 (not in Latin)
XXIV.25.8	in I.58.1
XXXV.35.18	in III.6.30
XXXVII.45.11–12	in III.31.2

The quotations are usually accurate and in most cases agree with our present text, for which I have used the Teubner edition. Variations, if of interest, have been indicated in the notes. Machiavelli is also remarkably accurate in the use he makes of Livy's text, but there are several slips, of which a list will be found in TABLE XV.

2. ARISTOTLE. Machiavelli certainly knew the *Politics,* to which he refers in D. III.26.2, and possibly also the *Ethics,* of both of which works numerous Latin translations were available in his day, and also a translation of the *Politics* into French. I select the following as instances:

ARISTOTELIS, *Op. omnia latina, interpr. Averroe, Ven. Ant. de Asula, 1483, folio 9 parts in 3 vols. (contained the 'Politics' and 'Ethics'). (E.1120.)*

——, *polit. lat. vers. a Ln. Aretino, c. comm. S. Thomae. Romae. Euchar. Silber, 1492, folio. (E.1172.)*

——, *Ethica, lat. e. interpr. veteri ac nova versione Ln. Aretini. Lovanii, Cr. Braem. 1476. (E.1155.)*

——, *le livre de politiques d'Aristote (trad. par N. Oresme). Par. Vérard, 1489, folio. Gothic letter. (E.1173.)*

There are far too many points of resemblance between Machiavelli's doctrine and Aristotle's for it to be possible to doubt that he had read the *Politics,* especially Book V, in which the resemblances mostly occur; not that there are any two passages, one clearly depending on the other, but that, since both Aristotle and Machiavelli are reflecting on the same subject-matter, they inevitably come at times to the same conclusion and make similar remarks. Thus, both ascribe class-conflict to the opposite tendencies of those who have honours or wealth and those who resent being without them (*Pol.* V.2 and cp. D. I.4.2; 5.3). Both would solve the problem by balance or proportion, not by eliminating one of the two classes (*ib.* and cp. D. I.61); but in yielding to the demand for equality, of which both have much to say, Machiavelli would go further than Aristotle (see A's remarks on equality in V.1 and for M on 'equality' see Index *sub voce*). Both also lay stress on the psychological factor in revolutions, e.g. on the love of gain and honour and superiority, on arrogance and avarice, and on the fear of punishment and of reprisals (V.2–3, and for M see Index *sub vocibus*). Aristotle also calls attention to the tendency of a wealthy democracy to become a government by families (V.3), as Florence did in the time of the Medici. He also points out in V.3–4 how great changes arise from small beginnings (cp. D. I.18.3), and in V.8 how difficult it is to recognise them at the start (cp. D. I.33.6). In V.4 he mentions inheritances and quarrels about marriages amongst the causes of revolutions (cp. D. III.6.5); and force and fraud as the two means which the would-be despot uses, with the stress on fraud since it is by this means that the populace is deceived (cp. D. II.13 and Index *sub* 'Appearances'). Another cause of revolution, mentioned in V.5, is the calumniation of the rich and powerful and the stirring up of the people against them, an evil on the consequences of which Machiavelli lays great stress, especially in D. I.8, and which was the cause of Soderini's fall (cp. D. I.7.6 and D. III.3.2–3). In the same chapter mention is made of the demagogue who becomes a general, and in V.6 of an army which becomes the arbiter between factions and ends by mastering both, to which cause Machiavelli rightly ascribes the fall of the Roman republic. Danger may also arise from those who are worthy of office, but have been passed over (V.7, and cp. D. III.17 on the danger of giving office to the disgruntled). It also arises when a person who is great desires to become greater (*ib.* and cp. D. III.6.9). Towards the close of this chapter Aristotle says that constitutional government breaks down when justice is maladministered (cp. what M says about courts in D. I.49), and, having pointed out its tendency to lapse either into oligarchy or into pure democracy, adds that 'the only stable basis for government is equality according to proportion and for everyman to enjoy his own'—a remark with which Machiavelli would be in whole-hearted agreement.

The correspondencies continue throughout this Book. In V.8 Aristotle recommends that, when the governing class is numerous, there should be many institutions (cp. D. I.2.17; 7.1; 16.8; 24.1), and that the tenure of office should be short, six months being specifically mentioned (cp. D. III.24 on military commands, and D. I.34.4–5 on dictatorship). There follow remarks on the need to control the notables by means of laws; on the difficulty the ordinary man has in discerning the beginning of evils; on innovations introduced by the private lives of citizens: on the importance of preventing magistrates from making money out of the offices they hold, and of preventing wealthy citizens from undertaking expensive and useless public services; all of which points Machiavelli also makes. (Cp. D. I.7.6; 37.8; and III.1.5 on the need to control ambition by laws; I.33.3 on discerning inconveniences in their initial stage; III.28 on the use of good works as a cover for ambitious projects; III.25 on the poverty of Rome's great men, and I.7.7 on judgeship being an honourable post.) In V.9 rulers are warned that even oligarchs should make it a principle to do no wrong to the people, and that, on the other hand, unless the young be trained by habit and education in the spirit of the constitution, not even the best laws will avail. It is all wrong to think it slavery to live in accordance with a constitution, for it is in this lies salvation; both of which principles Machiavelli often seeks to drive home. (cp. Index *sub* 'Populace, goodwill of'; 'Education'; 'Constitution'; 'Law'.)

In V.10 Aristotle draws the same distinction as Machiavelli does between a monarch and a tyrant. The monarch seeks, or should seek, the public interests; the tyrant looks only to private ends. The tyrant relies on mercenaries. The king takes as guards his own citizens; or should do so, Machiavelli would say, for the French kings had forgotten this principle (cp. D.I.21.2 and II.30.4). True kings will not mistrust their people and so will not deprive them of their arms. It is, moreover, to a passage in this chapter that Machiavelli would seem to be referring when in D. III.26.2 he writes that 'amongst the primary causes of the downfall of tyrants Aristotle puts the injuries they do on account of women, whether by rape, violation, or the breaking up of marriages.' Aristotle in V.4 has told the story of how the Syracusan constitution was once changed because two young men in the government fell out about the fiancée of the one and the wife of the other; and of how the beginning of troubles in Delphi was due to a bridegroom's deserting his bride; and how Timophanes stirred up a revolution in Mitylene and invoked the aid of Athens because the suits of his two daughters had been rejected. He now remarks that there are two forms of injustice which most commonly cause subjects to attack their rulers, insult and the confiscation of property. As examples he mentions the public dishonour offered to the sister of Harmodius; the killing of Evagoras by a eunuch whose wife had been carried off by Evagoras's son; the attack of Crataeus upon Ageselaus, who broke his word after promising one of his daughters in marriage.

Machiavelli does not cite the examples, but his remark sums up what Aristotle says in these two passages about women. He also points out in the chapter on Conspiracies (III.6.5) that 'injuries affecting a man's property or honour', especially the honour of his women-folk, 'are the two things which give men greater offence than anything else' (which is precisely what Aristotle says), and in this connection cites the case of Pausanias, just as Aristotle does, and also a marriage-case (*ib.*).

Next we have in V.10 the statement that 'the two chief motives which induce men to attack tyrannies are hatred and contempt'. This statement which may well have suggested P. 19, which deals with how hatred and contempt may be avoided, and mentions the violation of property and women as things which are to be avoided. And in V.11 occurs the passage in which Aristotle recommends as the third method by which a tyranny may be preserved that the tyrant should pretend to have the virtues of a true king, should care for the revenues, render an account of his expenses, appear to collect taxes for state purposes only, adorn and improve the city, and be particularly earnest in the services of the gods—a pretence of virtue which in P. 18 Machiavelli recommends all princes to maintain, since people expect it of them, though in point of fact there are many occasions, so he claims, on which they cannot afford to practise virtue, since this would mean ruin. (cp. *Introduction*, § 94.) Similarly, the advice Periander gave to Thrasybulus 'to cut off the tops of the tallest ears of corn', meaning that he must always put out of the way the citizens who overtop the rest (cp. V.10.1311a, 20 *sq.*; V.11. 1313a, 39), is applied by Machiavelli to all rulers who have just set up a new regime (cp. D. III.3 and 4, and III.30 on the need to remove the envious before good work can be done). Aristotle recognises the danger due to envy, but as his 'great preserving principle', oft repeated, he adopts the rule that care be taken that loyal citizens shall outnumber the disloyal, and that this be provided for by legal enactments (V.9. 1309b, 14–18). Machiavelli's approval of what Aristotle stigmatises as Persian or barbaric methods is, however, confined to the period immediately following a revolution. In general he agrees with Aristotle that 'the rule of a king is over voluntary subjects, though he is supreme in important matters', and that 'monarchy is preserved by the limitation of its powers'. This was why monarchy lasted so long among the Molossians and the Lacaedaemonians, says Aristotle. It is also to this reason that Machiavelli ascribes Sparta's stability in D. II.2, and to the constitutional procedure and the observance of law by the kings of France that he ascribes the stability of monarchy in that country (D. I.16.9; 19.4; 58.3; and III.1.9). On the other hand, to rulers who are anxious to get possession of an independent city Machiavelli recommends the use of an art which Aristotle says is characteristic of tyrants, namely, the sowing of quarrels amongst citizens, and the setting of the people against the notables and of the rich against one another (V.11. 1313b, 16–18, and cp. D. II.25.2 on keeping a city divided in order to induce it voluntarily to surrender).

Other points of agreement occur; for instance, in regard to the proposition that conspiracies against princes are almost invariably made by 'notables who either want to rule or to escape subjection' (V.10. 1311a, 18–19, and cp. D. III.6.8–11). Both except the case of those who do not mind getting killed. But though there are many who would like to kill tyrants, there are few, says Machiavelli, 'who do such things, and of them very few who do not get killed in the very act'; with which cp. Aristotle V.10 1312a, 30–9: 'It is rare, however, to find such men, since he who would kill a tyrant must be prepared to lose his own life if he fail . . . But this is an attitude to which few can attain.' There is substantial agreement, too, in regard to the causes which lead to the breakdown of a monarchy. Aristotle mentions two: (1) quarrels within the royal family, and (2) tyrannical methods and the violation of law (V.10. 1312b. 40–1313a, 3); and in the case of hereditary monarchies adds a third, namely, that kings often arouse contempt and are apt to outrage others (1313a, 10 *sq.*). Machiavelli in D. III.4 reminds kings of the danger due to rival claimants and that old injuries are never cancelled by new benefits; in D. III.5 warns them that they are likely to lose their kingdom, even though hereditary, should they break laws and disregard ancient institutions; and in D. I.19 he points out that a hereditary kingdom is likely to be lost should a weak monarch be succeeded by another weak monarch, where by a 'weak' monarch he means one who does not put his trust in war (*ib.*, 4); which is not quite the same thing as evoking contempt; this point, however, has already been discussed at length in P. 19.

In regard to inflicting injuries there is a discrepancy. Aristotle's warning against them is unqualified, but Machiavelli holds that a few will not matter, provided the prince has made sure of his people's goodwill (D. III.6.3). To prolonged injustice, however, he is not less averse than is Aristotle, whether it be directed against an individual (D. II.28.3, end) or against a class of people or people in general (D. I.45.3 and cp. P. 8).

Correspondences may also be found in other books. For instance, Aristotle's definition of a state as a 'community of citizens united by sharing one form of government' (III.3, 1276b, 1) expresses exactly what Machiavelli means by a '*vivere politico*', and also what he means by the term '*stato*' when this term signifies not merely a government but also the governed, as is often the case. So, too, does Aristotle's definition of a 'constitution' as 'the arrangement of magistracies in a state, especially the highest of all' (III.6.1278b, 8–10) agree with what Machiavelli says of the relation of the constitution to institutions and laws in D. I.18.2–5. What Machiavelli says in D. I.9 about the advantages of a constitution being formed by one man with adequate authority also agrees with what Aristotle says in III.13, 1284a, 3 *sq.* about the man whose virtue and political capacity is so outstanding that no one else can be compared with him. There is mention, too, in D. I.2.3–4 of the three good forms of simple state into which some divide politics, and of their opposites, a point with which Aristotle deals at great length in III.7. Both emphasise the tendency of the three good forms, Monarchy, Aristocracy and Democracy, to pass over into their opposites, and, though in describing their transitions Machiavelli follows Polybius, he is careful to point out that cyclic change is seldom completed (*ib.*, § 13). His view is that states alternately make progress and decline (cp. *Introduction*, § 149), which agrees with Aristotle's remark that the transition from a composite state to democracy, aristocracy or oligarchy, may be reversed (V.7.1307a, 20 *sq.*).

Machiavelli, then, had certainly read the *Politics* of Aristotle, probably the whole of it; but it is in Book V that he is especially interested, and of it that he retains the clearest recollection. Nor is this surprising, for it is on political movements, not on static analyses, that his thought centres, and Book V is not only concerned with revolutions, but considers them, just as he does, from the point of view alike of governors and governed, of those who aim at overthrowing a government and of those to whose interest it is to make it secure, be they monarchs or tyrants, aristocrats or oligarchs, constitutional rulers or demagogues. (Cp. for method *Introduction* § 95.)

3. CICERO, M. Tullius, b. 3 January, 106 B.C., executed by the orders of Antony on 7 December, 43 B.C., is cited in D. I.4.5 as having remarked that though the populace may be ignorant, it is capable of grasping the truth and readily yields when a man, worthy of confidence, lays the truth before it. The reference is presumably to the well-known passage in the *De Amicitia* in which Cicero first of all remarks that 'a public assembly, though composed of ignorant men, can usually tell the difference between a demagogue and a man who is constant, true, and grave *(gravis)' (XXV.95)*, and then in *XXVI.97* connects what he has been saying of this with 'friendship' by remarking that 'on the platform, i.e., in a public assembly, where there is the greatest opportunity for deceit and dissembling, truth none the less prevails provided it can be made plain and brought to the light of day' (cp. D. I.4, n. 4). This bears out what Machiavelli says elsewhere about the influence of 'grave men' on the mob (cp. I.13.4; 53.1–2; 54; 58.6; and III.22.10). The next reference is in D. I.33.5, and consists in a short quotation from the letters *Ad Fam. XVI.11*. In it Cicero speaks of Pompey as one *'qui Caesarem sero coepit timere'*. In neither of the references is Cicero quoted in Latin. The third and last mention of Cicero is in D. I.52.3, where we are told that his attempt to remove Mark Antony's supporters did but increase their numbers.

The fact that there are only two quotations from Cicero in the *Discourses*, neither of them in Latin and one of them inexact, and that in *The Prince* there is no reference to Cicero at all, suggests that with Cicero's works Machiavelli had no intimate acquaintance. Possibly the fact that his works were not published in Florence until 1514, but that the letters *Ad Fam.* had been published in 1510 may account for there being only one exact quotation which is from the letters *Ad Fam.* The existent editions were:

CICERO, M. TULLIUS, *Opera (ed. Alex. Minucianus) Mediol. Alex. Minucianus et Guilelmi fratres, 1498–99, folio, 4 vols. (E.4250.)*

—— *Opera rhetorica, oratoria et forensia. Par. in aedibus Ascens. (Kal. Dec. 1511), folio (E.4251.)*

—— *Opera epistolica.* ib. *6 kal. Dec. 1511. (E.4251.)*

—— *Opera philosophica.* ib. *kal. Dec. 1511, fol. (E.4251.)*

—— *Opera Epp. ad familiares. Flor. Ph. Junta, 1510, 8°. (E.4414.)*

—— *Opera Flor. Ph. Junta. m. Oct. 1514, 8°. (E.4286.)*

In the *De Officiis, II.vii. 24*, Cicero writes: *'Acriores autem morsus sunt intermissae libertatis quam retentae'*—a passage which may well have been in Machiavelli's mind when he wrote: 'Quite rightly do political writers say that peoples bite more savagely when they have just recovered their liberty than when they have had it for some time' (D. I.28.2). A remark which follows in *vii.24*, namely, *'qui se metui volent, a quibus metuentur, eosdem metuant ipsi, necesse est'*, is also akin to a paragraph in D. II.24.2 in which Machiavelli maintains that ill-treatment arouses hatred which in turn generates fear on the part of the prince. And it may be owing to what Cicero says of Phalaris and Dionysius in the same chapter, that Machiavelli links them together in D. III.6.6 as examples of men against whom conspiracies were formed because they had usurped their country's rights (cp. D. III.6, *n. 11*).

It is also from the *De Officiis* that Machiavelli borrows the metaphor of the 'lion and the fox', which exemplifies the two administrative principles on which all princes must rely, namely, force and fraud—cp. *De Officiis, I. xiii, 41,* and P. 18 (E. p. 142), P. 19 (E. p. 159); and see note 6 to D. I.18, and note 1 to D. II.13, and Guicciardini's comments at the end of this chapter. It is to be noted that, whereas Cicero *(in loc.)* and also Aristotle (in V.10.1313a, 9–10) regard force and fraud as methods to which only tyrants or would-be tyrants will resort, Machiavelli holds that all rulers and all who aspire to rule must use them as occasion demands. It is also probable (Burd says 'almost beyond doubt', *Il Principe,* p. 286) that Machiavelli was influenced by the chapters on *'beneficentia'* and *'liberalitas' (De Off. II. xv–xxiv),* especially in what he writes in his chapter on liberality and meanness in *The Prince* (P. 16). But to pretend to be generous when one is not really so, which is commended in D. I.51, or to use liberality towards one's neighbours in order that they may throw themselves into one's lap (D. II.20.4) would for Cicero be a misuse of this virtue. Similarly in regard to *'utilitas'*, Machiavelli's interest in the question of the relation of expediency to morality may well have been stimulated by Cicero's long discussion of the relation of *utilitas* to *honestas* in *De Officiis, Book II,* though actually Machiavelli's position is the opposite of Cicero's, for Cicero holds that expediency and morality should not be divorced and that to divorce them, as some do, is to subvert human society (cp. especially, *II. vi.21 sq.*). There is also a passage in *De Officiis, I. x* which has bearing on what Machiavelli says in D. III.42 about the conditions under which promises may be broken (cp. D. III.42, *n. 3).* It would seem, then, to be almost certain that Machiavelli had read the *De Officiis,* but the result was not that he found himself in agreement with Cicero's doctrine, as he finds himself in agreement with Aristotle's doctrine in *Politics, Book V,* but that he took up on the main issue a diametrically opposite position. (For other passages in which what Cicero says has bearing on the *Discourses,* see D. I.59, *n. 6;* II.30 and III.4, *notes at end;* III.20 *n. 2;* III.40, *n. 2.*)

There are other works of Cicero which Machiavelli may have perused. For instance, there is a passage in the *De Legibus* in which Cicero expresses the same views as Machiavelli not only in regard to the influence of great men (cp. D. III.1.4–7) but also in regard to the influence of rulers, especially bad rulers, on the behaviour of their peoples (cp. D. III.29). He writes:

'It is plain to see, if you care to call the times to mind, that a city has the same character as have its leading men, and that whatever change in behaviour takes place in rulers, a like change ensues in the people. This is much more to the point than what Plato says about the state of a city changing when the songs of their musicians change. In my opinion the manners of citizens alter when the life and mode of living of the nobility alters. Hence vicious princes are the more pernicious in their effects on a republic, in that they not only themselves introduce vices, but impregnate the city with them; so that they are a nuisance not merely because they themselves are corrupt, but because they corrupt others and by example do more harm than they do by sinning.' *(De Leg. III. xiv.)*

Another passage, in the *Tusculan Orations, II. 11,* is mentioned by Gilbert in connection with what Machiavelli says in P. 25 about fortune favouring the adventurous (see *The Prince and Its Forerunners, p.* 211); for Cicero also recommends that fortune be vigorously tested, since she seems to favour those who do this, but is 'hostile to those who do not risk anything'. Also Burd cites the *Pro Marcio, II.7,* where Cicero describes fortune as *'Rerum humanarum domina',* and another passage in the *Tusculan Orations, V.9.25,* in which Cicero says *'Vitam regit fortuna, non sapientia'* (p. 357). But, though Machiavelli ascribes great power to fortune, while at the same time recommending that she should be put to the test, and that in war much depends upon her favour, the passages mentioned (which comprise statements that anyone might make) in no wise either represent or account for Machiavelli's carefully worked-out theory of fortune, its functions, and its relation to virtue (cp. *Introduction VII, 79-83;* and Subject-Index sub 'Fortune'). Still less has Cicero's casual remark *'suscipienda quidem bella sunt ob eam causam ut sine injuria in pace vivatur' (De Off. I.xi.35)* anything to do with Machiavelli's views on the causes of war, which centre round empire-building; nor yet with his theorem that rulers should be content with victory, which is based purely on grounds of expediency.

4. DIODORUS SICULUS was the contemporary of Julius Caesar and of Augustus. His work is a general history of the world down to his own time, and was completed in the first years of the Christian era. He had spent some time in Egypt, about which he has much to say; but, as Machiavelli remarks in the only passage in which Diodorus is mentioned (D. II.5.2), histories which cover a period of some forty to fifty thousand years are not to be regarded as trustworthy. Latin translations of Diodorus Siculus were available in Machiavelli's day, e.g.:

DIODORUS SICULUS, *Historiarum priscar. Libri 1–5 a Poggio in lat. traducti. Bon. 1472, folio. (E.6161.)*

————— *libri duo, primus de Phillipi, alter de Alexandri rebus gestis (s. lib. 16 et 17). Utrunque latinitate donav. Aug. Cospus. Viennae. Hi. Victor. 1516, folio. (E.6162.)*

It is probably on Diodorus that Machiavelli relies for his remarks on the kings. of Egypt in I.1.9 and in I.58.3; and also for what he says about Semiramis in III.14.5, 6, and again for the fable of Antaeus in II.12.5. Other passages in which he may have been used occur in I.58, *see notes 3 and 5;* but for the siege of Tyre it is more probable that Quintus Curtius is used (see II.27, *n. 3);* and in III.13.4 *(see note 7).* For the influence of Diodorus on Machiavelli's method, see *Introduction,* § 97. There is no evidence that the second of the two works cited above was used; nor is it likely seeing that the work was not published until 1516 in Vienna.

5. HERODIAN was still living in the time of Gordianus III, who became emperor in A.D. 238. Of his life nothing is known, save that he lived for a long time in Rome. He was a Greek, and wrote his history, which covers the period from A.D. 180 to 238, in Greek. Translations, however, had been published before the end of the fifteenth century, namely:

HERODIANI *historiar. ll. VIII., lat., Aug. Politiano interprete. Romae (without printer's name), 20 June 1493, folio. (E.9532.)*

————— *a Caesare Aug usque ad Theodosium excerpta (together with excerpts from Eutropius, Paulus Diaconus, etc.) Flor. Ph. Junta, in Mart, 1517, 8°. (E.9533.)*

The full title of the first of these two works is: *'De Imperio Romanorum Imperatorum post Marcum'.* Though in *The Prince* Machiavelli does not mention Herodian, the opening words of the long passage in P. 19, in which he states that, in examining the lives and deaths of the Roman emperors, 'it seems to me sufficient to take all those emperors who succeeded to the Empire from Marcus the philosopher down to Maximinus', suggest that he has Herodian in mind. Anyhow, the whole passage is based on Herodian (cp. Burd's note in *Il Principe,* p. 316, n. 14). In the *Discourses*

Herodian is mentioned in D. III.6.31 in connection with the conspiracy of Plautianus against Severus and Antonius, both of whom Plautianus sought to kill. But Herodian does not say that the Emperor and his son dwelt in different countries, but merely that they were occupying different rooms (cp. D. III.6, *n. 43*). The quotation in III.6.30: 'The Senate sends you this', is also probably from Herodian *(see note 41)*.

There are several passages in the chapter on Conspiracies for which Herodian is almost certainly used. He is used, for instance, not only for the conspiracy of Plautianus, which is mentioned in D. III.6.21 as well as in 31 *(cp. notes 30 and 43)*, but also for the conspiracy of Laetus and Eclectus against Commodus (III.6.24 and 41, and *notes 32, 64)*, for that of Macrinus against Caracalla (III.6.25 and cp. *note 33)*; and for that of Quintianus against Commodus (III.6.30 and *note 41*). His work was probably used also as the basis for the discussion of the fates of emperors in I.10.5–7, just as in the case of P. 19.

6. PLUTARCH lectured in Rome in the time of the Emperor Domitian (A.D. 81–96) and is said to have been tutor to the Emperor Trajan, to whom he dedicated his *Apophthegmata Regum*, if indeed he is the author of this work. He lived for a long time in Rome, but died in Chaeronia, where he had been given a magistracy. Otherwise little is known of him in spite of his numerous works, which include not only the Parallel Lives but many other works with which Machiavelli seems to have been acquainted.

There is one reference to Plutarch in the *Discourses*. In II.1.1 Machiavelli describes him as a writer of great weight, but holds that he is wrong in thinking that Rome's successes were due rather to fortune than to virtue. Hence Machiavelli was obviously acquainted with the *De Fortuna Romanorum,* of which a Latin translation existed in his time, as also of many, but not all, Plutarch's works. The following Latin editions were available:

PLUTARCH I, *Vitae parallelae a variis interpretatibus latinae factae et a J. Ant. Campano collectae et editae. Large folio, without place or date, but certainly before 1471, and assigned by Ebert to U. Gallus, Romae, 1470. (E.17463.)*

—— *eaedem vitae. Romae, Sweynheim et Pannar, 1473, folio. (E.17465.)*

Fabricius in his *Bibliotheca Graeca* states that other Latin editions of the *Lives,* of which the originals have been lost, are mentioned in printed lists; e.g. an edition called '*Parallela. lat. per Guarinum e Graeco traducta.* Argentor, 1506, folio.' (Fabricius, V, p. 208.)

The earliest Florentine edition was not published until 1517, namely:

—— *parallelum* (sic). *Vitae Romanorum et Graecorum quadraginta novem in aedibus Philippi Juntae, 27 Aug. 1517. Greek. (Fabricus, p. 295 and E.17412.)*

Of the *Opera Moralia* the following works had appeared in Latin:

—— *de Fortuna Romanorum et Alexandri, Budaeo interprete, apud Oliverium Senant, ex aedibus Ascensianis, Paris, 1505. (Fabricius, p. 221.)*

—— *Apophthegmata regum et imperatorum, et Laconica, latine, Raphaele Regio interprete, Paris, apud Nic. Crispin, 1507, 4°. (Fabricius, p. 219); but of this work Ebert mentions an earlier edition:*

—— *Apophthegmata per Fr. Philelphum e graeco in lat. translata. (Ven.) Vindelinus (de Spira), 1471, 4°. (E.17474.)*

PLUTARCHI. *de Placitis philosophorum, libri V, latine Budaec interprete, Paris, apud Petit, 1505, 4°. (Fabricius, p. 224.)*

—— *de virtutibus mulierum, traductio per Alamanum Ranuntinum. Brix. Bonin de Boninis, 23rd Mart. 1485, 4°. (E.17476.)*

An edition of the whole of the *Moralia* was published in Greek:

—— *Opuscula LXXXXII (moralia, gr.) Ven. Aldus et And Asul. m. Mart, 1509, folio. (E.17404.)*

Fabricius also mentions a Latin edition, which has been lost, but is contained in old lists:

—— *Opera, II voll.*

Of the *Lives*, that of:

'Aemilius Paulus' is probably used in III.16.4, where he is mentioned as having been refused the consulate (see *note 4*); in III.25.4 for his poverty (cp. *note 9*); and almost certainly in III.35.5 for the story of Perseus (cp. *note 5*).

'Agesilaus' compared with Pompey is probably used for the remark in I.10.3 (cp. *note 4*).

'Agis' is used, according to Krappe, in I.9.5, but this I have ventured to question (see *note 8*).

'Alexander' may possibly have been used for the murder of Philip in II.28 (see *note 3*), but more probably Justin.

'Aratus' is used for the description of his peculiarities in II.32.7, (see *note 7*). He is mentioned also in III.5.3 see *note 3*.

'Brutus' is used in III.6.6 (see *note 11*) for the motives which led him and Cassius to murder Caesar; in III.6.33 (see *note 49*) for the events which disturbed the conspirators; in III.18.1 (see *note 2*) for the defeat of Brutus and Cassius; possibly also for the views expressed in D. I.10 (see *note 9*).

'Caesar' may well have been used in I.29.5 for the remarks on Caesar (see *note 6*); in I.33.5 (as well as Cicero) for the rivalry between Caesar and Pompey (cp. *note 3*); in I.34.1 for the remarks on his dictatorship (cp. *note 2*); in I.37.7, which also concerns the rivalry with Pompey (cp. *note 10*); certainly for the details of the murder given in III.6.35 (cp. *note 49*); and for the avenging of his death in III.6.36 (see *note 55*); possibly also for the revolt of the legions in III.13.4 (see *note 8*).

'Cato the Younger' is probably used in III.1.7, see *note 11*.

'Cicero' gives a criticism of Catiline which accords with Machiavelli's in D. I.10, see *note 8*; and is probably used also for his visit to the senate (see III.6.37 and *note 56*) and for his defeat (see III.6, *n. 51*).

Crassus' is almost certainly the source for the remarks on his having been deceived by Parthian promises in III.12.3 (cp. *note 5*).

'Dion' is almost certainly the source for the story of Calippus and Dion in III.6.45 (cp. *note 68*); and probably for the remarks about his good rule in I.10.3 and 17.1.

'Demetrius' is the source for the story of his treatment by Athens in I.59.2, where he is styled, as by Plutarch, the conqueror of cities (cp. *note 1*).

'Gracchus, Tiberius and Caius' may possibly be the source for the remarks about the Gracchi in I.37.9 and elsewhere (see Index *sub* 'Gracchi').

'Lucullus' may have been used in II.19.1 (see *note 2*); but not for III.12.3 (see *note 4*).

'Lycurgus' whose name is frequently mentioned (see Index *sub* 'Lycurgus') in connection with the constitution of Sparta, is probably the source of Machiavelli's information (cp. I.6 *n. 4*; I.11 *n. 8* II.3 *n. 4*).

'Marius' is used for the story of the Minturnian slave in III.6.29 (see *note 37*); also in III.37.6, see *note 8*.

'Pelopidas' may well have been used for the passages in which he is mentioned (see Index *sub* Pelopidas'), but there is a difficulty about the story told in III.6.32, for which see *note 48*.

'Pompey' is probably the source for the story of his end in Egypt, though Plutarch makes a clear distinction between the two Ptolemies, whom Machiavelli confuses (I.59.3 and see *note 2*), but Caesar's remarks on Pompey (in III.13.2) are not based on Plutarch. The early triumph mentioned (in I.60.3) is a point on which Plutarch says much.

'Pyrrhus' is probably used in III.20.2 (*see note 2*).

'Romulus' for the remarks about Romulus (see Index), and cp. I.9, *note 6*.

'Solon' for the remarks about the laws of Athens (see Index *sub* Solon, and cp. I.2 *n. 20*). The story of the ruse used by Pisistratus (cp. D. III.6.39) is also to be found in the Life of Solon (cp. *note 59*).

'Sertorius.' The opening paragraph of this life is suggested by Ellinger (p. 11) as a source for Machiavelli's remarks on recurrent events in I.39.

'Themistocles' may be the source for the story of his proposal to sink the Greek fleet (I.59.7), or alternatively Cicero (see *note 6*); and again for his having taken refuge with Darius (II.31.2 and cp. *note 2*).

'Theseus' contains the legend of the founding of Athens, mentioned in I.1.3 (cp. *note 2*).

'Timoleon' is probably used for the remarks about him in I.10.3 (see *note 5*); in I.17.1, where he is again conjoined with Dion; and again in III.5.3 (see *notes 2 and 4*).

Of the *Moralia* it is certain that Machiavelli had read the '*De Fortuna Romanorum*', for in D. II.1.1 he rejects the view which Plutarch therein expresses on this topic (cp. *note 1*; also 2.Pref. *n. 4*). It is also fairly certain that he had read the '*Praecepta gerendae reipublicae*' for Plutarch's remarks accord with his in regard to calumnies in I.8 (see *note at end*); to the treatment of suspect citizens (I.28.1 and cp. *note 1*); the accepting of lower offices (I.36, and see *note at end*); on the use of slogans (III.34, *n. 6*) and on the readiness of the populace to accept beginners (*ib.*, *note at end*); also on the danger of pretending to be a conspirator (III.6.45), and on taking note of the governed (see III.8, *note at end*).

The remark the Spartan made in regard to the walls of Athens (in II.24.13) is taken from the '*Sayings of the Lacedaemonians*' (see *note 14*). Possibly the '*Mulierum virtutes*' is the source for the story about 'Nelematus' (*sic.*) in III.6.19, but more probably the source here is Justin (see *note 26*).

There is also a fragment entitled '*De unius in republica dominatione, populari statu. et paucorum imperio*', in which these unusual terms replace those ordinarily used, e.g. monarchy, democracy, and oligarchy, and the second term '*popularis status*' is that by which Machiavelli denotes a democracy in D. I.2.4 (see *note c*).

Machiavelli may also have read the short treatise on '*De Cupiditate Divitiarum*' (see III.25, *n. 10*). (For his possible influence on M's method see Introduction, § 98.)

7. PROCOPIUS, a native of Caesaria, became secretary to Belisarius in Constantinople in A.D. 527, and accompanied him on his expeditions to Asia, Africa and Italy. He was made prefect of Constantinople by the Emperor Justinian in A.D. 565, and died a few years later. His work 'on the war Belisarius waged with the Vandals' is quoted in D. II.8.4 (see *note 9*). Ebert gives as the title of the work published in 1509:

PROCOPII, *de bello Gottorum, lat., Cp. Persona interprete, Romae, J. Besicken, 1506, fol.; de bello Persico, lat. Rph. Volaterrano interprete, Romae, Euchar. Silber, 1509, folio.* (*E.17995.*)

But according to Fabricius (VII, p. 557) the edition published in 1509 comprised also the *de bello Vandalico.* Its full title was:

PROCOPIUS CAESARIENSIS. *Libri primores quattuor de bello Persico et Vandalico ex versione Raphaelis Volaterrani, Mario, fratri, inscripta et Romae, 1509, fol. pridem edita, et libri de bello Gothero ex Christophori Personae, Prioris S. Balbinae, interpretatione . . . 1470 primum Fulgini editi sunt, deinde Veneti, 1471.*

It would seem, then, that at least one Latin translation of the '*de bello Vandalico*' had been published. Hence Machiavelli's use of this work cannot be cited as evidence that he knew Greek. Similarly in the case of the '*de bello Persico*', which may possibly be the source for the remark about Cobades in D. II.26.2 (see *note 1*). But the '*Historia arcana*', of which the authenticity is doubtful, was not published until 1623. Hence if Machiavelli did use this work in D. II.30.4, as Krappe thinks, he must have used a manuscript, which would almost certainly be in Greek. But, as I have pointed out in *note 6*, the reasons for supposing that this work was used are very slight. No Latin edition appeared before 1654.

Procopius may have been used also in II.8.5 for Dido (see *note 10*).

8. QUINTUS CURTIUS RUFUS is a writer about whom scarcely anything is known save that he wrote the life of Alexander the Great, a work with which John of Salisbury (d. 1182) was acquainted. Quintilian, who wrote in the first century A.D., refers to a Q. Curtius Rufus, but he may not have been the same person. Niebuhr thinks that he was contemporary with the emperor Septimius Severus, who died in A.D. 211.

Machiavelli mentions him in II.10.2–3 as having maintained that money is the sinews of war, and as having cited the defeat of Agis III by Antipater in support of his contention. The first edition of Q. Curtius Rufus's work was published about 1470, and a Florentine edition appeared in 1507.

CURTIUS RUFUS, Quintus, *De rebus gestis Alexandri M. (ed. Pomp. Laetus) (Romae) G. Lauer, without date (about 1470), large 4°. (E.5524.)*
—— —— —— *Flor. Ph. Giunta, 1507. (E.5530.)*

Between these two editions several others had appeared, namely, a Venetian edition by Vindelinus Spirensis, about 1471 (E. 5525); an edition at Milan by Zarotus in 1481; a Verona edition in 1491; an edition revised by Bm. Merula at Venice in 1494, of which a second edition was published in 1502. In all these early editions the first two books are missing, and though all relate the defeat of Agis III, none give the passage to which Machiavelli refers and which gives rise to the historical difficulty discussed in D. II.10 *n. 2.* There is, however, a passage missing here.

Machiavelli mentions Alexander the Great in other places, for which see Index *sub* 'Alexander the Great', but there is no other reference to Q. Curtius Rufus. He may well have been used, however, for the siege of Tyre in II.27.3 (see *note 3*); and for the conspiracy of Dymnus and Philotas in III.6.14 (see *note 23*).

The English translation of 'Quintus Curtius' *History of the Life and Wars of Alexander the Great, king of Macedon*', in ten books, translated by John Brende, and printed in London in 1561, contains a dedication to 'the highe and myghtye prince, John Duke of Northumberland, Earle, Marshall of Englande'. Since this was written only thirty-four years after Machiavelli's death and expresses in regard to history views which are remarkably like those of Machiavelli, it is worth quoting. John Brende in his Dedication says:

TO THE RIGHT

HYGHE AND MYGHTYE PRINCE, JOHN DUKE OF

Northumberlande, Earle, marshall of Englande,
&c. John Brende wisheth continuall
prosperities, wyth encrease of
honour

Manye have written, and experience besides declareth, how necessary historical knowledge is to all kynd of men, but specially to princes and to others which excel in dignitye or beare aucthorytye in eny commune wealth: the same beynge counted the most excellent kynde of knowledge, the chiefest parte of civyl prudence, and the mirrour of mans lyfe. There is required in all magistrates both a faith and feare in God, and also an outwarde policye in worldly thynges, whereof as the one is to be learned by ye scryptures, so the other must chiefly be gathered by readyng of histories. For in them men may see the groundes and beginnynges of commen wealthes, the causes of their encrease, of their prosperous mayntenance, and good preseruation: and againe by what meanes they decreased, decayed, and came to ruyne. There the vertues and vices of men do appeare, how by theyr good doynges they florished, and by their evil actes they decayed. How they prospered so long as they mainteined justice, persecuted vice, used clemencye & mercye, were liberal, religyous, vertuous, and voyde of covetnousness. And, contrariwyse, howe they fell into manifold calamityes, miseries, & troubles, when they embraced vice and forsoke vertue. In histories it is apparant how dangerous it is to begyn alteracyons in a comen wealth. How enmitye and hatreds oft rising upon final causes, have ben the destruction of great kyngdomes. And that disobeyers of hygher powers & suche as rebellyed agaynst magystrates, never escapyd punyshment, nor came to good end. In theym there be precydentys for all cases that may happen, in following the good, in escguing the evil, in avoidyng inconveniences, & in forsey-ing mischiefes. In them may be learned how to temper in prosperitie, how to endure in adversytye, & after what maner men should use them selves both in tyme of peace & warre.

> Preface to Quintus Curtius's *History of the Life and Wars of Alexander the Great, king of Macedon,* in ten books, translated by John Brende, London, printed 1561.

9. SALLUST was born in 86 B.C., the year in which Marius died; accompanied

Caesar in his African war in 46, and on his return wrote his history of Catiline's conspiracy, which took place in 63. This was followed by his history of the war with Jugurtha, king of Numidia, 111–106 B.C. He died in 34 B.C.

Machiavelli cites the *Bellum Catilinarium* in D. I.46.2 (see *note 4*); also without acknowledgment in D. II.2.2 (see *note 12* and cp. D. I.58.7). He mentions it in D. III.6.37 as the source for the account he gives of the conspiracy of Catiline in this chapter (see *note 56*). To the *Bellum Jugurthinum* there is a reference in D. II.8.1 (see note 2). Cp. also D. I.5, *note at end*; D. I.37, *note 4*; and D. II.29, *note 1*.

The *editio princeps* of both these works was published in 1470 at Venice, but it is more probable that Machiavelli used the Florentine editions, of which there were two.

SALLUSTIUS, *Caj. Crispius. De bello Catilinario et de bello Jugurthino. (Ven.) Vindelinus de Spira, 1470, large 4°. (E.19935.)*

—— *ib. Florence apud S. Jacobum di Ripoli, 1478, 4°. (E.19952.)*

—— *ib. Florence, Ph. Junta, 6 cal. Feb. 1503, 8° (E.19963.)*

The Jugurthan war may well have been used in regard to avoiding contempt and hatred in III.23 (see *note 3*); and the Catiline war has been suggested by Ellinger as a source for D. III.1, on returning to basic principles (Ellinger, p. 19).

10. TACITUS, who was the contemporary and friend of the younger Pliny, held office under Vespasian, Titus, Domitian, and Nerva, and may still have been living in the second century A.D., is mentioned by Machiavelli in three discourses. His *Histories* IV.3.7, are cited in D. I.29.1 (in Latin). A saying which occurs in the speech of Marcellus (*Hist.* IV.8) is mentioned in D. III.6.1. And in D. III.19.1 there occurs what purports to be a quotation from Tacitus: '*In multitudine regenda plus poena quam obsequium valet*', but in the only passage in which Tacitus compares *poena* with *obsequium*, he says just the opposite, namely, in the *Annals* III.55.5 (see *III.19, n. 2*). All the works of Tacitus had been published in Machiavelli's time, but the first five books of the *Annals* were not published until 1515.

TACITUS, *C. Corn. Annalium et historiarum libri superstites. (This work contains the last 6 books of the* Annals *and the first 5 of the* Histories*). Without place or date (Ven. Vindelin. de Spira, 1470), folio. (E.22134.) An edition of this work was also published at Milan in 1475. (E.22135.)*

—— *Libri quinque noviter inventi atque cum reliquis ejus operibus editi (a Ph. Beroaldo). Romae. St. Guillereti, cal. Mart. 1515, folio (E.22138.) This edition contained all the works of Tacitus.*

The passage D. I.10.8 is taken almost verbatim from the *Histories* I.2. The *Annals,* XV.68, are quoted in Latin in D. II.26.6, but the quotation is not ascribed to Tacitus. A quotation from the *Annals* (XIII.19) also occurs toward the end of P. 13, but is not referred to Tacitus. It has bearing on the theme of II.11 (see *note at end*). The *Annals* Book XV, are used for the Pisonian conspiracy in III.6.13, 15, 20 and 22, *and notes in loc.*; and the *Histories* for Antonius Primus in I.29, see *note 3*. The *Germania* may also have been read, for it has bearing on the migrations mentioned in II.8 and the incursions of German tribes mentioned in II.30.4, see *note 6*. The main source for this topic is, however, Procopius, and possibly also Blondus.

11. THUCYDIDES, the historian of the Peloponnesian war in which he played a prominent part in 424 B.C., is mentioned in III.16.1 and used there for the account

given of Nicias's opposition to the expedition to Sicily. He is also mentioned in A.W. III (B. 317; F. p. 81) as having said that the Spartans made use of flutes in their armies. Thucydides is the source for the massacre in Coryra (II.2.5, and see *note 6*); also for the story of Themistocles in II.31.2 (see *note 2*); and again perhaps for remarks about the constitution of Sparta in I.2.2 (see *note 4*), and in I.6.4 (see *note 4*). There are also several passages in which Machiavelli expresses views which agree with those of Thucydides. First there is the question of method, which has been discussed in the Introduction, § 98. Machiavelli may also have been influenced by Thucydides in what he says about the suspicion aroused by those who give advice in I.28 and I.53 (cp. *notes at end of these discourses*); about the troubles to which revolutions gave rise owing to ambition in I.46 (see *note at end*); about the folly of driving people too hard in II.23 (see *note at end*, and cp. III.12.2 and *note 2*); about the need to adapt oneself to the times in III.9 (see *note at end*); possibly also in his remarks on stratagems in III.40 (*see note at end*). For his method see Introduction, § 98.

Thucydides' works were translated into Latin and published about 1485.

THUCYDIDES. *historiar. Peloponnensium, libri VIII. lat. interprete Lr. Valla. Without place or date (Ven. about 1485), folio. (E.22946.)*

12. XENOPHON, the Greek historian, who was present at the battle of Delium in 424 B.C., and was still alive in 357 B.C., wrote two works of which Machiavelli, like other writers of the period, makes frequent use, namely, the *Cyropaedeia*, which is cited in II.13.1 and in III.20.3; 22.6; and 39.1; and the *de Tyrannide*, more commonly known as *Hiero*, which is cited in II.2.3. The *Cyropaedeia* is also mentioned in P. 14, towards the end. Xenophon's treatise *de Venatione* may also have been known to Machiavelli, for he speaks of Xenophon's views on hunting in III.39.2; but Xenophon treats of hunting also in the *Cyropaedeia* (cp. III.39.1 and *note 1*). Xenophon's works were published in Latin in 1490:

XENOPHONTIS. *Opera in hoc volumine impressa: 'Xenophon de Venatione' per Omnibonum (Leonicenum) Vincentinum in latinum traductus. 'Xenophontis liber de republica et de legibus Lacaedaemoniorum', Franc. Philelfus e graeco traduxit. 'Xenophontis oratio de regis Agesilai Lacedaemoniorum laudibus', per Philelfum traducta. 'Xenophontis apologia pro Socrate', per Ln. Aretinum in lat. conversa. 'Xenophontis opusculum de tyrannide', per Ln. Aretinum traductum. 'Xenophontis libellis de aequivocis'. 'Paedia Cyri Persarum regis' (interprete Fr. Philelfo).— Without place or date (Ven. about 1490), folio. (E.24128.)*

Ph. Beroaldus caused this translation to be printed afresh in 1502 (Bonon Bd. Hector, 1502, folio). There was also a translation of the *Anabasis* by Lampus Biragus, published about 1462, but now lost.

Ellinger suggests that the *Hipparchicus*, IV.13 and V, may have been used in III.12 on the pressure of necessity; and that the *Hiero*, 8–9, may have suggested to Machiavelli that monarchy would be the best remedy for Italy (Ellinger, pp. 23 and 40).

13. VIRGIL is quoted three times in the *Discourses* and once in *The Prince*. The *Aeneid* VI.813 is quoted in D. I.21.3, and I.155 in D. I.54.1. The third quotation, '*furor arma ministrat*' (*Aeneid* I.150) occurs in D. II.24.2 in conjunction with a few words from Juvenal. The quotation in P. 17 is from *Aeneid* I. 563. Virgil's works were published at Rome in 1469, and a Florentine edition appeared in 1510.

VIRGILIUS, Maro. *Opera et Catalecta. Romae. Sweynheym et Arn. Pannartz, without date (1469), small folio. Probably the first edition. (E.23632.)*
—— *Vergilius. Flor. Ph. de Giunta, 6 cal. Dec. 1510, 8°. (E.23668.)*

14. JUVENAL is quoted three times: the *Satires* VI.291–2 in D. II.19.8; the *Satires* VIII.124 in D. II.24.2, in conjunction with the quotation from Virgil, but without mention of Juvenal's name *('Spoliatis arma supersunt')*; and the *Satires* X.112–13 in D. III.6.6. The first edition of Juvenal's works was published in the same year as the first edition of Virgil's.
JUVENALIS, *Decimus Junius. Satirarum Liber. Without place. (Ven. Vindelinus de Spira) 1470, large 4°. (E.11188.)*
Another edition was published in Rome by U. Gallus, also in 1470 (E.11189), and a Florentine edition in 1513 by Ph. de Giunta, 8° (E.11220).

15. DANTE (1265–1321) is cited twice. A few lines from *Il Purgatorio, Canto VII.121–23*, on heredity are cited in I.11.5 (see *note 12*) and in I.53.2 a few words which purport to come from his *'Discourse on Monarchy'*, are cited: *'Vive la sua morte! e Muoia la sua vita'*. Actually they are to be found, not in the *'de Monarchia'*, which was not printed until 1559, but in the *'Convivio'* which was published in 1490. The *'de Monarchia'* existed only in manuscript in Machiavelli's time (unless there was some printed edition of which all trace has been lost), but from the fact that he mentions it we may infer that he had seen a copy. The early printed editions of the *Divina Commedia* and the *Convivio* were:
DANTE ALIGHIERI. *Comincia la comedia di Dante Alleghieri di Fiorenze nella quale tracta delle pene et punitioni de uicii et demeriti et premii delle virtu. (Foligno). J. Numeister, 1472, folio. (E.5680.)*
—— —— *la medes., col commento di Cp. Landino. Fir. N. (Todescho) di Lorenzo della Magna, 30 Aug. 1481, large folio. (E.5687.)*
—— —— *Commedia di Dante insieme con uno dialogo (di Ant. Manetti) circo el sito, forma et misure dello inferno. Fir. Ph. di Giunta, Aug. 1506, 8°. (E.5696.)*
—— *Convivio di Dante Alighieri. Fir. Fr. Bonaccorsi, 20 Sept. 1490—First Ed. (E.5745.)*

16. LORENZO DE' MEDICI (1448–92) is quoted in D. III.29.2, a chapter which claims that the faults of peoples are due to their rulers. The quotation, which is from the *'Rappresentazione di S. Giovanni e Paolo'*, bears this out. This work had been published in Florence during Machiavelli's lifetime, prior to 1500.
MEDICI, *Lr de'. Rappresentazione de SS. Giovanni e Paolo e di S. Costanza, Fir., Fr. Bonaccorsi, without date (but probably about 1490), 4°. (E.13537.)*
The reference given to this work by A. H. Gilbert in *Machiavelli's 'Prince' and Its Forerunners*, p. 44, is to the edition of Lorenzo de' Medici's works, published at Bari in 1914.

17. FLAVIUS BLONDUS is mentioned in III.27.5, where Machiavelli writes that to the fact that the encouragement of party strife in another city tends to produce divisions in your own, *Il Biondo* bears witness when he says of the Florentines that 'in their endeavour to restore unity to Pistoia, the Florentines themselves became divided'. Blondus was secretary to four popes, Eugenius IV, Nicholas V,

Callixtus III, and Pius II, to whom he dedicated his 'Roma Triumphans', and who in turn wrote an Epitome of his 'Decades Tres'. He died in Rome in 1463 at the age of 75. All his works had been published before the close of the fifteenth century, and copies of the early editions are to be found in Bodley, as well as of the Italian translations, which were not, however, published until after Machiavelli's death. I cite the editions in Bodley, which I have actually consulted:

BLONDUS, FLAVIUS, FORLIVIENSIS, *Roma instaurata, cum opusculo de gestis Venetorum, Verona, Bonin de Boninis, 1481, folio.*

—— —— —— *Roma triumphans, Brixiae, per Barth. Vercellensem, 1482, folio.*

—— —— —— *Italia illustrata, Roma in domo Phil. de Lignamine, 1474, folio (and another edition by Bonin de Boninis at Verona in 1482).*

—— —— —— *Historiarum ab inclinatione Romanorum imperii una cum abbreviatione Pii papae super eandem historiam. Ven. per Th. Alexandrinum, 1484, folio (and another edition, entitled 'Historiarum Romanorum Decades Tres'. Ven. Octav. Scotus, 1483, folio).*

I have spent many days perusing these five works by Flavius Blondus, and have come to the conclusion that in connection with Machiavelli they are of far more importance than is commonly supposed. *Roma Illustrata* contains a description of the various regions of Italy, and gives a brief account of their more important towns and of the events with which they are associated. *Roma Instaurata* is dedicated to Eugenius IV and contains an account, in part historical, in part descriptive, of the monuments, gates, and churches then existent in Rome, many of which had recently been restored. The *de (Origine et) Gestis Venetorum* is a short work, comprising but 13 pages, and is contained in the same volume as those just mentioned, in the Verona edition of *Roma Instaurata*, published by Bonin de Boniniis in 1481. It is dedicated to Franciscus Foscari, doge and senator, and gives an all-too-brief account of the history of Venice. These three works are comparatively small and to the student of Machiavelli are of minor importance. But it is otherwise when we turn to *Roma Triumphans*; for this work, which is dedicated to Pius II, who became Pope only three years before Blondus died, was written, as we are told in the preface, at a time when the Pope was gathering together the forces of Europe for a crusade against the Turks, and its aim is to explain how pagan Rome became triumphant, in the hope that the Pope by emulating Rome's methods may himself become triumphant. Hence the title. The contents are yet more remarkable. For the author divided his work (which contains ten books in all) under five main headings, in four of which he ascribes the greatness of Rome to precisely the same causes as Machiavelli does, namely, (i) to Rome's religion (Books 1 and 2); (ii) to her administration (Books 3 to 5); (iii) to her military discipline (Books 6 and 7); (iv) to her customs and institutions (Books 8 and 9); and then in (v) he describes her triumph (Book 10). The scheme is the same as Machiavelli's save that, for Blondus, Rome's greatness continued under the rule of the Emperors, and, in accounting for it, he cites events which happened not only in the time of the Republic, but also in that of the Empire.

The fifth work, though written before *Roma Triumphans*, in a sense completes it, for, as its title indicates, it deals with 'the decline of the Empire of the Romans' *(Historia ab inclinatione Romanorum imperii)*, and continues its history down to the time at which it was written. Rome's greatness, according to Blondus, began to wane after the death of Theodosius the Great in A.D. 395, when the Empire was divided between his sons and the invasions of Goths and Vandals began. Pius II regarded this work of such importance that of it he wrote an epitome, entitled: '*Abbreviatio Pii Pont. Max. supra Decades Blondi at inclinatione imperii usque ad tempora Joannis Vicessimi tertii, Pont. Max.*' This work is printed in the edition of the '*Historiae*' cited above. Blondus's work is divided into three Decades (or Books), each of them subdivided into 10 Libri (or long chapters), save the last, which contains 11. The period covered by the three decades, from 400 to 1415, is the period from which Machiavelli selects a number of incidents for which no source has been assigned. Of all, or almost all of them, the Gothic and Vandal invasions, the Saracens and the Tartars, Gregory the Great, Charles the Great, Louis XI, Carmignuola and the *condottieri*, and the history of Venice, Florence, Milan, and other cities in Tuscany and Lombardy, are all dealt with at considerable length. Hence for the events listed in TABLE v, from 400 to 700, and in TABLE VI, from 700 to 1415, this work of Blondus may well be the source on which Machiavelli relies. Anyhow, a comparison of what Blondus says about the events to which Machiavelli refers with what Machiavelli himself says would well repay careful study. A comparative study of Blondus' explanation of Rome's rise and fall with the account Machiavelli gives of it is also much to be desired, especially as Tommasini has shown that for numerous passages in *The History of Florence*, Machiavelli is dependent on the *Decads* of Blondus (*N. Machiavelli e suoi tempi*, Vol. III, pp. 215, 221–7, 231–69).

Blondus also wrote a second very short work on Venice, which has been published by Bartolommeo Nogara in *Studi e Testi*, n. 48, pp. 77–88. It is entitled *In Populi Veneti Historiam*. But neither this work nor the *De Gestis Venetorum* has been used by Machiavelli, so far as I can discover.

B. AUTHORS AND WORKS NOT MENTIONED, BUT CERTAINLY USED, IN THE 'DISCOURSES'

1. POLYBIUS (205–123 B.C.) was one of the noble Achaeans sent to Rome after the conquest of Macedonia in 168 B.C. He lived there in honourable captivity, but journeyed to Greece, Asia Minor, Egypt, northern Italy, and southern France in search of materials for his histories, the purport of which was to show why the whole of the civilised world had fallen under the dominion of Rome. Though the author is not mentioned by name, Polybius undoubtedly exercised a great influence on Machiavelli and more quotations from his work occur in the *Discourses* than from any other writer, save Livy. Polybius's words are actually cited, or better, perhaps, paraphrased only in D. I.2, and all the passages there used are taken from Polybius, Book VI. But dependence on Polybius is not restricted to this chapter, nor confined to Book VI. Other passages occur which correspond to what Polybius says in the earlier books. Those which concern method have been given in the Introduction, §§ 85 and 96, and the correspondence between the structure of Machiavelli's opening chapters, D. I.1–15 and that of Polybius, Book VI, has been pointed out in the Introduction, §§ 62–3.

Machiavelli had undoubtedly read Polybius, Book VI, or at least a summary of this book, for it is from this book that passages used in D. I.2 are taken. Yet—apparently—no translation of Book VI had been published in Machiavelli's day. Of Books I to V several Latin editions existed, namely:

POLYBII *historiar. libri superstites e graeco in lat. sermonem conversi a N. Perotto, Roma, Sweynheym et Pannartz, die ultima decembris, 1473, folio. (E.17703.)*
—— *Nicolai Perotti in Polybii historiarum libros proemium—libri quinque N. Perottus e Graeco traduxit. Ven. Bernardinus, Venetiis, 1498.*
Mentioned by Ebert (17703), and by Fabricius in *Bibl. Graec.* IV. p. 321.
—— *Historiarum reliquiae in Latium* (sic) *conversi linguam, Nicolao Perotto interprete. Ed. Aldinae Livii, 1520.*

Though none of these editions mentions Book VI, which is a kind of appendix to the first five books, and deals with the constitution of Rome, it is almost certain that Perottus knew of Book VI, and possible that he gave a summary of it in the *'proemium'* mentioned in the 1498 edition, though I have not been able to verify this. Anyhow, in the Catalogue of the Greek Codices preserved in the Laurentian Library in Florence, there is a codex (Pluteus LXIX), entitled:

Cod. IX. POLYBII *Historiarum Libri V cum notatis ad oram libri manu ut videntur Angeli Politiani. (Also) ex sexto Libro de Romanorum reipublicae principio et incremento, adhuc autem et ejus florenti statu ac differentia ab aliis.*

This manuscript is mentioned by Fabricius (*Bibl. Graec.,* IV, p. 319).

It is almost certain that Machiavelli would have known of it, and quite likely it is the manuscript he used, either translating it himself (if he knew Greek) or getting some friend to do it for him. But as to why he does not mention the author I have no suggestion to make, unless it be that he himself had discovered the manuscript and decided to appropriate its contents as if he himself were the author.

In the notes I have called attention to passages in the *Discourses* which correspond to passages in Polybius, and have given a translation of the passages in question. Most, but not all, come from Book VI, and the correspondence is most exact in D. I.2, where the citations follow one another in much the same order in which they occur in Polybius. But there are numerous other passages in which a correspondence between what Polybius says and what Machiavelli writes, is noticeable. Thus I.7 may have been used in II.20 (see *note 4*); I.14 in II.Pref. (see *note 1*); I.33–4 in II.18 (see *note 8*); I.35 in III.30 (see *note 8*); and I.65 *sq.* on mercenaries in III.32 (see *note 2*). Book II.26 *sq.* is of special importance as throwing light on the defeat of the Gauls referred to in II.1.3 and II.8.2 (see II.1, *n. 2,* and II.8 *n. 7*). II.39 on the rise of democracy in Greece may have been used in I.28 (see *note 2*); and II.43 on Aratus in III.5 (see *note 3*). With Book III there are correspondencies in II.Pref. with III.31 (see *note 2*); with III.81 *sq.* perhaps in III.40 (see *note 4*); with III.87 on Fabius Maximus, see III.49, *n. 6*; and with III.92 in III.40.2 (*n. 2*).

In regard to Book VI: for the Preface see I.1 *nn. 1 and 11*, and on equanimity III.31, *note at end*. For VI.3 see I.Pref. *n. 2*. For VI.5 see II.5, *n.5* on the wiping out of records. For VI.10 on Sparta see I.5, *n. 1*. For VI.14 on punishment by the people see I.7, *n. 1*. For VI.43 on Thebes see I.17; *n. 10*, and I.21 *n. 3*. For VI.48 on the authority of Lycurgus see I.9, *n. 1*. For VI.48 on the tranquillity of Sparta see I.6 *n. 5*, and on her decline see I.6, *n. 8*. For VI.49 on the coinage of Sparta see II.3 *n. 5*. The argument of VI.48–52 resembles closely that of Machiavelli in I.6. For VI.52 on mercenaries see II.20, *note at end*. For VI.53–6 on Rome's religion see I.11, *n. 2, n. 3 and 5*; I.12, *n. 4*; and I.15, *note at end*. For VI.57 on internal and external causes of decay see II.1, *note 3*; on the inevitability of class-conflict see I.3, *n. 1*; and on the opening words about growth and decay see II.Pref., *n. 3*. VI.57, in short, summarises neatly Machiavelli's view on the inevitability and the course of constitutional change. See also Introduction § 97 for his influence on M's method.

The references to Polybius may be looked up in Schuchburgh's translation, but I have not adopted this translation. My translations are based on the Latin version by Firmin-Didot (Paris, 1880).

2. HERODOTUS, the Greek historian (d. *circa* 425 B.C.), is almost certainly the source for the advice given by Croesus to Cyrus when he proposed to make war on Tomyris (D. II.12.1 and see *note 1*); and for the conspiracy of Ortanes against Smerdis, the pseudo-magus (D. III.6.19, and cp. *note 27*). Again, if Machiavelli has confused Sitalces, king of Thrace, with Cypselus of Corinth, as I have suggested in D. III.6, *n. 38,* then Herodotus is the source for the story of the conspirators who were put off by the graciousness of their reception (D. III.6.29). He may also be the source for what Machiavelli says about crucifixion in D. I.31.1 (see *note 3*); and again for the success of Athens after the Pisistratidae had been expelled, which is mentioned in D. I.58.7 and D. II.2.2 (see *note 3* to D. II.2). See, too, the note at end of D. I.43.

The *editio princeps* of Herodotus was published by Aldus in 1502; but a Latin translation of his works had appeared before this, namely:

HERODOTI *traductio e graeco in latinum habita per Lr. Vallensem. Ven. Jac. Rubens. 1474, folio (E.9559); which was followed by another translation published in Rome in domo Pt. de Maximis, 1475 (E.9560).*

3. JUSTIN, the historian, about whose life nothing is known, about whose date all we know is that it was not later than the fifth century A.D., and who used often to be confused with Justin Martyr, is certainly a source well known to Machiavelli and upon which he frequently draws. He is quoted in D. I.26.2, apropos of Philip II of Macedon, but not by name. The story of the quarrel between the populace and the nobles in Heraclea, of which Clearchus availed himself (D. I.16.7) is told by Justin in XVI.4-5 (see *note 6*). The story of the assault on Pausanias and his murdering Philip II of Macedon is also taken in all probability from Justin IX.6 (see D. II.28.3 and cp. *note 3*). The murder is mentioned again in D. III.6.7 (cp. *note 13*), and Clearchus is again referred to in D. III.6.32 (cp. *note 45*). In both cases the story told accords with the account given by Justin. The story of Hanno's conspiracy, told in D. III.6.38 and 40 is also based on Justin (cp. *notes 57 and 61*). So, too, in all probability is Justin the source for the remark about Thebes having called in a Spartan army (D. III.6.40 and see *note 62*). In the same chapter, D. III.6.32, the substitution of Diocles' name for that of Hipparchus is almost certainly due to Justin, who in II.9 makes the same mistake (see *note 44*). Justin is also the source for Machiavelli's account of the invasion of Greece by Gauls after the death of Alexander in II.10.5, *see note 8.*

Several editions of Justin's *Histories* were published prior to 1510, when there appeared a Florentine edition:

JUSTINUS. *Justini historici clarissimi in Troggi. Pompeji historias, ll. 44, Ven. N. Jenson, 1470, large 4°. (E.11113.)*

A Roman edition by U. Gallus was published in 1470-1, and another by Sweynheym and Pannartz in 1472; a Milan edition in 1474. Then the Florentine edition:

JUSTINUS *una cum L. Floro nuper castigatus (a Mariano Tuccio). Flor, Ph de Giunta, 3 Cal. Feb. 1510, 8°. (E.11125.)*

4. LUCIAN's *Charon* is the source for the story of Croesus in II.10.2 (see *note 7*). A Latin edition of his works was published in 1470, and another edition, translated by Erasmus and Thomas More in 1516:

LUCIANUS. *Dialogi VI, scil. Charon, etc. . . . lat Rinuccio et J. Aurispa interprete. Without place or date. (Romae, G. Lauer, 1470–2). 4°. (E.12418.)*

—— *Opuscula. (lat.) Erasmo Rot. (et Th. Moro) interprete. Ven. Ald. et And. socer, m Majo 1516, 8°. (E.12416.)*   •

5. SUETONIUS, who wrote numerous works in the early years of the second century A.D., is chiefly celebrated for his lives of the Caesars, of which no less than 15 editions were published prior to 1500. I give three of them below, one published in Florence in 1510:

SUETONIUS *Tranquillus, Caius. De XII Caesarum vitis libri XII. Romae, in pinea regione via Papae (per J. Ph. di Lignamine), mense sextili, 1470, folio. (E.21884.)*

An edition by Sweynheym and Pannartz appeared in Rome in the same year. (E.21885.)

—— *de vita XII Caesarum. Flor. Ph. Junta, 1510, 8°. (E.219898.)*

The lives of the Emperors were so well known that Machiavelli can scarce have failed to consult them, but there is only one passage in the *Discourses* in which he appears clearly to have used them, namely, in D. III.13.2 for the remarks alleged to have been made by Julius Caesar in regard to his battles with Pompey and with Afranius and Petreius in Spain (cp. *note 3*). Possibly also for the revolt of the legions in III.13.4 (see *note 8*).

6. VALERIUS MAXIMUS, who wrote, probably in the first century A.D., a treatise in 9 books on the doings and sayings of distinguished men, classifies them under various heads, and it may well be that this method of collecting examples illustrative of particular virtues and vices, etc., suggested to Machiavelli the idea of illustrating in this way his maxims and theorems (cp. *Introduction, § 92*). In the discourse on poverty (D. III.25) two of the persons cited by Machiavelli as examples, Marcus Atilius Regulus and Paulus Aemilius, are also used by Valerius Maximus to illustrate this virtue (cp. *notes 8 and 10*). See also I.14, *note 4*, and I.29, *note 8*.

The popularity of Valerius Maximus, whose work was used by numerous writers as a quarry in which to dig for examples, is indicated by the fact that no less than 14 editions were printed before 1490. Of these the *editio princeps* appeared in 1470:

VALERIUS maximus. *Factorum et dictorum memorabilium, libri IX. Without place or date (Arg. J. Mentelin, about 1470), folio. (E.23303.)*

A second edition was brought out in 1471, and in the same year appeared a Venetian edition by Vindelimus de Spira (E.23304). The first critical edition was published by Aldus, Venice, 1502, 8°.

7. VITRUVIUS, whose famous treatise on architecture is dedicated to Caesar, i.e. presumably Caesar Augustus, but about whose life little is known apart from what he says about himself in his work, is used—directly or indirectly—by Machiavelli

for the story told in I.1.10 about the proposal of Deinocrates to build a city in honour of Alexander on Mount Athos (see *note 8*).

Several editions of his works existed in Machiavelli's time, including one published at Florence in 1513.

VITRUVIUS, Pollio, M. *de architectura libri X (ex rec. J. Sulpicii Verulani), without place or date. (Romae, G. Herolt, about 1486), folio. Vacant spaces left for filling in Greek quotations. (E.23823.)*

—— —— *de architectura libri X. Without printer's name. Flor. 1496, folio. (E.23824.)*

A Venetian edition by J. de Tridino was published in 1511 (E.23825), and a Florentine edition by Ph. de Giunta in 1513.

8. ST. THOMAS AQUINAS and the *de Regimine Principum*.

(i) Machiavelli's knowledge of the doctrine of matter and form and his thesis that all states should look to the common good may have been derived direct from Aristotle, or from St. Thomas or, again, from any scholastic writer who follows the Aristotelian tradition. He was doubtless also familiar with some, if not all, of the numerous treatises which bore the title *de Regimine Principum* or an equivalent title, and which were much read in his own time, for in the opening words of P. 15 he calls attention to the fact that many have written about the way in which a prince should behave toward subjects and toward friends. (Cp. the Introduction to Gilbert's work *'Machiavelli's "Prince" and its Forerunners,'* which deals with 'The History of Books of Advice to Princes'. What Gilbert says here of Pontanus' *de Principe* may be said of all such works: 'Similarities there are, but they are features common to the type, not the necessary result of contact between the two works' (*op. cit.*, p. 11). In regard to the *de Regimine Principum* of Aquinas, however, the case is otherwise, as I shall presently proceed to show.

(ii) The opuscula of St. Thomas Aquinas, of which the *de Regimine Principum (seu de Rege et Regno ad regem Cypri)* is one, were published at Milan *'per Magistros Benignum et Johannem Antonium de Honate, 1488 in fol.'* The authority for this is J. G. T. Graesse in his *Nouveau Dictionnaire Bibliographique*, Vol. VI, pp. 140-1, in which he also mentions three early editions of this work, namely:

THOMAS DE AQUINO. *de Regimine principis. Without place or date (Col. Arn Therhoernen), in 4º.*

—— *Liber de rege et regno ad regem Cypri. Without place or date (Col. Arnoldus Therhoerem), in 4º.*

—— *De Regimine principis, de regimine Judaeorum, etc. Parisiis in aedibus Ascensianis. Jo. Parvus, 1509, in 8º.*

(iii) Of the *de Regimine Principum* only the first Book and the first four chapters of the second were written by St. Thomas (A.D. 1265-6). The rest is by a continuator, Ptolemy of Lucca. Similarly of the *Commentaries on Aristotle's Politics* in four books, only the first two and Book III up to *Lectio VI* were written by St. Thomas (*circa* 1269); the rest is by Peter of Auvergne. The first thing that strikes one about these two works is that the *Lectiones* and chapters are headed by theorems, as in the *Discourses* but not as in *The Prince*. With some of these theorems, moreover, Machiavelli is in whole-hearted agreement. For instance, Book I, *Lectio III* of the *Politicorum (seu de Rebus Civilibus)* is headed *Quod aliquibus natura servire conveniat, aliquibus autem dominari* (cp. D. I.4.2 and 5.3 on contrary dispositions, and D. III.8 on taking due note of the governed). *Lectio VIII* states that *Acquisitio pecuniarum finita est,* but that if it go beyond the necessaries of life it becomes *infinita et praeter naturam* (cp. II.Pref.7 on the insatiability of human appetites). Book II, *Lect. XII* is headed *Quod leges, etiam minus bonae, non sint facile immutandae* (with which cp. the chapter on Retrospective Laws—D. I.37). The heading of Book III, *Lect. III: non est idem bonum civem et bonum virum esse,* is a theorem basic to the distinction Machiavelli makes between political and ordinary morality. That of Book III, *Lect. V: Quod civitas sit liberorum hominum societas, cujus finis est utilitas communis, in quam omnis administratio publica tendere debet,* defines precisely what Machiavelli means by a republic.

(iv) The *de Regimine,* Book I, cap. 3, is headed *Quod regimen tyranni est pessimum.* Its opening words are: *Sicut autem regimen regis est optimum, ita regimen tyranni est pessimum,* with which cp. the heading of D. I.10: 'Those who set up a tyranny are no less blameworthy than are the founders of a republic or of a kingdom praiseworthy.' The application of the doctrine of matter and form to politics is also to be found in the *de Regimine,* namely in IV.8 where the continuator says that, 'if a form of government is to be changed, it should be borne in mind that countries differ alike with respect to their inhabitants and with respect to the way they live (their *modus vivendi)',* and that in consequence 'the form of government *(regimen et dominium)* should be adapted to the character of the people, as Aristotle says in the *Politics.* For some provinces are servile by nature and such provinces should be governed by an autocrat, including under the head of autocrat a king. Whereas those who are strong-minded alike in moral courage and in the trust they place in their own judgment, can be ruled only where there is a civic constitution *(principatu politico),* under which head is to be included an aristocracy.' With which compare what Machiavelli says in the chapter which is headed: 'He who would transform a republic should take due note of the governed' (III.8). Compare, too, what the continuator says about Italy's love of liberty with what Machiavelli says about it, and especially about Tuscany in D. I.55.8. In Italy especially, says the continuator, civic constitutions flourish. If you want to introduce an autocracy, it can only be done by tyrants. In the islands there have always been tyrants; but in northern Italy *(Liguria, Aemilia, et Flaminia quae hodie Lombardia vocatur)* no principality can perpetuate itself unless it be a tyranny, with the exception of the Doge of Venice, *qui tamen temperatum habet regimen* (IV.8; and cp. the contrast drawn in D. III.12.3 between the neighbours of Venice and those of Florence, and for Venice see D. I.35.2; 49.5; 55.10).

(v) Two other theorems, basic to Machiavelli's standpoint, are also to be found —somewhat surprisingly perhaps—in the *de Regimine Principum.* Machiavelli claims in II.29 that Rome's chastisement in 390 B.C., when she was taken by the Gauls, and her subsequent recovery, which paved the way to her future greatness, were decreed by 'fortune' or, as we should say, by providence. He also claims in II.1 that the principal cause of her Empire was virtue. In the *de Regimine* this topic is discussed in four chapters; in Book III, c. 4: *qualiter dominium Romanum fuit a Deo provisum propter zelum patriae;* c. 5: *qualiter Romani meruerunt dominium propter leges sanctissimas quas tradiderunt;* c. 6: *quomodo concessum est eis dominium a Deo propter ipsorum civilem benevolentiam;* and in c. 7 which ascribes disasters also to the providence of God. Furthermore, the main theme of the third Book of the *Discourses* which deals with the example set by Rome's great men, is also to be found in the *de Regimine,* in III.16: *ubi sanctus Doctor declarat quod isto modo aucta fuit respublica per exempla antiquorum Romanorum.*

(vi) Turning now to particular points in regard to which there is, or may be, a direct dependence on the *de Regimine,* we have first of all in D. III.12.1 the statement that 'some moral philosophers in their writings have remarked that neither of the two most noble instruments to which man's nobility is due, his hands and his tongue, would have attained such perfection in their work if they had not been driven to it by necessity'. In the *de Regimine,* I.1, we are told that 'whereas nature provides other animals with food, a covering of hair, and means of protection, such as teeth, horns, nails, or anyhow speed in flight, man is so constituted that nature provides none of these things, but, instead, he is endowed with reason, whereby he can prepare them all *by using his hands'.* . . . 'But for one man to do all this is impossible. Hence it is *necessary* that he should live in society, that one may be helped by another and different men use reason to discover different things, e.g., one medicine, another something else, and yet another something further. This is also made perfectly plain by the fact that it is peculiar to man to use *speech,* whereby one man is able adequately to express his ideas to others.' The essential points, the use of hands and of tongue, the arts which result, and the necessity which drives men to co-operate, are all there, and man's nobility is implied by the distinction drawn between his mode of life and that of other animals. Aristotle makes similar remarks in *Politics* I.2, but there is no corresponding passage.

(vii) The second book of the *De Regimine Principum* opens with a remark based on Vegetius which is wholly in accord with what Machiavelli says in D. I.1 about the founders of cities, and in I.10.1 and elsewhere about those who have founded republics and kingdoms. St. Thomas writes: *'Nam sicut Vegetius dicit, potentissimae nationes et principes nominati nullam majorem potuerunt gloriam assequi quam aut fundare novas civitates, aut ab aliis conditas in nomen suum sub quadam amplificatione transferre.'* He then goes on in this and the next chapter to discuss the question of sites, a topic with which Machiavelli deals in D. I.1. Both hold that a fertile site is best; both point out the dangers to which it may give rise; and both insist that the founder of a city or state should see to it that all men have work to do conducive to the good of the state. (Cp. with D. I.1 the *de Regimine* II, c. 4, and also I, c. 13, the paragraph beginning *Necesse est igitur institutoris civitatis.*)

(viii) Furthermore, in Book II, chapter 3, St. Thomas tells the story of the architect who proposed to build a city on a mountain, and of Alexander's reply, just as Machiavelli does in I.1.10, save that St. Thomas expressly mentions Vitruvius as his source, but (in Vives' edition) says that the architect was called Xenocrates, instead of Deinocrates. If in the older editions the name was given correctly, it may well be that Machiavelli took the story from the *de Regimine Principum* instead of taking it direct from Vitruvius. There is also mention in this chapter of the disastrous effects of idleness and of the need to prevent it by legislation, just as in D. I.1.

(ix) The need of instituting a *regia potestas* if a state which has become corrupt is ever to be reformed, upon which Machiavelli insists in D. I.18.5 is also the doctrine of St. Thomas' continuator who in the *de Regimine* II.9 says that 'with wise and virtuous men such as were the Romans of old a republican form of government *(politicum regimen)* is preferable, but, since "the perverse are difficult to correct and stupid people are numberless" as is said in *Ecclesiastes* I.15, when nature is corrupt monarchy *(regale regimen)* is more likely to be of use because, human nature itself being thus in a state of flux as it were, it has to be kept within bounds'.

(x) Two further correspondencies amongst many others are worth mentioning.

In D. I.37.7, after discussing the Agrarian Law which eventually led to 'the complete destruction of Rome's liberty', Machiavelli says, 'These animosities were revived in the time of Caesar and Pompey. For, when Caesar became the head of the Marian party and Pompey the head of Sulla's, they came to blows, and Caesar got the best of it and so became Rome's first tyrant.' The continuator in *de Regimine* IV.1 says: 'The government of Rome was republican (a *dominium politicum*) until the *imperium* was usurped, which came about when, his enemies having been disposed of in that Pompey and his sons had been killed, and the city having been subjugated, Julius Caesar took upon himself the sole dominium and monarchy, and converted a republic into a despotism or tyranny.' He also in the same chapter calls attention to the fact that cities in Germany and France still enjoy a civic life *(politice vivunt)*, and that there the *potestas regis sive imperatoris* is circumscribed since it is held in check by certain laws, with which compare Machiavelli's remarks on Germany in II.19.4 and on France in I.16.9.

(xi) To economics the *de Regimine* devotes many long chapters, whereas what Machiavelli has to say can be summed up in a single maxim: 'Well-ordered republics should keep the public rich but their citizens poor' (I.37.3; II.19.2; III.16.3). If by 'poverty' we understand 'a modest competence', as Machiavelli does, and if we apply what is said about the wealth that should appertain to a king in *de Regimine* II.5–7 to any state, as is implied by the words *regi et cuicumque domino* in the heading of chapter 5, the Machiavellian maxim would appear to be in no wise incompatible with the doctrine of the *de Regimine*. In fact, St. Thomas himself says at the close of a chapter on trading that 'it behoves the well-ordered state to use traders with moderation' (II.3).

(xii) There are, however, other points on which there is in part agreement, but in part also disagreement. I shall mention two such points. Both St. Thomas and Machiavelli hold tyranny in abhorrence. Hence both are faced with the problem how to get rid of tyrants. In Book I, chapter 6, St. Thomas says that 'there are those who hold that it is up to strong men to kill a tyrant even at the risk of their own lives', but this conflicts alike with Christian teaching and Christian practice. Moreover, to get rid of a tyrant in the old-fashioned way entails many dangers which may well be harder to bear than the tyranny (as Machiavelli admits in III.6.35). Hence, unless the tyranny is excessive, it is better to put up with it for a time (advice which is in accord with the 'golden saying of Tacitus' cited by Machiavelli in the first paragraph of the chapter on Conspiracies, III.6.1, and also with the chapter on temporising, I.33). Moreover, St. Thomas' main point in *de Regimine* I.6 is 'how to prevent a king from becoming a tyrant' and what he says about this is wholly in accord with Machiavelli's theory. 'Against the brutality of tyrants it is better to proceed not by the private and assumed authority of individuals, but by public authority', as the Romans did when they turned out the Tarquins and replaced them 'by consuls with less power'—a revolution which was 'bloodless', says Machiavelli, precisely because it was brought about not by violence but by 'the common consent of a whole people' (III.7.2). The continuator suggests other precautions, all of which Machiavelli endorses: the authority of governments should be circumscribed by laws (IV.1); care should be taken in a *politia* to select 'suitable rulers, i.e., *nec nimis potentes, quia de facili tyrannizant, nec nimis inferioris conditionis, quia statim democrizant*' (IV.8); nor should either consuls or other magistrates be 'perpetuated', but should be appointed to office in turn *(ib.)*. It is also necessary that every ruler should be *deo devotus et reverens, sed praecipue regi ad conservationem sui regiminis* (II.16 where the example of Romulus is cited).

(xiii) This brings me to my last point. *Discourses* II.2, reads to me almost like a running criticism of the first Book of the *de Regimine Principum*. In § 2 we are told that only free cities have increased either in dominion or wealth, as is exemplified by Athens after the expulsion of Pisistratus, and still more so by Rome after getting rid of her kings. In I.4 St. Thomas points out that the *regia dignitas rectorum* becomes odious to subjects when used as a pretext for tyranny. This 'is plainly exemplified in the Roman republic', in which, after the expulsion of the kings, 'it is, as Sallust remarks, incredible to note in how short a time the *Romana civitas* increased, once liberty had been acquired'. In § 3 Machiavelli remarks that the tyrant hesitates to reward good citizens lest they should give him cause for suspicion, and that it is to his interest to keep a state divided. In I.3 St. Thomas says that tyrants 'suspect anything like excellence in their subjects lest it should be prejudicial to their iniquitous rule'; and that for the same reason 'they strive to prevent their subjects from forming alliances' . . . and 'sow discord amongst them'. In § 4 we have a story about Hieronymus of Syracuse and another story about him, told by St. Thomas in I.6. In § 5 Machiavelli calls attention to the vengeance the populace is wont to wreak on those who have deprived them of liberty and cites Corcyra as an example. In I.5 St. Thomas calls attention to the dangers which may result from the rule of the many, which 'much more often becomes a tyranny than does the rule of one', as it did ultimately in the case of the Roman republic.

(xiv) In § 6 Machiavelli then asks how it comes about that men are less fond of liberty and also less bold than they used to be. He ascribes it to their education which under the influence of Christianity glorifies humble and contemplative men rather than men of action, assigns humility, abnegation and contempt for mundane things as man's highest good, and demands of men strength to suffer rather than strength to do bold things. 'The generality of men', he adds in § 7, 'with paradise as their goal, consider how best to bear, rather than how best to avenge their injuries'. With this compare I.6 in which St. Thomas, having cited the saying of St. Peter that subjects should submit reverently not only to good, but also to bad, rulers, adds that for conscience' sake men should be patient when treated unjustly, and praises that great multitude of converts who did not resist persecution, but patiently underwent death for Christ's sake. Then turn to I.15 where St. Thomas says that 'a kingdom should be ordered primarily for the attainment of beatitude' and that, since 'of this life celestial beatitude is the goal it pertains to the function of a king to see to it that the multitude leads a good life with a view to the attainment of celestial beatitude'.

(xv) Note, however, that St. Thomas goes on to say that (i) in view of the fact that men are both mortal and subject to numerous vicissitudes, the king should also see to it that they succeed one another so that the integrity of the whole may be conserved; and (ii) that, since they are sometimes perverse and become slack in doing what the state requires or disturb the peace by their transgressions, the king should constrain them to observe his laws by means of rewards and punishments; and (iii) that, since peace may be broken by external foes and the state be destroyed, he should 'also see to it that the multitude which is subject to him be made secure against enemies, for to ward off dangers within would be of little use if it could not be protected against dangers from without'. It is with this passage in mind, I think, that Machiavelli in § 7 points out that those who deprecate valour and let matters slide forget that Christianity 'permits us to exalt and defend the fatherland', which means that 'we should train ourselves to defend it'.

(xvi) Nor has he overlooked what St. Thomas said earlier about that 'pusillanimity' which he is so anxious to dispel. For instance, in I.3 St. Thomas says that 'it is natural for men, brought up in fear, to degenerate so that in mind they are servile and pusillanimous with regard to any action which is virile and strenuous.' And in I.4 as an example he cites the Romans who 'grew tired of continual dissensions which culminated in civil wars, and by these wars were deprived of the liberty they had so studiously cultivated and began to be subject to emperors . . . of whom many were tyrannical toward their subjects but toward their enemies grew slack and weak, and so brought the Roman republic to nought'. With which compare what Machiavelli goes on to say in § 8, namely that what has caused men to be less keen on liberty than they used to be, may well be 'the Roman empire which, with its armed forces and grandiose ideas, wiped out all republics and all civic institutions'.

(xvii) For the remaining paragraphs parallels can also be found if we turn to that part of the *de Regimine* which St. Thomas did not write, and there are numerous other similarities, intermingled with yet more striking dissimilarities, if we care to look for them. But from what has been said already it should, I think, be clear that in writing his *Discourses* Machiavelli does from time to time, and especially in D. II.2, revert to what is written in the *de Regimine Principum*.

C. AUTHORS PROBABLY USED, OR SUGGESTED AS HAVING BEEN USED, IN THE 'DISCOURSES'

1. AMMIANUS MARCELLINUS, XIX.1 *sq.* may possibly have been used for the story of Cobades in II.26 (see *note 1*). His histories were published in 1474.

AMMIANUS *Marcellinus. Historiae Lib. XIV–XXVI ex recognitione et c. praef. Aug. (Cneji) Sabini. Rom. G. Sachsel de Reichenhal et Bm. Golsch de Hohenhart, 1474, d. 7 Junii, folio. (E.525.)*

2. APPIAN may have been used for the account of Lucullus in D. III.13.3, in which case the erroneous statement that Lucullus was inexperienced may be due to Machiavelli's having confused him with Flaccus (see D. III.13, *n. 4*). Both Latin editions and a vernacular edition were available in Machiavelli's time, *scil.*:

APPIANI, *Alex. a Candido ling. lat. patrono romanus* (Ven), *Vind. de Spira, 1472, folio (E.849), with a second edition in 1477 (E.850).*

—— —— *hoc in volumine continentur bellum Carthag. Syr. Part. et Mithridat. in vulgari sermone* (da Als Bracchio), *Roma, Euch. Silber, 1502, folio. (E.851.) Of this translation a Giunta edition was published at Florence in 1519–20, in 2 vols. octavo.*

3. JULIUS CAESAR's *de Bello Civili* may possibly have been used for the civil war of which Machiavelli makes mention several times, but I can find no definite trace of this. An edition of Caesar's works was published in Rome in 1469, and there were two Florentine editions:

CAESAR, *Caj. Jul. Opera. Romae in domo Pt de Maximis (per Arn. Pannartz et Cr. Sweynheym), 1469, 12 Maii, folio. (E.3247.)*

—— —— *(Ed. Luc. Robia) Flor. Ph. Junta, 1508, m. Apr., 8°. (E.3254.)*

—— —— *Flor. Ph. de Giunta, 1514, 8°. Reprint. (E.3257.)*

4. DION CASSIUS may be the source for what Machiavelli says about the restoration of Ptolemy XI by Pompey in D. I.59.3, since Plutarch merely says that Ptolemy XII was under an obligation to Pompey on his father's account (cp. *note 2*). But Dion Cassius is not used either for the conspiracy of Laetus and Eclectus or for that of Quintianus in D. III.6 (cp. *notes 32, 64 and 41*). In fact, I doubt whether Dion Cassius was used at all, for no edition of his works was published in Greek until 1548 or in Latin until 1591 (see Ebert, 6138, 9).

5. DIONYSIUS HALICARNASSUS has been suggested by Krappe as the source for the passage in D. I.4.3, in which Machiavelli maintains that tumults in Rome did less harm than good (cp. *note 3*). Ellinger, on the other hand, suggests that Polybius VI.50 and Thucydides I.71 may be the source. All three suggestions seem to me highly improbable. Machiavelli's claim is the result of his own study of Roman history, and he is well aware that not everyone will be prepared to accept it (cp. D. I.4.1). There was, however, an edition of Dionysius in Latin, had Machiavelli chosen to consult it, namely:

DIONYSIUS HALICARNASSENSIS. *Originum S. Antiquitatum. Rom. Libri. lat interprete Lampo Birago, Tarvisii. Bn. Celerius de Luere, 1480, folio. (E.6227.)*

6. FRONTINUS, Sextus Julius, may well have been used in the chapter on stratagems (III.40, see *note 1*), but of this there is no evidence. The *editio princeps* of his *Strategematicon, Libri IV,* was published in Rome by Euch. Silber in 1487, 4°; and an English translation, dedicated to Henry VIII, was published in London in 1539. He is, however, used considerably in *The Art of War,* as Burd shows in *Le Fonte letterarie dell' 'Arte della Guerra'* (Rome, 1897).

7. ISOCRATES has been suggested as the source for several passages both in *The Prince* and in the *Discourses,* but the parallelism in the *Discourses* is in no case at all striking. The relevant discourses are II.20 on mercenaries, for which the *de Pace* is said to have been used (see *note at end of this discourse*); III.9 on adaptation to the times, for which Ellinger thinks that the *Archidamus* was used (see *note at end*); and the Preface to Book II and D. III.43, for which Ellinger (p. 13) suggests that *Nicocles* may have been used. He also suggests that the dedication of *The Prince* to Lorenzo de' Medici was based on this work, a suggestion which Burd ignores (rightly, I think). A Greek edition of Isocrates' *Orations* was published in 1493 at Milan (E.10579); but there was no edition in Latin. Hence, if Machiavelli consulted this work, he must have used the Greek edition, which is unlikely.

8. JOSEPHUS, or some secondary source based on Josephus, must have been used for the reference to Herod and Mariamne in I.58.3. They are mentioned both in the *de Bello Judaico* and in the Book on *Antiquities* (see *note 6*) and both works had been translated into Latin:

JOSEPHUS, *Flav. Libri Antiquitatum XX (lat., interprete Ruffino). An. J. Schuszler, 4 cal Jul. 1470. De Bello Judaico. ll. VII (lat). 10 cal Dec. 1470. Large folio. (E.10906.)*

9. MARSILIUS of PADUA, Rector of the University of Paris in 1312–13, and protagonist of the Imperial cause in the conflict between Louis the Bavarian and John XXII, took up the same attitude toward the Papacy and toward religion that

Machiavelli was subsequently to adopt. In his *Defensor Pacis* he criticises the Papacy, just as Machiavelli does, on the ground that it was mainly responsible for discord and civil wars in Italy and for its having been invaded by foreigners (*Dictio I*, c. 1, *n. 2* and c. 5, *n. 12*, with which cp. D. I.12). He conceives the state as essentially a *vita* (cp. Machiavelli's use of the term *vivere*); maintains that civic life (Machiavelli's *vivere civile*) is in itself a *vita sufficiens*, though liable to disorders owing to the fact that '*humanae mentes in malum plerumque sunt pronae*' (I, c. 16, *n. 5*, with which cp. D. I.3.3); and that the chief function of the *pars principians* (i.e. government) is to remedy disorders, for which it must have the requisite powers (see I, c. 12 and I, c. 14, and with what he says on the capacity of the people to govern themselves cp. D. I.58). Religion he holds to be useful whether it be true or false (I, c. 6, and cp. D. I.12.1–4 and D. I.14). It is the '*causa traditionis legum divinarum sive sectarum*', and is of value whether or not one believes in a future life (I, c. 19, 11 and cp. II, c. 23, 11—and note that the same term '*secta*' is used by Marsilius as is used by Machiavelli for a religious institution). The aim of the *Defensor Pacis* is to show precisely what Machiavelli seeks to show, namely, that the state is self-sufficing, not indeed apart from religion, but apart from any particular sect, under which head Christianity and the Papacy are included. On the other hand, Machiavelli does not criticise the claim of the papacy to be a divine institution or seek to disprove its supremacy, as does Marsilius in *Dictio II*.

That Machiavelli had read the famous work of Marsilius of Padua and that it influenced his attitude to religion can scarce be doubted, though he never refers to it, and no printed edition of it was published until 1522, when it was published at Basel by the protestant, Valentine Curio, under the pseudonym of Licentius Evangelus. The notice of his work in Fabricius is as follows:

MARSILIUS *sive* MASSILIUS PATAVINUS, *Ord. Minor. A. 1312 Rector Universitatis Viennae. D. 1328. Defensorem Pacis, dictiones sive libros III adversus usurpatam Romani Pontificis jurisdictionem, ed. Basileae, 1522, cum praef. Licentii Evangeli sacerdotis, atque in Goldasti Monarchia Imperii. (Fabricius V, p. 33.)*

There was a manuscript of the *Defensor Pacis*, known as M, in the Laurentian Library at Florence (Plut. XLIV, MS. XXVI). It is a fifteenth-century copy of an Italian translation, executed in 1362, of a French version. (See Previté-Orton's edition of the *Defensor Pacis*, Intro., p. xl.)

10. OROSIUS, the Spanish historian and friend of St. Jerome, may possibly have been used in II.8.6 for the migrations from Scythia (see *note 11*). The *editio princeps* of his *Histories* was published in Vienna by J. Schussler, in 1471, fol. Another early edition is given by Ebert:

OROSIUS, P., *historiae castigatae per Aeneam Vulpem (Vicentiae) Hm. (Levilapis s Lichtenstein) de Colonia. Without date. (About 1475). Folio. Several Venetian editions followed, in 1483, 1499, and 1500. (E.15242–5.)*

His work was translated into Anglo-Saxon by Alfred the Great.

11. PLINY (23–79 A.D.) may well have been consulted, but I cannot find any definite passage which comes from his work. There was available, however, not only a Latin edition, but also one in the vernacular:

PLINIUS *Secundus, Cajus. historia naturale di C. Plinio Secondo tradocta di lingua latina in fiorentina per Cp. Landino. Ven. N. Janson (sic). 1476, large folio. (E.17315.)*

—— *Historiae naturalis libri XXXVII. Ven. J. de Spira, 1469, large folio. (E.17257.)*
Eight editions were published in Italy before 1490.

12. AEMILIUS PROBUS (= CORNELIUS NEPOS). Several editions of a work bearing the title '*de Vita excellentium*', or some variant of this, were published prior to 1500, and subsequently numerous other editions appeared. All of them are ascribed to Aemilius Probus, but in 1569 Dionysius Lambinus brought out a new edition in Paris, which he ascribed not to the insignificant Aemilius Probus, but to Cornelius Nepos, the friend of Cicero. (For an account of the controversy and of the arguments in favour of Cornelius Nepos being the author, see Smith's *Dictionary of G. and R. Biography*, *sub* 'Nepos'.) The earlier editions were:

AEMILII PROBI, *de Vita excellentium. Venice, Jenson, 1471, quarto. (E.5248).*
This work contained twenty lives, including those of Themistocles, Aristides, Pausanias, Lysander, Dion, Epaminondas, Pelopidas, Agesilaus, Eumenes, Timoleon; followed by a section '*De Regibus*', giving lives of the kings of Persia and Macedon and of Alexander's successors; and concluded with the lives of Hamilcar and Hannibal.

—— *Historici excellentium Imperatorum vitae (et) de Virorum illustrium vita. Venice, Bernadinus Venetus. Without date.*
This is a second edition of the above work, but contains in addition the life of Cato.

—— *de Viris Illustribus. Without place or printer's name. (Milan, before 1496.)*
This was the third edition and contains the life of Atticus as well as that of Cato.
The work of Aemilius Probus was famous, and may well have been consulted by Machiavelli, e.g. in connection with Hannibal, where he mentions the use of stratagems (see III.40, *n. 3*). But I can find no clear indication that any of the lives comprised in Probus's work was used. Machiavelli prefers first-hand to second-hand authorities. Hence the scant use he makes of Valerius Maximus, except with a view to looking up examples whose lives he can study in the works of reputable historians.

13. SENECA's *de Beneficiis* (V.14) is the only source I can find for Sparta's leather coinage, mentioned in II.3.2. His *de Clementia* is recognised as a source for *The Prince* alike by Burd, by Ellinger, and by Gilbert. In the *Discourses* Machiavelli may, of course, have had in mind what Seneca says in praise of clemency when he wrote the two chapters (III.21 and 22) in which it is compared with severity in regard to its effects, as he may have had in mind what Seneca says on the pressure of necessity in I.12 when he wrote D. III.12, as Ellinger suggests (p. 24), but there are no corresponding passages so far as I can discover. Several editions were available.

SENECA, *Luc. Ann. Philosophus. Opera. Neap. Mthi. Miravus, 1475, folio. (E.20841.)*
Other editions appeared in 1478 and 1490. (E.20842–3.)
—— —— *Opera Omnia. Ven. Bernadinus de Coris, 1492, folio. (E.20844.)*

14. SEXTUS AURELIUS VICTOR, who flourished in the fourth century A.D., and wrote a work entitled '*De Viris illustribus Urbis Romanae*', may well have been consulted by Machiavelli and may possibly be the source for his statement that Aemilius Paulus was several times refused the consulate (III.16.4 and see *note 4*).

AURELIUS VICTOR, *C. Plinii secundi Nonocomensis, liber illustrium virorum incipit. (Rome about 1472.) 4°. (E.1404.)*

AURELIUS VICTOR, C. *Plinii II, oratoris Veronensis, de viris illustribus feliciter liber incipit. Without place or date. (Rome. G. Sachsel and Bm. Golsch, about 1475.) 4°. (E.1405.)* Other editions appeared in 1475, 1477 and 1480.

15. FLAVIUS VEGETIUS'S '*Epitome de re militari*' is a work which Machiavelli would have been likely to consult, and both Burd and Gilbert are of opinion that he used it. The passages which suggest Vegetius may, however, have been taken second-hand from some other work. The remark in D. I.10.1, for instance, may be based on St. Thomas, who quotes Vegetius in this connection in the *de Regimine Principum, II.1.* Similarly Vegetius is used by Aegidio Colonna, whose work is supposed to have had considerable influence on *The Prince* (cp. Gilbert, p. 214 and p. 8, n. 20). He is also quoted by Clictoveus (*ib.*, p. 72). The following editions were available:

VEGETIUS, *Flavius. Epitoma de re militari. Without place or date. (Ultraj. Ketelaer et Leempt, about 1473), folio, Gothic letter. (E.23433.)*

A Roman edition was published by Euchar. Silber in 1487, containing also the *Strategematicon* of Frontinus (E.23436), and there were others. Considerable use is made of the *de re militari* of Vegetius in *The Art of War.* See Burd, *Le Fonte Letterarie dell', 'Arte della Guerra'.* (Rome, 1897).

16. VELLEIUS PATERCULUS was a Roman soldier who in A.D. 15 at the age of 35 took to literature, compiled a compendium of Roman history from the earliest times up to date, and in A.D. 30 dedicated it to his friend, Marcus Vinicius, who had just been raised to the consulate. I mention it simply and solely because Ellinger suggests that one should compare Machiavelli's Preface to his second book with what Paterculus says in II.92, namely, that 'we are naturally more inclined to praise what we have heard than what has occurred before our eyes; we regard the present with envy, the past with veneration, and believe that we are eclipsed by the former, but derive instruction from the latter'. The text of Paterculus' work was only discovered in 1515 by Beatus Rhenanus in the Benedictine monastery of Murbach in Alsace. It was in an exceedingly corrupt state, and it was not until 1520 that the *editio princeps* was published in Basle. Hence Machiavelli cannot have made use of it unless we suppose him to have written the preface to Book II much later than the book itself. Nor to my mind is the parallelism between his remarks and Machiavelli's of the least significance, seeing that anyone might make such remarks, and no other parallelism has been found.

VELLEIUS, PATERCULUS, C. *Historiae Romanae. Duo volumina per Beat. Rhenanum ab interitu utcunque vindicata. Bas. J. Frobenius m. Nov. 1520, folio. (E.23470.)*

D. CONCLUDING REMARKS ON THE SOURCES USED IN THE 'DISCOURSES' AND IN 'THE PRINCE'

A general idea of the way in which Machiavelli handles his sources may be gained from the following table in which against each author mentioned I have indicated how often he is (i) mentioned, and (ii) quoted; (iii) whether his works are specified or not; and (iv) whether correspondencies between what Machiavelli says and what the author says are frequent, occasional, or negligible.

Name	Mentioned	Quoted	Works specified	Correspondencies
1. LIVY	In most chapters	*circa* 60 times	*The First Decad*	Continuous
2. ARISTOTLE	Once in III.26.2	—	*The Politics*	Numerous
3. CICERO	Three times, in I.4.5 I.33.5 I.52.3	Three times, in I.4.5 I.33.5 and without mention in I.28.2	—	Several
4. DIODORUS SICULUS	Once in II.5.2	—	*Histories*	Several
5. HERODIAN	Once in III.6.31	Once (probably) in III.6.30	—	Mainly in D. I.10
6. JUSTIN	—	Once in I.26.2	—	Numerous
7. PLUTARCH	Once in II.1.1	Views cited	—	Numerous
8. PROCOPIUS	Once in II.8.4	Views cited	*War with the Vandals*	Several
9. QUINTUS CURTIUS (RUFUS)	Once in II.10.2–3	Views cited in II.10.2–3	—	—
10. SALLUST	Three times, in I.46.2 III.6.37 II.8.1	*Catiline* quoted in I.46.2	*Catiline* in III.6.37 *Jugurtha* in II.8.1	Several
11. TACITUS	Three times, in I.29.1 III.6.1 I.19.1–2	Latin quoted Cited Misquoted Quoted in II.26.6	—	Several
12. THUCYDIDES	Once, in III.16.1	Views cited	—	Several
13. XENOPHON	Five times, in II.2.3 II.13.1 III.20.3 III.22.6 III.39.1–2	Views cited ,, ,, ,, ,, ,, ,, ,, ,,	*de Tyrannide* *Life of Cyrus* ,, ,, ,, ,, ,, ,, ,, ,, ,,	Several
14. VIRGIL	Twice, in I.21.2 I.54.1	Quoted Quoted Quoted in II.24.2	—	—

Name	Mentioned	Quoted	Works specified	Correspondencies
15 JUVENAL	Twice, in			
	II.19.8	Quoted	*Satires*	—
	III.6.6	Quoted	—	
		Quoted in		
		II.24.2		
16. DANTE	Twice, in			—
	I.11.5	Quoted	—	
	I.53.2	Quoted	Wrongly as-signed to *de Monarchia*	
17. LORENZO DE' MEDICI	Once in III.29.2	Quoted	—	—
18. FLAVIUS BLONDUS	Once in III.27.5	Views cited		See remarks above *sub* A.17

The works of all the authors mentioned above had been published at the time Machiavelli was writing, and of the Greek authors Latin editions existed in all cases. The works of Procopius, however, were not complete, nor—so far as our evidence as to printed books goes—were those of Plutarch complete. So far as Procopius is concerned this creates no difficulty, for there is no good reason for supposing that Machiavelli used the *Historia arcana*. If, however, it is legitimate to infer that a work has been used when between its contents and those of some other work there are *several rough correspondencies* (which is open to question; very much so, in my opinion), then we must put down Plutarch's *Praecepta regendae reipublicae* as a work which Machiavelli consulted; and, so far as we know, of it there was no Latin edition, nor, for that matter, any printed edition at all. Hence, *assuming that Machiavelli consulted this work, and assuming that no Latin edition existed,* for which the evidence is not quite negative, one must infer that he used Greek.

Of the eight authors listed in XIII.B as 'having been certainly used', the evidence is conclusive in the case of Polybius, Herodotus and Justin; and strong in the case of Lucian and Suetonius, though in Lucian's case it rests on a single instance, and in Suetonius's case on a quotation which has apparently been taken from his works. In the case of Valerius Maximus, the evidence seems to be sufficiently strong, and in the case of Vitruvius it is certain that the story of Deinocrates comes ultimately from him though Machiavelli may have read the story in some secondary source. Except in the case of Polybius, Book VI, Latin editions of all the works in question were available in Machiavelli's time; that no edition of the VIth book of Polybius' Histories was extant seems to be certain, and is confirmed by the fact that Machiavelli cites it *in extenso* without mentioning the author. Hence in this case he used a manuscript, presumably that of the Laurentian Library in Florence. For the claim that Machiavelli had read the '*De Regimine Principum*' the evidence is conclusive.

The evidence for the use of the authors mentioned in the third list (XIII.C) rests wholly on actual or supposed correspondencies, and differs considerably in strength.

In the case of the *'Defensor Pacis'* the evidence is fairly strong, but for the other authors mentioned the evidence in support of their having been used is very slight indeed. Josephus is ultimately the source for Herod and Mariamne, but the information may have been gained second hand, and similarly where there is a correspondence with Vegetius. In the other cases there is no definite correspondence to which one can appeal. The most one can say of these authors is that, save in the case of Marsilius, their works had been published in Machiavelli's time, were well known and often quoted, have bearing on what he says, and that Machiavelli was a great reader.

Nor is it without significance that of all the works listed above as having certainly or probably or possibly been used, all were extant in Latin editions (or in the vernacular), save in three cases. The exceptions are Polybius, Book VI, the *Defensor Pacis,* and Plutarch's *Praecepta regendae reipublicae.* Hence it is clear that Machiavelli preferred printed works, and consulted manuscripts only in rare and exceptional cases. It is also clear that he prefers the works of well-known historians and political writers to authors of secondary importance whose evidence had been culled from these works.

A preference for printed books as sources is no less conspicuous in regard to *The Prince.* Aegidio Colonna's *de Regimine principum* was published in 1473, without the printer's name (E.122). The *Opuscula* of Beroaldus were published in 1509 or 1517 (E.2020). The *de regendo magistratu* of Johannes Antonius Campanus was published, together with his other works, by Euchar. Silber in Rome in 1495 (E.3408). The *de Institutione principis* of Bernardo Giustiniano (a translation of Isocrates' *'Ad Nicoclem'*) was first published in 1472 and then in Paris in 1511 (Gilbert, p. 241). The *de Principe* of Joannes Pontanus, which is said by Tommasini to have exercised a great influence on Machiavelli, was published at Naples, by Mthi Moravius, 15th September 1490 (E.17741). Of the *Secreta Secretorum,* translated from the Arabic, several Latin editions existed before 1500 (Gilbert, p. 238). All of these works Machiavelli is supposed to have read prior to writing *The Prince,* and in most cases it is possible to find correspondences, if one cares to look for them.

TABLES XIV TO XVI
DATES, MISTAKES, TERMINOLOGY

Table XIV. Discourses indicating Dates

(1) The phrase 'in our times' is continually recurring (cp. below II.10.3—'*ne' nostri tempi*'; II.11.2—'*ne' di nostri . . . nel 1479*', etc.). The period referred to certainly includes events during Machiavelli's lifetime, that is from 1469 onwards, but may well refer also to events in his father's lifetime, that is from 1428 onwards. In short 'in our own times' covers the period subsequent to that with which Flavius Blondus deals in his *Historiae Romanorum decades tres*, which takes us down to 1415.

(2) I.1.9—The expulsion of the Mamelukes by Selim I occurred in 1517.

(3) I.12.5—'*essere propinquo . . . o la rovina o il flagello*'. In this reference to the coming scourge of the Church, it is to be noted that Luther's 95 articles were nailed up in Wittenberg on 31 October, 1517.

(4) I.19.3—'*Sali, presente signore*'. Selim I ruled the Turks from 1512 to 1520. This passage appears to refer to some date about 1517 (see *note 3* to this chapter).

(5) I.21.2—'*Un esemplo freschissimo*'. A reference to the invasion of France by Henry VIII which occurred *ne' prossimi tempi*, i.e. in 1513 (see *note 2*).

(6) I.23.5—'*Uno freschissimo esemplo, nel 1515*'. A reference to Francis I and his invasion of Italy in 1515 (see *note 5*).

(7) II.10.3—' . . . *ne' nostri tempi il duca Carlo arebbe vinti i Svizzeri*'. This refers to Charles the Bold, Duke of Burgundy, who was beaten by the Swiss in 1476.

(8) *ib.* '*pochi giorni sono*' (The war of Urbino). This refers to the quarrel between Pope Leo X and Francesco Maria della Rovere in 1516 and 1517.

(9) II.11.2—'*ne' di nostri . . . nel 1479*'. This refers to the war between the Pope allied with the Neapolitans and the Florentines in 1479.

(10) II.17.7—'*pochi anni sono*'. A reference to the death of Count Ludovico della Mirandola at Ferrara in 1509.

(11) II.17.10—The last sentence refers to the victories of Selim I over Ismail I of Persia in 1514–16, and against the Sultan of Egypt and Syria at Aleppo in 1516, and his successor in January 1517.

(12) II.24.14—'*ne' prossimi tempi*'. This refers to the attack of Francesco Maria della Rovere on Urbino in his war against Pope Leo X. The town of Urbino fell to him in January 1517 and this chapter must have been written shortly after.

(13) II.30.6—'*De' Viniziani si vide, pochi anni sono, la medesima pruova*'. This must be the defeat of the Venetians by the Spanish viceroy at Piacenza in 1513 (see *note 8*). In the same paragraph the invasion of France by Henry VIII in 1513 is also mentioned.

(14) III.6.7—A further reference to the 'present Turk', Selim I the son of Bajazet. Selim reigned from 1512 to 1520.

(15) III.10.7—'*ne' tempi nostri*'. Two cases are cited here, the first that of the battle of Morat in 1476, and the second that of the battle of Novara in 1513.

(16) III.12.3—'*come intervenne a Firenze ne' prossimi tempi*'. This reference is plainly to the fall of the Medici in 1512 (see *note 4*).

(17) III.14.2—'*pochi anni sono*'. This refers to the failure of the Oddi to recover Perugia from the Baglioni in 1495. A few years means here at least eighteen years.

(18) III.27.2—'*quindici anni sono*'. The incident quoted is the strife which broke out between the Panciatichi and the Cancellieri in Pistoia in October 1501 and January 1502, so this passage must have been written either at the end of 1516 or beginning of 1517.

(19) III.35.2—The incident related here is the invasion of Persia by Selim I in 1514–16 in which his army suffered great privations.

(20) *The passage in II.24.9.* If the incident referred to in this section is the attack on Genoa, to which Villari and Burd think that it refers, the date is 1521. But I have given reasons in *note 10* showing that the incident referred to took place in 1515.

Table XV. Machiavelli's Mistakes

Machiavelli is a careful writer, and does not make many mistakes. Almost all his quotations from Livy are exact and almost all his facts agree with the sources once one has found the right one. There are, however, some mistakes, most of them of minor importance. In about half of them two persons are confused or the wrong name is used, which may, of course, be due to a defect in the early edition used.

The mistakes are as follows:

(1) I.13.4. The senator who tried to quell the tumult caused by Appius Herdonius was Publius Valerius, not Publius Ruberius, and the person who succeeded him as consul was Lucius Quintius (Cincinnatus), not Titus Quintius. (see *note 5* and Livy III.17.1 and 19.2).

(2) I.26.1. The quotation from the *Magnificat* = '(who) filled the hungry with good things and sent the rich empty away' is not said of David, but of the Lord (see *note 1* and cp. Psalm 22).

(3) I.33.1 and 6. There would seem to be in this chapter a confusion between the first Latin war in which a dictator was appointed and the Great Latin war in which 'full forty peoples formed a league against Rome' (see *note 6*).

(4) I.53.2. The quotation from Dante is from the *Convivio*, not from the *de Monarchia* (see *note 3*).

(5) I.59.3. The Ptolemy with whom Pompey sought refuge in Egypt was not the Ptolemy whom he had reinstated, but his son, Ptolemy XII (see *note 2*).

(6) II.2.6. Blood shedding and ferocity were not characteristic of Roman ceremonial in republican days.

(7) That the coinage instituted by Lycurgus was *di cuoio* (of leather) is open to question. More probably it was of iron (see *note 5*).

(8) II.10.2. The defeat of Agis III by Antipater did not precede the death of Alexander by a few days, but by a few years. The mistake here, however, is probably due to the text Machiavelli was using, for the early texts were very corrupt, and modern texts do not contain the passage Machiavelli is using (see *note 2*).

(9) II.19.8. The text of Juvenal's *Satires* VI.291-2 does not contain the words '*gula et*' (see *note 12*).

(10) II.31.2. The king with whom Themistocles sought refuge in Asia, and to whom he made promises he was unable to fulfil, was not Darius, but Artaxerxes (see *note 2*).

(11) III.6.19. It was not Nelematus, but Hellanicus, who organised the conspiracy against Aristotimus (see *note 26*). So too in III.6.26.

(12) III.6.29. The story told of Sitalces, King of Thrace, does not appear in any records, so far as I can discover; but, if for Sitalces we substitute Cypselus, Tyrant of Corinth, it agrees with the story told by Herodotus (see *note 38* and Herodotus V.92).

(13) III.6.31. If Machiavelli wrote '*abitanti in diverse paesi*', (B. p. 202), this is a

mistake, for Herodian says '*diversis habitantes cubiculis*', but for '*paesi*' the *Filadelfia* edition reads '*luoghi*' (see *note 43*).

(14) III.6.32. It was Hipparchus, not Diocles, who with Hippias became tyrant in Athens after the death of Pisistratus, and got killed (see *note 44*); and Phillidas, not Charon, who was counsellor to the tyrants of Thebes (see *note 48*). The mistake, however, in the first case is due to Justin.

(15) III.13.3. It is possible that in this section Machiavelli is confusing Lucullus with Flaccus, for Lucullus was by no means inexperienced when he was sent to the second Mithridatic war (see *note 4*).

(16) III.17.1. It was Lucius Salinator, not Claudius Nero, who made the remarks ascribed to the latter toward the end of this paragraph (see *note 4* and Guicciardini's remarks at end of the chapter).

(17) III.18.1. The saying with which this passage opens is wrongly ascribed to Epaminondas: it should be Chabrias (see *note 1*).

(18) III.18.3. For *Aequi* read *Volsci*: there is no mention of the *Aequi* in Livy IV.37–41. And in I.40.8 read *Aequi* for *Volsci* (see *note 20* and cp. Livy III.38.3 *sq.*).

(19) III.19.1. The words ascribed to Tacitus are not to be found in his works, and in the *Annals* III.35.3, he says just the opposite (see *note 2*).

(20) III.32.2. Only the troops from Sicily, not those from Sardinia, went to Africa after the First Punic war, and the ambassador sent to treat with Spendius and Matho, was not Hasdrubal, but Gesco (see *note 2*).

(21) III.33.3. Gaius and Publius Manlius were military tribunes, not consuls, in 379 B.C. (see *note 7* and cp. Livy VI.30.3).

(22) III.22.10. If *Vettor Pisani* is the gentleman of whom Machiavelli writes in this paragraph, the passage is full of inaccuracies (see *note 17*).

(23) III.48.1. The ambush here mentioned took place after the dictator's return. Machiavelli would seem to be confusing it with an earlier ambush described by Livy in X.3 (see *note 1*).

There are also some mistakes in the spelling of proper names. In I.5.6 *Menenius* is better written *Maenius* and the *praenomen* should be Gaius. Also *Fulvius* should be *Folius* or *Foslius*. In I.47.3 *Calavio* is written *Calano*. In III.6.14 for *Cebalino* we have *Ciballino*. In III.6.17 *Teodoro* for *Teodoto*. In III.6.19 *Ortanes* instead of *Otanes*. In III.6.43 *Rutilio* for *Rutilo*. Again in III.6.19 the number of foot-soldiers should be 1000 not 200; in the heading of II.21 *first prefect* would be more accurate than *first praetor*; and in Barbèra's text we have *fragello* for *flagello* in I.12.5.

Thirty-odd mistakes in a work of such length comprising some 750 names and almost as many incidents is not very many. I shall be quite content if my own notes are as accurate as the text on which I am commenting.

Table XVI. Some Remarks on Machiavelli's Terminology

Below will be found comments on some of the terms Machiavelli uses to which attention has been called in the footnotes at the end of the chapters.

Accidente by derivation means an event, something that happens to a person or a state. Usually it has a pejorative sense and means a misfortune (cp. the heading of D. I.56.1: *Innanzi che seguino i grandi accidenti;* and III.11.1: *è nascoso qualche proprio male che fa surgere nuovi accidenti;* where the context requires 'misfortunes'; cp. also III.49.1, where we have *accidenti che abbiano bisogno del medico*). In I.2.1 and 2 it would seem to be used in a more general sense, *secondo li accidenti* (as occasion arose), and *per la occorrenzia degli accidenti* (through the happening of something which provides an opportunity). So, too, in the heading of I.39, where we are told that the same *accidenti* happen to different peoples. But even here it may well be 'misfortunes' that Machiavelli has in mind, for it is integral to his theory that rulers and states can learn from events which fortune brings about, and usually these events are disasters, as in the case of Rome in 390 B.C. (cp. D. II.29, and see *Introduction, VII*).

Capitano usually means a general (cp. I.23.4; 29.1; II.33.4; III.9.2), but in the plural it may mean 'officers' or 'commanding officers', as in I.44.1. For the office of *il Capitano* in Florence see D. I.8.4 and 49.2.

Capo means a 'head' or 'leader' as in the heading of I.44: '*Una moltitudine sanza capo*', but in the plural it may mean 'officers' as in I.29.2 '*per prudenza degli altri capi*'. Cp. also the phrase '*capo di sacrificio*' (master of ceremonies) in I.25.3; *capi della religione* in III.1.8.

Città, a city, but, since the cities which Machiavelli envisages are those, which became the capitals of states, Athens, Rome, Florence, the word usually signifies a 'city-state'. Hence I have often translated it by 'state', indicating the term *città* in a note. So, too, in the plural, *cittadi*.

Cittadini d'entro (II.27.4), people who are described in II.1.6 as 'ladders by which to climb in', or 'gates by which to enter', a city or province, i.e. as we should now say 'fifth columnists'. Cp. II.32.5.

Civile, concerned with civic affairs or politics. Thus, in I.33.4, *nelle cose civili espertissimo*, an expert in politics; cp. II.18.3: *che danno delle cose civili regola*. See also sub '*vivere*'.

Civiltà has much the same sense. Thus I.28.2 *scrittori della civiltà* (writers on civic government or civic affairs); and in I.55.8 *che delle antiche civiltà avesse cognizione*; I.55.7 *inimici d'ogni civiltà* (hostile to any form of civic government).

Comità, the characteristic of one who gets on well with other people, hence sociability, as in the heading of III.22.

Congiura, usually a conspiracy, but in general persons (or states) who have bound themselves together in opposition to some other person (or state). Hence a confederation or league, as in I.33.6; 53.3, and cp. II.2.9, where in translating I have

313

used the word 'combination'. Cp. also III.11.3: *Congiurò nel 1483 tutta Italia contro ai Viniziani.*

Diliberazioni, decisions (not 'deliberations'), e.g. in I.38.1.

Dimestichezza, behaviour characteristic of members of the same family, but applied by Machiavelli also to states. Cp. III.2.2, where it is applied to a person (and has been translated by 'familiar intercourse'), with II.21.5, where it is applied to Rome and her allies and has been translated by 'easy-going ways':—'*umano e dimestico con loro,*' and then '*Questa dimestichezza e liberalità.*'

Esecuzioni, administrative acts. See III.49.2–3, where we have both *la potenza delle esecuzioni* (the power of administration), and *tutte le altre esecuzioni.*

Fastidio, vexation, troublesomeness (cp. I.16.7).

Gentiluomini, gentry or gentlefolk. See I.55.7 for their definition as people who live on their estates and do no work, and note the exception made in the case of Venetian 'gentlemen', who derive their wealth from merchandise, not from their estates. (Cp. also I.6.2.)

Giornata, an open battle; see the definition in II.17.1.

Grandi, the leading men in a city or state, almost equivalent to *nobili,* save that they were not in general titled. In Florence '*grandi*' was a technical term for the nobility (as in Spain for the upper nobility); but Machiavelli uses it in a more general sense. In I.2.16; 4.2 and 5.1, the *grandi* are contrasted with *l'universale* and with *la plebe,* and *uomini grandi* with *uomini popolari.* Hence I have translated *grandi* here by 'upper class', but elsewhere have translated it by 'leading men'. (I.16.7) or by 'men of standing' (III.6.8).

Ignobili, the common people as contrasted with the *nobili* or upper class (cp. I.5.3; 30.3; and III.6.7).

Imperio, a position of authority such as that held by a military commander; cp. the heading of III.24, where *imperii* means military commands. It does not, however, always connote a military command, but is used in a more general sense, e.g. in I.17.5, *forma di republica e di imperio,* a republican form of government; and II.13.1, *pervenuti o a regno o a imperii grandissimi,* to attain either a kingdom or very great power. *Imperio* also means 'empire', cp. the heading of II.1.

Libero as applied to a city or state means primarily that it is not subject to some other state or power; cp. the definition of *liberi edificatori delle cittadi* in I.1.6 as 'peoples who under a prince or of themselves have found a new place of residence'. It is essential that a free state should be able to choose its own form of government. Hence tyranny is excluded, but not necessarily principality. A state loses its *libertà* when it becomes subject to a tyrant or to some other state. The term is often combined with *vivere* (*vivere libero*—a free community), and with *stato* (*uno stato libero*—a free government), q.v., sub '*vivere*' and '*stato*'. I have translated such phrases somewhat differently according to the context, but the essential meaning of the term '*libero*' is retained by Machiavelli throughout. For instances of its occurrence see I.1.6; 7.1; 16.5; 18.1, and heading; 49.1 and 6; II.2.2 and 3; III.3.1 and 4; 24.1; 25.1.

Licenza, anarchy I.47.4, and cp. *licenzioso,* anarchical, applied to a form of government in I.2.4.

Modo, a way of doing something, method, custom; sometimes combined with the term *straordinario*—abnormal methods (I.7.1); or with *vivere* in *modo di vivere,* custom (III.25.1) or type of polity (II.19.4 and 6). In III.1.6 *modo del vivere,* political standpoint.

Moltitudine, a term frequently used by Tacitus. To mark the distinction between *una moltitudine* and *la moltitudine* I have in general translated the term by 'a crowd' when *una* is used, and by 'the masses' when *la* is used (cp. I.44, heading, and I.57.2 with I.58, heading, and I.2.9, 10; also I.53.4). But the difference is very slight, as is clear from I.44 where the *moltitudine* mentioned in the heading is at once exemplified by the Roman plebs; and from I.16.5 where both articles are used in the same paragraph. *Moltitudine,* in short, is but a synonym for the 'populace', with the stress laid on its plurality.

Nobili. The term *nobili* and the corresponding term, *la nobilità,* are used to denote the upper class whether in ancient Rome or in an Italian state in Machiavelli's day. For other terms distinguishing the two classes between which conflict is apt to arise, see *Introduction,* § 159.

Ordini. The term *ordine* sometimes means class or rank. For instance, in II.17.10 it is used for 'ranks' in the military sense. It may also mean an enactment, as in III.11.1. But, when used in the plural, its most common meaning is 'institutions'. Cp. I.18.2 where *ordini* are contrasted with *leggi* (laws), and a list of institutions illustrating the meaning of the term *'ordini'* is given. In the same paragraph Machiavelli speaks of *l'ordine del governo, o vero dello stato,* in Rome, where the term *ordine* comprises all Rome's institutions, and is equivalent to 'constitution', though the term *'constituzione'* is also used (e.g. in I.2.15, B.61).

Ossequio in its Latin form, *obsequium,* is a term frequently used by Tacitus in the same sense as that in which Machiavelli uses it. It signifies the attitude of a ruler who is seeking to win favour with the populace; hence 'considerateness', as in the heading of III.19. The corresponding English term 'obsequiousness' signifies a similar attitude, but of subjects toward their rulers, not *vice versa.*

Ottimati is another term used by Machiavelli to signify the upper class or the nobility (cp. I.16.7; 28.2; and also 52.3, where he speaks of *la parte degli ottimati*). But the term is also used in I.2.3 and 14 in a technical sense 'Aristocracy', i.e. a state ruled by the aristocracy.

Ozio, idleness, in I.Pref.3; I.1.7; 10.1; 55.7 and II.25.1. But in II.2.7 Machiavelli speaks of those who have interpreted our religion *secondo l'ozio e non secondo la virtù,* where the meaning is that religion, as thus interpreted, recommends men to do nothing about the evils which beset them, the policy of *laissez faire.*

Popolo, the populace or people, in contrast with the *nobili* or *grandi,* e.g. in the heading of I.5. The word is of frequent occurrence and I have translated it by 'populace', unless the context required 'people' as in II.1.1, *il Popolo romano,* the Roman people. It is also the term most frequently used for the Roman plebs, cp. I.6.1, where *il Popolo* is opposed to *il Senato,* but *la Plebe* is also used (e.g. in I.5.1). In I.5.1 occurs also the cognate term *'uomini popolari'* (in contrast with *uomini grandi*); and in I.6.2 the Venetian term *'popolani'* in contrast with *'gentiluomini'* (cp. I.55.10, where *'popolari'* is used instead of *'popolani'*). *'Popolare'* or *'Governo popolare'* is the technical term for a democracy, i.e. a state in which the government is drawn exclusively from the populace (cp. I.2.3, 4 and 14, and *notes 7 and 8*).

Principe. This term is used not only in the technical sense in which it is used in *The Prince* to signify a ruler in whom all the powers of government are centred, i.e. an autocrat or sole ruler or monarch, but not necessarily a tyrant, of course; it is also used in a more general sense of any ruler or commander. Thus in I.12.3 we have *i principi d'una republica* or *d'uno regno* (cp. I.16.5 and 33.6); in II.26.3 *principi di eserciti*, army-commanders (cp. I.36.1; III.10.5 and 22.5); in I.14.3 *principe de' pullarii*, the head-poultryman; and in I.38.1 we are told that the Roman senate wanted to be *principe delle diliberazioni*, to take the lead in decisions.

Qualità ordinarily means character, as in the opening words of P. 10 in which Machiavelli examines the 'character' of principalities with a view to determining their military strength; or again, in the phrase *di qualità che*. In I.2.17 it is used to denote the three *potenze* essential to a properly constituted republic, *la potenza del Principato* or *la potestà regia*, *la potenza degli Ottimati*, and *il governo popolare*. I have translated the term *qualità* in this case by 'estate'.

Republica. This term is used in two senses: (1) in the old Roman sense of *res publica*, the commonwealth, all that is common to a people including the people themselves; and (2) a republic of the Roman type, involving the three factors mentioned in the previous note. The term *republica* in the first sense may be either a principality or a republic in the technical sense. It has been translated in this case by 'commonwealth' or 'state' (cp. I.9, heading, and III.1, heading), and the term '*republica*' is given in the notes. In the second case a 'republic' is opposed to a 'principality' (see Index *sub* 'Principality'). Thus in the heading of III.8 occurs the phrase '*chi vuole alterare una republica*'—he who would transform a *republic*, and the chapter which follows deals only with one kind of transformation, that from a republic to a principality.

Sbanditi, those who have gone into banishment, compulsory or voluntary. See the heading of II.31, where I have translated the term by 'refugees'. One might, of course, say 'exiles', but nowadays the other term is preferred.

Setta is used to denote an organised body of men, distinct from others. Thus in I.7.5 we have *una setta contraria alla sua*, a rival party; cp. the sequence: *odio— divisione—sètte—rovina* in I.8.3. In II.Pref.5 we have first *quella setta Saracena che . . .* that Saracen tribe which . . .; then *sette* and *provincie* are used to denote the parts into which the Roman empire broke up. In I.12.2 we have *la setta degli indovini e degli aruspici*, the body of soothsayers and diviners. In II.5, heading, we have *la variazione delle sètte e delle lingue*, where *sètte* has a religious significance—changes of religion and of language (cp. *ib.*, § 1, *una setta nuova, cioè ùna religione nuova*). So, too, in III.1, heading, *una setta o una republica* means a religious institution or a commonwealth; and in II.5.1 Machiavelli, following in the wake of Marsilius of Padua, speaks of Christianity as *la setta Cristiana*.

Stato. This term is used constantly, as appears from the notes at end of the chapters, in which its occurrences have been indicated. It means primarily a form of government, e.g. principality, aristocracy, democracy, as is apparent from its first occurrence in I.2.3; and from the fact that in I.2.4 it is replaced by the phrase *ragioni governi*. In its technical and proper sense it does not mean simply government, for in I.18.2 Machiavelli distinguishes it from *governo*, where he is describing what he calls *l'ordine del governo, o vero dello stato*. *Governo* signifies the actual government: *stato* signifies its form, or a government of some particular form. Hence such phrases as *uno stato libero*, a free form of government (I.18, heading, I.7.1 and III.3.1); *stato di pochi*, an oligarchy, (I.2.4); *stato popolare*, a democracy (I.2.3; 18.7); and again such phrases as *mutare lo stato*, to change the form of government (II.27.5; III.3.1; 7.2); *mantenere nello stato* and *perdere lo stato* in II.15.6 and III.3.3; *riordinato nello stato suo* and *offende uno stato assai* in I.45.2–3, where also occurs the phrase *casi di stato* (cases of treason). See also II.24.9, *a variare lo stato di Genova* (to change the form of government in Genoa); and I.7.1 where we have both *peccassono contro allo stato libero* and *tentano cose contro allo stato*; and III.3.4 where *uno stato libero* is contrasted with *uno regio*.

Not infrequently, however, the term *stato* means government, as in II.24.9, where we are told that Ottaviano Fregoso *prese lo stato*, seized the government (of Genoa), or in the phrase *stato che regge*, government in power (II.25.3). Or again it may have the same connotation as the modern term 'state', and be used in the same sort of ambiguous way to mean either the government or the governed in conjunction with the government (cp. I.7.1; 26.1; 40.2; II.21.1 and III.6, 10, where I have translated it by 'state', e.g. in I.26.1 we have *principe o d'una città o d'uno stato*, ruler of a city or of a state). Cp. also such phrases as *conto di stato*, reasons of state (I.45.2); *coloro che tenevano stato*, ministers of state (II.18.4); *tengono stati*, to hold office (II.31.1).

Stato libero (a free government or self-government) occurs in I.7.1; 16.3; 18.1 and heading. *Vivere libero* (a free or self-governing community) occur in I.16.5; 49.1, 6; II.2.2, 3; III.24.1; 25.1. The phrase *liberi edificatori delle cittadi* occurs in I.1.6 (and cp. the heading of I.49).

Universale. A clue to the significance of this term is given in I.2.16, where it is opposed to the *grandi*, and hence is more or less equivalent to *il popolo*; in I.40.11, where we have *hanno amico l'universale ed inimici i grandi*, in contrast with *hanno per inimico il popolo e amica la Nobilità*, there being in the case in question but *pochi nobili*; in I.16.5 where we have *ha per nimici i pochi* in contrast with *ha per nimici l'universale*; and I.17.4 where renaissance is ascribed to the action of individuals not to *la virtù dello universale*. Hence *l'universale* is not identical with the populace but rather with the general public as opposed to nobles or eminent men. I have so translated it in I.2.16; 7.2; 32.1; 39.2 (twice) and in III.3.2; and as 'the public as a whole' in I.17.4 and 40.11.

It is clear from the context that the cognate term *universalità* (with the indefinite article, *una*) in II.28.2 and III.7.2 means a whole people, but in I.50.3, with the definite article, *l'* it is applied to the Venetian Grand Council, which consisted exclusively of patricians but had a very large membership. Hence I have translated the *universalità* of this Council as 'the Council at its general meeting', and so for the phrase *quella universalità di quel Consiglio*.

Virtù. For the meaning of this term see *Introduction X, 109–111.*

Vivere. This term when used as a substantive signifies a community, i.e. a set of people living together in a city or state in accordance with a certain *modo di vivere*, pattern or mode of life (cp. II.2.7; 19.4, 6; 25.1; and III.1.6 for *modo di vivere*; and I.26.3 *nimici d'ogni vivere*). Usually, however, the word *vivere* is qualified by some adjective, e.g. *un antico vivere in una città* (an ancient form of constitution in a state) in I.25.4; *uno vivere politico* in I.6.2 and 25.5 (a body politic or a political regime). The two adjectives with which *vivere* is most commonly combined are *civile* and *libero*.

Uno vivere civile is a community living in accordance with some constitution, whether republican or monarchic, cp. I.26.1, *si volga o per via di regno o di republica alla vita civile*. The community will in such a case have *viveri civili* (civic institu-

317

tions, II.2.8), and will thus be incompatible with tyranny, but not with absolutism if the absolutism be constitutional. If a *vivere civile* is to be incompatible with absolutism (in this sense) it must also be *libero* (cp. I.9.1 where Romulus is spoken of as the founder of *uno vivere civile* (a state which in fact was a monarchy), and I.9.4 where we are told that Rome's institutions were more in conformity with *uno vivere civile e libero* than with *uno (vivere) assoluto e tirannico*. One is tempted to translate *uno vivere civile* by a 'democratic' state or regime, but, quite apart from the ambiguity with which the term 'democratic' is fraught, it would be better in view of what Machiavelli says about such a '*vita*' to translate it by 'constitutional regime' or 'constitutional state' or simply 'state'.

Uno vivere libero means primarily a state which is free from foreign domination; but, as in Tacitus the term '*libertas*' is opposed to '*principatus*' (*Agric.* 3), to '*rex*' (*Ann.* 1.1), and to '*domini*' (*Hist.* 4.64), so Machiavelli often uses it, not merely in opposition to tyranny as in I.16.3 and II.2.2–3, but in the sense of a self-governing state, or at any rate a state which has chosen its own form of government (cp. its use in P. 3, Burd 186).

The phrase *uno vivere libero* occurs in I.16.3 (twice); 49.1, 5; II.2.2, 3; and III.24.1; 25.1. The phrase *uno vivere civile* in I.3.1; 9.1; 55.8 and II.19.2. In II.23.3 occurs the phrase '*campi che per vivere gli mancono*', they lack living space or *lebensraum*.

INDICES

REFERENCES in the Indices are to Book, Chapter, and to the numbered sections into which the chapters have been divided for convenience of reference.

References to the Notes are given only when the note is of special importance. In the page-headings of the Notes, however, are given not only the Book and Chapter or Chapters to which the notes refer, but also (i) the index-numbers of the notes comprised on the page, and (ii) the number of the Book, Chapter, and Section to which the first and last notes on the page refer. Hence, if so desired, the indices can be used in order to look up the notes on some particular person, place, or topic without first looking up the index-number in the text.

The Introduction has not been indexed, but a detailed analysis of its contents is given in Volume I, pp. ix to xiii.

INDEX OF PROPER NAMES

N.B. *The names in italics are not mentioned in the text, but the person or incident is referred to there.*

⚔ = *battle;* † = *killed; q.v. after dates refers to the Chronological Tables in which details of the incidents will be found.*

Where names occur also in 'The Prince', this has been indicated by putting P., followed by the number of the chapter, in brackets at the end of the references.

SUBJECT INDEX

___

N.B. Subjects which form the headings of discourses are indicated by italics

Subject Index

351

COMMON GOOD (*cont.*)
Roman populace lovers of I.58.6
rule by common consent III.7.2
COMPETITION
Free competition recommended
II.2.10
CONCESSIONS
Avoid appearance of yielding to force
when granting III.11.5
when to grant II.14.2
'CONDOTTIERI'
II.18.4, and cp. *n. 3*
CONFEDERATIONS
*More reliable if made by republics than
princes* I.59
Three kinds of II.4
*How a single state or individual can pre-
vail against a confederation* III.11
Between Latins and Romans
II.15.1, 5
means of dealing with enemy con-
federations II.14.3 (cp. II.21.6)
on equal terms, disadvantages of
II.4.4, *n. 3*
the Swiss II.19.5
CONFESSORS
St. Francis and St. Dominic popular
as III.1.8
CONFIDENCE
Essential in armies before battle III.33
*How a general should act to acquire that of
his army* III.38
Importance of II.12.6
necessary to inspire it in face of un-
familiar enemy III.37.6; 38.1, 2
religion means of inspiring it in
troops I.14.4; 15.1–3; III.33.2–4
CONQUEST
*Everything to be made new in a conquered
province or city* I.26 (cp. II.3.4)
When mishandled, leads to ruin II.19
*To encourage divisions in a city not the
way to conquer it* II.25
The Roman method of conquering towns
II.32
Causes and effects of II.8
change of place-names due to
II.8.3

CONQUEST (*cont.*)
conquered admitted to citizenship
II.23.2
desire and need for II.19.3 (cp. I.6.5–
10)
harm done by II.19.6, 7, 8
Rome's II.17.1–6 (would have been
helped by artillery)
use of Fifth columnists by Rome
II.1.6; 32.5
CONSERVATISM
Men naturally averse to change I.18.5
CONSPIRACIES
General III.6
Against own country I.16.4; III.6.37
against prince I.2.9; 58.10; III.2.2,
3; 5.4; III.6.1–36
against the common good I.58.10;
III.6.37–40
against towns II.32.5, 6; III.6.2
as a method of taking towns
II.32.5, 8
by men of standing usually III.6.8
dangers of III.6.1–10; 12–17
dangers in carrying out III.6.18–34
dangers of writing in III.6.21, 37
dangers resulting from a bad conscience III.6.33; from change of
plan III.6.27, 28; from nervousness
III.6.33; from perturbation of mind
III.6.29, 30; from trying to kill
more than one prince III.6.31, 32
dangers subsequent to III.6.35, 36
failure due to false impressions and
unforeseen events III.6.34
futility of III.6.1
of the Bacchanals III.49.2
one-man conspiracies III.6.7
punitive action in dealing with
III.6.42–3
use of poison in III.6.38, 40, 41;
III.20.2; 21.4
sometimes used in sense of Leagues
(*q.v.*)
CONSTITUTION
And institutions I.18.2–5
should allow for expansion I.6.5–10;
II.19.3

Subject Index

LEAD
  Danger of taking the lead in advising
    an unusual course III.35
LEAGUE
  Based on inadequate grounds II.11
  Against Rome II.4.3; 13.3
  See also CONFEDERATION, and
    Index of Proper Names *sub*
    LEAGUES
'LEBENSRAUM'
  II.23.3
LEGAL OUTLETS
  required owing to the ambitions of
    the populace I.4.4; I.7 *passim*; I.8.2
LEGISLATION
  *Bad if retrospective or contravening ancient
    custom* I.37
  Becomes corrupt I.18.3
  good legislation provides for indict-
    ments III.34.5
  kings better legislators than republics
    I.58.8
  necessary when custom breaks down
    I.3.3
  needs renewal III.1 *passim*; 8.6; 11.1
  no need of if things go well I.3.3
  procedure in Rome I.18.3, 4
  supposes that man is wicked I.3.1,
    n. 2
  to be initiated by a strong man I.17.4
LETTERS
  Men of I.10.1
LIBERALITY
  Men conspicuous for, revolt against
    tyranny I.2.9
  towards neighbours II.20.4
LIBERTY (see *sub* FREEDOM, and for
    Machiavelli's use of '*libero*', see
    TABLE XVI *sub* '*Libero*', '*Stato*',
    '*Vivere*')
LICENCE
  Preferred to liberty I.40.7
LICENTIOUSNESS
  Absence of under good emperors
    I.10.7
  equivalent to anarchy I.2.4 and see
    n. 8
  hereditary princes lapse into I.2.8

LICTORS
  At first twelve I.25.2; 40.3
  increased to 120 under the Decem-
    virate I.40.5
LIFE
  Not long enough for one man to cor-
    rupt state I.11.5; III.8.5
  not long enough for one man to estab-
    lish reforms I.17.5; III.1.7
  shortness of, universal III.1.1
LIQUIDATION OF RIVALS
  Need of, before good work can be done
    III.20
  Of 'the Sons of Brutus', after a revolution
    III.3
  By kings, when they have despoiled others
    III.4
  Of revolted enemies and towns
    II.23.3–6
  of the Spartan ephors I.9.5
  of tyrannical princes I.2.9
  of tyrannical rulers I.2.10
  opposed to generosity II.23.3, 4
LOYALTY
  Not to be expected from the servile
    II.23.4
  not to be secured by fortresses
    II.24.1, 15
LUXURY
  II.19.8; III.6.38

MAGISTRATES
  Afraid of powerful citizens I.29.6
    (cp. 37.5)
  appointment of, in Rome I.18.2
  army to obey in a republic III.22.9,
    10
  better for a conquering power not to
    appoint II.21.3
  election of, by populace I.58.7
  honoured in non-corrupt states I.10.7
  period of office I.25.4
  powers suspended during Decem-
    virate I.40.2
  prejudicial if authority usurped or
    self-appointed I.34.3; 40.12; if
    appointment irregular I.34.3; if not
    appointed I.50.3

MATTER (*cont.*)
matter and form III.8.5
people are the material of the state
II.23.2; III.8.2
when free from corruption I.16.2;
17.4

MEAN
See MIDDLE COURSE

MEDICINE
A record of experiments I.Pref.2
dictum of medical men III.1.2
heart and vital parts II.30.5
incidents calling for a doctor III.49.1
purgation restores health II.5.4

MEN OF STANDING (*grandi*)
Retain their equanimity in adversity III.31
Conspiracies chiefly formed by
III.6.8–10
great men passed over in time of
peace III.16.1
influence of on populace I.4.5; 13.4;
53; 54; 58.6; III.22.10; 34.2

MERCENARIES
*Rulers should employ own subjects as
troops* I.21 (cp. 43.2)
dangers of employing II.20 (cp. III.31.5)
Useless as troops I.43.2

METHOD
Of Machiavelli claims to be a new
one I.Pref.1
Cp. *Introduction* VIII

METHODS OF OBTAINING POWER
Abnormal required if people hostile
I.16.5; 17.5
abnormal to be used when normal
not available I.7.2
normal sometimes inadequate
I.18.5, 6
unconstitutional I.7.5; their use undesirable I.34.7

MIDDLE COURSE
To be avoided in dealing with subject people
II.23 (cp. 24.10)
Harmful I.26.3; III.40.2
impossible to keep to I.6.10; III.21.3
impracticable III.2.3

MIGRATIONS
Causes of II.8

MILITARY COMMANDS
*Prolongation of, the cause of Rome's servi-
tude* III.24 (and see *sub* COMMAND)

MILITARY COMMANDERS
But few acquired reputation after prolongation of consulate III.24.3. See
sub GENERALS

MILITARY DISCIPLINE
Slack in Machiavelli's day II.16 (cp.
18.7; III.36.4)
And valour III.36.2
method of Camillus III.31.6
need of III.36.2, 3
Rome's neglect of II.29.1; III.14.1, 2;
22.4, 5
security based on III.31.5
victory presupposes III.33.1, 3

MILITARY INSTITUTIONS
In Machiavelli's day III.15.5
kept up in England I.21.2
neglected III.10.1 (cp. II.16; 18.7;
III.36.4)

MILITARY ORGANISATION
Makes for good order I.4.1

MILITARY PAY
Why introduced in Rome I.51; 52.1;
cp. II.6.3

MILITARY TRAINING
Given training all men may become
soldiers I.21.3
Livy on III.31.5
need of I.1.8; II.17.8; 19.2
sham fights II.17.8; III.38.3
should be given in peacetime
III.31.5, 6

MIRACLES
Belief in to be encouraged I.12.3
plenty in Rome I.12.4
See also PRODIGIES

MISFORTUNE
Preceded by prodigies I.56
(see *sub voce* '*Accidente*' in TABLE
XVI)

MISTAKES
*Generals never punished for severely by the
Romans* I.31
*The Populace makes mistakes about
generalities but not about particulars* I.47

Subject Index

Subject Index